AIR BATTLES BEFORE D-DAY

AIR BATTLES BEFORE D-DAY

HOW ALLIED AIRMEN CRIPPLED THE *LUFTWAFFE* AND GERMAN ARMY IN FRANCE

COLONEL JOSEPH T. MOLYSON JR., USAF (RET)

STACKPOLE
BOOKS
Essex, Connecticut
Blue Ridge Summit, Pennsylvania

STACKPOLE
BOOKS

An imprint of The Globe Pequot Publishing Group, Inc.
64 South Main Street
Essex, CT 06426
www.globepequot.com

Distributed by NATIONAL BOOK NETWORK

British Library Cataloguing in Publication Information available

Library of Congress Cataloging-in-Publication Data

Names: Molyson, Joseph T., Jr., 1947- author.
Title: Air battles before D-day : how Allied airmen crippled the Luftwaffe
   and German army in France / Joseph T. Molyson, Jr..
Description: Essex, Connecticut : Stackpole Books, 2025. | Includes
   bibliographical references and index.
Identifiers: LCCN 2024055796 (print) | LCCN 202405579—7 (ebook) | ISBN
   9780811777063 (hardcover) | ISBN 9780811777070 (epub)
Subjects: LCSH: World War, 1939-1945—Campaigns—France—Normandy. | World
   War, 1939-1945—Aerial operations, American. | World War,
   1939-1945—Aerial operations, British. | Normandy (France)—History,
   Military.
Classification: LCC D756.5.N6 M65 2025 (print) | LCC D756.5.N6 (ebook) |
   DDC 940.54/420944—dc23/eng/20250212
LC record available at https://lccn.loc.gov/2024055796
LC ebook record available at https://lccn.loc.gov/2024055797

∞™ The paper used in this publication meets the minimum requirements of American National Standard for Information Sciences—Permanence of Paper for Printed Library Materials, ANSI/ NISO Z39.48-1992.

For the five sons who went to war, of which three came home . . .

SK1c Irwin John Langhoff Sr., US Coast Guard

LT Daniel Joseph Lyons, US Navy

SSGT John Patrick Lyons Jr., US Army

SSGT Patrick Michael Damien Lyons, US Army

SGT Robert Alexander Lyons, US Army

and their mothers . . .

Gold Star Mother Margaret Burke Lyons

Blue Star Mother Alice Jeanne Doebele

Contents

CONTENTS

Maps, Illustrations, and Tables

MAPS

ILLUSTRATIONS

TABLES

Preface

This is my second book on the aviation contribution to Operation OVER-LORD, the D-Day invasion of northwestern France on June 6, 1944. The first book was *Six Air Forces Over the Atlantic*, which covered the airpower contribution to victory in the Battle of the Atlantic campaign. For context, it also covered the early war period and the development of the six air forces described. It was the first step on the Allied path to Normandy.

In this second book, I attempt to describe the tapestry of efforts in preparation for the invasion of Normandy even as the Battle of the Atlantic continued to be fought. Like any tapestry, it involves multiple threads interwoven to produce a final product. As an airman, I will focus the narrative on airpower's contribution to this tapestry. The Allies, weakened by worldwide defeat in 1939 to 1942, resurrected and focused their air forces on defeating the Axis in 1943 and 1944. Problems were encountered and solutions formulated and implemented. None of these solutions were perfect or without great cost, yet in the end they enabled the Western Allies to invade France in Operation OVERLORD.

Joe Molyson
Lilburn, Georgia
June 2024

In 2003, I had the privilege of preparing an oral history of the World War II service of South Carolina senator John "Ace" Drummond. Drummond was a captain in the 510th Fighter Squadron flying P-47Ds from RAF Christchurch, England, in 1944. His decorations included the Distinguished Flying Cross, two Purple Hearts, nine Air Medals, the European–African–Middle Eastern Campaign Medal with three Battle Stars, and the Presidential Unit Citation. Not bad for a young guy from the small town of Ninety Six, South Carolina.

Drummond later became an accomplished South Carolina senator. At age eighty-four in 2003, his memories of wartime service remained sharp.[1] Drummond clearly remembered his many squadron mates:

The pilots were young; the average age for the 510th Fighter Squadron 405th Fighter Group was twenty-seven, although many were much younger. What strikes me about the war is how young we were. I was an old man, I was twenty-five.

There was a boy I was friends with in the squadron. We called him K-Kid [Lieutenant Boleslaw Kociencki]. The most handsome kid you'd ever seen. On his plane he had a cartoon of a kid with two pistols. We called him our "trolling bait." When we went out on the town all the girls came to him! He was brave, he would drive through hell. He was a hell of a good pilot.

Somewhere on the Seine River we were going to skip-bomb a bridge. We had delayed-action bombs and we would try to stick that bomb in the bank underneath it. I had just gone in and was pulling out and I heard K-Kid hollering "Get him off my tail! Get him off my tail!"

Jenkins [the section leader] had gone in first and was already above. He said, "Does anyone know what those two fires are?"

Somebody said, "K-Kid and a bogie [enemy aircraft]."

When we got back someone said two Me 109s were on the river, evidently trying to escape from something else, and they ran into us. And they said they thought they had run into one another and crashed. And I said, "No way! He [K-Kid] hollered, 'Get him off my tail!'"

Nobody heard that but me. He shot that one down and the other one shot him down. Eight years later, we found out that a French woman had found his dog tags. When I went last year [in 2002] to France, I found his grave.

I remember earlier when K-Kid got a medal pinned on him by General Quesada. Quesada himself was young, only forty-one or forty-two years old. When he pinned that medal on him, he looked up at him and said, "Lieutenant, how old are you?" K-Kid said, "Nineteen, sir." So help me, he looked like he was sixteen.

Quesada said, "Does your mother know you're over here?" We all laughed then, see? Two weeks later he was gone.

Now when I tell this story I wonder if his mother knows he's still over there.

Introduction

The focal point of World War II in Europe was the invasion of Normandy on D-Day, June 6, 1944. That invasion did not come easily; it required years of preparation in headquarters, factories, depots, airfields, ships, and foxholes. Britain had to be established, reinforced, and maintained as a base from which the Allies could launch the eventual—but not inevitable—return to France.

Peacetime Britain was a net importer of natural resources and food. After war began, the import of weapons was an additional requirement to be met. Therefore, maintaining the lifeline between Britain and its overseas sources of supply across the world's oceans, particularly the North Atlantic, was a necessary first step on the road to D-Day. Aviation was a key component in the defeat of Germany in the North Atlantic.

The Second Step to Normandy

World War II began with the German invasion of Poland, *Fall Weiss* (Case White) in September, 1939. The *Wehrmacht* (German military) was designed for quick, offensive operations. The Germans intended it to be a short war, a continuation of Hitler's aggressive diplomacy that had defeated British and French attempts to restrain him. Hitler wanted to fight only Poland, but Poland's allies Britain and France finally understood that the time for diplomacy was long past.

By taking Poland, Hitler cleared a path for a future invasion of his archenemy, the communist Soviet Union. It also garnered him a resourceful and stubborn enemy, Great Britain, who remained a threat to his west throughout the war. By June of 1940 the Allied armies in Continental Europe had been defeated and the British army driven back across the Channel from France to Britain.

By December 1940, the British had successfully prevented the Germans from crossing the Channel and invading the British homeland. From that time, the British plotted and planned their return to France. In France patriots made the occupation as painful as possible for the Germans, tying down Nazi resources.

In June, 1941, the German invasion of the Soviet Union changed World War II from a British war to an Allied one. The Allied war expanded to the Pacific in December of 1941 when America joined as an active belligerent.

Germany and Italy declared war against the United States a few days after Pearl Harbor. These strategic mistakes by the Germans, Italians, and Japanese doomed them to defeat.

Hitler's unified military, the *Wehrmacht*, dominated all of Continental Europe.[1] The *Luftwaffe* was the most powerful European air force; the German army (*Heer*) supreme on land. The *Kriegsmarine*, the German navy, maintained a partial blockade of Britain's lifeline across the Atlantic to force its surrender. All three forces had to be reduced or paralyzed before any return to France was possible. This was essential for what became Operation OVERLORD, the Allied invasion of northwest France on June 6, 1944, to be successful.

I use the term "Britain" to refer to the United Kingdom, which includes England, Wales, Northern Ireland, and Scotland. US troops were billeted throughout these regions. Most US-controlled airfields were located in eastern England.

There are also some additional terms concerning aviation terminology. A *sortie* is one flight by one aircraft. Simultaneous sorties intended to accomplish one job is a *mission*. The term mission can also be used to describe a major function of an air force. An *abort* is the cancellation of a sortie before it reaches its intended goal. A *chandelle* is a climbing turn. A *jettison* is the intentional act of dropping an object from an aircraft. Distances given in this book are in *statute miles* (5,280 feet), as was used in most army and air force documents of the time. During World War II, *nautical miles* (6,076 feet) was used in some long-range navigational computations and to describe airspeed, but may be less familiar to most readers.

CHAPTER ONE

The Channel and the Narrow Seas

The English Channel divides southern England from the northwestern coast of Continental Europe. It provides access from the North Atlantic to the North Sea. The waterway is about 300 miles long and about 100 miles across at its widest point. Its average depth is about 200 feet. At its most narrow, it is only 21 miles from Dover to Calais, and is called the Straits of Dover.

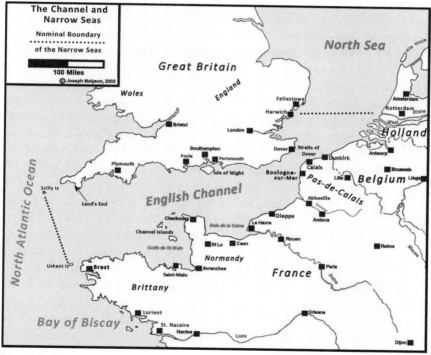

Map 1.1. The Channel and the Narrow Seas. MOLYSON[1]

3

Dover is in the English county of Kent. Calais is in the French department of Pas-de-Calais (note hyphens). To the west of the Channel is the North Atlantic Ocean and to the east is the North Sea. The Channel is not only a waterway connecting the Atlantic to the North Sea, but also a major pathway to world commerce from ports as far east as St. Petersburg, called Leningrad during World War II.

The Channel has several names. Formally, in Britain it is the English Channel. To the French, it is *la Manche* (the Sleeve). To the German fliers of World War II, it was *der Kanal* meaning "channel" or "ditch." The latter term was derogatory. Some American aircrew, returning from bombing Germany, also termed the North Sea between the Netherlands and Britain "the Channel," but this is a geographic misnomer.

The Channel is the most formidable water obstacle between Berlin and London, dwarfing any river on Earth. Intrepid merchants have been crossing the Channel for many thousands of years, but it has stopped all but a few invaders over the centuries and intimidated the rest. There has never been a bridge across the Channel, and only recently has a successful tunnel been built. Until the eighteenth century, the Channel was crossed only by boat.

It was first crossed by balloon in 1785 with aeronauts Jean-Pierre Blanchard, a Frenchman, and John Jeffries, an American. Blanchard earned a pension from French king Louis XVI for this feat. They flew from Dover to Guînes in the Pas-de-Calais in less than three hours, drifting on the wind. In 1909, after an English newspaper offered a £1,000 prize (about £120,000, or US$152,000 today), the competition was on to fly over the Channel in a powered aircraft.

The first attempt for the prize was by Frenchman Hubert Latham on July 19, 1909, and ended 6 miles shy of Dover with a splash. He became the first man to ditch an airplane in the Channel, but far from the last. Six days later, Louis Blériot made the first actual crossing in his Blériot XI. He flew at 250 feet, at a speed of 45 miles an hour. Without a compass, he navigated using a picket ship and dead reckoning. The entire flight took about 37 minutes. The crossing was only six years after the Wright brothers' first flight, and five years before World War I.

Wind has always been a factor in cross-Channel flight. The prevailing winds and weather are from the west and bring in storms from cold North Atlantic waters, mixing with the warmer water of the Gulf Stream. The prevailing winds were the dominant factor in the Age of Sail and are still a major contributor to navigational calculations. To accurately predict the weather over and near the Channel, weather observations were required from stations to the west until the advent of meteorological satellites long after World War II.

The Atlantic and the North Sea both have strong tidal currents, which sometimes collide in the Channel to cancel or reinforce each other. This sometimes adds to the complications of navigation between France and southern England. This makes Channel ports and harbors important; in fact, they were the first points fortified by the occupying Germans in World War II.

Because of the tides and other factors, including geology and hydrology, some Channel beaches are soft sand. Others are covered with large pebbles called "shingle." Sand can bog down wheeled vehicles and make even walking difficult, especially carrying heavy loads. The pebbles can foul the tracks of tanks and other tracked vehicles, jamming them to a stop. In both cases, mobility across the beach is an important factor in planning an invasion along the Channel coast.

The most important commercial port on the French side of the Channel is Le Havre, once home of the great French transatlantic passenger ships, an easy train ride to and from Paris. It lies at the mouth of the River Seine, the only major river to drain directly into the Channel. The British liners berthed across the Channel at Southampton, an easy train ride to and from London. Southampton is also protected from the Channel tides by the Isle of Wight, which is separated from the English mainland by a narrow strait, the Solent.

Naval bases on the Channel include Plymouth and Portsmouth in southern England and Cherbourg in northwestern France. Smaller ports and coastal sheltered places host vessels destined for faraway destinations and fleets of commercial fishermen. The Channel ports—Calais, Dunkirk, Boulogne-sur-Mer, and Dieppe—through which British troops, equipment, and supplies could easily be delivered from Dover to northern France, were major German ground objectives in both World War I and World War II.

THE NARROW SEAS

The Channel is the major component of the Narrow Seas, over which English kings formerly claimed sovereignty and demanded tribute. Except for brief interludes at the hands of the Spanish and Dutch, these waters have been dominated by the Royal Navy since medieval times. The Narrow Seas' nominal western boundary is the same as that of the Channel, a line drawn between the French island of Ushant (Ouessant) and the English Isles of Scilly. Its eastern boundary is a line drawn between the English port of Harwich and the Dutch port of Rotterdam.[2] This extension east from Dover was the route most often taken by English and American bombers striking into Germany during World War II.

CHAPTER TWO

The Beach

The machine-gun rounds neatly pocked the sand, dotted lines interrupted only when an obstacle was encountered—wood, steel, or flesh. Their Russian allies, desperate for relief from the German onslaught that would consume their country, had encouraged the invaders. Someone far away had a bold concept—push through to Russia—and now young men were attempting to make the great idea a reality. Even the sailors offshore were not safe; many ships had been lost to mines on the approach to the target area. Now coastal artillery was hitting others.

The legion of landing craft dwindled as they made hazardous multiple trips back to the transports to bring in more desperately needed troops and supplies. Aircraft did not hamper defensive fire from the beach. There was no coordination between the leadership afloat and the trapped men ashore. Allied generals and admirals peered through the smoke, trying to sort out the confusion. No war college prepared you for this, carnage on a grand scale some called "strategy."

The defenders on the bluffs above the beach were well dug in and dominated the shoreline with automatic weapons and artillery fire. With mobility unhindered by Allied bombardment or airpower, their defending army moved behind the beach at will to concentrate strength where required. They would lose other battles, but in this place and at this time, they would win.

In London, Churchill listened to the reports as they came in. Much of this was his plan, and now the plan was dying along with his soldiers and sailors. Berlin must be happy. It was obvious that Churchill's grand scheme would not work; the enemy was holding, and the far shore would remain theirs. The Allied troops were pinned down. They couldn't break the line and move inland. When enough of them had died, London ordered them withdrawn. Under fire, the survivors slowly re-embarked. While a few wanted another chance, most just wanted to live long enough to go home.

Gallipoli Peninsula, Ottoman Empire, 1915.

THE NEXT WAR

The Gallipoli Peninsula controlled the maritime straits between the Mediterranean and the Black Sea. It was also the outer defense of the imperial capital of the Ottoman Empire at Constantinople. Military aircraft were operated by both sides but did not affect the outcome of the invasion. The commanding position dominating the straits helped to isolate the landlocked Russians from their French and British allies in the Mediterranean. This in turn led to the eventual collapse of czarist Russia and its surrender to the Germans, who then turned their full might to the West.

The Turks prevailed in the defense of Gallipoli, but in the end, they joined Germany and the other Central Powers in World War I defeat. It was, after all, Germany's turn to lose. The Germans had beaten and embarrassed the French in 1870, laying siege to Paris in the process. The French never forgot it, and would eventually avenge it. The Allied survivors of Gallipoli would go on to other battles; many would later fall on other fields. The ashes of their war would nurture the seeds of the next.

Map 2.1. The Gallipoli landing, February 1915. MOLYSON

STALEMATE IN THE WEST

In World War II, neither the Allies nor the Germans could afford the trench-warfare bloodbath they had endured in the Great War. When negotiations, prevarications, and demonstrations failed against Poland and its Allies in 1939, Hitler seized most of Western Europe, including France, by lightning attack—blitzkrieg. The British were pushed back across the Channel, where they mounted a successful defense. In reply, the Germans also transitioned to a defensive stance, as most of their forces were transferred south and east to new adventures. Only the 21 miles of the Straits of Dover separated Germany from victory over Britain. It was now Führer Adolf Hitler's newly seized castle on one side of the Channel and British prime minister Winston Churchill's threatened castle on the other. The result was a stalemate, but not inaction.

The Germans were determined to defeat any future liberation of France before an Allied beachhead could be established. Hitler's generals attempted to re-create the conditions that had allowed the Turks to defeat the English at Gallipoli, a *Festung Europa* (Fortress Europe) that could repel any likely Allied invasion.

The British began working on a return to France soon after their desperate victory in the Battle of Britain. It was obvious to even the earliest invasion planners that the German air force and navy would have to be decisively defeated before the German army in France could be engaged on the beaches, and beyond. The British, joined by the Americans in 1941, used airpower to achieve the prerequisites for a return to northwestern France less than three years later.

CHAPTER THREE

The Airpower Factor

The Allied air forces contributed in many ways to preparations for the invasion of northwestern France. All of these efforts began modestly and grew in effectiveness over time. Some were directed by national leaders, others by sheer necessity. With the benefit of hindsight, it is easy to see there were at least six missions for which airpower was critical.

The first mission was the defense of the maritime routes to and from Britain. This goal began modestly along the coast but eventually extended to the mid-ocean defeat of German surface warships and U-boats. The last *Kriegsmarine* surface raiders were driven by Royal Air Force (RAF) bombing from their lair at Brest, France, by February 1942. By May 1943, German submarines were driven from the North Atlantic by better intelligence exploitation, increased numbers of surface escorts, and longer-ranged antisubmarine aircraft. This allowed Britain to become a well-supplied base from which to launch attacks against Occupied Europe.[1]

The second mission was the defense of Britain, especially after the British Expeditionary Force was withdrawn from France in 1940. Without an effective army, the RAF prevented a German invasion across the English Channel or North Sea. Britain became the bastion from which the Allies launched OVERLORD. Even on the eve of D-Day, the RAF and US Army Air Forces (USAAF) were required to forestall impending German missile attacks against southern England by V-1 cruise missiles and V-2 ballistic missiles.

The third mission was the defeat of *Kriegsmarine* coastal forces that could threaten an approaching Allied invasion fleet. The RAF crippled the 1940 German invasion fleet hastily assembling in French, Belgian, and Dutch ports, and went on to attack the German coastal convoy system and the ports from which they sailed. The threat posed by German coastal warships led to the development of RAF Coastal Command "strike wings," especially created to defeat small German warships and coastal convoys in the Channel, the Bay of Biscay, and the North Sea.

The fourth mission was the strategic attack of German installations and military and naval forces (see appendix 2), which began in 1939 and greatly expanded by the end of 1941. Such attacks required aircraft able to carry and deliver adequate bomb loads to targets in occupied territory and in the German homeland. It was quickly determined that air superiority was necessary to get the bombers to their targets in daytime. It was this mission that best achieved the crippling of the German air force and severely impeded German industry.

The fifth mission was the development of transport aircraft that could carry cargo and troops quickly from where they were based to where they were needed. This capability was readily available once exploited, due in large part to the pre-war civilian airline industry. This enabled the delivery of thousands of aircraft and tons of critical equipment around the world, less than twenty years after Lindbergh's solo crossing of the Atlantic. By 1944, the Allies were able to land complete airborne divisions in enemy territory and sustain them by air.

The sixth mission was the application of aviation resources to the tactical and operational requirements of the land forces. The general failure of air support and cooperation between the British Air Force in France (BAFF) and the British Expeditionary Force (BEF) in 1940 led to the reluctance of the RAF to engage in Army Co-operation.[2] Conversely, the Royal Army insisted on better methods of getting air support from the RAF. The RAF and the Royal Army redefined and improved their relationship during the fighting in North Africa. This would come to fruition on D-Day.

The evolution of expertise in conducting air operations occurred worldwide. Lessons learned in one theater of operations were passed to airmen in other theaters. The various missions evolved in parallel, not sequentially. This is reflected in the narrative, which frequently switches from one mission to another. Fortunately, the industrial base in the United States, Canada, and Britain was able to build enough planes and train enough aircrew to accomplish all six almost simultaneously.

Chapter Four

Arsenal (March 1935–August 1941)

In 1935, Hitler's Germany abrogated the Treaty of Versailles, resuming conscription to build a new German army of thirty-six divisions. The German air force, resurrected as the *Luftwaffe*, was revealed. By mid-1936, the Germans and Italians were actively supporting Francisco Franco's Fascist rebels in Spain, sending some of their most advanced weapons and skillful warriors.

The British yielded to domestic political pressure and concluded the Anglo-German Naval Agreement, permitting Germany to openly build large surface warships and submarines. Quietly, the Royal Air Force began to explore technological solutions to the future defense of Britain. This included the building of advanced fighter aircraft, better bombers, and extensive defensive radar installations. The radars and fighters were linked with an increasingly sophisticated command and control system.

The Yanks

The Munich Crisis of September 1938, when Hitler expanded German territory at the expense of the Czechs, clarified American president Franklin Roosevelt's fear of resurgent German militarism. Roosevelt, former assistant secretary of the navy during World War I, ordered the chief of naval operations to begin refurbishing large numbers of inactive World War I destroyers in reserve at Philadelphia and San Diego. He also ordered the transfer of a squadron of cruisers to the Atlantic. FDR's first objective was to secure access to Britain and France via the North Atlantic.

The Atlantic Squadron was not the only benefactor of Roosevelt's reaction to Munich. On November 18, 1938, FDR ordered top cabinet and military leaders to prepare for war. Roosevelt wanted airplanes, lots of airplanes, including an air corps of 20,000 aircraft. He envisioned an eventual annual production rate of 24,000 aircraft for the air corps, naval aviation, and for American allies.[1] Roosevelt settled for a near-term objective of 10,000 for the air corps, the maximum that was politically possible in the current congressional climate. These 10,000 would include 2,500 trainers, 3,750 bombers and fighters in combat units, and 3,750 aircraft in reserve.[2]

Of course, in a future war, getting airplanes to America's allies in Africa and Europe would be a challenge. The northern route via Canada, Newfoundland, and Labrador to Scotland was identified, but was always challenged by weather, especially during the winter. The Roosevelt administration, with the assistance of Pan American Airways and its founder Juan Trippe, began developing a series of airfields across Latin America that could be used to ferry aircraft from Natal, Brazil, to the west coast of Africa. The route, which was open throughout the year, was first established in July 1941.

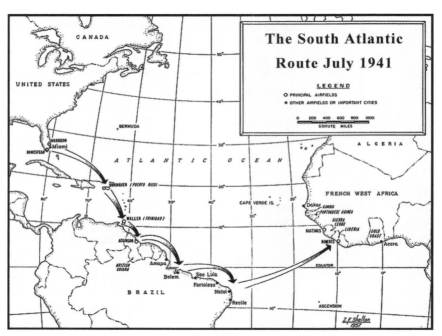

Map 4.1. Southern air ferry route. MOLYSON AFTER CRAVEN[3]

Natal was the closest Latin American city to Africa and Europe, and with its generally good weather would be a natural jumping-off point. There were several airfields in West Africa controlled by France and Britain. After crossing the Atlantic, newly delivered aircraft could travel north and then along the European or North African coast to their destinations.

The United States instituted the Selective Training and Service Act in September 1940, the first peacetime draft in American history, at the height of the Battle of Britain. While President Roosevelt supported the British, the United States did not declare war on Germany until December 1941, in reciprocity for the German declaration.

No other industrialized country began the war years with such a gap between its actual and potential productivity as did the United States.[4] The memories of the Great War were in the minds of the voters, and they did not want another overseas adventure. After World War I the Senate did not ratify the punitive Versailles Treaty nor join the League of Nations. It was felt that European problems were theirs to resolve, and this feeling was still pervasive in 1941.

America was an economy in recovery from the Depression and did not aspire to a large air force or army. The navy defending America's coastal frontiers, it was thought, provided sufficient protection from foreign threats. The United States was preparing to grant the Philippines independence in the mid-1940s. Roosevelt used New Deal tools and the force of his personality to circumvent existing Neutrality Laws and the public misperception of the threat to the Americas. It was Roosevelt and his close advisors who envisioned and developed "The Arsenal of Democracy."

Table 4.1. Conversion of Civilian to Military Production.[5]

Civilian Product	Military Product Equivalent
2,500 tons of tin plus 190,000 tons of steel	5,000 tanks
30 lipstick cases	30 ammo cartridges
2,300 pairs of nylons	1 parachute
1 pound fat	0.3 pound x gunpowder
30,000 razor blades	50 0.30 caliber machine-gun rounds

America's economic mobilization—the transition from mainly peacetime civilian production to maximum production of military goods—took many months. Real progress was made by February 1942, and it reached a plateau in November 1943.[6] Military equipment was more complex than what it replaced on the production line. The B-24 bomber, for example, had two orders of magnitude more parts than a passenger car.[7] This in turn required more subcontractors to produce parts, and more skilled workers to put them together.

Table 4.2. Partial List of New Products Developed for Military Requirements.[8]

Requirement	Product
Antibiotic	Penicillin
	1943: 7,500 ampules
	1944: 10,276,000 ampules
Fabrication	Epoxy
Field transportation	Jeep
Improved aviation engine performance	100-octane gas
Faster combat aircraft	Jet engine
Aircraft detection in reduced visibility	Radar
Logistics	Standardized cargo (Liberty and Victory ships and standardized tankers (T-1/T-2), landing ship, tanks (LSTs), and front-ramp landing craft
Lubrication	Teflon
Manufacturing	Electron microscope
Nutrition	Improved field rations, including M&Ms
Packing material and insulation	Styrofoam
Public health insecticide	DDT
Weatherproof shelter	Quonset hut

Even without enemy action, it took time to gather the money, to recruit and train the workers, to convert or build factories, and to develop synthetic substitutes for materials controlled by the Axis. It took time to prepare the military and naval forces to use the tools the new economy was producing. Many men were drafted out of production jobs and into the military. They had to be replaced by women and men who were unsuited to active military service, who in turn required training in nontraditional skills. Although Lend-Lease aid to threatened democracies and other government industrial programs had begun the transition after the Munich Appeasement, Pearl Harbor was the impetus for the great acceleration of wartime production.

In World War I, the American airmen in Europe were dependent on the British and French for airplanes and other kinds of support. US Air Corps chief General Henry "Hap" Arnold did not intend for a similar dependency to develop in World War II. As he worked with President Roosevelt and other leaders to build a war-winning air force, he was quite specific in his concept of airpower:

Air power is not made up of airplanes alone. Air power is a composite of airplanes, air crews, maintenance crews, air bases, air supply, and sufficient replacements in both planes and crews to maintain a constant fighting strength, regardless of what losses may be inflicted by the enemy. In addition to that, we must have the backing of a large aircraft industry in the United States to provide all kinds of equipment, and a large training establishment that can furnish the personnel when called upon.[9]

Before they could fight the Axis as a team, Britain and the United States had to establish lines of communication and a mutual understanding of their joint interests and expectations. This included not only the civilian governments but also the senior levels of their military establishments. British prime minister Winston Churchill led a Commonwealth clearly feeling the effects of total war. Britain's army had been soundly beaten on several occasions and now was holding on grimly in North Africa. Roosevelt clearly recognized the precarious position of the British and had taken the initial steps to assist them, just short of war.

The Royal Navy convoy escort force was clearly overmatched in the North Atlantic. The Royal Air Force Fighter Command adequately defended the

Figure 4.1. Women in an A-20 factory. LOC 2017694234

homeland but could do little over occupied France with its short-range fighter aircraft. RAF Bomber Command was evolving into a nighttime strategic bombing force after excessive daylight bombing losses. Their attacks did little to deter the Germans from further aggression, but Bomber Command was the sole military force in Britain able to strike offensively at the Germans.

Yet Churchill, like Roosevelt, was able to look beyond immediate problems toward the ultimate objectives of the liberation of Europe and victory. Naively, the Soviet government of Josef Stalin assisted in the partition of Poland and maintained economic ties with Germany until Hitler attacked Russia. Somehow the movement of German military might to his western border seemed to have escaped him. Perhaps he had never read *Mein Kampf.*

THE ABC-1 STAFF AGREEMENT (JANUARY–MARCH 1941)

By the beginning of 1941, American Lend-Lease aid was flowing across the Atlantic. The American, British, and Canadian (ABC) governments began military conversations to ascertain how a future Anglo-American alliance might fight the Axis of Germany–Italy–Japan.[10] By March, it was decided that Hitler's Reich was the most powerful and dangerous of the three. The nascent alliance would first seek to defeat Germany and liberate Europe, with or without a declaration of war by the United States. This was the origin of the so-called "Germany first" policy.

Of particular interest was the emphasis on a strategic air campaign against German military power. Such a campaign was already under way, being flown by British and Commonwealth airmen. In June, Hitler invaded the Soviet Union, and at the time it seemed it would defeat Russia before the end of the year. This confirmed the worst fears that Nazi Germany would continue to expand its conquests until defeated on the battlefield.

The ABC-1 agreement called for strategic offensive operations against the European Axis Powers as a maximum effort and strategic defensive operations against Japan in the Far East, with minimum diversion of forces from the European war. ABC-1 specifically stated: "Offensive measures in the European area will include a sustained air offensive against German military power, supplemented by air offensives against other regions under enemy control which contribute to that power."[11]

ARGENTIA CONFERENCE (AUGUST 9–12, 1941)

In July, President Roosevelt asked the secretaries of war and the navy for the overall production requirements necessary to defeat the Axis. Roosevelt planned on meeting Churchill within the next sixty days and wanted to know what assistance America could offer. The president would build America's grand strategy based on military inputs, as well as those of his political, diplomatic, and industrial advisors.

The Joint Board of the Army and Navy, the precursor to the US Joint Chiefs of Staff, was unable to build consensus on a strategy upon which to establish military requirements, let alone what could be spared for the British. Therefore, the War and Navy Departments each decided to answer the presidential inquiry in their own way.

In August, Roosevelt and Churchill synchronized the wartime and postwar goals of the Western Allies at the Argentia Conference. Argentia, on Newfoundland's Placentia Bay, was the site of a new US Navy air base leased in exchange for earlier US aid to Britain. There were many in the United States who would avoid war, if possible, yet Roosevelt came to Argentia to represent America as the Arsenal of Democracy.

CHAPTER FIVE

Theory into Practice (1914–1939)

The British way of war in France from the time of the AD 1066 Norman Conquest has been to fight with several Continental allies against a stronger common enemy. In the nineteenth century, the main enemy was France, and one of the allies, German Prussia. In the twentieth century, the main ally became France and the enemy was Germany. The way of war was the same; it was only the enemy and allies that changed over time.

The British army sent to France in 1914 was called the British Expeditionary Force (BEF). The term "expeditionary" meant an armed force organized to fight in a foreign country. It grew from 150,000 men in 1914 to a peak strength of over 2 million later in the war. By the end of the war, almost 420,000 of these men were casualties.

The scourge of trench warfare led to widespread pacifism in Britain, France, and America after the Armistice. It also suggested that an alternative means for victory should be sought if Britain were ever to fight again in Continental Europe. Using land armies to win wars was hideously expensive, both in treasure and lives.

The Royal Flying Corps (RFC), part of the Royal Army, developed as a powerful adjunct to the army, as well as undertaking separate missions including bombing of industrial targets in western Germany. After the war, it was established as a separate military service, the Royal Air Force (RAF). This included a separate air ministry as part of the government and an air staff to run the new service. The senior RAF officer was Chief of the Air Staff (CAS).

The RAF joined the annual contest between the Royal Army and Royal Navy for funding priority. It also promoted airpower as a new way to win a future war in Europe, a strategic bombing strategy against the enemy homeland independent of supporting the ground war.

In March 1922 it was revealed that the French *Armée de l'Air* had 300 bombers and 300 fighters which could strike Britain from coastal bases. Relations had cooled rapidly between the two allies once the Armistice had been signed in

1918. The RAF at the time had less than 40 fighters to oppose such an attack.[1] It seemed that the French, suitably aroused against its erstwhile ally, might conduct its own strategic bombing campaign against Britain. This led to calls to expand the RAF, but available funds and the imperative to disarm restricted its growth. Fortunately, the French had no reason to go to war against Britain.

Calls for disarmament continued, fed by the fear of another land war and concern that London and other British cities could be bombed without warning. Some factions of the civilian government thought such attacks could not be prevented. Japan's 1931 massive air attacks against Chinese cities brought more despair than action. In a November 10, 1932, speech in the House of Commons, once and future prime minister Stanley Baldwin said, "It is well . . . for the man in the street to realize that there is no power on earth that can protect him from being bombed . . . *the bomber will always get through.*"[2]

For Baldwin, this may have been an appeal to disarm before Doomsday. For airmen, it was a justification to rearm and refocus on discrete missions. In 1936, the RAF was reorganized into various commands by function, a structure maintained throughout World War II. These included three combat commands: Fighter Command, Bomber Command, and Coastal Command.

The Germans had other ideas. Hermann Göring and others formulated a different theory of air war, called blitzkrieg (lightning war). The dive-bomber would be the basis for a ground-support air force combined with mechanized formations to provide an army that could quickly strike deep into an enemy's heartland. German officers were trained to automatically concentrate at the *Schwerpunkt*, the critical point at which an enemy could be overcome.

Medium- and dive-bombers ranged ahead of the army, clearing a deep path into enemy defenses. *Luftwaffe* fighters swept away opposition to German air operations. There was no strategic bombing force established. Enemy economic resources were not to be attacked unless necessary to win the land war. They must be preserved, captured, and exploited for Germany.

WORLD WAR II EARLY RAF OPERATIONS

In the late 1930s, the RAF developed four primary combat missions for applying British airpower against Germany.

The first mission was to defend the airspace over Britain from air attack. This was the domain of the RAF Fighter Command, flying short-range fighter interceptors.

The second was to cooperate with the Royal Navy to control the seas around Britain and the maritime lines of communication originating and terminating in the home islands. This was assigned to RAF Coastal Command, operating flying boats and maritime patrol bombers.

The third was an independent strategic bombing campaign against the German heartland conducted by Bomber Command. At the start of the war, Bomber Command flew twin-engine medium bombers for this purpose. Four-engine heavy bombers, which could carry larger bomb loads to more distant targets, were under development. At no time did the RAF contemplate developing long-range escort fighters to support these bombers, because "the bomber will always get through."[3]

The fourth mission was for the RAF Fighter and Bomber Commands to jointly support the Royal Army and its allies in a ground war, preferably on the European continent. Army coordination and support was secondary to their primary missions of homeland air defense and strategic bombardment. Fighter Command would employ their short-range fighters to protect the army from enemy bombing. Bomber Command would use its light bomber force to attack enemy land forces just beyond the front line.

In March 1939, the British government allied with France to guarantee the sovereignty of Poland. When the Germans invaded on September 1, neither Britain nor France was in a position to help. Geography and prewar complacency worked against them. On September 4, 1939, the independent strategic bombing mission began when Bomber Command sent home-based twin-engine medium bombers in daylight to attack coastal targets and ships on the German North Sea coast. Results were disappointing and casualties heavy due to German day fighters and antiaircraft fire.

Soon, Bomber Command turned to dropping propaganda pamphlets at night over Germany when day fighters were not a factor. This had a positive effect on future Bomber Command operations, for the pamphlet mission taught the aircrew how to better navigate at night and in bad weather.

On September 9, 1939, a hastily assembled second British Expeditionary Force was sent across the Channel to defend France from a possible German attack. They sat in northern France until May 10, 1940, a period they nicknamed "The Phony War." The BEF was accompanied by an RAF element, the British Air Force in France. The BAFF was divided into two forces: the RAF Air Component, to directly support the BEF, and the Advanced Air Striking Force (AASF), for independent bombing operations beyond the front line.

The German *Fall Gelb* (Case Yellow) operation began on May 10, 1940. The Fighter Command allocation to the BAFF never exceeded the number of fighter squadrons that could be spared from the defense of Britain. Once the Germans

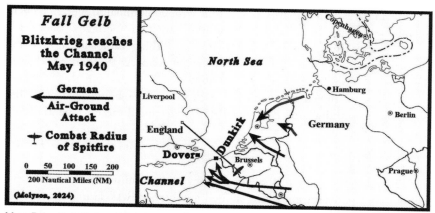

Map 5.1. *Fall Gelb*—blitzkrieg reaches the Channel. MOLYSON

invaded, neither the limited number of RAF nor French fighters were able to establish air superiority, or even parity with the *Luftwaffe*. The British had not brought their sophisticated but bulky radar-directed control system with them, and the French lacked an effective system to defend its airspace.

Attacking through Holland, Belgium, and northern France, German columns with extensive air support cut through the Allied armies and reached the Channel and North Sea coasts at several points by May 10, 1940. In the process, they isolated Allied armies from one another, overran Allied airfields, and terrorized cities in their path with selected bombing. This was blitzkrieg expertly applied.

The AASF light bombers were decimated by German fighters and FLAK (an acronym for *Flugzeugabwehrkanonen*—antiaircraft artillery) while conducting daylight attacks to stop the German onslaught. The attacks were both valiant and suicidal, and the damage they inflicted was negligible. Short-range British Hurricane fighters, driven from their airfields, evacuated back to England. Spitfires, withheld until the British troops in Belgium were pinned against the sea at Dunkirk, provided valuable air cover as a motley fleet of naval and civilian vessels evacuated the BEF.

Later in May, Bomber Command began bombing into Germany using its medium bombers based in England. The BEF, the BAFF, and the French were soundly beaten by the *Luftwaffe* and German army in France and Belgium. The decision to bomb Germany ultimately rested with Churchill and his war cabinet, since it invited reprisal raids by the German air force.

The initial RAF night attacks, this time with bombs instead of leaflets, were intended to hit precise oil and transportation targets in Germany. They failed to inflict much damage, or even find their targets. The desired effect of drawing German fighters and flak back into Germany did not occur. Nothing could deter the *Luftwaffe* from the *Schwerpunkt* at Dunkirk.

The French signed the Armistice with Germany on June 22, 1940. The operations to withdraw the BEF and BAFF were completed on June 25, 1940. Britain stood alone.

There were three main conclusions to be drawn from the RAF experience in France in 1939–1940.

First, direct support to the Royal Army by light bombers was ineffective without air superiority, something limited numbers of RAF Hurricane fighters could not provide. Second, strategic night-bombing operations could be conducted independent of and distant from the ground war. Third, day bombers required an escort fighter of sufficient range to accompany the bombers to their targets. Escort fighters were not required if the bombers attacked by night.

In the Battle of Britain, from June through September of 1940, the *Luftwaffe* reached similar conclusions concerning the survivability of bombers in daylight and the need for adequate fighter escort. Although the Germans had the Messerschmitt Bf 110 (also known as the Me 110), a twin-engine long-range fighter, it was no more survivable against RAF single-engine day fighters than the bombers it escorted. By the end of 1940, the British and German air forces were strategic bombing only at night.

THE TACTICAL SCHOOL

In the 1930s, the Air Corps Tactical School at Maxwell Field, Alabama, developed the doctrine of daylight precision bombing as its model for American heavy bomber operations. The premise of strategic bombing was that a society's "fabric" could be destroyed by highly selective attacks on its economy. For the airmen at the Tactical School, this meant precision daylight bombing against key targets.[4] Future US Army Air Forces (USAAF) leaders—Spaatz, Eaker, and the rest—would pass through this school on their way to war.

The Americans prepared to enter the war with the rugged B-17 as its main heavy bomber. The Fortress was a direct result of Tactical School thinking. Its one job was to carry bombs deep into enemy territory in daylight and drop them precisely on specific enemy targets. The plane was supposed to be so heavily armed that it could resist attacks by enemy fighters and operate with acceptable losses. Visionaries though they were, Air Corps leaders failed to appreciate that the airspeed and firepower of enemy fighter interceptors would also evolve. Therefore, the Air Corps did not press for a long-range escort fighter to augment the defensive firepower of the B-17. When the Americans began strategic bombing of Germany in 1943, the battered bombers did get through—but not all of them.

All of this capability came at a cost: The B-17 had a lower bomb-carrying capability than contemporary lightly armed British heavy bombers that bombed by night. After heavy British bomber losses in daylight raids, a heavily armed American daylight bomber seemed a good investment.

Chapter Six

Darkness (September 1939–February 1942)

The Navy can lose us the war, but only the Air Force can win it. Therefore our supreme effort must be to gain overwhelming mastery in the air. The Fighters are our salvation, but the Bombers alone provide the means of victory!
—Winston Churchill, June 1940[1]

During the first year of World War II, it seemed the German emphasis on clearing a path for their ground forces was the most effective employment of airpower. The *Luftwaffe* enabled the German army to seize territory rapidly using blitzkrieg tactics. This worked well as long as the enemy countries were weak and their capitals easily overrun. Once the German army reached the Channel ports in May–June 1940, the easy victories in Western Europe were over.

In the 1940 Battle for France, the traditional method to employ Allied airpower to support the army was predominant. Primarily occupied in supporting their respective armies, neither side was able to deliver decisive strategic bombing on the other's homeland. The RAF was forced by circumstances to abandon almost 180 unserviceable Hurricane fighters out of the 450 sent to France. More were lost in combat.

In addition to aircraft losses, both the Royal Army and the RAF left significant amounts of ground equipment in France. Fortunately, surplus RAF pilots and ground crews were evacuated by transport aircraft or on the vessels rescuing the army. The RAF's other modern fighter type, the Spitfire, joined with the Hurricanes to cover the Dunkirk evacuation from airfields in southeast England.

Even as the depleted RAF Fighter Command prepared to fight the Battle of Britain beginning in July 1940, Churchill knew that Bomber Command was his last hope to win the European war. Germany now had access to the Channel and North Atlantic, and the Royal Navy was forced into a defensive mode. The French army was gone and the British army needed to rebuild. It was no longer a matter of supporting the army; it must be defended until it could be reconstituted.

An attempted German invasion of Britain loomed. If it succeeded, Britain would be conquered. If it was repulsed, the chastened Germans might move south and east to leave Britain to wither on the vine. Churchill, however, had the vision to look beyond today's defeats toward tomorrow's victory; to keep Hitler engaged in Western Europe:

> *There is one thing that will bring him back and bring him down, and that is an absolutely devastating, exterminating attack by very heavy bombers from this country upon the Nazi homeland. We must be able to overwhelm them by this means, without which I do not see a way through.*[2]

DAY OR NIGHT

It was combat experience that made existing American and European theories of strategic bombing diverge. Both believed in bombing to deliver a "knockout blow." American bombing theory emphasized accurately delivered attacks on precise targets with heavily armed bombers in large self-defending formations. Britain's Bomber Command entered the war with lightly armed twin-engine Whitley and Wellington bombers as their main means of executing a strategic bombing campaign. The *Luftwaffe* bombers—Heinkel 111s, Dornier 17s, and Junkers 88s—also were lightly armed for self-defense and were not intended for strategic bombing.

German bombers in the Battle of Britain could not penetrate the RAF defenses by day. Similarly, the RAF bombers could not punch through German daylight air defenses. Unescorted daylight bombing was found to be impractical over Europe. It was thought the American theory would not work. Therefore, nighttime area bombardment became the principle around which the *Luftwaffe* and RAF conducted attacks on each other's homelands.

As the Battle of Britain ended in October 1940, the bloodied *Luftwaffe* switched to night area bombing. The British nicknamed this new campaign "the Blitz." The British also began to do their strategic bombing under cover of darkness. Most German industry, after all, was located in or near urban areas. Cities were also where industrial workers lived.

Night area rather than night precision bombing was undertaken because most precise targets could not be located at night with 1941 technology. This was especially true in the Ruhr Valley industrial zone in western Germany, which was perpetually shrouded in smog. The RAF and the *Luftwaffe* continued their mutually destructive night urban raids as war raged along the periphery of Europe in late 1940 through 1941.

Thanks to the *Luftwaffe*'s area bombing of British cities, there was plenty of evidence to support this strategy. Churchill's scientific advisor, Lord Cherwell, collected data that indicated the destruction of one's own house was the worst possible blow to morale. Some people seemed to mind it more than the loss of relatives or friends. With Germany's population concentrated in its fifty-eight largest cities, it should be a simple matter of mathematics to "de-house" (Cherwell's term) about a third of the German population in about eighteen months.[3] This quite Teutonic calculation was henceforth applied to RAF targeting philosophy.

Even the gift of twenty new Boeing B-17C bombers in early 1941 did nothing to change the RAF's mind about daylight raiding. They failed to heed American advice on how the big planes should be employed in large, self-defending formations, bombing precise targets from high altitude. As new British-built four-engine aircraft began entering German night skies in the summer of 1941, the RAF evaluated the American-built Flying Fortress I (B-17C) as a potential day bomber.

Unfortunately, the RAF employed it in small formations and from too high an altitude. There were insufficient numbers of aircraft to provide the wall of defensive machine-gun fire envisioned by the Americans. The bombsights provided with these aircraft were not effective above 25,000 feet. The first RAF Fortress lost in combat was shot down over Scandinavia during this test period.

On September 8, 1941, pilots of *Jagdgruppe Stavanger* (Fighter Group Stavanger) shot down one of the big new bombers of RAF No. 90 Squadron over Norway. Ironically, the victorious pilot flew a Bf 109T, one of the aircraft that was supposed to be embarked on the abortive German aircraft carrier *Graf Zeppelin*. Thus, a fighter that had already lost its original mission downed an aircraft that would transform daylight bombing in Europe.[4] The Fortress tests were not successful for the Brits, and the surviving RAF Fortresses were transferred to other duties. This confirmed British night-bombing doctrine.

Both the British and Germans were learning to better use technology to lift the veil of darkness. For the attacker, various electronic navigation aids enabled bombers to better find enemy target areas in the dark. Both sides accomplished this by broadcasting radio beams from fixed ground stations that were received and interpreted by navigational electronic equipment on their bombers. Both sides knew the limited capacity of such equipment and how it could be made ineffective by jamming. Each development was met by the adversary's countermeasures.

THE KAMMHUBER LINE

Defensively, the *Luftwaffe* evolved a nighttime system similar to the British system used to win the daylight Battle of Britain. As RAF night bombing increased, the Germans in April 1941 began operating a string of ground radar stations across the RAF approach routes into Germany. The system, named *Himmelbett* ("four-poster bed"), included the radar stations, flak belts, ground-based fighter controllers, and interceptor aircraft. The line of defenses in depth arrayed along the western German border became known as the Kammhuber Line, after night defense commander General Josef Kammhuber.

The Kammhuber Line was the main zone in which German night fighters hunted. The defenses started at the coastline and ended in the area of Berlin. Aided by this radar network and depending on natural lighting for the final attack, single- and twin-engine interceptors were employed to find and destroy RAF bombers. The Germans also increased the number of flak installations

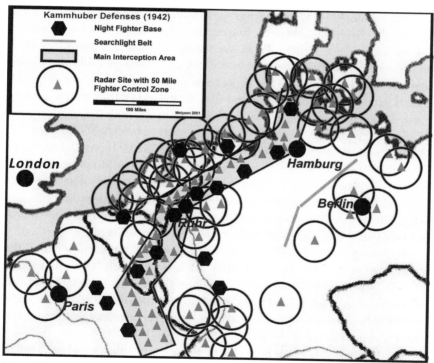

Map 6.1. Kammhuber Line Defenses by 1942. MOLYSON AFTER MURRAY

around their major cities and in belts along the Line. Flak was a static defense weapon; *Luftwaffe* interceptors were required to hit the bombers before they arrived over their target and to harass them on their withdrawal. A similar defensive program was being used to defend English skies at night.

By August 1941, the Germans had combined the use of ground and experimental airborne intercept (AI) radar to lead night interceptor pilots to enemy bombers. The ground radar would get the fighter to within 3 miles of the target bomber, and then the new AI radar would guide the fighter to within visual range. The disappointing twin-engine Bf 110, maligned as a day escort fighter in the Battle of Britain, came into its own as a night fighter. It was here that the Bf 110 had the advantage over German single-engine fighters, for it had a second crew member to spot targets, and later, to man the air-to-air radar.

Searchlight batteries were also fed location information by the ground radar, improving their chance of catching an RAF bomber in a light cone. Once illuminated from below, the bomber could be engaged visually by nearby flak batteries. This increased RAF bomber casualties significantly.

After June 1941, Germany was overcommitted, fighting on three fronts against the British in Western Europe and the Mediterranean, as well as the Soviets on the Eastern Front. Added to this was the increasing RAF night-bombing campaign over the homeland. The *Luftwaffe* could not significantly expand; it simply switched major units from place to place to meet emergencies and Hitler's ill-considered priorities. At the end of 1941, things got even worse as the Japanese dragged the Third Reich into war with the United States.

Luftwaffe generals Galland and Kammhuber approached *Reichsmarschall* Göring about the increased British night raids and the air defense of the West. Göring ignored their advice to emphasize the production of more air defense aircraft, delaying effective German response to the worsening night-bombing situation. Germany seemed to be winning in Russia and victory was expected before Christmas. Overcoming the Soviet Union would allow Germany to turn and finish off the British, ending the RAF night-bomber offensive.

Kammhuber continued his efforts despite lack of support from the *Reichsmarschall*, keeping pace with RAF advances. By early 1942, production AI radar sets were reaching German night-fighter units in quantity. British countermeasures were devised and the fighting continued. The rest of the night war would be a series of technological surprises, at various times debilitating the other's ability to attack or defend.[5]

On February 14, 1942, Secretary of State for Air Sir Archibald Sinclair issued a directive for continuing the strategic bombing of Germany. By the end of the month, the man who would implement that directive so effectively was named Air Officer Commanding-in-Chief (AOC-in-C) Bomber Command. He was Air Marshal Sir Arthur Harris, who because of his singular obsession with pulverizing Germany soon became known simply as "Bomber" Harris.

If Harris ever had any doubts as to where to drop his bombs, they were put to rest by his boss, RAF chief of air staff (CAS) Air Marshal Sir Charles Portal. Portal's comments on the directive were clear enough:

> *The key words of the directive indicate that the "primary objective" of British bombing in Germany should now be focused on the morale of the enemy civil population and, in particular, of the industrial workers. Ref the new bombing directive: I suppose it is clear that the aiming points are to be the built-up areas, not, for instance, the dockyards or aircraft factories where these are mentioned in Appendix A. This must be made quite clear if it is not already understood.*[6]

The gloves were off. By "built-up," Portal meant residential and downtown areas, where the workers and their families lived.

CHAPTER SEVEN

Bomber Crews

For the strength of the Pack is the Wolf, and the strength of the Wolf is the Pack.

—RUDYARD KIPLING, *THE JUNGLE BOOK* (1894)

The men who flew combat in the British and American bombers were somewhat different than the common perception of aviators as individualists. Bomber crews were a team. Each member of the team was responsible to the others for the success of the mission, and if possible, the survival of the crew.

Warplanes are machines. They don't come alive until they are tended to and flown by people. These people sacrifice, sometimes everything, so that warplanes can deliver the goods. A warplane cannot fix itself, experience frustration or terror, exhibit courage, or foresee its own demise. People can, and people do.

Bomber crews were most often trained to do a particular job depending on the design of the aircraft, including pilot and copilot, navigator or observer, flight engineer, bombardier or bomb aimer, radio operator or gunner. Sometimes a crew member was trained to do a secondary job, most often as a gunner in those crew stations where a mounted gun was available. American multiengine bombers had pilots and copilots. In February 1942, the British removed the copilot from the RAF bomber crews, assigning the flight engineer to assist the pilot.[1]

As American heavy bomber formations became larger, it was customary to have a lead navigator and bombardier for the squadron or group. The lead navigator was an experienced flying officer and combat veteran. He was a man of known navigational skill and could use the limited electronic aids of the time. He flew in the formation leader's aircraft. Alternate formation leaders had an alternate lead navigator on board in case the original formation leader's aircraft was shot out of the formation.

American formation leaders and their alternates also had lead bombardiers in their crew. To concentrate the formations' bombs on the target, the skilled

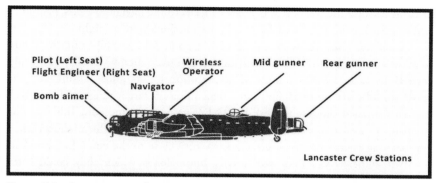

Figure 7.1. Arrangement of crew in a British Lancaster heavy bomber. MOLYSON

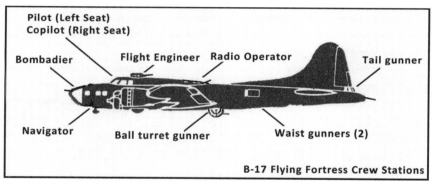

Figure 7.2. Arrangement of crew in an American B-17 heavy bomber. MOLYSON

lead bombardier would open his bomb bay doors on approach to the target, a visual cue to the other bombardiers in the formation to also open their aircraft's bomb bay doors. The other bombardiers dropped when the lead aircraft's bombs began falling. If the formation was tight and well disciplined, this large salvo of bombs would produce a tight impact pattern on the ground around the target. The larger the bomber formation, the wider the track of bomb explosions would appear on the ground.

Flight engineers were a necessity on some heavy bombers because of the complexity of these four-engine aircraft. On most American bombers, the flight engineer doubled as the top turret gunner, since this station was close to the flight deck where the engine controls were located. Navigation in Europe was difficult because the weather was often bad, electronic navigation aids, primitive, and at least for the RAF and *Luftwaffe*, the missions were at night.

American bombers were armed with a powerful .50 caliber machine gun to allow the bomber to defend itself in daylight over enemy territory. Officially, each B-17 carried 8,000 rounds of ammunition for its guns. Unofficially, the crews would carry up to 10,000 more depending on target range and fuel load. The British used the less powerful .303 Browning machine gun. This was due to ordnance availability and the fact they were carried on night missions, when approaching enemy fighters were not seen until close to the defending bomber.

British heavy bombers had heavier bomb loads which they could carry greater distances than the contemporary B-17 and B-24. American bombers were designed for precision bombing in daylight and were provided with highly accurate bombsights. The British performed area bombing and their aiming system was adequate to accomplish this mission. Later in the war RAF heavy bombers received better bombsights and flew some daylight precision bombing missions over France.

The most critical crew member was the pilot. He commanded the aircraft and the crew. Allied pilots could eliminate an unsatisfactory crewman from the crew if a replacement was available. It was the pilot—or, as necessary, the copilot—who would order a bailout, crash landing, or ditching if the airplane was unflyable. On American heavy bombers, the pilot and copilot had no hand-held machine gun at their station and no way to aim bombs. Their job was to fly the airplane and get it to the target.

When the German fighter pilots learned how vulnerable the B-17 and B-24 were to frontal attack, the pilots and copilots became the preferred target. German night-fighter pilots normally did not perform frontal attacks, and the injury or death of the bomber pilot was incidental to the damage or destruction of the aircraft. Depending on duty station, casualties among the crew members varied. On RAF bombers, the "safest" position was the bomb aimer. The most dangerous was the pilot. In American bombers, the most dangerous was the pilot/copilot, followed by the ball turret gunner.[2]

On the August 1943 Schweinfurt–Regensburg raid, sixty bombers were lost with about six hundred crewmen aboard. On average, 1.7 percent of the crew members per downed bomber were killed and most of the rest captured. "Average" includes bombers that exploded, killing all the crew, and some in which all the crew escaped.[3]

CHAPTER EIGHT

Lübeck (February–December 1942)

We are going to scourge the Third Reich from end to end. We are bombing Germany city by city and ever more terribly in order to make it impossible for her to go on with the war. That is our object, and we shall pursue it relentlessly.
—AIR MARSHAL ARTHUR "BOMBER" HARRIS[1]

The British suffered a long history of strategic bombardment at the hands of the Germans, beginning in World War I. The Germans resented their British cousins joining as allies with the French in August 1914. Germans prayed *Gott strafe England* ("God punish England") as they invoked the Almighty's aid in defeating their unexpected foe. The British had been allied with the German states during the Napoleonic Wars, and neutral during the Franco-Prussian War in 1870. The French, not the British, were their ancient enemies, and the Germans had long memories.

Resentful of the emerging Anglo-French alliance, a popular German children's song in the autumn of 1914 called on the Kaiser's zeppelin rigid airship fleet to destroy England by fire. On January 19, 1915, zeppelins raided the south of England by night as they began their *Luftschiffangriff gegen England*, and forty-two civilians were killed.

The German airship bombing campaign was intended to hit only military and related targets. The night bombing, however, soon degenerated into area terror bombing of London. For the Germans, night was a refuge from British defenses. By the end of the zeppelin flying season in October, twenty-two raids had been conducted and over two hundred civilians killed. In the following years, German Gotha biplane bombers replaced the zeppelin attacks.[2]

In World War I, the Royal Flying Corps officer who commanded the revenge bombing against Germany for the attacks on London was Lord Trenchard. After World War I, Trenchard became the chief of staff of the new Royal

Air Force and promoted the RAF doctrine of striking against an enemy's economy and civilian morale as a war-winning strategy.[3]

During the Battle of Britain twenty years later, the Germans attempted to selectively destroy the RAF by day to facilitate invasion. When that was unsuccessful, the *Luftwaffe* initiated the Blitz, the area bombing of British cities by night. Again, night provided some protection from the defending RAF fighters. The idea was not to destroy the RAF, but British civilian morale.

In the end, the *Luftwaffe* achieved neither objective. RAF aircraft production priorities were adjusted and new, heavier bombers for retaliation were introduced. Justified or not by the German attacks, Portal's expanded RAF bombing charter to Harris in February 1942 was quickly implemented. By March, the first German city to burn under its auspices was attacked.

On the night of March 28–29, 1942, 234 RAF bombers dropped about 300 tons of incendiaries and high-explosive bombs on the old city of Lübeck, Germany. The city center with its many wooden buildings was destroyed, and the situation on the ground was chaos, with 320 civilians killed and many more wounded and displaced. Although Hitler agreed that the *Luftwaffe* must retaliate, he would not bring home air units operating in the East to reinforce the *Luftwaffe* in the West. The invasion of the Soviet Union was well under way, and the Führer would not deviate from his plans to conquer Russia.

Instead, only the German air force bombers still based in northern France were sent on a series of *Baedeker* raids, named after the prewar tourist guides, on the English towns of Exeter, Bath, Coventry, Norwich, and York. The towns were selected for their cultural and historic value rather than their military significance. The attacks failed to deter the RAF from its own strategic bombing. Improving RAF night defenses imposed heavy losses on the German bombers. The *Baedeker* raids on cultural targets gradually became less frequent and blended with German attacks on more productive areas.[4]

Major RAF night attacks continued against Cologne, Essen, and Hamburg in April. Then the old section of ancient Rostock burned down on April 23–24, 1942, and three subsequent raids were conducted against this city. The Heinkel aircraft factory located nearby was also damaged. Nazi propaganda minister Joseph Goebbels described it as a *Terrorangriff* ("terror raid") in his diary, the first time he referred to an RAF night attack in these terms. He further stated that "community life is at an end."[5] Much worse lay ahead in May.

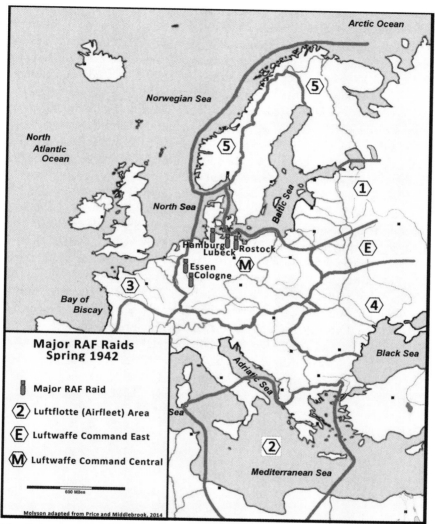

Map 8.1. Major RAF raids, March–April 1942. Note the targets and the widespread areas of responsibility for the Luftwaffe air fleets. MOLYSON AFTER PRICE AND MIDDLEBROOK[6]

On the night of May 30–31, 1942, the British conducted the first "Thousand Bomber Raid" on a German urban area. The target was Cologne, a major city on the Rhine, already bombed but still designated a lucrative night target. RAF Training and Coastal Commands were scoured for enough aircraft and crews to make up the magic number.[7] Over 1,500 tons of bombs were dropped, including 8,300 stick incendiaries, 81 firebomb canisters, 4 liquid drum incendiaries, 3 heavy "mines,"[8] 116 phosphorus bombs, and 90 high-explosive bombs.[9]

The mines and high-explosive bombs were meant to shatter dwellings and other structures, to provide fuel for the fires, and to damage the firefighting organization. The target was the center of the city; the major transportation, production, and military targets within the urban area were only an afterthought. Terror bombing on an industrial scale had arrived in Western Europe.[10]

The inventory of RAF four-engine bombers grew rapidly. By midsummer 1942, the RAF was hitting several targets a month with hundreds of bombers. The first four-engine RAF bomber was the Short Stirling, introduced into strategic bombing in early in 1941. The Handley Page Halifax, a more effective bomber, entered service in July 1941. The best and most versatile of the three, the Avro Lancaster, joined in early 1942. Its first target in Germany was Essen, bombed March 10–11, 1942. Along with the assignment of Harris as AOC-in-C Bomber Command, the RAF had the aircraft required to implement the Portal-Harris doctrine of de-housing the German industrial workforce.

Neither side had an effective night-bombing sight or operational bombing radar in 1942, so "accurate" bombing was a matter of finding a whole city rather than bombing somewhere out in the countryside. Targets in the smog-shrouded Ruhr Valley industrial area at night were particularly hard to bomb accurately. Killing each other's cows would not bring victory.

CHAPTER NINE

Cooperation (June 1940–August 1941)

I believe that the first and great principle of war is that you must first win your air battle before you fight your land and sea battle.
—GENERAL BERNARD LAW MONTGOMERY, 1943[1]

After Dunkirk, the RAF resisted demands to establish a formal Army Co-operation Command on par with the other combat commands. It was thought by some that the RAF could make up for the weakness of the depleted British army formations recently evacuated from France. The British airmen thought the air war over Britain and the Narrow Seas, the Battle of Britain, was more critical. If they could keep the German army out of Britain, the crippled British army could rebuild. This required all remaining British fighters to ward off the *Luftwaffe*, while British bombers went after the *Kriegsmarine* invasion fleet assembling across the Channel.

Once the Battle of Britain was won, the RAF Army Co-operation Command (ACC) was reluctantly established under Fighter Command. For the British Air Staff, establishing an effective night-bombing campaign against Germany, preventing mass *Luftwaffe* night raids, and fighting the Battle of the Atlantic were still priorities. Cooperating with the Royal Army seemed like a mission that could be deferred well into the future.

The Air Officer Commanding (AOC) of the ACC was Air Marshal Arthur Barratt, who had commanded the BAFF (British Air Force in France) before Dunkirk. Barratt had watched support for the Allied army fail due to poor communications and muddled doctrine as much as the prowess of the German air force. He vowed to do better. He became a champion of the army cooperation mission, which put him at some odds with other senior RAF leaders.

The ACC consisted of No. 70 (Training) Group and No. 71 (Army Co-operation) Group.[2] In August 1941, the No. 71 Group was disbanded and became six army cooperation wings directly under Fighter Command. Each was firmly under the control of the RAF, although officially each reported directly to an army regional headquarters.

Aircraft included Lysander and civilian-type liaison and observation aircraft; American-built Tomahawk low-altitude fighters; and assorted light transports. The Lysanders were STOL (short takeoff and landing) aircraft with sufficient range to carry and land agents deep in enemy territory. The civilian-type aircraft were designed by the American firm Taylorcraft and designated "Auster" in RAF service. They were used to observe for friendly artillery and as couriers. The Tomahawks were useful for tactical reconnaissance, the visual observation of the terrain and the enemy forces operating there.

Significantly, these aircraft were generally unsuitable for night strategic bombing into Germany, air defense of Britain, or antisubmarine warfare. Therefore, they could be spared from the RAF's "real" missions. The ACC trained and operated only in Britain, although some of its personnel and aircraft were rotated into the North African campaign. It was in North Africa that the army cooperation doctrine evolved under combat conditions. It was up to Barratt and his staff to make the ACC combat-ready for a return to France.

CHAPTER TEN

Allies (December 1941–March 1942)

The Japanese attack on Pearl Harbor, followed by the German and Italian declaration of war a few days later, profoundly changed the nature of the Anglo-American relationship. Neutrality laws no longer limited Roosevelt's range of action. More importantly, the average American was now committed to fighting and winning the war.

ARCADIA: THE FIRST WASHINGTON CONFERENCE (DECEMBER 22, 1941–JANUARY 14, 1942)

Shortly after Pearl Harbor, Churchill undertook another hazardous trip to North America, attending the Arcadia Conference in Washington. This time Churchill arrived aboard the powerful new battleship *Duke of York*. Churchill's route avoided German air bases in western France, as the dominance of airpower over seapower close to enemy coastlines had again been demonstrated within the last month.[1] Among other disasters in the Pacific, Japanese land-based aircraft had sunk the battleship *Prince of Wales*, sister ship of the *Duke of York*, off Malaya. Churchill had traveled aboard *Prince of Wales* to the Argentia Conference the previous summer.

The Americans wanted to quickly land their army on the coast of France and come to grips with the Germans. From the beginning of the alliance their British cousins had counseled a more circumspect assault. Large armies require man-power. Britain's available manpower, always limited, had been drastically reduced by World War I losses. Not only had the Great War cost millions of Allied casualties, but the sons of the war dead would also never be born, let alone serve. The British called it their "Lost Generation."[2] BEF losses in 1940 reinforced the British viewpoint.

Unlike the earlier Argentia Conference, Arcadia addressed urgent war issues rather than postwar goals. Circumstances had at last pushed the United States firmly and openly into the Allied camp with the United Kingdom and the Soviet Union. Now, even with America's Pacific Fleet in ruins, General Secretary Stalin

39

insisted from afar on an immediate Second Front to be established by an Allied invasion of France. Churchill knew this was folly and said so. He had no intention of fighting the German army in France in the near future. He would not risk another Dunkirk.

Arcadia reconfirmed the ABC-1 objective of "Germany first." It also established the concept of a "Supreme Allied Commander" in each theater of operations.[3] The first so designated was General Sir Archibald Wavell, the British commander in India. Wavell's command, called ABDA (American-British-Dutch-Australian), included the entire Southwest Pacific and Southeast Asia, most of which was currently being overrun by the Japanese. The respective services were placed under a local theater commander, rather than working under the orders of their respective staffs back in London or Washington.

In Washington, Army Chief of Staff General George Marshall added Lieutenant General Hap Arnold to the Joint Board, affirming the key role American airpower was to play in the war. The United States at the time had no independent air force, Arnold now being the commanding general of the US Army Air Forces (USAAF). Previously, the principals of the Joint Board included only the army chief of staff and the chief of naval operations. Arnold's assignment transformed the Joint Board into the first US Joint Chiefs of Staff (JCS).

Marshall made the decision to bring in Arnold as a counterpart of Air Marshal Portal, head of the Royal Air Force and a member of the British Chiefs of Staff (BCOS). The combined JCS and BCOS, a third of which were airmen, became the Allied Combined Chiefs of Staff (CCS) for the rest of the war. General Marshall's visionary decision made the eventual creation of an independent US air force inevitable. It was as a JCS member that Arnold attended Arcadia.[4]

The Arcadia Conference set the theme for Anglo-American discord over an invasion of northwestern France that would continue to echo throughout 1942 and the first half of 1943. What the Soviets thought of as the "Second Front" and Americans thought of as the direct path to Berlin was to the British the main highway to disaster. In 1940, under conditions of air parity, the *Luftwaffe* had made the BEF's escape from French beaches a near debacle. The RAF quickly returned the favor in the Battle of Britain by demonstrating that the previously invincible German army could not cross England's shore unless the *Luftwaffe* gained air supremacy.

FRANCE OR NORTH AFRICA?

The British knew that an invasion of northwestern France would demand and consume huge amounts of war materials and people, and they had other priorities. Most of the material and people would come from America and be shipped to Britain, the most likely base for such an attack across the Channel. To move such quantities, the Allies must win the Battle of the Atlantic against the U-boats then raging just off America's coast and all across the North Atlantic shipping lanes. That would take time.

The British also wanted to immediately extend the strategic encirclement of the Axis. Now that the Americans were in the war, they could help to win the protracted campaign in North Africa and the Mediterranean. This would complete the Allied ring around Germany and Italy, possibly forcing the capitulation of Italy and maintaining the neutrality of Turkey.

While all of this was occurring, bombing and subversion could wear down the German economy and the forces of occupation, respectively. The British also identified increased requirements to sustain the Soviet ally and maintain essential defensive positions in the Far East and Pacific, especially India and Australia. All of this required American economic and military power far beyond the capability of even the entire British Commonwealth.

There was also a British agenda for the Vichy French[5] regimes of North and West Africa. "Vichy" referred to the capital of the collaborationist French government in unoccupied southern France. At Arcadia, the British identified the desirability of countering Vichy French military power threatening their vital air and maritime routes in the South Atlantic. Vichy regimes controlled key airfields at Casablanca and Dakar, on Africa's Atlantic coast.

The British Chiefs of Staff intended to meet the Vichy challenge in Africa and to maintain the movement of economic and military assets between their European, African, and Far Eastern possessions. They proposed Operation MAGNET to replace Commonwealth troops in Northern Ireland with American troops. The Commonwealth troops in turn would move into active combat areas to provide additional manpower.

They also proposed Operation GYMNAST, an invasion of the three Vichy territories in Northwest Africa: French Morocco, Algeria, and Tunisia. This assault would be conducted primarily by US forces. The British and Vichy were not on good terms. The Vichy government felt the British had deserted them at Dunkirk. The British had also attacked a portion of the French fleet in North Africa to prevent it falling into German hands.

At that time, the Vichy air force had retaliated by bombing the British fortress at Gibraltar. Vichy troops would resist a British invasion of North Africa but might accept an American landing. Churchill hoped such a move would

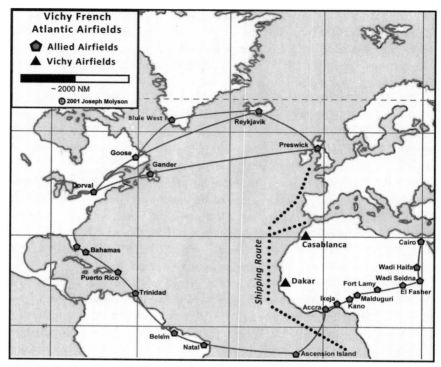

Map 10.1. Vichy French air bases threatening Allied shipping routes in the South Atlantic. MOLYSON ADAPTED FROM CRAVEN AND CATE

sever ties between the French forces in this region and the Vichy government, allowing former Vichy French forces to reenter the war against the Axis.

At the very least, military conquest would bring this part of Africa under Allied control. Roosevelt liked MAGNET but objected to GYMNAST. General Marshall advised FDR that a North African adventure would delay a cross-Channel attack well beyond 1942. In addition, he stated that such a diversion to the Mediterranean seemed more aimed at maintaining Britain's imperial lines of communication than destroying Hitler's regime.

Both MAGNET and GYMNAST were delayed due to lack of ships rather than the desires of either Roosevelt or Churchill. The United States entered the war short on merchant ships. The U-boat campaign in the Atlantic and Gulf of Mexico exacerbated the situation, as did conflicting demands for limited resources for the Pacific. US troops did not reach Northern Ireland until April, and it would be November before they landed in North Africa. The Soviet request for a Second Front by invading France was thus tabled, victim of American shipping shortages and British misgivings.

Direct Western assistance to Russia remained confined to sending equipment and goods via Murmansk in the north, through the Persian corridor to the south, and to Siberia to the east.[6] Of course, the Allied air campaign against Germany was in fact a kind of Second Front. Albert Speer, Hitler's armaments minister—and therefore the top authority on the effect of Allied airpower on Germany's war effort—was the best witness on the decisive effect of Allied air operations in Germany's eventual defeat. He gave airpower credit for starting a "second front" two years before the invasion of German-occupied Europe. Speer said that the day-and-night Allied bombing forced Germany to keep a million men on the "West Wall" at antiaircraft stations, fighting fires and repairing bomb damage to weapons production.[7]

Immediately after Arcadia, the JCS evaluated the results and began planning future US activity. There was general American agreement with the British that the strategic air bombardment of Germany must be increased using American forces. The Americans also began preparing to join the British SOE (Special Operations Executive) in subversive and intelligence-gathering activities in Occupied Europe. It was the matter of an invasion of North Africa versus northwestern France that continued to vex the US military leadership. Major General Dwight D. Eisenhower, chief of the US Army Operations and Planning Staff in 1942, wrote:

> We've got to go to Europe and fight—and we've got to quit wasting resources all over the world—and still worse—wasting time. If we're to keep Russia in, save the Middle East, India and Burma, we've got to begin slugging with air at West Europe; to be followed by a land attack as soon as possible.[8]

CHAPTER ELEVEN

BOLERO (July 1941–April 1942)

In July 1941, when Roosevelt asked the army for its overall production require-ments to fight a war against its potential enemies, the new Army Air Force provided a comprehensive airpower plan that addressed not only what needed to be built, but also how it should be used. This was Air War Plans Division Plan 1, or AWPD-1. The plan was approved by General Marshall as army chief of staff and sent to the president.

AWPD-1 called for the production of sufficient aircraft, especially heavy bombers, to defeat the logical unspoken enemy, Germany, by precision daylight attacks on essential industries. The huge air force required for such a task must be built in America, transported across the Atlantic, and established in Britain. After Pearl Harbor, the plan evolved into AWPD-4 to provide additional com-bat airpower for the Pacific Theater. The European Theater, however, remained the top priority. The Japanese would get only 10 percent of the effort.

General Arnold, as commanding general of the Army Air Forces, was told by Marshall to push as many aircraft across the Atlantic as possible. Arnold established the VIII Bomber Command in Britain to arrange for the bombers' arrival and employment. The VIII's commander was newly promoted brigadier general Ira Eaker. Both Marshall and Arnold knew the VIII Bomber Command could engage German forces long before an American army could invade France from Britain.

Eaker arrived with a staff of five men in February 1942, without so much as a paper clip. Major General James E. Chaney, commander of all US Army forces already in the British Isles, was not happy to see Eaker or to accept Arnold's initiative to set up outside of his purview a separate operational chain of com-mand for the Army Air Forces in Britain. Chaney's attitude was problematical but did not stop Eaker's mission. What Chaney may not have realized was how much Marshall wanted the Army Air Force to aggressively begin the daylight air attack against Occupied Europe.[1]

The RAF could have been a problem, too, but instead facilitated Eaker's determined effort to begin daylight operations. Bomber Harris thought the Americans should give up their day bombers to Coastal Command, which was already using similar planes to hunt submarines. The Yanks could then fly night bombers provided by the RAF. Eaker graciously but firmly refused to integrate his nascent command into the RAF night-bombing force in exchange for food, tents, and new bombers from the RAF Bomber Command.[2]

Even after Eaker's refusal to join the British night effort, the RAF was generous and supportive of the arriving American airmen. The RAF provided the Yanks with existing airfields, ground for new airfields, and air–sea rescue in the Narrow Seas.

Harris—along with many other British leaders, such as Churchill and Air Chief Marshal Portal—were impressed by Eaker's no-nonsense approach. Eaker knew the British had been fighting the Germans for three years and were in no mood for a long-winded lecture on how the Americans were going to win the war. Instead, soon after arrival he gave the assembled townspeople at High Wycombe a thirty-second speech: "We won't do much talking until we've done more fighting. After we've gone, we hope you'll be glad we came. Thank you."[3]

BOLERO

Marshall never wavered in his determination to build a million-man American army and a 10,000-airplane air force in Britain, and to subsequently invade France across the English Channel. The American military buildup in the United Kingdom began in April 1942, code-named Operation BOLERO. Two British airfields in Iceland came under American control as stepping-stones to Britain, and more were built by American engineers in Greenland. Aircraft flying from the United States, including USAAF- and American-produced aircraft destined for the RAF and Royal Navy, traveled through these bases. The British renamed the existing air route from Canada to the United Kingdom via Iceland the "Arnold Line" in honor of the head of the US Army Air Forces.[4]

At the height of the U-boat campaign along the US East Coast, shipping aircraft by sea was both slow and dangerous. Airplanes with sufficient range were flown directly across the Atlantic. In support of the VIII Bomber Command buildup, on February 20, 1942, Arnold ordered the all-out development of auxiliary ferry tanks[5] for the new twin-engine P-38 Lightning fighters. This would give these aircraft sufficient range to fly across to Britain via Iceland. The US Army Air Material Command was slow to respond, and it would be a year before it provided a usable ferry tank. Fortunately, Lockheed was more forthcoming, and within months the first P-38s bound for England were using Lockheed tanks.

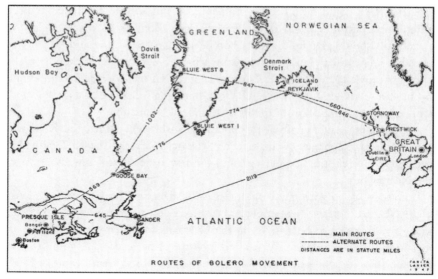

Map 11.1. The North Atlantic ferry route, the "Arnold Line." MOLYSON AFTER CRAVEN
AND CATE[6]

Getting airplanes to Britain via the Arnold Line presented significant problems. Unlike the South Atlantic Route, cold, wet weather in the sub-Arctic was a continual challenge. With their external "ferry" tanks, five P-38F fighter groups traveled the long and hazardous Arnold Line in formation with B-17E navigation aircraft.[7] American four-engine bombers, the B-17 and B-24, had the range to make the trip; however, single-engine American fighters did not. They were shipped intact on aircraft carriers or broken down and carried as cargo. USAAF ground personnel and equipment were brought over mainly by ship. This significantly added to the time necessary to build an individual unit. Of course, the sea transport of many tons of ordnance and other supplies was also necessary.

It was estimated that it took a full six months to transport and establish an operational fighter squadron from the United States to England.[8] Despite foul weather and German radio-deception efforts, by August 31, 1942, 164 P-38s, 119 B-17 bombers, and 103 C-47 transports made the Atlantic crossing by air. By the end of 1942, almost 1,000 aircraft had attempted the flight with less than 40 lost to all causes.[9] Success against the U-boat allowed increasing numbers of aircraft to be brought in by ship, and this later became the primary method of delivery for single-engine fighters and light bombers.

One hundred new military airfields were built in Britain by American engineer aviation battalions and British civilian construction firms. Meaningfully, many of the runways incorporated rubble trucked in from previously bombed British cities. Five million tons of military supplies were sent to support the eventual invasion across the Channel coast. All other military activity, including the Anglo-American operations in the Mediterranean, Southeast Asia, China, and the Pacific were secondary to Operation BOLERO.

SLEDGEHAMMER

As BOLERO began, Marshall traveled to London to confer with the British leadership. He brought two draft operational plans for the BOLERO troops being moved to Britain to cross the Channel and engage the Germans in France. He proposed a landing in the fall of 1942 called SLEDGEHAMMER. It would be a limited assault into the Pas-de-Calais where the Channel was most narrow. The lodgment would be held until early in 1943, when it would be used as the base for an expanded attack called ROUNDUP.

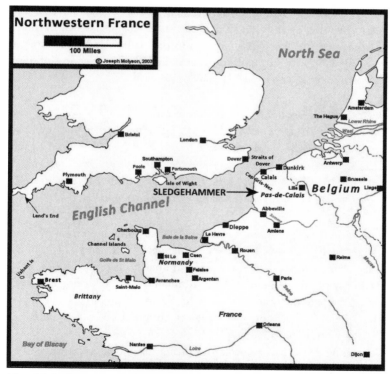

Map 11.2. Operation SLEDGEHAMMER, an invasion the Americans wanted to conduct in the fall of 1942. MOLYSON

Such an invasion of northwestern France would provide an immediate threat to the German homeland and the occupied portions of Western Europe. Hopefully, Hitler would divert significant forces from the east to defend France, easing the pressure on the beleaguered Russians. The north of France had mainly flat terrain, much easier to traverse than the mountainous areas of southern Europe. If the coastal defenses could be breached, there was little in the way of natural defenses between the coast and the German frontier.

The British had originally proposed ROUNDUP as the capstone of a series of campaigns around the periphery of Axis-held territory, but the Americans felt such a long war could be avoided if Germany was attacked directly through France. The British agreed, but with many reservations, and Marshall was able to travel to Northern Ireland at the end of the conference in order to welcome some of the first American ground troops arriving for BOLERO on April 17, 1942.[10]

Marshall also took the opportunity to visit the nascent VIII Bomber Command, whose intended function was daylight precision bombing with four-engine B-17 and B-24 aircraft. Marshall, as the US Army chief of staff and senior officer, believed in airpower as an essential part of overall army capability. In June 1941, he had converted the Army Air Corps into the Army Air Forces as a coequal partner of the US Army Ground Forces and the US Army Services of Supply.

Eaker later commented on Marshall's visit:

> *In April 1942, General Marshall came to the US VIII Bomber Command during a visit to the British Chiefs of Staff. After hearing my report on our plans at that early date, he said to me, "Eaker, I do not believe a cross-Channel invasion of Europe will ever be possible until the Luftwaffe is destroyed. Do your plans provide for that?" I assured him that the destruction of the German air force was our prime intermediate objective.*[11]

Returning to Washington, General Marshall soon appointed Major General Dwight D. Eisenhower to be the commander of US Army Forces in Britain, replacing Chaney. It was literally a war-winning transition. Chaney, a veteran pilot, went back to the United States to command the 1st Air Force, whose mission was to prepare operational aircrew and combat aircraft for the expanding war. Like Marshall, Eisenhower was a fan of both SLEDGEHAMMER and of the USAAF's ability to immediately attack German forces.

General Marshall had a knack for putting his people in positions that best utilized their talents.

CHAPTER TWELVE
Kanalfront (January 1941–August 1942)

In January 1941, as German air force units were resting and rebuilding in Occupied Europe, the *Luftwaffe* flyers along the so-called *Kanalfront* bordering the Channel were settling into a predictable routine. After the rigors of the Battle of Britain, the pace on German airfields was almost leisurely. Across the Narrow Seas from Britain was *Luftflotte 2* (Air Fleet 2), headquartered in Brussels. Its area of responsibility (AOR) included the Netherlands, Belgium, and northern Germany. It controlled a fighter wing, JG26 (*Jagdgeschwader 26*), with three fighter groups each of three squadrons of Bf 109E fighters, with more in reserve, some 108 aircraft.[1] Along the French coast and inland to central Germany was *Luftflotte 3*. Its fighter wing was JG2 (*Jagdgeschwader 2*), also with three fighter groups of three squadrons.

LEANING INTO FRANCE

The RAF achieved daytime air superiority over Britain when they stopped the massive German daylight raids in the early fall of 1940, achieving their RAF mission of *defensive* air warfare to protect the homeland. After October, the German bombers came only in very small numbers by day and in much larger numbers at night, when the Spits did not fly. At the end of the Battle of Britain, Air Marshal Sholto Douglas assumed command of Fighter Command. He was soon directed by RAF chief of air staff Air Marshal Charles Portal to "lean forward" toward France. Portal wanted to pave the way for a later return to France by the Allies by inflicting crippling losses on the German fighter force.

This meant conducting RAF *offensive* air operations against *Luftflotte 3* across the Channel. The job fell to the Spitfire squadrons, as many Hurricane fighters were being dispatched overseas. Only the Spit was thought capable of holding its own against the most current models of the Bf 109E over enemy territory. Neither the planes nor most of their pilots were ready for this task.

The Spitfire was designed to defend airspace over Britain within a sophisticated radar-directed air defense system. The Spitfires and Hurricanes had shredded

German bombers escorted by their kindred enemy, the Bf 109E, the Emil, in the Battle of Britain. The Spitfire, however, lacked the range to fly much beyond the French Channel coast, up to perhaps 175 miles from their base to the far northern suburbs of Paris or Lille.

Map 12.1. *Luftwaffe* areas of responsibility, January 1941, at the beginning of the "lean forward" operations into France. Note short combat radius of Spitfire.
MOLYSON ADAPTED FROM PRICE[2]

Fighter Command was rebuilding from its extreme effort to defend British skies. It had lost many experienced pilots, and others were sent to Training Command and overseas assignments. In their place arrived new pilots inadequately trained to take on the veteran *Luftwaffe* pilots over France. There was a dearth of tactical air-to-air practice in the Training Command of 1941. These men had many less flying hours than their prewar predecessors, with predictable results.

Spitfire pilots had to be as wary of their fuel gauges as they were of the German fighters hunting them. Now it was the *Luftwaffe* who had the advantage of radar and ground control. British fighter losses were severe and greatly exceeded those of their German opponents. When Spitfire pilots were shot down, if they survived, they most often were taken prisoner. Some damaged aircraft made it to the cold water of the Channel where surviving a ditching or parachute escape was no sure thing.

The Spit was never intended to be a bomber escort, although later it would be tasked with escorting shallow daylight bomber raids over France. It was not courage that was lacking, it was range. Orders are orders, and the RAF tested an augmented Spitfire Mark IIa with an additional 48-gallon (US) fuel tank mounted on the port wing. These were designated "long-range" and assigned to escort shallow-penetration bomber missions.

By May 1941, Air Marshal Douglas was informed that the pilots of the three "long-range" squadrons felt that they could not compete on equal terms with the upgraded models of the Bf 109. Douglas told Portal and Portal informed Churchill. The "lean forward" effort continued, however, despite lack of success. The idea of longer-range RAF fighters was abandoned, at least until 1943.[3]

FUTILITY

The first offensive RAF missions over France began in December 1940. This was during the period known as the Blitz, when concentrated German bomber attacks against British cities were conducted only at night. British day fighters could do little at the time to stop these attacks, which meant they were available for other chores. The initial "lean forward" missions were called "Rhubarbs," which later evolved gradually into more complex attacks.

Rhubarbs were small patrols of Spitfire fighters of less than squadron strength, generally ignored by the outnumbered Germans. Efforts to bring them up to fight by strafing airfields came to naught. German airfields soon became nests of light and medium antiaircraft guns. The increased German flak deterred the RAF fighters from strafing. This, in turn, reduced *Luftwaffe* ground casualties on German airfields. Substantial numbers of Spitfires were lost to ground fire without ever seeing a German fighter.

"Circuses" were larger formations of Spitfires escorting a small bomber contingent as "bait" for enemy fighters. Bomber Command objections to this role were ignored. The British repeated the German Battle of Britain mistake of close escort of bombers. The bombers were not bait for the *Luftwaffe*; they were anchors for the Spitfires. Always, remaining fuel was an issue on the way to the target and on the return.

The Circuses intermittently forced German interceptors to react. When the Germans chose to attack a Circus, their expertise was evident. The RAF faced a disadvantage flying into the sun, heading east toward their targets, and away from it on the way home. When success was likely, German pilots would be waiting for the hapless and unlucky up in the sun.

Rhubarbs were later expanded to "Rangers"—full fighter wing sweeps of three squadrons totaling thirty-six to forty-eight aircraft, also called "big wings."[4] Disappointing as a defensive tactic in the 1940 battle, the idea of the big wing sweeping into France to kill German fighters was resurrected for offensive purposes in 1941. It was a good idea, until the range of the Spitfire was considered.

Like Rhubarbs, Circuses normally failed to elicit much of a German Air Force (GAF) fighter response. Circuses were expanded to "Ramrods," even larger bomber formations escorted by Spitfires. The limited range of the Spitfire

Table 12.1. RAF "Lean Forward" Attacks Against Airfields and Coastal Vessels, January 1941–August 1942.

Mission Designation	Description
Circus	Formation of 20 to 30 light and medium bombers escorted by up to 16 squadrons of fighters to draw up German fighters
Ramrod	Similar to Circus, but usually with a specific ground target for the bombers
Ranger	Fighter-only sweeps of any size intended to wear down the German fighter force
Rhubarb	Low-level, small-fighter-only sweeps operating under low cloud cover, protected from enemy fighters at higher altitude
Roadstead	Low-level armed reconnaissance attack on enemy coastal shipping and ports
Rodeo	Large offensive fighter-only sweeps over enemy territory
Rover	Code name for a Roadstead by Coastal Command aircraft against German vessels and ports

made these shallow raids of nuisance value only. None of these measures prevented the *Luftwaffe* from using French airspace and air bases. A condition of air parity was maintained within Spitfire range and German air superiority where the Spits could not reach.

While RAF losses mounted, the British could also cause casualties. RAF fighters wiped out the entire 9./JG2 (9th Squadron Fighter Wing 2) on June 28, 1941. In the end, however, the Germans won the 1941 campaign. From June to December, 1941, the RAF lost 411 aircraft to some 103 GAF fighters shot down; 51 other GAF fighters were lost to non-combat causes. This would not help a future Allied invasion of France. The 75 RAF fighter squadrons—over 900 aircraft held at home to conduct these attacks—starved RAF operations in the Mediterranean and Far East.[5]

OWNING THE AIR

Air parity means simply that on the average day, an air force can use airspace but cannot prevent an enemy from also using it. This was the situation in northwestern France and the Low Countries (Belgium and the Netherlands) along the coast during 1941–1942. German bombers, reconnaissance, and transport aircraft were all of course at risk. German radar tracked the RAF missions over France so that its vulnerable support aircraft could avoid them.

Air superiority means an air force can use airspace while denying the enemy effective use of it. It means flying more fighters in the area than your adversaries, or at least flying fighters superior to your enemy in sufficient number to win most fights. Air superiority derives from *presence*, a daily form of King of the Mountain in which the air force most often using airspace controls it. Air superiority allows an air force to pick the fights it is likely to win.

The Spitfire could not reach deep into French territory, giving the Germans de facto air superiority beyond the coastal zone. Short-legged Spitfires, despite superior numbers and adequate performance, never established the presence required to beat *Luftflotte 3* over its own ground.

The numbers of RAF missions over France continued to increase throughout 1941 as German fighter strength in Western Europe actually declined. From June 1941, the bulk of the *Luftwaffe* (60 percent) was fighting on the Eastern Front. Even then air superiority eluded the RAF.

Luftflotte 2 departed the Low Countries in the spring of 1941 and was sent east to help with the invasion of the Soviet Union. It left behind *Jagdgeschwader 26* (JG26). *Luftflotte 3* remained in France, adding JG26 to its own JG2. The two fighter wings had perhaps 240 single-engine fighters spread along coastal bases

53

in groups (*Jagdgruppen*) of 25 to 35 aircraft. The River Seine divided their two operating areas, with JG2 to the west in France and JG26 to the east in northern France and the Low Countries. JG26, flying largely from the airfield complex just across the Channel from Dover, soon became known by the RAF as the "Abbeville Boys." Abbeville was an airfield and town near the center of this complex.[6]

Map 12.2. *Luftwaffe* areas of responsibility, June 1941. Note extension of German operations into Russia and in the Mediterranean, impeding reinforcement of *Luftflotte 3*. Also note that *Luftflotte 3* replaced *Luftflotte 2* in the Low Countries and the Pas-de-Calais. MOLYSON AFTER PRICE

German fighters on the *Kanalfront* generally retained yellow-painted "Battle of Britain" engine cowlings for ease of recognition. They were known colloquially as the "Yellow Nose Bastards" by RAF fighter pilots. Their nickname reflected both the paint job and grudging respect for their highly effective fighting skill.

UPGRADING THE ADVERSARIES

Both the RAF and *Luftwaffe* replaced their Battle of Britain vintage fighters on the Channel front during 1941. The Spitfire V became the standard RAF fighter in England with a strengthened airframe to take a more powerful version of the superb Merlin liquid-cooled engine. The Mark V appeared in February 1941, for a time besting the old Bf 109E Emil being flown by *Luftflotte 3*. It became the most numerous Spitfire model built.

The Germans countered with a new model, Bf 109F, the Friedrich. The Emils went to quieter sectors along the coast or back into Germany. The Bf 109F soon became the primary German fighter on the *Kanalfront*. While its added range and speed were significant, it was delivered too late to influence the Battle of Britain. It was a better performer than the Battle of Britain vintage Spitfire Mk I and Mk II, and a good match for the Mk V.[7]

In late 1941, the Germans began deliveries of the new FW 190A, a radial-engine fighter with great promise. It soon earned the nickname "The Butcher Bird" for its effective air-to-air capability. The Spitfire Mark V had a formidable new adversary. Designed to be simple, reliable, easy to maintain, and highly effective, it proved to be one of the best fighters of World War II.[8] By the end of 1941, both JG2 and JG26 had large numbers of these aircraft.

Inability of the RAF to establish air superiority over coastal France culminated in the German Operation CEREBUS in February 1942. The German navy evacuated its remaining heavy warships from Brest, where they were being pummeled by RAF bomber attacks, through the Channel and back to Germany. For that occasion, the Germans mustered extra fighters and maintained a bubble of air superiority over the *Kriegsmarine* ships that the RAF was unable to pierce.

JAGDBOMBERS

In March 1942, JG2 and JG26 created a tenth squadron in each wing, 10./JG2 and 10./JG26. These consisted of Bf 109F-4 aircraft able to carry one SC 500 (1,100-pound) or two SC 250 (550-pound) bombs suspended from newly installed bomb racks under the belly and wings. These were *Jagdbombers* ("fighter-bombers"), or *Jabos*, tasked with harassing the Channel coastline. The RAF maintained air superiority over Britain, but this did not stop the speedy *Jabos* from sneaking in at low level over the Channel and terrorizing coastal towns and facilities.

In March 1942, FW 190 *Jabos* also began to appear. They were faster than the 109s and could carry a heavier bomb load. Attacks on Britain continued for several years, not ceasing until after D-Day. The RAF response was standing patrols over the Channel, which impeded but did not stop the attacks.[9] It was on these patrols the British first employed their new Typhoon fighter. Although much larger than the Spitfire or Hurricane, it proved to be an able opponent to the FW 190. Between October 1942 and June 1943, Typhoons shot down no less than fifty-seven FW 190 *Jabos*.

UPGRADES CONTINUE

In June 1942, a confused FW 190 pilot landed at RAF Pembrey and gave the RAF their first FW 190A to test. The superb qualities of the Butcher Bird forced another burst of RAF fighter development.[10] The engine of the Spitfire Mk V was replaced with an even more powerful version of the Merlin engine, creating the Spitfire Mk IX.[11] Although deliveries of the Mark IX began in July 1942, it would be many months before significant numbers of these aircraft were available.

The 190 was inferior to the Spitfire Mk IX above 25,000 feet, equal or superior below that altitude. The technological balancing act continued as new models of the FW 190 and Bf 109 were matched by later upgrades of the Spitfire. The RAF continued its expansion and maintained a higher percentage of new pilots than their German counterparts. This was reflected in the 3:1 monthly kill ratios the Germans maintained during the 1941–1942 fighting on the *Kanalfront*.

CHAPTER THIRTEEN

Death of a Kondor (August 1942)

Although both Roosevelt and Churchill supported the BOLERO buildup, during the spring of 1942 the American and British military staffs made repeated attempts to divert some of the buildup to the Pacific and Mediterranean. The British also continued to press for a US invasion of North Africa. Marshall blocked most of these attempts, and the UK-bound equipment and troops arrived as scheduled.

Fast-paced Japanese conquests in the Pacific caused another problem for the air buildup in England. In June 1942, the Battle of Midway and other activity in the Pacific caused some P-38 Lightning fighters to be sent to the US West Coast rather than to England. There seemed to be a real threat the Japanese would follow up any victory they might achieve at Midway with attacks against the continental United States. Fortunately, it was the US Navy that won the fight. It wasn't until late June that Lightnings began to arrive in England via Iceland over the cold northern routes of the Arnold Line.

KONDOR

The German air threat continued in the Iceland area in the form of the FW 200 Kondor. These maritime bombers were operated by *Fliegerführer Atlantik* (Aviation Command Atlantic), the *Luftwaffe* headquarters assigned to conduct operations against Allied convoys approaching Britain. Kondors could attack ships and provide reconnaissance for U-boats only as far as Iceland. The Kondor's flight path around Iceland was defined by the range of the FW 200 and the expected combat radius of Allied interceptors based in southwest Britain, Northern Ireland, and Scotland. The aircraft would fly north from France to the west coast of Iceland and turn east to land in southern Norway. After servicing, they would return on the same route.

The heyday of the Kondor as a ship-killer was in the past because the Allies had installed antiaircraft batteries on most merchant ships. Some merchant ships were also converted to carry war-weary Hurricane fighters to be catapult-launched when an FW 200 approached. These ships were blended into some

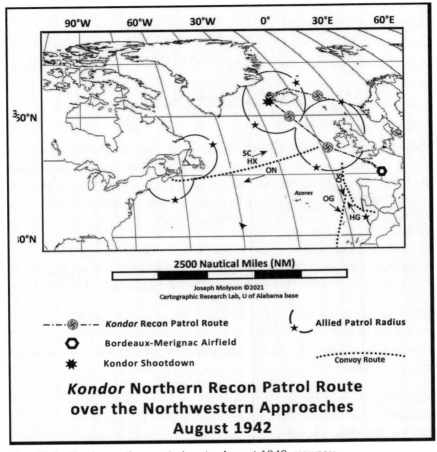

Kondor Northern Recon Patrol Route over the Northwestern Approaches August 1942

Map 13.1. Kondor northern patrol route, August 1942. MOLYSON

convoys, causing the German bombers to keep their distance unless an opportune target presented itself. Therefore, they still carried bombs on reconnaissance missions. The Hurricanes ditched at the end of their interception attempt unless within range of friendly airfields. Not all the pilots were recovered from the water. It was that kind of war.

Figure 13.1. Lockheed P-38F Lightnings at Iceland. Lieutenant Shahan's number 42 is at the left. USAF[1]

On July 3, 1942, the P-38F Lightnings of the 27th Fighter Squadron (USAAF) arrived in Iceland and were temporarily attached to the local command, the 342nd Composite Group. The squadron had flown in from Presque Isle, Maine, en route to England. Among the pilots of the 27th FS was its commander, Major John Weltman, and his wingman, Second Lieutenant Elza Shahan. The USAAF was sending Curtiss P-40 Warhawk aircraft by sea to Iceland to provide local air defense, but they would not arrive until early August. The P-38s would fill in for air defense until then.

The P-40C Warhawks of the 33rd Fighter Squadron (USAAF) arrived on August 6, flying off the aircraft carrier USS *Wasp*. Among the thirty-two pilots assigned to the 33rd FS was Second Lieutenant Joseph Shaffer. He and his squadron mates had a unique experience as US Army pilots, because the Warhawk was not normally flown off a carrier deck. On August 14, Shaffer was on airborne patrol just a week after his arrival. An approaching Kondor would be his first air-to-air combat.

In the early morning of August 14, 1942, at Bordeaux-Mérignac airfield in France, *Oberfeldwebel* Fritz Kuhn and his crew prepared their FW 200C-4 Kondor maritime bomber for a long patrol. Kuhn and his crewmates were all veteran

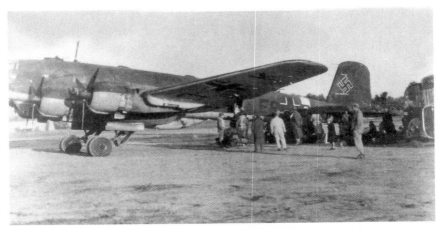

Figure 13.2. FW 200 with crew boarding, probably at Bordeaux-Mérignac. AIR
FORCE HISTORICAL RESEARCH AGENCY, KARLSRUHE COLLECTION

enlisted aircrew, not unusual for a *Luftwaffe* bomber. They included *Oberfeldwebels*
Fritz Kuhn (pilot), Philipp Haisch (copilot), Ottmar Ebener (radio operator),
Artur Wohlleben (flight mechanic), Albert Winkelmann (gunner), and *Unteroffizier* Wolfgang Schulze (flight mechanic). Like combat aircrew on both sides,
they knew that takeoffs were mandatory but landings were optional. Kuhn's crew
would not finish the final eastward Iceland–Norway leg this day.

The bomber's flight was uneventful until the aircraft approached the southwest coast of Iceland, possibly tracking a convoy 30 to 40 miles to the southwest
of Keflavik. German maritime bombers flew fast and high near Iceland, hoping
to escape before an intercepting fighter could reach them. Radar operated by
the 556th Signal Battalion (Aircraft Warning) detected the approaching aircraft
and initially identified it as friendly. Friendly aircraft most often were the ones
approaching from that direction. When the German failed to enter the approach
path for Reykjavik airfield, the track was reclassified as hostile.

At 1000 hours it was spotted by an RAF No. 330 (Norwegian) Squadron
N-3PD floatplane and reported to ground control as a Kondor. With radar and
visual confirmation the track information was passed to the Flight Operations
Center in Reykjavik.

When the radar track information was received, Weltman and Shahan in
their P-38s scrambled to intercept the German bomber. There was a broken
overcast at 1,500 feet over the airfield. As the Lightnings climbed through it,
they spotted the Kondor, who had turned north. Weltman's element found the

Kondor first and shot up the enemy bomber. The FW 200 fired back with its battery of machine guns. Weltman's guns and an engine were hit and he descended to exchange his aircraft for an undamaged Lightning from the airfield.

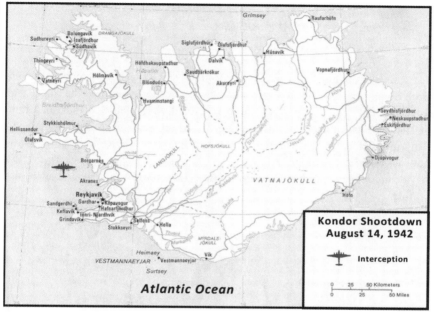

Map 13.2. Kondor shoot-down area, Iceland, August 14, 1942. MOLYSON[2]

Shahan continued the fight, joined by Shaffer in a P-40.[3] Both Shahan and Shaffer made passes at the FW 200, with the P-40 knocking out a Kondor engine. Shahan, with a faster climbing aircraft, made a chandelle (climbing turn) to hit the Kondor from the side with a deflection shot. The German's markings, "F8+BB," must have been very visible. The "+" in the number was the *Luftwaffe* iron cross insignia.

Shahan opened fire from about 100 yards, hitting along the fuselage in the vicinity of the bomb bay. As he attempted to dive below the German, the Kondor exploded in his face and showered Shahan's P-38 with debris. The remains of the Kondor fell into the ocean less than 10 miles southwest of Hvalfjörður Fjord, the big convoy anchorage and navy base north of Reykjavik. There were no parachutes from the stricken aircraft. Members of the German aircrew that weren't killed by American bullets died from the explosion of German bombs.

Weltman and his damaged P-38 landed safely, as did Shahan and Shaffer. Weltman commented in his after-action report:

> One of the crew was washed up on the shore later on, and he was found to be full of bullets. So we knew we had been scoring an awful lot of hits on that big clunk. Shahan and the P-40C pilot, 2nd Lt. Joseph Shaffer, each got half credit for the kill.[4]

This was the first air-to-air victory for the USAAF in the European Theater. Both Shahan and Shaffer received a half credit for the victory and the Silver Star for valor. The 33rd Fighter Squadron remained, defending Iceland until June of 1945. Weltman and his 27th Fighter Squadron went on to England later in August and then to the Mediterranean for Operation TORCH. Weltman was not unscathed crossing the Atlantic. A U-boat sank the transport carrying the squadron's luggage, and he flew for a time in a borrowed British battledress uniform.

CHAPTER FOURTEEN

The New Guys (May–August 1942)

Far to the south of the Arnold Line, Iceland, and the *Kanalfront*, other American planes used the southern route to deliver multiengine USAAF aircraft to North Africa, the Middle East, and India. They flew from Florida across the Caribbean to Natal, Brazil. From there they crossed the South Atlantic to West Africa and beyond. In May 1942, two dozen USAAF B-24 Liberator bombers bound for Asia were halted in Egypt. Colonel Harry A. Halverson led this bomber unit, termed the Halverson Detachment and code-named HALPRO.

The B-24 Liberator was another four-engine American heavy bomber that had entered production after the B-17 Flying Fortress. Of somewhat newer design and "high-tech" for its day, the B-24 could carry more bombs than a B-17 to a somewhat longer range. Liberators were especially valuable as heavy bombers in the Mediterranean, where their extra reach was needed to hit strategic targets in southern Europe and along the coast.

The slab-sided Liberator was not as attractive an airplane as the Fortress. Some critics called it "the box the B-17 came in." Also, the Liberator could not fly quite as high as the Fortress, nor was the airframe quite as tough. The B-17 was a stable aircraft and a pilot's dream to fly. The B-24 was a challenge to control and did not keep formation as well as the B-17. German fighter pilots would later exploit these facts by preferentially attacking the looser B-24 formations when both types of American heavy bomber were present.[1] Yet despite some negative characteristics, the B-24 was instrumental in the strategic bombing campaign in Europe.

Lieutenant Colonel Jimmy Doolittle's April 1942 Tokyo raid induced the Japanese to overrun potential American bomber bases in China. HALPRO and the other US bomber forces headed to Asia, intended for follow-on attacks against the Japanese homeland. They suddenly lost their mission, redirected to support Allied operations in the Eastern Mediterranean and Middle East. Soon, they were attacking Axis troops in Libya and Italian naval vessels in the Mediterranean.[2]

At dawn on June 11, 1942, thirteen HALPRO aircraft were sent to bomb the vital oil refinery complex at Ploesti, Romania. One turned back early with fuel-line problems. Damage to the target was negligible, but Hitler had been put on notice, American heavy bombers were attacking strategic targets from Mediterranean bases in daylight. Four of the B-24s were interned in Turkey and one crash-landed on its return to Africa.[3] It was two months before the Eighth Air Force in England mounted its first heavy bomber mission.

In July, ten B-17 Fortresses were transferred from their bases in India to reinforce the Allied forces defending Egypt and the Suez Canal. In August, the Liberators and Fortresses were used to build the 1st Provisional Bomb Group (Heavy) assigned to the US Middle East Air Forces.

BUILDING AN AIR FORCE

As the American men and planes of the Eighth Air Force appeared in Britain after traveling the Arnold Line, they were met, supported, and mentored by the RAF. The Brits might not have agreed with American bombing philosophy, but from day one they provided much of the critical equipment and bases the Yanks needed to operate.

The Americans, however, did not immediately go into combat. Arriving American fighters were not integrated into British air defenses. Their mission was to attack across the Channel. Upon arrival in England, the P-38s thirsting for first combat with the German air force found themselves virtually grounded. First, they had to learn the areas in which they were to fly. Their HF (high frequency) radios were replaced with superior British VHF (very high frequency) systems. The Americans had to fit into the system of air traffic control to find their airfields in bad weather and avoid "friendly" antiaircraft guns and balloon barrages.[4] There was also the matter of aircraft recognition. Spitfires looked a lot like Bf 109s.

There was modification after modification to the P-38F to better its chances against the *Luftwaffe*. By the end of July, all they knew about the P-38F against a German fighter were the results of a mock combat with a captured FW 190A flown by a British pilot. The results were mixed. The Focke-Wulf apparently had better acceleration and a superior rate of climb. Surprisingly, at lower altitudes the P-38 could turn slightly better than the 190, and more than held its own in acrobatic maneuvers.[5]

EARLY OPERATIONS

Much of the success of the Eighth Air Force during its first year in England was due to the efforts of three generals: Lieutenant General Hap Arnold, Major

General Carl "Tooey" Spaatz, and Major Ira Eaker. Arnold, of course, was commanding general of the Army Air Forces, a direct subordinate of General George Marshall, army chief of staff. It was Arnold who would direct the air portion of Roosevelt's "Germany First" national strategy. He would pick the planes, the units, and the leaders who would form all the overseas air forces, and the Mighty Eighth would become the largest of these.

"Tooey" Spaatz was the first Eighth Air Force commander. Eaker commanded VIII Bomber Command, that portion of the Eighth Air Force that flew the American heavy and medium bombers based in England. Spaatz and Eaker forged a brilliant working relationship with their counterpart at Bomber Command, Air Marshal Harris. Arnold, Spaatz, and Eaker were colleagues and friends, and all believed in daylight precision bombing. When Arnold had become chief of the air corps in 1938, Spaatz was his operations officer and Eaker his executive staff officer. The relationship continued into World War II, when Arnold sent Spaatz to set up the Eighth Air Force at Savannah, Georgia, and Eaker to establish VIII Bomber Command in England. Eaker and the others were influenced by theorists at the Tactical School, totally committed to winning the war through strategic bombing.[6]

The fighters of the Eighth Air Force were assigned to VIII Fighter Command, headed by Brigadier General Frank O'Driscoll Hunter. Hunter was a World War I ace who had downed eight German aircraft. Hunter fit the public perception of a fighter pilot: brave, reckless, and prone to fast cars and fast women. Unfortunately, his idea of air superiority was the fighter sweep, the most successful air-to-air tactic of World War I. The Brits had already realized that fighter sweeps were unproductive during the "lean forward into France" operations, yet Hunter persisted in his beliefs. In its first nine months of operation, VIII Fighter Command downed only fifteen German planes against seventeen American losses. Most of these victories were accomplished while escorting bombers, not during fighter sweeps.[7]

As part of BOLERO, the 15th Bomb Squadron had been sent to England as a night-fighter unit. The British had used their American-made Boston light bombers as night fighters, equipping them with Turbinlite airborne searchlights to illuminate German bombers. The 15th also flew the Boston, in USAAF service called the A-20 Havoc. By the time the 15th had arrived in England, the British had switched to airborne radar for attacking German aircraft at night. This left the 15th with no mission, so it was attached to RAF No. 226 Squadron, which flew the Boston III bomber version. The A-20 pilots of the 15th had little trouble sharing aircraft with their British mentors.

FIRST BLOOD

By July 4, 1942, the 15th Bomb Squadron was ready for their first mission with the RAF squadron. General Eaker later said the Germans partially provoked the early raids. "They'd been boasting, 'Where are the Americans?' dropping messages on our airdromes, chiding us and all that sort of thing."[8] The mission was flown against four *Luftwaffe* airfields in the Low Countries. Six American and six British crews flew in the attack in twelve aircraft.

Flying from their grass strip at Swanton Morley, the speedy light bombers quickly crossed the Channel. Unfortunately, they were spotted by German coastal patrol boats and reported to the German defense headquarters. The planes were met with heavy flak over their targets. Bombing effectiveness was questionable, but not the bravery of the combined squadrons pressing home their attacks. Three of the aircraft were lost, two of them flown by American crews.[9] The RAF and USAAF had shed blood together. Before the end of July, the squadron had mounted its own low-level attack against Abbeville/Drucat airfield in France (see map 15.1).

ENTER THE FORTRESS

By August, the VIII Bomber Command B-17s were ready to fight. On August 17, 1942, twelve B-17s bombed the railroad marshaling yards and repair facilities at Rouen-Sotteville, France. Leading the mission and the first flight of six aircraft was 97th Bombardment Group commander Colonel Frank Armstrong, aboard the B-17 *Butcher Shop*. Leading the second flight was Major Paul Tibbets, who would later fly Eisenhower to Gibraltar for Operation TORCH and the A-bomb to Hiroshima to end the war in the Pacific. Aboard Tibbets's plane, the *Yankee Doodle*, was Brigadier General Ira Eaker of the VIII Bomber Command.

Four squadrons of the new Spitfire Mark IX escorted the twelve B-17s. Rouen was within their expanded 225-mile combat radius. Six additional B-17s flew a diversionary mission. The escorts would down two German fighters in exchange for two Spitfires. An FW 190A, flown by German *leutnant* Herbert Horn, was probably downed by ball turret gunner Staff Sergeant Kent West.[10] The ball turret, which was fitted to the rear underside of B-17 and B-24 bombers, was a novelty in the European Theater.

Over the target, flak was light and only two bombers were hit. About half of the bombs fell within the target area, causing scattered damage. The Eighth Air Force was in the daylight precision bombing business. *Leutnant* Horn, a pilot in 3./JG2,[11] is listed as "Killed in Action" on the same day and same area; however, that listing implies that one of the escorts shot him down. Horn was credited with three victories before his death. Staff Sergeant West, the first American aerial gunner credited with downing a German aircraft in World War II Europe, was killed in North Africa in December.

General Eaker changed into a dress uniform for *Yankee Doodle*'s landing at Grafton. His pictures that day showed a rare smile; he was obviously elated at the results and the safe return of all his bombers. Eaker's boss, General Spaatz, and the Anglo-American press corps, were waiting for the bombers' return. The reporters duly noted that Eaker had flown in B-17 *Yankee Doodle*, a fact that was featured in British and American papers the next morning. This inspired Air Marshal Harris to send his congratulations to Spaatz and Eaker: "*Yankee Doodle* certainly went to town and can stick another well-deserved feather in his cap."[12]

Chapter Fifteen

JUBILEE (June–August 1942)

I want you to turn the south coast of England from a bastion of defence into a springboard of attack.
—Churchill to Air Marshal Lord Mountbatten, Chief of Combined Operations, March 1943[1]

In June 1942, Churchill and Field Marshal Alan Brooke (General Marshall's British counterpart) returned to Washington to discuss the Allied atomic bomb project and the prospects for an early invasion of France. The Allies could land less than a division of troops with the limited British shipping and landing craft then available.

The Germans had over twenty divisions in France. It was obvious that the landing of one division would not draw any additional German forces from the east for a "Second Front." SLEDGEHAMMER was canceled, and ROUNDUP was rescheduled as a stand-alone attack to be executed sometime in the second half of 1943.[2] The BOLERO buildup was to continue.

Even though the British blocked SLEDGEHAMMER, strategists in Washington and London understood that to liberate Europe required an eventual landing on the northwestern French coast. This meant developing the means for delivering troops under fire from German air, ground, and naval forces. It also meant breaching fixed defenses. Another Gallipoli was to be avoided at all costs.

On August 19, 1942, two days after the supporting Eighth Air Force attack on the Rouen-Sotteville marshaling yard, Operation JUBILEE was conducted at Dieppe, France. Dieppe was a French Channel port town to the west of the Pas-de-Calais. JUBILEE was an Allied amphibious raid. The mission was not to hold the beachhead, but simply to see if such a landing could rapidly capture a moderately fortified Channel port.

The raiders included 5,000 Canadians, 1,000 British, and 50 US Rangers. The landing would assess various new Allied technologies and tactics for a future

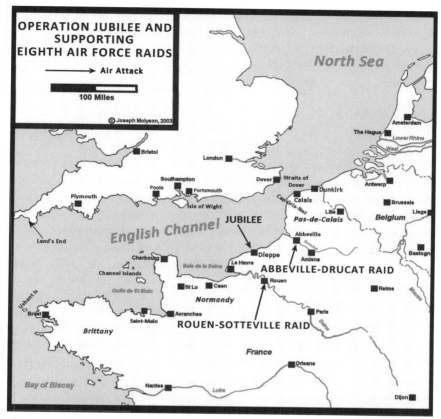

Map 15.1. Operation JUBILEE and supporting Eighth Air Force raids, August 17–19, 1942. MOLYSON

invasion, as well as the German defenses. To exploit any invasion of northwestern France, it was thought a harbor must be seized. This was required to bring large numbers of Allied troops and heavy equipment and supplies quickly into the new bridgehead.

The role of Allied airpower was a major factor in this experiment. Part of the test was to determine how well Allied fighters based in England might defend the landing and the newly acquired port. By this time, USAAF pilots in Spitfires from the 31st Fighter Group were flying their first combat missions with the RAF. The great air battle associated with the Dieppe raid was the culmination of the RAF 1941–1942 "lean forward" offensive.

It started as a normal day at Abbeville/Drucat, a German fighter base for 5./ JG26 in northeast France. Unknown to the base personnel, four combat squadrons of B-17s (twenty-four aircraft) across the Channel were being dispatched to bomb their airfield.[3] The *Luftwaffe* duty pilots rode into the base as usual from their billets in town. Arriving at their dispersal, or aircraft parking area, they began to look over their FW 190s. Then, the *Oberwerkmeister* (line chief) passed them an order he had received from the *Gruppe Gefechtsstand* (Group Command Post): "Scramble two aircraft immediately, fly to the coast, and check out the area." There were no other details, but obviously something was up.

The only officer present among the duty pilots was *Oberleutnant* Horst Sternberg. Sternberg was a *Schwarmführer* (flight leader) in the *Staffel*. He grabbed novice NCO pilot *Unteroffizier* Peter Crump as his *Katchmarek* (wing man). Sternberg ordered him to fly "Black 8," the Focke-Wulf assigned to squadron commander *Oberleutnant* Wutz Galland. Galland was the brother of General of the Fighters Adolf Galland; his aircraft was always kept in top-notch condition.

They climbed away in the dawn twilight, contacting the *Jafü* (fighter control) for instructions. They were ordered to fly at medium altitude toward Dieppe. In a short time, they were flying southwest parallel to the coast, able to see the ground below but not the surface of the fog-shrouded sea. As they approached Dieppe, they began to see streams of sparks, followed by geysers of earth silently lifted into the air by the impact of naval artillery. Finally, they began to perceive the dim outline of approaching enemy destroyers firing their guns and landing craft approaching the beach.

Invasion!

As they flew over Dieppe, several strings of white lights that looked like pearls but were actually incandescent German flak rounds reached up toward the two aircraft. One luminous string transfixed the pristine Black 8 for an instant, but Crump's plane motored on. Relief! Galland treated his aircraft like personal property; it wouldn't do to have it shot down by friendly fire.

Sternberg's orders were to do a quick reconnaissance and get the word back to the *Gruppe* headquarters as quickly as possible. Therefore, he avoided flying over the town again, or the "hot" areas of the beach. He also ignored several Spitfires spotted by Crump. The 190s were higher and well illuminated by the sun. The Spit pilots failed to spot the German planes. As the Focke-Wolfs crossed the southern edge of the town, German light flak again began to fire at them. When a German ground unit was under attack, it was unhealthy for an airplane—any airplane—to fly over.

On Sternberg's landing, Galland was of course furious that the new guy had flown his fighter. The flak holes didn't help either. There was a full day ahead for

JG26; the invasion, or at least a major amphibious raid, was on. Now Galland was going to have to risk his neck in someone else's plane.[4]

The assigned Allied air forces for the raid included 56 fighter squadrons, or about 750 planes. Commanded by Air Marshal Sir Trafford Leigh-Mallory, they included only 4 squadrons of Spitfire IXs, the only Spitfire of comparable performance to the FW 190A or the new model Bf 109G. The RAF pilots were well trained, but because of continuous expansion still had a much higher percentage of non-veterans than the Germans. By August JG2 and JG26, still defending the *Kanalfront*, each had about 110 operational FW 190As and Bf 109Gs. The Germans went into the Dieppe air battle outnumbered over three to one in fighters, but with a qualitative advantage both in pilots and their aircraft.

Only 5 squadrons of RAF bombers (Blenheims and Bostons) were in the attack, the ratio of fighters to bombers nominal for a "lean forward" Circus. This was a full assault, however, and the Germans committed more than just fighters to the battle. *Luftflotte 3* also committed 20 FW 190 *Jabos* and 220 Ju 88 and Do 217 medium bombers. The German bombers, veterans of the Blitz night bombing, were not used to working with a day escort, and some fell to Allied fighters.

The first German fighters to attack the bridgehead arrived shortly after Sternberg's *Rotte* (element) had completed its reconnaissance. While each side would later claim it had achieved air superiority over the beachhead, neither attained it. Although significant numbers of RAF fighters were flying over Dieppe, they were unable to keep the *Luftwaffe* out of the landing area. German fighters and flak downed about 88 Spitfires and 12 other Allied aircraft, while 48 *Luftwaffe* fighters were lost. American pilots had flown 8 of the lost Spitfires. While the air fighting stalemated overhead, the unhindered German army won the land battle and killed or captured much of the landing force. German ground forces inland from the beach arrived unimpeded throughout the day.

Although the Allied air cover achieved air parity with the defending German air force, they were unable to provide the close air support so desperately needed by the troops ashore. There were no Allied artillery observation aircraft to direct naval gunfire on the German reinforcements as they approached the beach. The Germans lost only some 300 ground troops. Of the 6,100 Allied soldiers landed, some 1,400 were dead and another 1,600 wounded. The Germans took over 2,000 prisoners.[5]

The RAF effort to defend the Royal Navy ships offshore was only partially successful. The German medium bomber units were able to fly about 145 sorties[6] against the ships, which were their primary target. Ships were easier to pick out than Allied troops on shore. The *Luftwaffe* would lose 16 medium bombers during all-day attacks for a loss rate exceeding 10 percent. These attacks were supplemented by FW 190 *Jabo* attacks. The only major warship sunk was HMS *Berkeley*, a destroyer, hit on the stern by a *Jabo* 1,100-pound bomb and later scuttled by its crew. Some smaller vessels were also sunk and many were damaged.

In addition to the combat air patrol over the landing area and escort of RAF medium bombers, the Allied air effort included a supporting attack against Abbeville/Drucat airfield by 24 American B-17 heavy bombers. The flak defending the field scored several hits, but the German interceptors were busy elsewhere. Although damage was done to this base, there weren't enough American bombers to shut down all twelve German fighter bases within range of Dieppe.

The Allies would fly almost 2,500 sorties in support of the Dieppe landing. Dieppe was close to the English coast. Allied air cover should have been easy, but German tactical proficiency trumped Allied operational advantages. Although the ships offshore received adequate protection, the troops received little direct or indirect support from the air.

It was obvious to the future Allied invasion planners that something had to be done about German airpower over France. Obviously, the *Luftwaffe* was as strong as ever in France despite eighteen months of offensive RAF operations. The "lean forward" offensive had cost almost 1,000 pilots and planes.[7] After Dieppe, the RAF discontinued the Circuses in favor of unescorted low-level incursions by fast American and RAF medium bombers.

Despite the disaster, there were several positive effects from JUBILEE.

First, Hitler was firmly convinced that an early German ground counterattack could stop an Allied landing. He failed to consider the fact that the Allies had never established air superiority. The beach defenders and their support on the flanks were able to concentrate on killing the assault troops and sinking their landing craft. Mobile German reinforcements were able to approach the beachhead unhindered by Allied airpower.

Second, Hitler was also convinced that the Allies would land very close to or in a French port, not on an open beach. Dieppe was seen as an experiment, which it indeed was.

Third, the Allies now understood that air superiority would be required if inferior numbers of assault troops were to break through the beach defenses. This was necessary to pin the defenders and prevent their rapid reinforcement. More effective naval bombardment, better means of crossing the beach, envelopment of the defenders using airborne and glider troops, and other force multipliers would also have to be employed.[8]

CHAPTER SIXTEEN

Decisions, Diversions, and Missteps (July–October 1942)

With SLEDGEHAMMER canceled, it was time to address Roosevelt's objective of getting American ground troops into combat in Europe in 1942. In July, Roosevelt and his military leaders accepted the necessity of an Allied landing in French North Africa, formerly designated GYMNAST and now code-named Operation TORCH.

Prospects for TORCH were good; however, British naval attacks against the collaborationist Vichy French fleet in July 1940 had alienated the British from their erstwhile allies. The Vichy French might accept a predominantly American landing, but not a British one. TORCH had a great negative impact on the BOLERO buildup in Britain, especially on the American Eighth Air Force.

SPLIT DECISION

Although much of the airpower for Operation TORCH in North Africa would be shipped from the United States, it was decided to transfer 400 of the 700 planes that had been provided to Eighth Air Force by BOLERO to a new Twelfth Air Force.[1] The Twelfth Air Force would control all American air units supporting TORCH. Eighth Air Force was essentially gutted to prepare the Twelfth for war in the western Mediterranean.

Eaker complained bitterly to General Arnold that diversions of Eighth Air Force aircraft and men were a greater problem for the bombing offensive than the *Luftwaffe*.[2] Some of the veteran groups transferred were replaced by new units from the United States. The only positive effect of TORCH on the Eighth Air Force was the looting of the German air force training system by *Luftwaffe* chief of staff Hans Jeschonnek to send additional German aircraft to the forces in Africa. This would adversely affect the quality of new German fighter pilots for the rest of the war.

The 78th Fighter Group, flying VIII Fighter Command's only operational P-38 Lightnings, eventually lost all its planes and most of its pilots to equip other units of the Twelfth Air Force. General Arnold sent every P-38 he could find to support TORCH, because of all fighters then available, only this one could fly the Atlantic or move from the United Kingdom down to North Africa. If the P-38s were not sent, then the African invasion must be abandoned altogether.[3] The P-38F with two 150-gallon drop tanks had a combat radius of over 600 miles, about the direct distance from London to Berlin.[4] With the Lightnings went the Eighth Air Force's only long-range fighter capability. No more P-38 fighter groups would be seen in England for a year.

Brigadier General Hunter was only too happy for his VIII Fighter Command to give up its Lightnings. Colonel Cass Hough, who ran fighter technical development for Hunter, said, "I couldn't get Hunter into a P-38."[5] It left Eighth Air Force with only short-range Spitfires, gifted from the RAF, as the sole fighter available for bomber escort.[6] The B-17s were on their own anywhere beyond Paris until the following summer. In Hunter's defense, then-current American doctrine had never suggested a long-range escort fighter was needed.

ACHTUNG SPITFIRE!

The VIII Bomber Command continued its own daylight B-17 bombing campaign over France.[7] On September 1, 1942, the first major sweep by Eighth Air Force fighters crossed the French coast. These were 78th Fighter Group Lightnings awaiting the movement order to the Mediterranean for TORCH. Hunter had finally released them for combat. The thirty-two Lightnings had a simple mission: to provoke a *Luftwaffe* interception, win the subsequent air battles, and get some combat experience. It did not pay to ignore the advice of RAF veterans, who warned that the frugal Germans would send no fighters to intercept. When these aircraft and pilots transferred to Twelfth Air Force, they were yet to be battle-tested against a German fighter.[8]

The "tyranny of range" continued to plague the short-legged Spitfire attempting to escort American heavy bombers to targets in France. It became worse as autumn weather obscured European skies. On September 26, twelve new Spitfire IXs of the veteran RAF No.133 Squadron escorted a dozen B-17s to the JG2 airfield at Morlaix, France. France was covered in clouds, and with an inaccurate weather report, the formation drifted over 130 miles south of the target. Fuel-wise, this was a minor problem for the Fortresses, but a dilemma for the Spits.

Attempts by the RAF fighters to fly under the clouds looking for a landmark brought an immediate response from German flak. The bombers and fighters became separated, and then a group of FW 190s bounced 133 Squadron. Although at least one FW 190 was downed, twelve Spitfires were lost to enemy aircraft, flak, or fuel exhaustion.[9] Three 133 Squadron pilots were killed, seven were MIA (missing in action—that is, simply gone without a trace), and one was taken prisoner. One pilot made it back to crash-land at Kingsbridge. Although 133 Squadron was RAF, all the pilots were Americans.

American fighter pilots first entered the European air war as RAF volunteers in 1940. After training, most were assigned to three so-called Eagle Squadrons: 71, 121, and 133. The three units did not become combat-ready until after the Battle of Britain. Their operational careers had begun during the more frustrating period of Rhubarbs and Circuses that characterized RAF Fighter Command operations in 1941. By August 1942, each Eagle Squadron was a veteran outfit and participated in Operation JUBILEE over Dieppe as RAF pilots.[10]

On September 29, 1942, just three days after the Morlaix incident, the Eagle Squadrons were transferred to the USAAF and became the VIII Fighter Command's 4th Fighter Group. This brought many of the Eagle Squadron veterans together for the first time, for while in British service the three units had never been assigned to a single RAF wing. There was some initial friction as old barriers broke down and new friendships were forged.[11]

Both pilots and aircraft were transferred immediately, while the ground staff slowly transitioned from RAF to USAAF personnel. The pilots would have problems adjusting to a new and vastly different air force culture. Unlike the American Flying Tigers in China, none of these men were American military veterans. The uniforms and rank insignia were new.

Confusion about rank insignia was sorted out quickly since the Eighth Air Force brass had shown up for the transfer ceremony. Former pilot officer and now second lieutenant "Deacon" Hively was approached by a gentleman who seemed a bit old to be a fighter pilot. The older guy introduced himself simply, with "My name is Spaatz." Hively replied innocently and without a salute, "Mine's Hively." The rest of the conversation between the lieutenant general and the lieutenant must have been interesting; unfortunately, it was not recorded in the unit history.[12]

CHAPTER SEVENTEEN

TORCH (November–December 1942)

In North Africa, the situation for the Axis was about to deteriorate. German and Italian forces were deployed in Libya and western Egypt fighting the Battle of El Alamein. If they succeeded, they could cut the British Commonwealth in half by seizing the Suez Canal. Not only did they lose the battle, but they were out of position to readily counter the Allied landings far to the west in Morocco and Algeria.

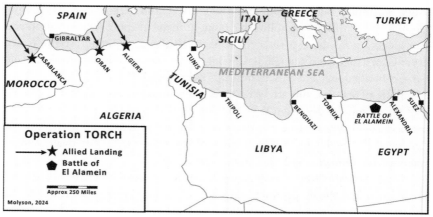

Map 17.1. Operation TORCH, November 8–16, 1942. MOLYSON[1]

SHUFFLING THE BRASS

The former Eighth Air Force groups sent to Twelfth Air Force were joined by thousands of US ground troops originally sent to Britain under the BOLERO buildup. One of these men was Lieutenant General Dwight D. Eisenhower, who was sent to England to plan the SLEDGEHAMMER landing and was now picked by Marshall to lead the Allied forces for TORCH. Eisenhower was to become commander in chief of the North African Theater of Operations (NATOUSA), later renamed the Mediterranean Theater of Operations (MTO).

Spaatz was promoted to senior American air commander for the new theater, leaving Eaker in Britain in command of a much-reduced Eighth Air Force. Twelfth Air Force, commanded by Jimmy Doolittle, controlled American air forces in the western Mediterranean. Lieutenant Colonel Doolittle had bombed the Japanese in Tokyo the previous April; eight months later, Major General Doolittle was bombing Vichy French and Germans in North Africa.

Eisenhower was known both to national leaders and lowly privates as "Ike," although very few men could address him as such. Ike had the common touch when working with American and foreign political and military leaders. He was diplomatic and accommodating to other ideas and concepts but uncompromising in his priorities. He was just the man to lead a coalition military force.

Ike's TORCH command post was located at Gibraltar, the British fortress at the mouth of the Mediterranean. He appropriated a B-17F, *Red Gremlin*, as his personal transport. As the invasion date approached, Ike and his headquarters staff were bundled aboard six B-17s for the trip. The weather report was poor and the mission delayed. Finally, Eisenhower said simply that he had to go. Major Paul Tibbets advised that the weather was too bad to fly, but Ike had confidence (perhaps born of desperation) in the B-17 Fortress and its crew.

Red Gremlin led the other five B-17s into the overcast skies and proceeded south. Ike spent the flight from England to Gibraltar in the cockpit sitting on a blanket-padded board between the two pilots. One bomber had to return to England with mechanical problems. The rest flew on under low clouds to complete the trip. Tibbets later said that it was his only sortie of the war where he had to *climb* to get high enough to land.

Six hundred ships carried the 90,000-man TORCH invasion force across U-boat-infested seas. The total distance was 3,000 miles from the US East Coast and some 1,500 miles from the BOLERO bases in the United Kingdom. Remarkably, no ships of the initial landing force were lost to enemy air or submarine attack until after the landings.

Although bombers could fly from Britain to North Africa via Gibraltar, single-engine fighters could not. American P-40 fighters were delivered by Allied escort carriers from United States ports. They could take off from these small ships but had to land on captured French airfields, or wherever they could.

The troops were successfully landed and briefly engaged the French defenders, an army of some 200,000 men supported by 500 planes. Few were fans of Hitler. By the end of November 1942, Eisenhower's Operation TORCH invasion force was ashore and the fate of the Axis in Africa sealed. The Vichy French were overpowered and convinced to come over to the Allied cause.[2] Their capitulation led Hitler to occupy Vichy France, another country crushed.

Eisenhower's plan to seize hard-surfaced airfields in Tunisia using paratroopers was trumped by German air-landed troops.[3] The Germans occupied Tunisia, flying in more troops from Sicily. For the remainder of the campaign, Allied air forces in the west flew from muddy airstrips in Morocco and Algeria while the *Luftwaffe* enjoyed the all-weather facilities in Tunisia. Eisenhower learned his first hard lesson from the Germans; the German military appreciated all aspects of airpower and would concentrate the *Luftwaffe* to oppose any Allied invasion. The lessons of Dieppe were reinforced.

The surrender of Vichy French airfields in northwestern Africa included the key bases at Casablanca and Dakar, long a threat to the Allied shipping routes to and from Gibraltar and the Indian Ocean. Among other benefits, the aircraft delivery and communications "Southern Route" through Latin America and across the South Atlantic to Africa was enhanced. This allowed for increased multiengine aircraft movement to the Mediterranean and continued supply when the Arnold Line was temporarily closed due to winter weather. Once aircraft had arrived on the west coast of Africa, they could move cross-country northeast to Egypt. Some aircraft continued on to India and China.

CHAPTER EIGHTEEN

Autumn over France
(November–December 1942)

As Operation TORCH grabbed the headlines, the remainder of 1942 saw the much-reduced Eighth Air Force continue its campaign against German facilities in France and the Low Countries. It was a time of experiment and the gaining of combat experience. The Americans had great faith in the rugged construction and defensive machine guns on their Fortresses and Liberators.

A group of eighteen B-17s could bring 162 .50 caliber machine guns to bear on German interceptors with longer range than the weapons mounted on contemporary models of the FW 190 and Bf 109.[1] Even with this disadvantage the Germans sometimes scored victories against the big American bombers, especially when the formations could be broken up. A bomber that drifted out of formation was an easy target.

Attacking a formation of B-17s was not a job for the fainthearted. As a German ace recalled:

> To fight against twenty Russians that want to have a bite of one, or . . . against Spitfires, is a joy. And one doesn't know that life is not certain. But to curve into seventy Fortresses allows all the sins of one's life pass before one's eyes. And when one has convinced oneself to do it, it is still more painful to force it on every pilot in the wing, down to the last young newcomer.[2]

The VIII Bomber Command was determined to decrease losses to German fighters while increasing bombing accuracy. Whatever formation was flown, it was important the bombers be tucked in tight together. This was harder for the pilots to fly, but it made the formation look more formidable. Colonel (later Lieutenant General) Archie Old made this point to his men:

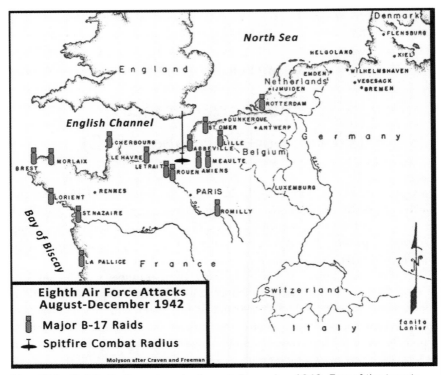

Map 18.1. Eighth Air Force targets, August–December 1942. Few of the targets were within Spitfire escort range. MOLYSON AFTER CRAVEN

There was one thing that every man in my outfit heard me harp on all the time: "Get that goddamn formation in there and keep it there if you are interested in a long life and you are interested in doing a good job." The tighter that formation is, the better the bomb pattern; particularly if the airplanes are not seesawing back and forth, right and left, you will do a better bomb job.

Also, those damn [German] fighters out here are looking at you and a hell of a lot of other units there, and if you have that compact bunch of airplanes together in a nice, tight formation, if they are compact, they know there is a hell of a lot of guns that can start unloading on them when they come in there. So the idea is, "Don't get that guy. Look at that outfit back yonder that is scattered all over the goddamn sky." It paid dividends from that standpoint.[3]

Various arrangements of aircraft were tested both to optimize defensive fire and to allow for more accurate bombing. It was Colonel (later General) Curtis LeMay who developed the so-called "combat box," a complex formation that presented a wall of machine guns to approaching German aircraft. The combat box was an effective, but not perfect, defense against German fighter attack.

LeMay also determined that evasive maneuvers to avoid flak over the target did little to protect bombers and actually ruined the bombing pattern. The Eighth Air Force developed a policy that the best way to beat flak was a rapid, steady passage over the target to ensure accurate bombing and to saturate the flak defenses with too many targets. The Eighth adopted the use of a master bombardier in the lead aircraft of each combat box to drop the first bombs in a

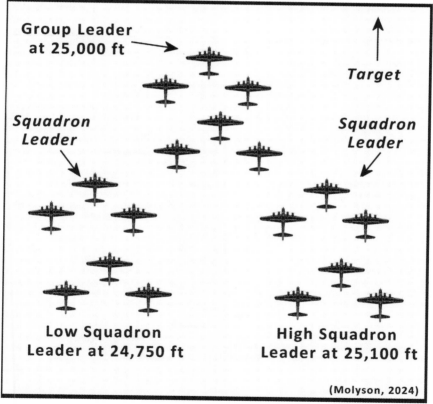

Figure 18.1. Combat box of an eighteen-bomber group in three six-plane squadrons (top view). MOLYSON ADAPTED FROM US ARMY AIR FORCES DIAGRAMS

formation, the other aircraft bombing off the leader. This greatly improved the concentration of bombs into the target.[4]

The B-17s often ventured beyond the range of USAAF and RAF Spitfires to deliver attacks along the French Atlantic coast. A common and frustrating target was the German U-boat pens located along the Bay of Biscay. The B-17 crews called the heavily defended target port of Saint-Nazaire "Flak City." Even without enemy fighters in the vicinity, flak could ruin your whole day. The sub pens in the U-boat harbors had thick concrete roofs that could not be penetrated by any bomb the B-17 could carry. Damage was limited to structures and equipment outside the pens. Attacks against war-related industrial plants, *Luftwaffe* repair facilities, and German airfields in France and the Low Countries were more lucrative.

The fighter pilots of *Luftflotte 3* in France and the Low Countries were severely challenged by the big bombers. Against the sporty German fighters

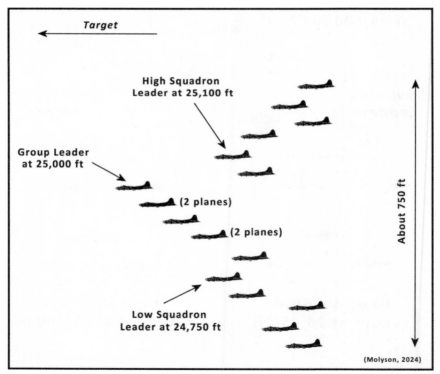

Figure 18.2. Eighteen-bomber combat box (side view). MOLYSON ADAPTED FROM US ARMY AIR FORCES DIAGRAMS

they seemed like huge dump trucks. The German pilots called them *Dicke Autos* ("fat cars"). Another nickname was *Viermot*, literally, "four-motors," a nickname the B-17 shared with the B-24 and the RAF Stirling and Halifax and Lancaster bombers.

It took twenty to twenty-five 20mm cannon hits to down a B-17. The Bf 109F was under-gunned for this task, having only one 20mm cannon and two rifle-caliber machine guns. The FW 190 was better armed but did not perform well over 21,000 feet, where the B-17s most often operated.[5] Both sides began developing new tactics and equipment in response to the other's daylight successes just as the RAF Bomber Command and the German night fighters were doing after dark.

The first lesson learned by the German day fighters about the Fortress was that each B-17 had twin tail and belly turret guns and that these guns had a longer effective range than the guns of their fighters. Attacks on B-17

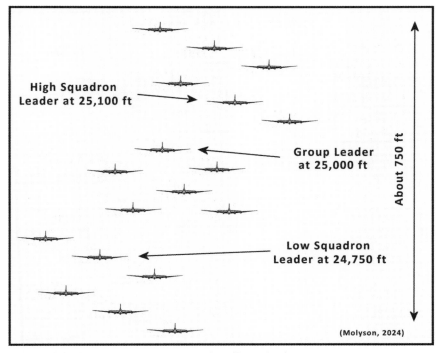

High Squadron
Leader at 25,100 ft

Group Leader
at 25,000 ft

Low Squadron
Leader at 24,750 ft

About 750 ft

(Molyson, 2024)

Figure 18.3. Eighteen-bomber combat box (front view). MOLYSON ADAPTED FROM US ARMY AIR FORCES DIAGRAMS

formations from the stern were suicidal; in fact, the belly turret guns of its intended target destroyed the first German fighter downed by a B-17 over Europe. Major Egon Mayer of *Jagdgeschwader 2* developed the head-on attack against LeMay's combat box formation.

The German fighters would fly a parallel course to the bombers, gauging altitude and course while remaining outside of the .50 caliber machine-gun range. The German interceptors would then speed ahead and turn into the front of the bomber formation. The head-on attack brought heavy firepower against the front of the target bombers while exposing the German to a minimum of defensive machine-gun fire.[6]

The bomber pilots and engines were more at risk than in a stern attack, and the German fighter avoided the fatal tail guns. Since the front of the formation was hit, losses to unit commanders and lead master bombardiers and navigators went up. Executing this attack was very demanding, and in the beginning few German pilots could perform it and still hit the target.

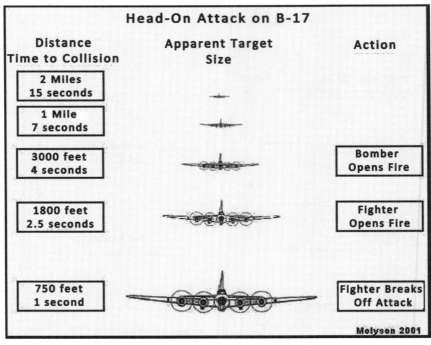

Figure 18.4. Head-on attack on a B-17. Not for the faint of heart. MOLYSON ADAPTED FROM SPICK[7]

The main defense of the nose of the B-17, at this time, was a single .30 caliber machine gun—no match for a German fighter's armament. The top and belly turrets provided some protection if the fighter was somewhat above or below the level of the bomber, but basically the nose machine gun bore the brunt of driving off the attacker. This forced the Eighth Air Force to develop more firepower at the front end of the B-17. The first response was to put more handheld machine guns through the Plexiglas nose and side windows. This solution was neither elegant nor particularly effective. Eventually, another turret with two .50 caliber machine guns was added to the chin of the airplane.[8] The B-17 had been armored against rear attack only. An Air Material Command report soon called for bulletproof glass and additional armor for the cockpit.[9]

The Eighth Air Force honed its tools over France. By December 1942, however, the Eighth had yet to bomb a target within Germany.

CHAPTER NINETEEN

The End of the Beginning (January 1943)

The next major Allied meeting, code-named SYMBOL, took place at the Anfa Hotel, Casablanca, on the Atlantic coast of Morocco in January, 1943. Roosevelt was tired of running the war from so far away; he wanted to visit the troops and meet with Churchill—and perhaps Stalin—on liberated ground. It was the first time in history a president had ridden in an airplane while in office. Unfortunately, Stalin refused to come, citing that his duties as generalissimo of the Soviet armies forced him to remain in Moscow.

Eisenhower's troops in Northwest Africa were attacking eastward into Tunisia. Montgomery's units were driving westward to crush *Generalfeldmarschall* Rommel's *Afrika Korps* between the two Allied armies. In Russia, German general Friedrich von Paulus and his 300,000-man *6th Armee* was disintegrating at Stalingrad on the Volga River. German hopes to cut the Volga River, lifeline of the Soviet Union, had been impaled on the wreckage of Stalingrad.

The Nazi leadership, notably armaments minister Albert Speer and propaganda minister Joseph Goebbels, recognized Stalingrad as "Germany's Dunkirk." The civilian economy was not fully mobilized for war and must change. Casualties on the Eastern Front would soon cause the drafting of 800,000 additional skilled workers into the army. This redirected manpower was replaced with women, men not fit for military service, and more "guest" workers.[1]

The Nazi Party hardened its domestic security rules, and for the first time the average German began to really doubt German press reports. It seemed that only after Stalingrad did the Nazi regime try to put Germany on a true total war footing. Real efforts were made to bring women into the workforce. On February 11, 1943, all male secondary school students born in 1926 and 1927 (fifteen- and sixteen-year-old boys) were called up as *Luftwaffe* auxiliaries to help man the flak forces. Germany could ill afford to tie up over half a million troops it maintained on domestic antiaircraft duty.[2]

The Casablanca Conference (January 14–24, 1943)

At Casablanca, the Allies again confirmed the "Germany first" strategy. BOLERO would continue with massive amounts of new planes being sent overseas from the United States as well as the return of some "borrowed" aircraft and crews used in TORCH to England. The Battle of the Atlantic would be intensified with the addition of massive amounts of new antisubmarine aircraft and ships. Although Axis troops were still holding out in Tunisia, Allied focus was already turning northward across the Mediterranean.

The Combined Chiefs of Staff at Casablanca ordered that the defeat of the U-boats should be the first priority for resources. This directive was caused by the staggering Allied shipping losses in 1942, amounting to nearly 9 million gross registered tons (GRT),[3] or an average of about 650,000 GRT per month. Unless these losses could be stopped, the U-boat campaign clearly would win the war by making it impossible for depleted merchant shipping to supply food, petrol, and munitions from the United States to the United Kingdom, and later, to France.[4]

To support the future invasion, destruction of German airpower was mandated in the air, on airfields, and in the aviation industry. The lessons of Dieppe were still fresh. The Germans had a simple choice: come up and fight the streams of American daylight bombers and suffer mortal attrition of their pilot force, or allow the bombers to destroy the aircraft industry and fail from lack of new aircraft.[5]

When asked by the press if these events were the beginning of the end of the war, Churchill declared it to be "the end of the beginning."

Round-the-Clock

The British were still not keen on American daylight precision bombing. Churchill was a leading critic of the American concept. Their own tragic daylight bombing attempts had sustained enormous casualties. General Arnold ordered Eaker from Britain to Casablanca. He was to convince Prime Minister Churchill that daylight bombing combined with the RAF's continual night bombing would produce "round-the-clock" attacks, offering no rest to the Germans.

Churchill was yielding to RAF doubts that the Eighth Air Force could successfully bomb Germany by day, and was trying to convince President Roosevelt to switch the USAAF to night operations. After a half-hour discussion between Churchill and Eaker, the prime minister said:

You have not convinced me you are right, but you have convinced me that you should have a further opportunity to prove your case. When I see President Roosevelt at noon today, I shall withdraw my request that the Eighth Air Force discontinue daylight bombing and suggest instead that they continue their campaign for a time. How fortunate it would be if, as you say, we can "bomb the devils around the clock."[6]

The successful result of Eaker's meeting with Churchill was codified in the Combined Bomber Offensive (CBO), established to "bomb the devils around the clock." Target lists for the CBO, including USAAF daylight precision bombing and RAF night area bombing of German cities, would be centrally coordinated. The Eighth Air Force, and its VIII Bomber Command, was not yet ready to hit the German homeland, but continued to pummel German facilities in occupied France.

The British pushed for the momentum gained in the Mediterranean to be maintained, even if it was a secondary theater. Although the Axis would continue to hold out for several more months in Tunisia, an invasion of Sicily was approved. Eisenhower was appointed supreme commander, even though he was junior in rank to several of the British officers involved. In conjunction with continued landing operations, an attempt would be made to lure Turkey into the war as an ally.

Finally, and most dramatically, at Casablanca was the call from President Roosevelt for "unconditional surrender" of the Axis countries. This was a fight to the death. Unconditional surrender would resonate the following summer in the skies over Germany, as the *Luftwaffe* fought with ever-increasing determination to avoid the consequences of such an ultimatum.[7]

Chapter Twenty

The Med (January–December 1943)

The war in the Mediterranean continued after the Casablanca Conference. The Americans and British depleted German and Italian forces in the air, on the ground, and at sea. While the Allies could replace losses, the Germans could not without robbing other combat areas. Axis aircraft and convoys fought an unsuccessful battle to keep their forces resupplied. *Luftwaffe* combat units were repeatedly sent to fight in North Africa and were shredded there. Aircraft production in Germany was accelerated to replace losses, and the Eastern Front was robbed to provide more airpower to stem the Allied advances. None of it worked for very long.

On May 13, 1943, the Axis forces in North Africa surrendered, with 150,000 enemy troops captured. Less than a month later, reporters attached to Eisenhower's headquarters in North Africa could clearly see preparations being made for another invasion somewhere in the "Med," where Eisenhower was now the commander in chief of the Allied Forces. At a press conference on June 12, Ike briefed them on the entire plan. The operation was code-named HUSKY and the objective was Sicily. He then charged them with preserving security until the attack commenced, and they did not disappoint him.[1]

HUSKY began in July 1943 and was completed by mid-August. General Marshall held firm on the return of major American forces to Britain as soon as possible. The British managed to again convince their American partners to continue limited offensive operations in the Mediterranean, if for no other reason than to divert German attention away from France. Italian support for the Axis began to waver.

By September, Montgomery had jumped across the narrow Strait of Messina from Sicily to land his British Eighth Army in the toe of Italy. The Americans quickly followed with Operation AVALANCHE, an attack at Salerno near Naples. Italy surrendered at the start of AVALANCHE, the first major Axis country to capitulate.

General Marshall rejected an attempt by Eisenhower, still commander in chief in the Mediterranean, to retain the four B-17 heavy bomber groups due to return to the Eighth Air Force in Britain. Ike also failed to retain the surviving aircraft of the four B-24 heavy bomber groups that had flown the costly August 4, 1943, attacks against the oil fields at Ploesti, Romania. Four medium bomber groups from Eighth Air Force were dispatched south from Britain to the Mediterranean to offset transfer of the heavy bombers back to Britain.

By mid-September, the Germans had concentrated against the Salerno beachhead. In response, Eisenhower unleashed his remaining medium and heavy bomber units (as well as substantial amounts of naval gunfire) to defeat the attack. This was the first use of US heavy bombers in a direct attack to support a beachhead. Soon the Allies were firmly ashore, and the Germans withdrew north to new defenses. Marshall's loyalty to the BOLERO buildup, the future invasion of France from Britain, and the ongoing strategic bombing campaign against Germany would be to Ike's benefit.

Eisenhower's time in the Mediterranean was ending.[2]

CHAPTER TWENTY-ONE

Radar

Of all the arcane military hardware to emerge from World War II, radar was among the most effective means of detecting an enemy attack or target.[1] Radars emit a radio signal, or "radar emission," which reflects off various objects called "targets." Metal objects, such as airplanes, are especially reflective of radio waves. The radio waves that are reflected can be received by the source radar. This is called a "target return." The target return signal is processed by the radar set and presented to the operator on a video display. Various kinds of radar were developed in several countries, and by the beginning of World War II both Britain and Germany had effective early warning (EW) search radars to protect their homelands.

The Freya radar, developed before World War II and deployed along the German North Sea coast, detected an incoming daylight raid of twenty-two RAF Wellington bombers on December 18, 1939. The bombers, some 70 miles out to sea, were on an anti-shipping mission and were ordered not to fly over the German mainland, or under 13,000 feet, to avoid warship antiaircraft fire. The radar site alerted *Luftflotte 2*, which launched sixteen Bf 110 and twenty-four Bf 109 fighters to intercept. Fourteen Wellingtons and their crews were shot down. This forced the RAF into night-only area bombing of Germany.[2]

Scientists in and out of uniform who worked on radar and other such devices were nicknamed "Boffins" by the Brits. It was the integration of radar with the fighter control network that allowed the outnumbered Royal Air Force to successfully defend the United Kingdom in the Battle of Britain. The RAF turned the tables on the German air force with radar. The *Luftwaffe* lost the element of surprise that had been the hallmark of its previous victories against enemies without effective radar early warning.

Late in 1940, the Germans extended their own EW radar coverage from Germany's North Sea coast to the coasts of France, the Low Countries, Denmark, and Norway to ensure that British bombers were quickly detected as they approached the Reich. Like their British counterparts, German EW radars had large antennas and long detection ranges. They provided the general location of incoming aircraft but could not provide data accurate enough to aim weapons.

Both the British and Germans developed smaller radar sets called GL (gun laying) radars to direct antiaircraft guns. Other small sets, called AI (air intercept) radars, were developed for installation on night fighters. To bring fighters within visual or AI range of their targets, GCI (ground control intercept) radars were used to bridge the information gap between the EW and AI radars.

Radar is a kind of weapon, and like any weapon it is subject to countermeasures. Radar receivers could be flooded with energy at the same frequency as the energy they were designed to detect. This was called *jamming* and could be accomplished actively, using powerful jamming transmitters, or passively, using strips of reflective foil. The jamming transmitters had to overpower the radar they were trying to jam. A common British-developed jamming transmitter was *Mandrel*, used to protect bombers from German EW radars.

A passive countermeasure employed was a reflective foil strip called *chaff*. It was cut in long strips whose length was matched to the frequency of the radar it was supposed to jam. Chaff was developed independently by both sides, but neither the British nor the Germans were eager to disclose its existence. It used the victim radar's own energy to blind it. Dispensing of chaff became and remains the most common kind of countermeasure to radars.

The British also developed a night / bad-weather bombing navigation radar called H2S, ironically nicknamed "home sweet home." The American derivative was called H2X. RAF night bombers were also equipped with detectors to warn the crew when a German AI radar was watching them. Since AI radars had only about a mile of range, such a warning meant the enemy fighter was closing in. The defensive–offensive seesaw continued so that by D-Day radar was a significant factor in detecting, avoiding, and attacking the enemy.

Chapter Twenty-Two

Flak

Organic defense of the troops and the homeland by the flak [was] indispensable.
—Generalfeldmarschall Albert Kesselring[1]

Dedicated German antiaircraft guns came into existence during the Franco-Prussian War of 1870–1871. After a rapid advance, the Germans surrounded Paris. The French remained in the fortified city, communicating with the outside using balloons. The Germans responded by quickly developing a 36mm BAK (*Ballonabwehrkanone*) anti-balloon cannon mounted on a cart. Only six of these guns arrived at the Paris perimeter, downing one of the sixty-six balloons known to have escaped Paris.

The victim was the French balloon *Daguerre*, lost on November 12, 1870. The crew crash-landed and was captured by the Prussians. Considering the extent of the perimeter, it was quite a feat for such a small number of guns to be within range. The gun's aiming system was primitive and the balloon was a moving target. The guns' bullets damaged the airbag but it took time for the gas inside to escape. The French responded to the BAK by flying only at night, a solution that was still in vogue seventy years later.[2]

Between 1870 and 1914, the Germans continued to slowly develop better guns and tactics. They recognized heavier-than-air aircraft as a major threat to their field armies and homeland. Guns designed to bring down these aircraft were redesignated as flak. Improved aiming devices, engine sound detection gear, and better guns and organization made more effective defense possible. During the Great War, flak brought down over 1,500 Allied aircraft over the front and in Germany.

During the years between the two world wars, development of the German flak forces continued. In 1935, Göring brought the flak arm under *Luftwaffe* control from the German army. By the start of World War II, strong *Luftwaffe* antiaircraft defense was provided to the field armies, airfields, and key parts of the homeland. Hitler and Göring considered flak to be the main defense of the homeland, supplemented by limited fighter forces.

There was never a question of prioritizing fighter versus flak as a defense against Allied aircraft. The Germans entered the war well equipped with both types of weapon. In fact, the German air force was organizationally divided between the *Flieger* (aviation) and *Flak* (antiaircraft artillery) arms. Both branches were supported by a sophisticated command-and-control system manned mostly by *Luftwaffe* communications troops and other specialists. Radar, searchlights, and sound detectors were fully integrated into the structure.

Once the *Luftwaffe* had absorbed existing flak assets, the German army established new flak batteries to have some antiaircraft capability under its control, but these were generally limited to 20mm and 37mm weapons and local defense machine guns. Only a few army 88mm heavy flak battalions were authorized, and they lacked much of the sophisticated aiming equipment enjoyed by the *Luftwaffe* units. All calibers of flak, both *Luftwaffe* and army, were used to hit ground targets when required. They were quite lethal in this role.

In World War II, flak was normally categorized into three classes by the caliber of the gun. The *light flak* category consisted of various-caliber machine guns with solid bullets and 20- to 23mm rapid-fire machine cannon with explosive shells. This included weapons mounted for self-air-defense on trucks and tanks as well as purpose-built antiaircraft vehicles. The *medium flak* category consisted of rapid-fire 37- to 57mm machine cannon with explosive shells. *Heavy flak* included hand-loaded cannon above 75mm. Although not "rapid fire," a proficient crew could fire multiple rounds per barrel per minute. The terms "light," "medium," and "heavy" were also used to describe the intensity of fire received around a flak-defended target, regardless of gun caliber.

Table 22.1. Approximate Effective Slant Range of Antiaircraft Guns.[3]

Weapon Category	Weapon Caliber (mm)	Approximate Effective Range (feet)*
Light Flak	7.62–23	0–7,500
Medium Flak	30–57	3,000–12,000
Heavy Flak	75–128	13,000–36,000

* Approximate ranges based on a study of multiple sources with multiple variables. Flak guns could also fire at ground targets. Flak guns could not fire straight up. Generally, aircraft above 10,000 feet were engaged only by heavy flak guns.

Flak guns were initially deployed in a battery of three to four weapons with associated equipment such as range finders and analog computer gun directors. During the war years, this was increased to as many as ten guns, but six was a more typical number. Batteries in turn were assigned to battalions, sometimes with a mix of medium and heavy guns. In the field, light flak 20mm guns operated with heavier batteries or on their own. These were a major threat to low-flying aircraft.

Flak was a threat whenever attacking targets on the ground, or simply flying over enemy territory. Hitler threatened at least once to terminate the fighter defense of the Reich and rely strictly on flak after repeated failure to stop American bombing. "Flak suppression" via attacks on flak batteries by aircraft was generally unproductive as measured by the ratio of flak batteries destroyed to attacking aircraft downed.

Aircraft attacking at low altitude were often hit by rapid-firing light and medium flak guns. This was a particular problem when attacking German army units and *Luftwaffe* airfields in France and the other occupied territories. Some guns were mounted on trucks or railroad flatcars. Others were static, mounted on the ground or on the tops of buildings. Aircraft above 5,000 feet could expect heavy flak from 88, 105, or 128mm guns.

Over German territory, on a clear night, a bomber crew could not recognize roads and small villages from above 6,000 feet. Structures such as factories could not be discerned from above 4,000 feet.[4] This led to blind-bombing of the terrain below, and eventually to low-flying Pathfinders to mark targets for the bombers high above. A Pathfinder flying at 4,000 feet on a clear night was an easy target for even medium antiaircraft fire.

Flak was a particular threat over cities and industrial areas, day and night. Medium and heavy flak were arranged as area defenses of major cities. Other defenses, such as barrage balloons, dummy installations, smoke generators by day, decoy fires at night, and other measures supplemented the guns. Civil defense workers, mostly civilians, established and maintained a blackout, making decoys more effective.

As they were introduced, night fighters most often worked outside of flak-defended areas, but sometimes even within flak zones. The fighters were separated (hopefully) from "friendly" antiaircraft fire by coordination of maximum altitudes for the flak. By 1942, about a quarter of German military spending was for the flak arm.[5] The homeland flak force continued to grow even as the *Luftwaffe* called home many of its day fighters to defend the Reich.

The bomber men feared flak. It killed at random, and there was little you could do about it. The guns were primarily close to major targets, so that as the bombers flew their straight bomb runs without evasive maneuvers, they would be subjected to aimed and "box" barrages of flak. Box barrages were fired ahead of aircraft formations so that the victims would fly through.

With enemy fighters you could fight back, but flak was impersonal and deadly. Even with the advent of fighter escort, the threat from flak never diminished. Approximately half of American combat aircraft losses were due to flak.[6]

In 1940, almost all flak personnel were men. By 1944, one-third to one-half were women, selected prisoners of war, partially disabled soldiers, and pre-service-age youngsters. Older age groups were also represented.[7] Able-bodied flak men were often transferred to antiaircraft units in occupied territories. The buildup of flak defenses inside Germany included the increase of flak personnel from approximately 528,000 in 1940 to 573,000 in late 1944. Perhaps 400,000 additional personnel manned flak stations on the Western and Eastern Fronts. There was always a manpower shortage in the flak branch because after the losses of 1942, there was a general shortage of troops for the *Wehrmacht*. By 1943, the

Figure 22.1. 88mm flak 36—the famed "88." AIR FORCE HISTORICAL RESEARCH AGENCY, KARLSRUHE COLLECTION

worsening fuel situation also detracted from adequate training of both regular and volunteer flak troops.[8]

In April 1942, Göring authorized the development of unguided flak rockets and guided flak missiles. By 1943, the *Foehn* ("mountain wind") light flak rocket was in service, but only three batteries were delivered to the field. Four German surface-to-air guided missiles (SAMs) were also developed, but none of these weapons affected D-Day or the strategic bombing of Germany.[9]

Allied countermeasures to flak included active and passive jamming of radars and fighter control radio frequencies. As flak downed or damaged Allied bombers, more armor was added when possible, including "flak jackets" and helmets for bomber crews. Flak forced daylight attackers to bomb from higher altitudes where most heavy flak batteries were less effective. Released from higher altitude, bombs became more dispersed away from the target. Bombing became less precise.

Flak damage also slowed some aircraft, forcing them from defensive formations and making them more vulnerable to German fighters. Flak often killed or maimed crew members even when the aircraft survived damage. The USAAF lost almost 18,500 aircraft in the air war in Europe. At least 7,800 were shot down by enemy flak, 6,800 by enemy aircraft.[10]

Chapter Twenty-Three

Into the Reich (January–April 1943)

The Casablanca Conference ended on January 24, 1943, with the approval of the Combined Bomber Offensive (CBO). That night, RAF Bomber Command bombed Düsseldorf in the Ruhr Valley industrial district through thick cloud. Only a few bombs hit the city.[1] The Ruhr target cities were hard to hit due to poor visibility and the smog associated with heavy industry.

The Eighth Air Force conducted their first daylight raid into Germany with fifty-five heavy bombers on January 27. This was a shallow-penetration raid—that is, the American bombers did not fly very far into German airspace (see map 23.1). That night, the RAF Düsseldorf raid was repeated, using accurate Oboe navigation equipment and ground-marking target indicators dropped by Pathfinder aircraft.[2] This made the bombing, again conducted through cloud, more accurate. Round-the clock all-weather bombing had arrived over Germany less than a week after the CBO was approved at Casablanca.

For the American raid, sixty-four B-17s and twenty-seven B-24s were launched. The Fortresses' target was the Bremen-Vegesack shipyards, while the Liberators were to bomb the Wilhelmshaven-Emden port area. Both were considered prime targets due to their connection with the U-boat campaign. The Liberators were unable to locate their target and returned to base without bombing. Over Germany, two Liberators were shot down by German fighters. The Liberators claimed 12 / 8 / 6 (destroyed / probably destroyed / damaged) German fighters; the numbers were probably inflated by double-claiming kills in the heat of combat. Double-claiming was the unintentional consequence of two gunners claiming the same aircraft.

The Fortresses were unable to bomb Vegesack due to cloud cover. Fifty-three of their number dropped the first USAAF bombs on Germany on their alternate target, the Wilhelmshaven docks. Two Fortresses bombed another alternate target at Emden. Over 137 tons of general-purpose high-explosive bombs were dropped. One Fortress was shot down by German fighters. Nine

Fortresses did not bomb for various reasons. The Fortresses claimed 10 / 6 / 7 enemy fighters. Double-claiming again probably inflated the numbers.

The targets were beyond the range of available USAAF or RAF Spitfires. The approach route was over the North Sea, and the initial targets required only a shallow penetration into German airspace to minimize interception by German fighters.[3] A new phase in the Battle over Germany had begun, the Americans by day joining the British by night, as noted by German ace *Leutnant* Heinz Knöcke:

> *At noon comes the first attack by American bombers on the North Sea Coast of Germany. We have been expecting it for several weeks. . . . It is obvious to me that today, with the first massed daylight attack by the Americans on Germany, marks the opening of a new phase of the war in the air.*[4]

Interceptors from *Jagdgeschwader 1* repeated the earlier German mistake of attacking American bombers from the tail. Three US bombers were shot down at a cost of seven FW 190As.[5] Göring underreacted to the raid, hoping that minimum fighter reinforcements in the Low Countries and northwestern Germany would make the attacks too expensive to continue. In this he discounted the tenacity of Eaker's Eighth Air Force, the potential for massive American bomber production, and the eventual deployment of a longer-range escort fighter.

Inspector of German fighters General Adolf Galland wanted to concentrate his fighters centrally in Germany, beyond the range of the American escorts. He knew that Göring's dispersed perimeter defense would never work with the few hundred fighters the *Luftwaffe* had available in the West.[6] When no increase in the day or air defense of the Reich was authorized, Galland brought additional fighters home by subterfuge.

General Galland knew that 1943 was a year of decision for the GAF. German fighters needed more powerful engines, longer range, more effective aircraft armament, higher speed, greater rates of climb, and an increase in operating ceiling. A jump to a new-model fighter was not possible, both because of Hitler's intransigence and the necessity to avoid the temporary cessation of production that would accompany an entirely new aircraft. Upgrades were limited to existing models.

Göring's fighters began to lose their technical edge over their Allied counterparts. The delay in introducing new aircraft designs made obsolescence an increasing problem. In 1942, for example, the Germans had fielded yet another version of their Bf 109, the Gustav. The Bf 109G would be the most-produced version of the Messerschmitt fighter, but it wasn't the clean design its predecessors had been. Upgraded equipment was installed under protruding fairings on the narrow fuselage, leading to the nickname *Die Beule* ("the bulge").

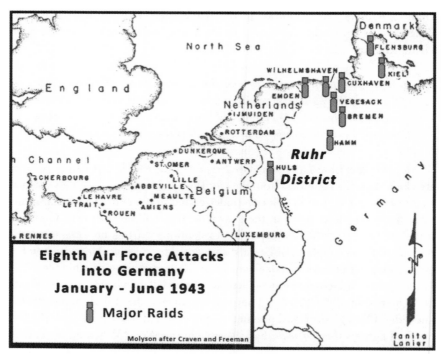

Map 23.1. Eighth Air Force shallow penetration attacks into Germany, January–June 1943. MOLYSON AFTER CRAVEN AND FREEMAN[7]

In February 1943, as scheduled, the Eighth Air Force in Britain gave up all its P-38s to the Twelfth Air Force in the western Mediterranean. Doolittle's Twelfth Air Force began raiding Axis airfields in Italy. The Ninth Air Force in the eastern Mediterranean continued to threaten Axis forces there. This not only paved the way for the later Allied invasion of Sicily, but it also forced the German air force to spread its fighters ever thinner along the shrinking Axis perimeter.

Most American heavy bomber missions were still being conducted against German targets in France and the Low Countries. The ones within Spitfire range were escorted. It was obvious that having an escort reduced bomber losses, but that did not save more distant targets in western France or Germany from unescorted daylight attack.

SPECTER

General Galland confronted German armaments minister Albert Speer with a new specter—increasing American daylight precision bombing of the Ruhr District, Germany's most important industrial area. The British were already area-bombing in the Ruhr at night. "Despite considerable damage and losses, these nightly area bombings did not produce a decrease in our war production," Galland noted. "Speer therefore felt most apprehensive when I told him that I foresaw the early possibilities of American daylight raids on the Ruhr."[8]

The VIII Bomber Command scheduled attacks on Hamm, in the Ruhr Valley, on February 2 and 14, 1943. The bombers approached Germany across the North Sea to reduce the time German fighters could intercept them. Both were canceled due to weather over the North Sea. The first successful USAAF daylight attack on the Ruhr was on March 4, when forty-four B-17s penetrated the North Sea weather to bomb the Hamm railway marshaling yard. Although Wilhelmshaven was again attacked on February 26 and March 22, it was the Hamm bombing that placed the Ruhr into American bombsights.

By May, RAF bombers intensified night bombardment in the Ruhr. As part of this "Battle of the Ruhr," the RAF bombed three dams that provided power and regulated water flow through the industrial region. Unlike urban area bombing, these were night precision bombing attacks using specially trained crews flying modified Lancaster bombers. Two of the three dams were breached, causing some destruction and loss of production. Neither urban area bombardment nor the precision bombing of the dams was decisive; Germany continued to produce much of its armaments from this region.

Galland was called to confer with Hitler in early May. Hitler, apparently cautioned by Speer on the emerging American precision bombing threat, asked what could be done to prevent daylight raids. Galland insisted he needed four times as many defending single-engine fighters as attacking bombers, plus equal the number of twin-engine *Zerstörer* heavy fighters.

The *Luftwaffe* night air defense organization was drawing large numbers of *Zerstörer* into the *Nachjagdwaffe* ("night-fighter force") and away from day missions. This was a direct result of round-the-clock bombing. The requisite low-visibility equipment on night fighters decreased their daytime capability. Night-fighter pilots could not fight all night and then rise to fight all day. Hitler agreed on the force ratio but disagreed that the Americans could field an escort fighter with sufficient range to penetrate deeply into the Reich. Göring had already told him such a thing was impossible, and Hitler apparently agreed.[9]

By March, Eighth Air Force still had only about one hundred bombers available for operations. It must have seemed like more to the Germans, who desperately tried new tactics to break up the tight combat boxes of Fortresses and Liberators. Each box consisted of one combat group of eighteen bombers. Ideally, a combat wing consisted of three of these groups, or fifty-four aircraft. Eaker could muster at most only two of these combat wings with the aircraft he had available.

On March 22, German *Leutnant* Knöcke led his squadron on the first air-to-air bombing of a B-17 formation, downing one bomber. The idea was not so much to hit a bomber as to make the bombers in a particular squadron break up their formation. Individual bombers could then be attacked piecemeal. The attackers used time-fused 500-pound bombs dropped from their FW 190s. Knöcke was personally commended by Göring for his initiative in a phone call

Figure 23.1. Me 410s deliver salvo of BR 21 rockets during head-on attack. US ARMY AIR FORCES

that night. He laid at attention in his pajamas to receive the accolade. The next day General Kammhuber, commander of *Fliegerkorps XII* and apparently out of the loop, reprimanded him for use of unauthorized weapons![10] The bombing technique had limited success, and rockets were eventually introduced to accomplish the disruption of bomber formations.[11]

The most successful of these weapons was the *Werfer-Granate 21* artillery mortar adapted from army ordnance. *Werfer-Granate* literally means "thrown grenade," the German term for a mortar round. The grenade was boosted out of its carrier tube by a rocket. In *Luftwaffe* service, it was known as the BR 21 *Bordrakete* ("aircraft-mounted rocket"). A BR 21 was carried under each wing of the attacking fighter and launched into the bomber formation to scatter the target squadron.

In April, German fighters defending the Reich began using drop tanks to carry extra fuel externally, extending their flying time to two hours. It took almost fifty minutes to assemble an interceptor force and reach the bomber stream, and the drop tanks allowed more time in the combat area. Galland still felt this was not enough to provide the required endurance for three-hour sorties unattainable with current German aircraft designs.[12]

CHAPTER TWENTY-FOUR

The Tyranny of Range (January–July 1943)

For the VIII Bomber Command, the inability of available friendly fighters to accompany bombers all the way to their targets became an increasing concern. *Luftwaffe* pilots were learning how to kill the big American bombers by day. Penetrating enemy defenses to attack the enemy homeland was the key function of strategic bombing. Berlin was 600 miles from London and much too far away to be escorted by the Spitfires flown by the RAF and USAAF. This was the "tyranny of range" with which Eighth Air Force had to contend.

Map 24.1. Escort fighter radius, April 1943—only as far as the German border.
MOLYSON

The RAF actively opposed developing long-range versions of the Spitfire. Although the British provided escort for the 1942 B-17 raids over France, the Spit could not reach beyond Lille.[1] With the P-38s sent to Twelfth Air Force in February 1943, the Spits were all that was available. Even missions with targets in western France such as the submarine pens on the Atlantic coast were too far to be escorted. The newly delivered P-47C Thunderbolt had better range than the current Spitfire but would not be combat-ready until April.

How Far?

The *range* of a plane is the total distance it can fly without refueling. Range is affected by weather, model of aircraft, maintenance history, and crew proficiency. The *maximum range*, or *ferry range*, is achieved by using all available space for additional fuel and carrying little or no ordnance or cargo. This factor was the most important consideration in delivering aircraft to distant locations where combat en route was not intended.

The dominant factor in operating combat planes was their *combat range*. Combat range was less than the ferry range because the plane carried ordnance or cargo and only the fuel required for the mission. Also, combat missions often were conducted on irregular routes to patrol or to avoid terrain and enemy defenses.[2]

Combat radius, also called *tactical radius*, was the maximum distance an aircraft could fly from takeoff with a normal combat load, travel to the combat area, engage an enemy and return for landing. This calculated figure was considerably less than half the combat range because it allowed for safety, fuel reserve, assembly of formations, and time in the mission area. During World War II, combat radius was considered to be three-eighths to two-fifths of the combat range.

JUGS

The first Republic Aviation P-47C Thunderbolts arrived in the European Theater of Operations (ETO) by ship on December 20, 1942. Three fighter groups were initially slated to fly the P-47. The first aircraft went to the three former Eagle Squadrons of the 4th Fighter Group. The robust Thunderbolt was nothing like the slim British fighters previously flown by this unit, and the 4th soon nicknamed it "the Jug." The 4th would not grudgingly give up their last Spitfires until April 1943.[3] The much-beloved Spitfire Marks V and IX flown by the 4th Fighter Group were designed to get to altitude quickly, fight briefly, and then land close by.[4]

The Mark IX could provide escort only as far as the Paris area or central Holland, and initially the P-47C had similar range.[5] Neither could reach

Germany. In every other way the Spit and Jug were dissimilar. The Spitfire had a poor rate of roll, the motion around the long axis of the aircraft. Although light and highly aerodynamic, the plane could climb well but was very poor in the dive. At medium to high altitude to escape the Spit, a German 109 or 190 could perform a split-S, a maneuver in which the plane rolled in an inverted position and then dived. The Spitfire simply couldn't roll as quickly or catch them in a dive.

The new Thunderbolt had exactly the opposite characteristics. It was heavy and aerodynamically challenged by its wide radial engine, but it had excellent roll authority and dived like a boulder. Pity the German fighter that tried to dive away from a Thunderbolt.

The 56th Fighter Group arrived in England soon after the 4th received their Thunderbolts. The 56th had flown the P-47B in the States and would upgrade to the more capable P-47C in England. From the beginning, they loved their massive fighter. The 78th Fighter Group replaced its P-38s, given up to TORCH, with Thunderbolts. The P-47s would suffer through the same kinds of airframe and engine problems that plague all new warplanes. The P-47C was not equipped with drop tanks. Initially, the average Thunderbolt pilot in formation

Figure 24.1. P-47 Thunderbolt, the "Jug." AIR FORCE HISTORICAL RESEARCH AGENCY

gave a P-47C a combat radius of something less than the advertised 225 to 230 miles, about the same as the Mark IX.[6]

The Jug had a passing resemblance to the German FW 190, and soon the dark green Thunderbolts sported a white QID (quick identification) band around the cowling and vertical stabilizer. The new marking probably prevented at least some P-47 losses to friendly fire.[7] The veteran 4th Fighter Group pilots were at first unenthusiastic about their new planes. Their concerns were shared with the RAF pilots indoctrinating the new guys of the 56th Fighter Group. Could the Jug hold its own with the German fighters?[8]

The pilots of the 56th Fighter Group, never having flown Spitfires, developed tactics that worked to the strengths of their own machines. The RAF provided opportunities to try out the Thunderbolts in a training environment, helping to prepare the Americans for the inevitable meeting with the Yellow Nose Bastards just across the water.

Future ace Robert S. Johnson of the 56th Fighter Group engaged in a mock dogfight with an RAF Spitfire IX. He noted the British plane could turn more sharply and climb faster than the Jug. Conversely, the Thunderbolt was faster and could roll more rapidly. Since a roll could position the airplane to climb, dive, or turn, the pursuing airplane had to roll to match the maneuvers of his target. It was here that a pilot who knew the strengths and weaknesses of his plane versus those of an enemy came to the fore.

By refusing to turn, but simply rolling and threatening to turn, Johnson was able to evade the more maneuverable Spitfire and pull ahead of the RAF plane. As the Spit pilot attempted to catch the P-47, Johnson suddenly dived and then pulled up in a zoom climb. No plane could match the Thunderbolt in a dive, certainly not a Spitfire.

At the bottom of the dive, the P-47 had tremendous energy that Johnson used. He pulled up suddenly, and the P-47 zoomed high above the Spit. He then reversed into another dive, hammering down on the hapless Brit. With eight .50 caliber guns pointed at the Spitfire's cockpit, the mock fight was over. Perhaps one less RAF pilot thought the Thunderbolt no match for the Germans.[9]

The veteran 4th Fighter Group was declared fully operational with the Jug on April 8, 1943, and took it on its first combat mission over France. Members of the other groups (56th and 78th) manned four of the P-47s as observers. This mission was a Circus over the St. Omer area in the Pas-de-Calais. This was the home territory of the Abbeville Boys, the yellow-nosed fighters of JG26.

The Thunderbolts flew in four-aircraft "finger four" formations developed by the Germans in Spain and adopted by the RAF after the Battle of Britain.

Within a week the P-47 found its first *Luftwaffe* victim over France. On April 15, Major Don Blakeslee of the 4th FG downed an FW 190 south of Dieppe. The Thunderbolt's eight .50 caliber machine guns could deliver a total of 120 rounds per second. It didn't take long to disassemble an enemy fighter.

The Thunderbolts were as tough as they were heavily armed and could absorb more punishment than any other fighter flying in Europe. Experience soon proved to the P-47 pilots how rugged their new planes were. In one instance, an FW 190 attacked Robert Johnson after his Jug had sustained severe battle damage in an earlier dogfight with *Oberst* Egon Mayer.[10]

Damaged rudder cables meant the battered P-47 could not be maneuvered; Johnson watched helplessly as another FW 190 fell in behind his Thunderbolt. All he could do was place as much of his body behind the armored seat back as he could. The German emptied his guns into Johnson's plane from behind, Johnson getting in only one shot when he chopped power and forced the FW 190 to overshoot. The German was wary of the Jug's eight .50 caliber machine guns and would not attack from the front. The German, later identified as Major Georg-Peter Eder of II./JG26, returned to a tail attack but could not fatally damage Johnson's Jug. Out of ammunition, the German left with a final, frustrated salute by rocking his wings.

Surely the encounter made the *Luftwaffe* gossip circuit.[11]

When Johnson landed, the ground crew had to pry the cockpit open over torn metal in the fuselage. After being treated for two flesh wounds at the emergency field in England, Johnson viewed the wreck that had brought him safely home. There were twenty-one gaping holes from 20mm cannon hits. Johnson counted over one hundred other bullet holes. The Jug was literally covered with holes, including five in the propeller. The lower half of his rudder was gone. Inside the cockpit, there were three 20mm impacts against the armored seat that saved Johnson's life. The flap control handle was also blown away.[12] Republic Aviation knew how to build a combat airplane.

CHAPTER TWENTY-FIVE

Little Friends (January–August 1943)

Back in 1942, VIII Fighter Command's General Hunter had directed Colonel Ben Kelsey and Lieutenant Colonel Cass Hough to set up an Air Technical Section at Bovingdon Airfield. Now the investment had begun to bear fruit. When the P-47 Thunderbolt arrived in early January 1943, this center did much to improve its capabilities. The necessary work was extensive, and the Jugs would not enter combat until April. Hough informed General Hunter that despite Eaker's directive for bomber protection, the heavy P-47 would never be a useful escort fighter. Hunter replied, "Figure out a way to do it."

The answer, of course, was external fuel drop tanks that could be jettisoned[1] for combat. In February 1943, Eaker made an official request for fighter drop tanks to Air Material Command and British industry. Problems with both the US and British bureaucracies prevented a more rapid solution for a cheap metal drop tank strong enough to be pressurized at high altitude.

On June 14, 1943, the POINTBLANK Directive was issued to the Allied air forces. The U-boats had been pushed out of the North Atlantic; the convoy battle there was being won. The German air force, not U-boat facilities, became the primary target of the Combined Bomber Offensive (CBO). While attacks against German airfields and support facilities in France were to continue, VIII Bomber Command was to prioritize the aircraft manufacturing system within Germany and Occupied Europe.

The need for a mission-capable escort fighter increased as VIII Bomber Command's attacks penetrated into German airspace, beyond the combat radius of the P-47. In an April 17 raid on Bremen, 16 of 115 attacking bombers were lost, a rate of 14 percent. A loss rate of 4 percent was considered the upper level of "acceptable losses."[2] On June 13, 22 of 76 bombers were lost on a raid against the Kiel U-boat base, a rate of 29 percent. A July 26 raid against Hannover, northeast of the Ruhr, cost 16 of 121 bombers dispatched for a rate of 13 percent.

Increasing German prowess by day caused General Eaker to direct VIII Fighter Command to begin close escort of the bombers to the maximum extent of fighter range. This order robbed all initiative from the escort fighters and wasted fuel. This decision also ignored the German experience of close bomber escort in the Battle of Britain. The initial order to stay physically close was soon opened to a looser arrangement. If the escorts were too close, they masked some defensive fire from the bombers. The German response was to wait until the escorts left at the Belgian border and then pounce on the bombers.

Only 27 percent of Germany's fighters remained on the Eastern Front where they were sorely needed to fight a resurgent Soviet air force and Red Army. The rest of the fighter force had been redeployed to counter increasing American bombing campaigns and the growing Allied airpower in the Mediterranean. During the spring and summer of 1943, about 40 percent of all German fighter production was sent south and destroyed by attrition. An entire air fleet, *Luftflotte 2*, was sent from Russia to be split between Italy and the Balkans. To meet its requirements to defend the Reich in the west and the south, the *Luftwaffe* lost air superiority on the Eastern Front.[3]

With only air parity, the Germans began their ill-fated attack at Kursk, Russia, on July 5, 1943. Kursk was about 450 miles northwest of Stalingrad, where the Russians had swallowed the German Sixth Army the previous winter.

Figure 25.1. Close escort failed to adequately protect bombers and wasted gas.
NATIONAL ARCHIVES AND RECORDS ADMINISTRATION, USAAF PHOTO 25501

The distance and direction from Stalingrad was important, as the Russians were recovering lost ground and the Germans were trying to reconquer it. This developed into history's greatest tank battle and marked the end of German offensive operations in Russia. Despite defending *Luftwaffe* fighters, Soviet aircraft and tanks demolished the Nazi panzers, and the long German retreat west to Berlin had begun.

BLITZ WEEK

During Blitz Week, July 24–30, 1943, the Eighth Air Force greatly expanded the daylight bombing of Axis territory. This began with strikes on Herøya and Trondheim, Norway. At Herøya, the new IG Farben nitrate works[4] was put out of action for over three months. New factories for producing aluminum and magnesium were permanently destroyed. At Trondheim, both the U-boat base and shipping were hit, while a similar attack on Bergen was aborted due to weather.

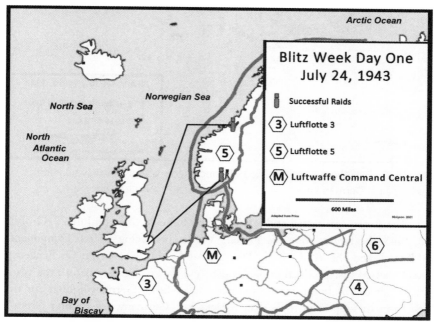

Map 25.1. Blitz Week, Day One, July 24, 1943. MOLYSON[5]

On July 25, Hamburg and Kiel shipyards were attacked and damaged. Despite POINTBLANK, U-boats still had high priority in the CBO bombing. Smoke from a previous British attack on Hamburg impeded the Eighth Air Force bombing. An attack against the Heinkel aircraft works at Warnemünde, producing FW 190 fighters, was prevented by adverse weather. On July 26, the U-boat yards at Hamburg were struck and the synthetic rubber and tire manufacturing facility at Hannover was badly damaged. This cut production there by 25 percent for almost a month.

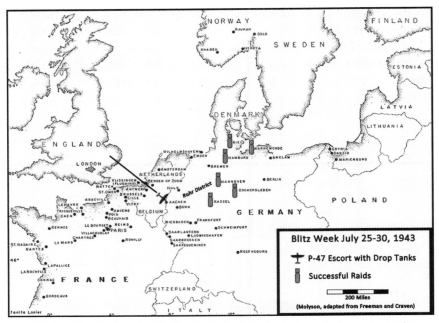

Map 25.2. Blitz Week, July 24–30, 1943, included relatively shallow penetration raids against German targets. MOLYSON AFTER FREEMAN AND CRAVEN[6]

The Americans rested and repaired their battered force on July 27. On July 28, 1943, the targets were the Fieseler Works, producing aircraft components at Kassel, and the AGO FW 190 plant at Oschersleben. The Oschersleben attack caused lost production of some fifty FW 190 fighters before the plant was repaired. The bombers encountered rocket-firing German fighters for the first time. In support of these deep attacks into Germany, 4th Fighter Group's Thunderbolts flew as far as Aachen in western Germany, using unpressurized half-full 200-gallon ferry tanks.[7] Suitable or not, they did the job. The mission was an impressive 280-mile round-trip from the P-47 base at Debden.

Pilot skill and Eagle Squadron experience made this an unusually proficient unit, able to stretch their fuel to the maximum possible. The unpressurized fuel in the tanks would not draw above 23,000 feet; therefore, the aircraft were limited to that altitude until the tanks were empty. Rather than dropping the tanks at the coastline, they kept them on the aircraft until they were empty or in a fight. With these tanks, 75 critical miles of combat radius was added to the short-legged P-47. This surprised the Germans, who lost six FW 190s and three Bf 109s to the unexpected escort.[8]

On July 29, Kiel shipyard was hit again and over 750,000 propaganda leaflets dropped. Hamburg, 50 miles south, was burning in a firestorm inflicted by the RAF. A dark column of smoke, 10 to 20 miles wide, rose to 3,000 feet and drifted northeast toward the Baltic.[9] The message was simple: There was no place to hide in Germany, day or night. The Heinkel aircraft factory at Warnemünde was attacked again, and this time the weather was acceptable for bombing. Eighteen of twenty-seven production buildings were damaged. On July 30, the Fieseler Works at Kassel was bombed again.

Within six days, 1,000 bomber sorties struck 15 targets all over Germany. Eighth Air Force lost 87 bombers in these attacks, some 6.4 percent of the bombers on the mission. The raids into Germany also produced a backlog of damaged American bombers that had to be repaired by the overstretched maintenance crews.[10]

Escorts that could not penetrate beyond Aachen lowered bomber losses during the approach and departure to Germany, but not enough. By the end of Blitz Week, some 100 aircraft and 90 combat crews had been lost, a prohibitive rate of 10 percent although bombing results were good.[11] It would be two weeks before the bombers could return to strike deep German targets.[12]

The VIII Fighter Command development center at Bovingdon continued to source locally produced drop tanks in Britain. Impressed by the Thunderbolt's accomplishments during Blitz Week, the British Air Ministry officers visiting Washington urged General Arnold to extend the range of the P-47 even more. They also hoped the USAAF would field an improved escort fighter that could accompany the American bombers all the way to targets deeper in Germany.[13] General Arnold was already pressuring Air Material Command on this issue.

Bovingdon soon fielded improved drop tanks for the P-47. These included pressurized metal 75-gallon tanks formerly intended for the P-39, and glue-impregnated pressed-paper 108-gallon drop tanks. These became standard equipment for the P-47 and later for the P-51. By August 1943, a well-flown P-47 had a combat radius of 375 miles.[14] The P-47 became even more useful in providing entry and withdrawal bomber escort up to and from the German border.

The partnership between the bomber crews ("Big Friends") and the escort fighter pilots ("Little Friends") grew strong. The escorts never left the bombers until forced back by fuel. The bombers learned to fire the green flares that signaled "I need help now" to the escort fighters when they were still around.

American fighters were now over the western Reich, a fact that Inspector of Fighters General Galland promptly reported to Hitler. Galland told the Führer that the situation could only grow worse as American technical prowess solved the escort fighter range issue. He was soon called to account by Göring. By the summer of 1943, Göring was more worried about the effect of the air war on Hitler's opinions than anything else, so Galland was immediately attacked by his outraged boss.

"What's the idea of telling the Führer that American fighters have penetrated into the territory of the Reich?"[15]

Galland replied that American fighters have been shot down over Aachen, in Western Germany. Göring said it was impossible; they must be damaged fighters that glided that far east. Galland invited Göring to travel to the site of the crashes. He refused and kicked Galland out of his office.[16]

Galland revealed after the war that before long-range escort was provided, the GAF lost on average one fighter for each American heavy bomber it shot down. After escort was provided the rate increased to two to three fighters per bomber. Escort fighters saved bombers and increased the depletion of the *Luftwaffe*, the primary objective of POINTBLANK.[17]

CHAPTER TWENTY-SIX

GOMORRAH (July 25–August 3, 1943)

By the summer of 1943, *Luftwaffe* night-fighter tactics against the British bombers had become more effective. Bomber Command attrition began to approach levels that could not be sustained. Then, in the middle of July, there was an ominous lull in the night raids into Germany.[1]

What followed was the massive round-the-clock bombing of Hamburg, the largest German city after Berlin. Situated on the Elbe River near its estuary, it was Germany's gateway to the world's oceans and the largest port in Europe. Shipping and shipbuilding, from U-boats to cargo ships, fueled its economy and that of all of northern Germany.

Sir Arthur Harris, chief of the RAF Bomber Command, set a simple goal. The objective of the attack was "to destroy Hamburg." It was the large, productive, and vulnerable civilian working population that particularly invited RAF attack. The RAF started a series of devastating firebombing raids against the city, burning a quarter of Hamburg's dwellings.

Eight hundred RAF night bombers, Wellingtons, Stirlings, Halifaxes, and Lancasters opened the battle on the night of July 24, 1943, the same day the American daylight "Blitz Week" bombing campaign began. It was their 138th visit to the city, one that neither side would ever forget. The RAF navigators found their target using their new H2S bombing radar, for the city's location on a well-defined waterway allowed it to be picked out by radar even on the darkest of nights.[2] Ironically, for a city that built U-boats, the H2S was a variant of the same ASV (air-to-surface vessel) radar used to hunt surfaced German submarines at sea.

The RAF crews dropped 40 tons of chaff, code-named "Window," in combat for the first time. The small aluminum strips defeated the radar-equipped German night fighters and flak guns. H2S bombing radar was unaffected by the chaff since it operated at a different frequency. The H2S radars made the city visible to the bombers, while the chaff made the bombers virtually invisible to the defenders.

The first wave of bombers dropped high-explosive bombs that smashed the structures below into kindling and damaged the Hamburg firefighting service.

Then came many more waves of RAF bombers dropping incendiary bombs.[3] A total of 2,284 tons of bombs were dropped for a loss of only 12 bombers. This was only the beginning. Hamburg began to burn.[4]

The following day, one hundred VIII Bomber Command B-17 bombers of the 1st Bomb Wing dropped 196 tons of bombs. Hamburg's location meant the Americans could hit the city without much penetration of German airspace, thus avoiding most of the defenders' fighters and flak batteries. It was the first American attack on Hamburg and the first real confirmation of synchronized Anglo-American "round-the-clock" bombing so confidently proposed by American general Ira Eaker to Winston Churchill at the Casablanca Conference six months before.

Fifty-four more aircraft from the 1st Bomb Wing dropped 134 tons on July 26, both attacks concentrating on the dockyard area.[5] Dense smoke from the previous night's raid made precision bombing difficult, and many bombs went awry. Therefore, American bomb impacts were not confined to the selected industrial targets. Extensive destruction of firefighting equipment and water mains had already occurred and additional damage was caused.

The RAF returned on the night of July 27, dropping another 2,326 tons of ordnance for a cost of seventeen aircraft.[6] The weather had been hot and dry for weeks. In the city environs were Germany's largest lumberyard and an oil refinery and storage facility. Fuel stored in the city (mainly coke and coal) for industrial use and for next winter's heating, combined with the combustible elements of structures and property, created a giant firestorm that consumed Hamburg. The asphalt streets sizzled and many human victims burst into flame. A witness later termed the result a "lake of fire."

Cyclonic 150-mph winds sucked trees 3 feet thick into the flames along with many of Hamburg's unfortunate citizens. Thousands of others asphyxiated in the bomb shelters. It was unimaginable devastation and carnage, the kind that Hitler had wanted to inflict on London since 1940.

During World War II, less than 52,000 people would die in all of Britain from bombing, despite Germany's best efforts. Some 50,000 would die in Hamburg alone that week, with another 800,000 made homeless. The RAF code-named the attack Operation GOMORRAH; the survivors would call it the *Katastrophe*.[7] A final RAF night raid was launched on the night of August 2, but it was broken up by thunderstorms over Germany. In any case, it would have been anticlimactic. The city was gone.

The effectiveness of the attack—including the first use of accurate bombing radar *offensively*, and radar-defeating chaff *defensively*—caused widespread general despair among the ruling political and military circles.[8] Still in denial, Hitler refused to visit the burned-out city.[9]

CHAPTER TWENTY-SEVEN

Surrounded (July 1–August 13, 1943)

Map 27.1. USAAF numbered air forces with heavy bombers, July 1943.
MOLYSON AFTER PRICE[1]

By the time Hamburg burned, Occupied Europe was surrounded by three USAAF numbered air forces, the Eighth, Ninth, and Twelfth. These operated in cooperation with the Bomber Command in England and other RAF units in the Mediterranean. All operated heavy bombers as well as other combat aircraft. The Eighth Air Force remained in Britain. The Ninth Air Force operated in the eastern Mediterranean, within range of much of southeastern Europe. The Twelfth Air Force, which had arrived as part of Operation TORCH, controlled USAAF units in the western Mediterranean and was bombing targets in Italy.

TIDALWAVE

On August 1, 1943, in the midst of the RAF destruction of Hamburg at night, a significant daylight attack was being executed. Far to the south, 177 B-24D bombers of the Ninth Air Force again struck the Romanian oil refinery complex at Ploesti in Operation TIDALWAVE. The bombers attacked at low altitude to avoid enemy radar. Although there were significant navigational errors compounded by enemy fighters and flak, about 40 percent of the refining capacity was destroyed. Without efficient damage control by Romanian fire crews and bomb disposal personnel, much more would have been eliminated.[2]

Much of the lost capability would be restored within a month; Ploesti was Hitler's major source of fuel. The aircraft losses were the most severe to date: 532 airmen were lost; 57 bombers were shot down and another 7 interned in Turkey, a loss rate in excess of 37 percent. Over half of the surviving aircraft that returned to North Africa had battle damage and many were scrapped.[3]

Some of the planes were Eighth Air Force Liberators "on loan" to the Ninth Air Force, and many were lost or damaged. Yet General Arnold did allow one more major attack with these borrowed aircraft, one directly related to Operation POINTBLANK.[4] On August 13, 1943, the Ninth Air Force sent sixty-one B-24s from its North African bases to bomb the Messerschmitt production center near Vienna at Wiener Neustadt. It was the first American daylight raid into Germany from the south. A coordinated second raid against Regensburg, also a Messerschmitt assembly facility, by Eighth Air Force bombers based in England was called off because of weather.

GAF fighter reaction was particularly weak as there was no day fighter defense organized for this area. Only two bombers were lost. There were few fighters assigned in the south, and the radar perimeter had gaping holes. After the attack, the *Luftwaffe* sent three squadrons to this new gap in Göring's perimeter defense.[5]

It was not enough.

CHAPTER TWENTY-EIGHT

The Schweinfurt–Regensburg Raid (August 17, 1943)

I am impressed by the precision with which these bastards bomb. It is fantastic.
—HEINZ KNÖCKE, GERMAN ACE[1]

In July and August of 1943, B-17s, P-47s, and B-26 Marauder medium bombers hit daylight targets in France, Belgium, and Holland. On August 16, 1943, 4th Fighter Group Thunderbolts escorted B-17 Fortresses to Paris. They claimed eighteen German fighters for the loss of only one P-47. The pilot successfully evaded capture and later returned to the unit.[2] The Jugs returned home and prepared to escort the first deep strikes from England into Germany for the month.

The August 17 double attacks were against two critical facilities on the POINTBLANK target list: the Messerschmitt fighter production complex at Regensburg (postponed from August 13) and the ball-bearing factories at Schweinfurt. The ball bearings were an essential component of aircraft assembly; each Junkers 88 bomber, for example, required over 1,000 of them. It was hoped that destruction of ball-bearing manufacturing capability would strangle the German aircraft industry.

Eighteen squadrons of P-47s and sixteen squadrons of RAF Spitfires would escort the bombers in relays as far as the German frontier, return to England for refueling, and meet them again to cover the withdrawal. RAF Typhoon fighters and USAAF B-26s would attack German airfields in France to tie down the fighters based on these fields. None of these activities prevented the *Luftwaffe* from assembling over 300 single- and twin-engine interceptors to meet the main attack over Germany.

The Regensburg force was Colonel Curtis LeMay's 4th Bombardment Wing (4th BW). It consisted of three "combat wings," each of two or three bomb groups flying as combat boxes. Each combat box was a bomb group. These

B-17s were all equipped with so-called "Tokio" tanks, giving them the range to travel on to North Africa after bombing the target. ("Tokio" was the spelling then currently used in the USAAF for the Japanese city of Tokyo. These tanks theoretically provided sufficient fuel to allow B-17 and B-24 bombers to bomb Tokyo from bases in China.)

Flying south would hopefully confuse the Germans and avoid the aroused defense that would be encountered by aircraft returning to England. The 4th BW would be followed a few minutes later by the Schweinfurt force, the 1st Bombardment Wing (1st BW). The 1st BW was a larger force, consisting of four combat wings each of three bomb group combat boxes. It was hoped the 1st BW would benefit from enemy fighters exhausting their fuel and ammunition attacking the 4th.

The day of August 17, 1943 was one of the most significant in World War II, certainly in regard to POINTBLANK and the Combined Bomber Offensive. This would be the first Allied daylight attack against Schweinfurt, a town that would become one of the most bombed of any in Europe. After bombing, the 1st BW would be returning to England through the heaviest defenses and needed all the help they could get.

The Regensburg force was launched as scheduled on the morning of August 17, but the Schweinfurt force was fatally delayed due to heavy fog at its bases.[3] The delay meant that the approach P-47 escorts accompanying the 4th BW (Regensburg) would now have to return and refuel before the 1st BW (Schweinfurt) could take off. This ruined the original plan, which was to saturate the German defenders with incoming bombers.

REGENSBURG

Weather delayed the assembly of the 4th BW once airborne, and two hours of circling was fully monitored by German radar. The Germans were ready for them when they crossed the English coast. For bomber-interception missions, *Luftwaffe* fighters now usually carried a 66-gallon drop tank under the fuselage. Standard armament for a typical Bf 109G was the 20mm cannon and two machine guns. Some aircraft also carried two BR 21 rockets under the wings. The Germans had also reorganized their technique for quickly launching an entire fighter group more or less simultaneously.

After the escort left the 4th BW of the Regensburg force at the German border, the bombers were subjected to ninety minutes of intense fighter attack. Fourteen bombers were lost by the time the target was reached. Six Bf 109s were downed in the process, while 127 of their original 146 B-17s were able to bomb the target. The Regensburg force then turned south for Africa. This confused the defense, and only two more B-17s were lost to enemy action. Three more crash-landed in Switzerland and Italy due to battle damage; five more ditched in the Mediterranean with fuel exhaustion. Fortunately all the crews of the ditched aircraft were rescued.

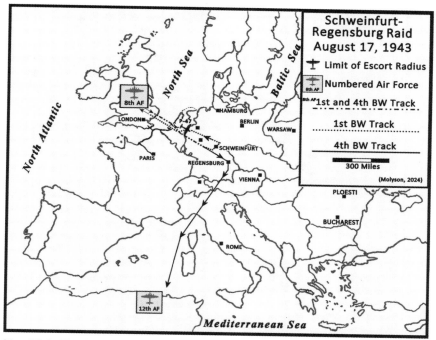

Map 28.1. The Schweinfurt-Regensburg Raid. MOLYSON AFTER CRAVEN ET AL.[4]

About fifty-five surviving but damaged B-17s could not make the trip back from Africa and were left with the Twelfth Air Force for later repair or scrapping.[5] Days later the 4th Bomb Wing's fifty-eight serviceable B-17s returned to England, bombing Bordeaux-Mérignac airfield on the return trip.

One of the veteran *Luftwaffe* pilots who intercepted the bombers that day was Gustav Rödel, who was based in Vienna:

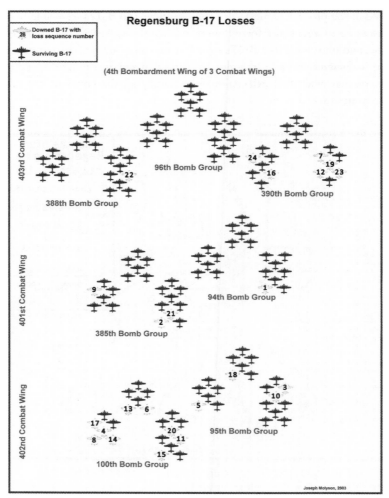

Figure 28.1. Regensburg mission B-17 losses. MOLYSON AFTER MIDDLEBROOK[6]

*We could see the flak bursts, which were always a signal to us that the bomb-
ers were over their target. We arrived from the northeast, with just enough
time to get behind the formation. I personally didn't score any kills that day,
but I saw the burning bombers and crash fires, as well as some of our own
fighters going down.*[7]

Schweinfurt

As the fog lifted at the 1st BW bases, the bombers destined for Schweinfurt launched and assembled into formation. A total of 230 B-17s crossed the coast; although they lost 24 aircraft by the time the target was reached, 188 B-17s were able to bomb the target effectively. One *Luftwaffe* pilot estimated that there were 60 parachutes in the air at one time, some German but mostly American. Along the way 9 Bf 109s, 8 FW 190s, and 1 Bf 110 had been shot down. About 80 bombs fell within the target factory complex and the adjacent rail facilities; 2 more bombers were lost near the target, at least 1 of these to flak.

With the mission accomplished, the bloodied 1st Bombardment Wing turned north and then west for England, running the gauntlet a second time. On the way home the men could see the smoke columns from crashed German and American aircraft. Ten more B-17s would fall, as well as three P-47s and two Spitfires of the withdrawal escort on the return leg. Later, American veterans completing their twenty-five mission combat tours said that Schweinfurt was the worst and most frightening combat they witnessed in Europe.

The bright spot, if there was one, was the action of the 56th Fighter Group. Instead of jettisoning its pressed-paper drop tanks as they crossed the coast of Holland to meet the bombers, they kept them and ambushed a group of German fighters 15 miles east of Eupen, the bomber rendezvous point. The German fighters were focused on bomber interception, not air-to-air combat against P-47s dropping down from the west out of the sun. The Germans were hammered, losing at least eleven fighters while downing only three Thunderbolts.[8] More than that, it gave some respite to the battered Fortresses returning home.

Effects

Ball bearings were the most simple and necessary of all aircraft components. Albert Speer, *Reichsminister* of armaments, estimated that ball-bearing production at Schweinfurt immediately dropped 38 percent, but the damage was repaired by mid-September.[9] Unfortunately, there were stockpiles of sufficient quantities for production of aircraft to continue until the factory was repaired. Speer believed that subsequent attacks on critical component production would cripple the German war machine.[10] He ordered the dispersal of aircraft component and assembly facilities to multiple locations. This greatly reduced the efficiency of German aircraft production.

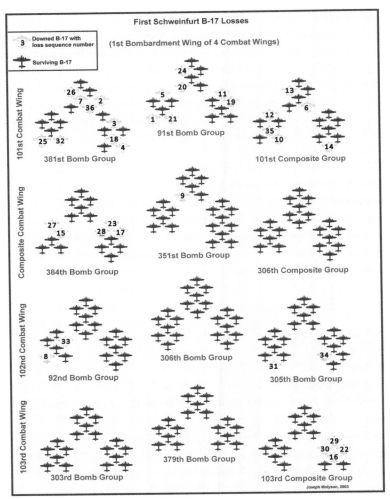

Figure 28.2. First Schweinfurt mission B-17 losses. MOLYSON AFTER
MIDDLEBROOK[11]

The decision to disperse aircraft component production to other German cities was met with resistance. The city of Würzburg, for example, correctly assumed that relocation of some of the Schweinfurt production to its city would bring American or British bombers, endangering both their homes and the cluster of hospitals located within the urban area.[12]

Professor Willi Messerschmitt, whose assembly plants at Regensburg and Wiener Neustadt had been badly damaged, was able to maintain and even increase aircraft production in dispersed locations. Later, however, he estimated that Speer's dispersal order cost Germany some 50 percent of the production possible if the factories had remained unmolested.[13]

Without the daylight bombing that led to the dispersion of aircraft factories, the Allies would have faced twice as many German fighters later in 1943 and 1944.

CHAPTER TWENTY-NINE

HYDRA (August 17–18, 1943)

GOMORRAH had burned down Hamburg and the ruined city must be avenged!

Hitler ordered acceleration of Germany's secret *Vergeltungswaffen* ("vengeance weapon") programs at Peenemünde, a rustic setting on the shores of the Baltic Sea. Extensive facilities had been built there to support research and development of rocket- and jet-powered weapons. With the failure to subdue Britain due to lack of effective strategic bombers and escort fighters, Germany was developing long-range missiles to provide the kind of strategic bombardment the *Luftwaffe* could not provide with conventional aircraft.

Peenemünde scientists and engineers produced two kinds of long-range missiles for the German air force and army. The first, under *Luftwaffe* guidance, was the Fieseler 103 *Kirschkern* ("cherry stone"), a pilotless jet-powered flying bomb, today called a cruise missile. By necessity, launch ramps would have to be located on the French Channel coast to hit its primary target, London. Once accepted by Hitler as a revenge weapon, it became Vengeance Weapon 1 (*Vergeltungswaffen 1*), or "V-1." The missile was vulnerable to Allied air defenses

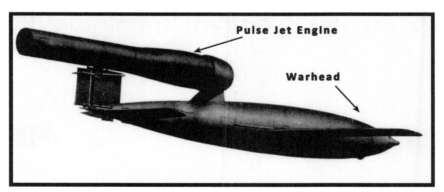

Figure 29.1. Fi 103 (later called the V-1). AIR FORCE HISTORICAL RESEARCH AGENCY, KARLSRUHE COLLECTION

because it was slower than the fastest Allied fighters. It flew a straight flight path from ramp to target in a preset direction, until a timer shut down the engine and it fell onto its victims. Its low flight path also brought it within range of Allied antiaircraft guns. The *Luftwaffe* intended to overcome British defenses with swarms of these relatively low-cost weapons.

Under army artillery experts, the A-4 rocket-powered ballistic missile was developed and redesignated as "V-2" (*Vergeltungswaffen 2*). With a range of about 220 miles, it could easily reach London if based in France or the Low Countries. The closer the launch site was to the Channel coast, the farther it could reach into southeast England. The V-2 flew a parabolic course reaching up to 60 miles into outer space before falling back toward its target on the Earth's surface. The V-2 was the first human-built device to reach outer space.[1] It was a

Figure 29.2. V-2 launch beyond trees. AIR FORCE HISTOR-ICAL RESEARCH AGENCY, KARLSRUHE COLLECTION

very serious threat, because no defense was possible once it was launched. Hitler ordered 1,800 V-2 missiles a month to be built by April 1944, to be used in a devastating and sustained attack.[2]

The British had detected and tracked the threat posed by the weapons and intended to destroy the German capability to further develop and produce them. The missiles threatened their capital, and possibly Allied air bases and the invasion ports. On August 17, the night of the Schweinfurt–Regensburg Raid, the RAF launched Operation HYDRA, a "maximum effort raid" against the Peenemünde facilities. About 600 RAF bombers attacked the facility to forestall the potential missile attack on their homeland.

Map 29.1. Section of German restricted flying zone map showing Peenemünde.
LUFTWAFFE VIA AIR FORCE HISTORICAL RESEARCH AGENCY

HYDRA was conducted in moonlight to increase the chances of bombing success. It was the only occasion after mid-1943 that the RAF attempted night precision bombing over Germany. Most of the bombs dropped were high-explosive weapons, since Peenemünde was too dispersed to support a firestorm. The target was not so much the production facilities as the human resources housed near the laboratories and factory. Peenemünde West, where the *Luftwaffe* conducted research on the V-1 and other types of missiles, escaped serious damage.[3]

The residential area, or "Settlement" of Peenemünde East, was leveled, killing almost 200 German men, women, and children. A key casualty was the lead propulsion engineer Dr. Walter Thiel, who perished with his family.[4] Unfortunately, 600 forced laborers, mostly Polish, also died when their camp was hit during the initial bombing phase.[5] Within days, *Luftwaffe* chief of staff Hans Jeschonnek, committed suicide. The combined effects of Göring's bumbling, Hamburg's destruction, the assault on Peenemünde, and American daylight attacks on Ploesti, Wiener Neustadt, Schweinfurt, and Regensburg proved too much for the youthful general.

Total losses to Bomber Command in HYDRA were 40 heavy bombers destroyed. The Germans had begun to adjust to "window" and RAF tactics. The moonlit attack made the bombers more vulnerable to night fighters. The bombers dropped 3.6 million pounds of bombs on Peenemünde, the equivalent of over 1,600 V-1 or V-2 warheads. The war had become more brutal and personal, and what the Germans hoped to inflict on British civilians in London had been visited on them at Hamburg and Peenemünde instead.

It was later estimated that HYDRA delayed German V-weapon attacks by six to eight weeks. Without the attacks, the Germans could have advanced the bombardment of southern England by V-1 cruise missiles to April 1944, five weeks before D-Day. Initial V-2 ballistic missile attacks could have been advanced to July 1944 and used both against England and the Allied bridgehead in Normandy. Bomber Command did, however, overestimate the results of its attack. On August 19, thirty hours after the last RAF bomber had come home, the British declined an American offer for VIII Bomber Command to finish the job in daylight.

The head of the V-2 program, Major General Walter Dornberger, learned from captured British aircrew that the RAF bombers would be sent back repeatedly until they had completely knocked out the research station. Dornberger decided to simulate a knockout blow by HYDRA using bomb debris, camouflage, and other means. He dispersed the surviving personnel and equipment throughout Germany.[6] Bomber Command did not touch Peenemünde for nine months; by that time it was no longer an important V-weapon production center.[7]

Earlier air raids on Friedrichshafen by the RAF on June 20 and the Africa-based Ninth Air Force at Wiener Neustadt on August 13 had unwittingly damaged alternate V-2 production facilities. After HYDRA, it was decided to begin construction of a massive subterranean V-2 production facility at Nordhausen, Germany, code-named *Mittelwerk* ("Central Works").

Germany's professional army and the Nazi Party's private army—the *Schutzstaffel* (SS), under Heinrich Himmler—fought over control of the V-2 program. Eventually, the SS absorbed the V-2 program at the expense of the army. Inevitably, the SS introduced prisoners as a solution to the chronic labor shortage. *Mittelwerk* would employ massive amounts of slave labor in its construction and eventual production of V-2 rockets. At least 60,000 prisoners were involved, of which at least 10,000 died working on some facet of the V-2 project.[8]

The move underground to avoid further air attack and the reorganization of the V-2 program took time. Whatever the morality of selectively killing the enemy's scientists in the Peenemünde bombing and chasing the survivors underground, V-2 development was delayed for almost a year—well beyond D-Day.

During August 1943, heavy losses of Allied day and night bombers were matched by German fighter losses of almost 250 aircraft.[9] Along with these planes died some of Germany's best fighter pilots, the German pilot loss rate for July through September 1943 being about 16 percent per month.[10]

Hitler was impatient; he did not want to wait over eight months for the missiles to begin hitting London. He refused to allow the *Luftwaffe* to prioritize defense of the Reich by diverting bomber production into fighter production. *Luftwaffe* leaders knew both pilots and planes needed to be husbanded, and new types of fighter aircraft built. Instead, Hitler ordered assignment of a *Luftwaffe* coordinator to resume the conventional night air bombardment of England.[11] This would provide a program of retaliation until the V-weapons were ready. The Führer's orders facilitated continued Allied air attacks against the homeland.

CHAPTER THIRTY
COSSAC and OVERLORD
(January–July 1943)

At the Casablanca Conference in January 1943, it was decided to establish an American supreme Allied commander (SAC) to lead the cross-Channel invasion. Shortly thereafter, the British General Staff appointed Lieutenant General Frederick E. Morgan to be chief of staff (COS) to a yet-to-be-appointed SAC. Morgan was given the initial responsibility for planning the attack. Few men were as responsible for the success of D-Day as Freddie Morgan.

Figure 30.1. Lieutenant General Frederick E. Morgan, the lead planner for D-Day. POGUE[1]

By April 1943, Morgan had established the planning organization and had named it COSSAC, after the initials in his new title. He warned his officers at that time to avoid thinking of themselves as planners, and to see themselves, instead, as the embryo of a future supreme headquarters. "The term *planning staff* has come to have a most sinister meaning," he observed. "It implies the production of nothing but paper. What we must contrive to do somehow is to produce not only paper but action."[2]

COSSAC inherited a great body of background information on how to conduct a landing on a hostile shore as a result of the Dieppe and North Africa landings. There was an even greater wealth of information on how *not* to conduct such an operation. Also available were the ongoing reports of an army cooperation effort called Exercise SPARTAN, conducted in Britain in March of 1943. This exercise demonstrated how air forces could be employed to support a combined operation directly and indirectly, as OVERLORD was intended to be.

All of this information from combat and exercises pointed to one essential fact: *Air superiority* must be seized and maintained over the invasion area. The enemy air force must be rendered ineffective in attacking the invasion fleet or the troops landed on the shore. German air attacks must be intercepted well inland. The short-range Spitfire, Britain's mainstay air superiority fighter, was clearly inadequate to fight the *Luftwaffe* outside of the coastal zone.[3] Longer-range American fighters must be employed for this purpose until forward airfields were established in France.

In June 1943, just after the surrender of Axis forces in North Africa and the withdrawal of U-boats from the North Atlantic, Morgan published his first plan for the invasion of France across the Channel, Operation OVERLORD. He called air superiority over the German fighter force "an essential pre-requisite" for any attempt to return to the Continent. Morgan used his intelligence information well. Published only a few weeks after the June POINTBLANK Directive that detailed the air offensive against the *Luftwaffe*, it echoed the means by which the German fighter force must be destroyed.

Sir Arthur Harris of AOC Bomber Command interpreted POINT-BLANK to mean that the Americans would go after daylight precision targets while he continued to burn down the workers' factories and neighborhoods at night. Harris eschewed what he called "panacea" targets—precision targets whose destruction some thought could quickly end the war. So it was the Americans, with significant RAF intelligence support, that developed the list of critical fighter-related targets for precision bombing.[4]

Morgan, in his "Attainment of the Necessary Air Situation," stated what airpower was required to do in order for OVERLORD to proceed:

1. The infliction of heavy casualties on the German fighter force by air battles brought about at an early date in areas advantageous to us.

2. Long-term bomber offensive against the sources of supply and production and first-line fighter units of the German Air Force.

3. The disorganisation of the German Air Force units and the disruption of airfield installations within enemy fighter range of the CAEN area. [Note: Caen was the major city within the projected initial invasion area.]

4. The disorganisation of the German Fighter Command and control organisation in the CAEN area.[5]

Clearly, the first two OVERLORD air objectives fell within the realm of the Eighth Air Force. RAF Fighter Command had been unable to bring much of the German fighter force to battle, and Bomber Command seldom attacked specific targets like aircraft factories. The Combined Bomber Offensive was "combined"—that is, it involved the forces of the RAF Bomber Command and the Eighth Air Force's VIII Bomber Command. It was not truly "coordinated" because British and American bombing strategy had diverged too far for that to be possible on a regular basis. American and British bombers seldom went after the same targets or attacked a particular area at the same time.

On July 30, 1943, the War Office in London published a "Digest of Operation OVERLORD."[6] The Digest reflected the guidance given at previous conferences and the influence of the hardworking COSSAC staff. The bulk of the document dealt with criteria for selecting a landing site and the means by which the Allies would attack.

The invasion of northwestern France was set for May 1944.

CHAPTER THIRTY-ONE

The Plan (July–November 1943)

COSSAC's OVERLORD Digest was neither a war plan nor an attack order, but it formed the basis of all subsequent preparations for D-Day. Among the most critical elements of the OVERLORD study was the selection of Normandy as the so-called "Lodgment Area," the place where Allied armies would enter France and gather strength before moving on toward Germany.[1]

Estimates of German ground strength varied depending on current intelligence, but it could be assumed that as many as sixty Axis divisions might be in France, Belgium, and Holland for the defense of Fortress Europe. These were assigned to four field armies, including the Italian 4th Army in southeast France. Their infantry divisions were spread along the French coast with little armor or vehicles. Much had been abandoned in North Africa, and the Eastern Front was a great consumer of German army equipment. Most were regular infantry who could maneuver and fight, but some were dug-in static divisions of limited offensive potential. An agile Allied army of thirty to forty divisions might be capable of invading France and establishing itself onshore, especially if adequate ports were eventually provided and air superiority maintained.[2]

Due to the Dieppe debacle (Operation JUBILEE), it was decided early in the planning process that a port would not be attacked directly on D-Day. Instead, open beaches would be assaulted and necessary support provided by specially designed vessels and structures protected by Allied fighters. Expeditionary airfields in France would be established to provide additional protection from the *Luftwaffe* and air support for the advance. Only then would the invaders move laterally along the coast to seize ports.

Before the ground troops could fight, they had to be delivered into Continental Europe. Even with no *Atlantik Wall*—the coastal defenses of France and the Low Countries—the intended delivery of over 100,000 men in twenty-four hours would be a monumental accomplishment, and that was only on D-Day. In the days following the invasion, sustaining and expanding this force would place ever greater demands on Allied logistics. The eventual needs of a million troops on D+90 (three months after the first landing), both for daily living and for combat, would require mountains of supplies and equipment.

For a Normandy attack to work, when the invasion began, no more than twelve German mobile divisions could be present in France west of the Seine and north of the Loire. This was because the intended initial Allied force would be no more than four divisions, including two light airborne brigades landed on the flanks. Sufficient interdiction had to be accomplished so that no more than

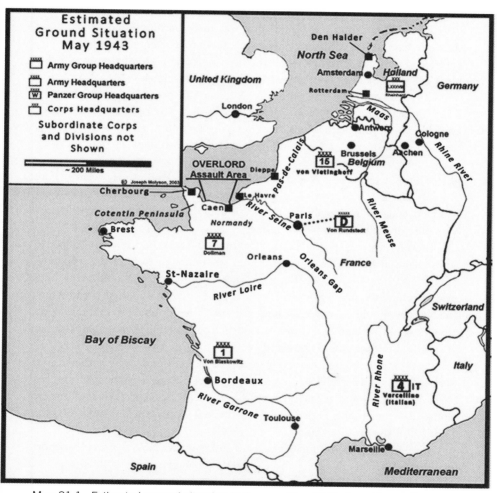

Map 31.1. Estimated ground situation in France, May 1943. Army Group D in Paris also functioned as the headquarters for all German forces in France, Oberkommando Wehrmacht West (OKW). MOLYSON

three additional enemy divisions could enter the operational area within two months of landing the Allied troops.[3]

Interdiction is the interruption of the orderly flow of troops and materiel from their source to the point at which they are employed. Destruction of one or more ammunition trains traveling from an ammunition factory or storage facility to a military unit is an example of interdiction. Interdiction requires knowledge of the source, the method of transportation, the delivery route, and the destination. To accomplish interdiction, one of more of these elements is attacked. For OVERLORD, pre-invasion interdiction was to be accomplished primarily by the Allied air forces, with supplementary attacks by the French Resistance just before and after the landings. After the invasion began, interdiction would also block the movement of German units reacting to the attack.

COSSAC's study began with the analysis of all potential landing beaches from Bordeaux, France, to Den Helder in Holland. The right combination of available ports, suitable beaches, tidal data, distance from airfields in England, roads to move inland, and known German defensive strategy all were included in the equation. This was more than a desk exercise; thousands of reconnaissance photographs were taken. Allied combat swimmers clandestinely went ashore in many places to take soil samples. Vacation picture postcards of France were collected, collated, and analyzed. From this data the physical characteristics and suitability of each beach was determined.

The physical criteria included a continuous beach of sufficient length to rapidly land at least a single division and solid enough to hold the weight of combat and support vehicles. Remembering Gallipoli, there should be no high ground behind the beach from which the defenders could dominate the invaders. The beaches should be within striking distance of major ports, so that follow-on supplies could be landed through the ports from general-purpose ships rather than those built for amphibious warfare.

As the study proceeded, the potential beaches and ports were gathered into "sectors." The total capability of each sector to permit the movement of supplies across its beaches and through its ports was then calculated. The results were expressed as the number of divisions a sector could support on D-Day, D+30 (one month after the invasion), and D+90.

Since no sector had sufficient beaches and ports available to provide support for thirty-plus army divisions, the COSSAC planners next assembled adjacent sectors into six so-called "groups." These groups were again analyzed according to a set of operational criteria.

The first criterion was the geographical relationship with the ultimate target, Germany. This quickly removed the Biscay coast and Brittany groups from serious contention, as they were too far from the German border for consideration. The Germans could destroy the Loire River bridges to prevent Allied armies moving up from the Bay of Biscay. The Brittany Peninsula could be blocked across its neck in a manner similar to German strategy in Italy. The short average combat radius of British fighters also made the Biscay coast and Brittany unfavorable.

Conversely, geographically the best groups were those furthest east: the coasts of Holland, Belgium, and the Pas-de-Calais west to the Seine. Unfortunately, the Germans could also read maps. The combination of suitable beaches, good ports, and short distances to the German border was not lost on Hitler or *Generalfeldmarschall* Gerd von Rundstedt, leading Army Group D and the senior army commander in France. The strongest segment of the *Atlantik Wall* fortifications had been built on this most favorable coastline.

The powerful 15th Army had been stationed along this coast from Le Havre to Rotterdam. The well-entrenched LXXXVIII Corps defended Holland north of Rotterdam. Breaking into Fortress Europe east of the Seine was simply too tough, although Allied deception plans would continue to suggest to the Germans that just such an attack was contemplated.[4]

With the other sectors eliminated, only the coastline from Cherbourg to the Seine River remained. It was here, close—but not too close—to the German border, where the Allies would strike. On this coast, Caen was initially picked as the focus of an amphibious and airborne attack.[5] Amphibious divisions would be landed on the selected beaches and airborne brigades would be dropped to guard the flanks.[6]

The invaders would then move westward to cut off the Cotentin Peninsula, seizing it and Cherbourg from the land side before moving eastward into Germany. Cherbourg was the prewar sailing point for many French transatlantic liners; it had an excellent port and was served by a major rail line running south and east to Paris. A secondary landing near Marseille would be conducted using Allied forces in the Mediterranean. Even as the planning proceeded, the Combined Bomber Offensive was beginning the process of attrition that would remove the *Luftwaffe* as a serious impediment to the invasion.

NEPTUNE

The actual assault phase of OVERLORD was so complex it received a special designation, NEPTUNE. Information about the NEPTUNE/OVERLORD operation received a special code name, BIGOT. BIGOT was a prefix to compartmentalize the information to a very limited group of people. A document marked with the classification "Top Secret" received extensive procedural and physical protection. A document marked "Top Secret BIGOT" received even more.

Personnel within the highly selective group were said to be "BIGOTED." Violation of the stringent security protocols could mean the deaths of thousands of men; such criminal malfeasance was not tolerated. When an American major general mentioned the potential invasion date at a London restaurant, he was demoted to lieutenant colonel and sent home by order of Eisenhower.

The original NEPTUNE/OVERLORD Plan called for an assault of three amphibious divisions and two airborne brigades. General Montgomery, the land commander, insisted on a more robust landing of five amphibious divisions and three airborne divisions on both sides of the invasion area, which was expanded into the Cotentin sector. The expanded force would include two US infantry divisions (the 4th and a composite unit of the 1st and 29th), two British infantry divisions (3rd and 50th), and the Canadian 3rd Infantry Division.

Two US airborne divisions, the 82nd and the 101st, would be delivered by parachute and glider on the west flank of the landings. The British 6th Airborne Division would be similarly delivered on the east flank. The employment of the airborne divisions would allow early seizure of some exits from the landing beaches and secure both flanks of the landing area. Ike felt the additional effort would facilitate the early seizure of Cherbourg. Early use of both the ports of Caen and Cherbourg were thought necessary to sustain the invasion army in its Lodgment Area.[7]

CHAPTER THIRTY-TWO

Troop Carrier

The troop carrier air crews are flying the most vulnerable of all the tactical aircraft in our air force. There is no armor on these planes for defense against ground fire; they don't even have rubber-covered leakproof gasoline tanks. They fly at slow speed when dropping paratroopers or towing gliders, and at an altitude—500 feet—which our armored and protected Flying Fortresses would consider too hazardous. It is essential that missions planned for these planes be worth the risk involved.

—Colonel R. B. Bagby G-2 SHAEF
(Eisenhower's intelligence officer)[1]

It was General Montgomery's insistence that the invasion front be expanded to the west that brought both American airborne divisions into the forefront of the invasion plan. Not everyone was pleased with the expanded role of the American airborne units, least of all Air Chief Marshal Leigh-Mallory, head of the Allied Expeditionary Air Force (AEAF). The RAF had performed a seminal role in helping the British army establish its airborne forces.[2] Leigh-Mallory's AEAF also controlled all the troop carrier aircraft of the US Ninth Air Force and the RAF Transport Command.

In a COSSAC study of aviation requirements for the invasion, the AEAF was responsible for "lift and continual supply and protection of airborne elements during the assault."[3] So, Leigh-Mallory had reason to be interested in how the American airborne units would be employed. At the Quebec Conference, COSSAC had been allotted 632 transport aircraft (predominantly C-47/C-53 medium transports) to lift a force of less than two airborne divisions proposed in the original plan.[4] Over a thousand would be required in the enlarged plan. Troop carrier aircraft in those numbers had yet to arrive in England. Also, Leigh-Mallory thought the swampy terrain and stiff German defenses of the intended airborne assault zones would destroy the two American units.

Brigadier General James M. Gavin, assistant division commander of the 82nd Airborne Division and Eisenhower's point man on airborne operations, met on February 18, 1944, with Leigh-Mallory at Bentley Priory. British lieutenant general Frederick "Boy" Browning and other key British officers were at the meeting, as well as Major General William O. Butler, senior USAAF officer at AEAF. The British had set up an airborne corps commanded by Browning and were eager to absorb the two American airborne divisions into it.

The plan to absorb American divisions into a British corps was actively resisted by Eisenhower's American staff. Gavin later recalled the discussion to an interviewer:

GEN. GAVIN: A very high-powered meeting, you couldn't get any more high-powered unless you went to Montgomery and Eisenhower himself. So, Leigh-Mallory said to me, "Now, General," he said, "tell me about these things. I want to understand how you make these parachute operations work." So, I went over the whole thing. I soon began to realize that he was very cold to the whole idea. He didn't believe a word I was saying, I guess. He didn't think it was possible for the Americans. He didn't say a word about the British. And . . .

INTERVIEWER: He didn't think it was possible for the Americans?

GEN. GAVIN: To carry out an American operation . . . to carry out an airborne operation. But I didn't realize at that moment that he wasn't talking about the British. He was talking about the Americans, but he didn't sort of isolate them as such. . . . In this situation the meeting broke up, and I was very discouraged.

I realized that this absolute top airman, reporting right to Eisenhower, didn't believe we could do what we said we were going to do. On the other hand, I had worked closely with General Bradley [the American ground forces commander for the invasion], and he had told me he would not go into Normandy without the airborne divisions in front of him, because he had seen their work in Sicily, and he knew we had to have them.[5]

Churchill understood the absolute necessity of a maximum effort to break into Fortress Europe. He was not pleased that two American airborne divisions might be squeezed out of NEPTUNE. The prime minister asked Eisenhower what airborne operations he required. Ike stated he must have at least a division and a half, with another to drop twenty-four hours later. At the February 8

(British) War Cabinet meeting, Air Chief Marshal Portal told Churchill that increasing the troop carrier force would dilute its quality. A near-disastrous airborne operation in Sicily the previous summer were still fresh in everyone's memory. Now that the troop carrier pilots were much better trained, no one wanted to decrease quality again. Leigh-Mallory said that training bottlenecks would make any expansion impossible.[6]

In the end, it was American productivity and Eisenhower's willingness to postpone the landing in southern France that solved the troop carrier dilemma. In August 1943, during the Quebec Conference, there had been no active American troop carrier units in the United Kingdom. By postponing the landings in southern France, Eisenhower gained the troop carrier and airborne assets he needed for NEPTUNE/OVERLORD. The Army Air Force also came through.

By April 1944, three wings with a total of fourteen troop carrier groups each of four squadrons had been assembled. All were placed under IX Troop Carrier Command (IX TCC), part of Ninth Air Force. Each squadron had up to twenty-five aircraft, although not all aircraft would be flown on a particular mission. No less than thirty-eight wing and three larger IX Troop Carrier Command exercises were conducted to train all of these new airmen, culminating in Exercise EAGLE on May 12.[7] Unfortunately EAGLE was blessed with excellent weather, so the planners failed to build in adequate bad-weather procedures in the actual invasion orders. This would have great negative impact during Operation NEPTUNE.

Even with enough aircraft, the commander in chief of the AEAF continued to oppose the planned American airborne operation. Leigh-Mallory clashed directly with Lieutenant General Bradley during the first airborne planning meeting at St. Paul's School. Montgomery chaired the meeting, and he watched silently as two of his senior commanders argued. After Bradley explained that he wanted the two American airborne divisions included, the Olympians began their battle as recorded in Bradley's *A Soldier's Story*.

Both men were anxious for the safety of their troops. Leigh-Mallory said that he could not accept dropping the paratroopers to seize the exits to Utah Beach, one of Bradley's objectives. Bradley replied that he would not land amphibious troops on the beach if the exits were not cleared of Germans. Leigh-Mallory turned to Montgomery and stated that if Bradley insisted on dropping the paratroopers, he (Bradley) would have to accept full responsibility for the operation. Bradley replied quickly that he was in the habit of accepting responsibility for all his operations. At this point, Montgomery rapped his knuckles on the table. "That is not at all necessary, gentlemen. I shall assume full responsibility for the operation."[8] Montgomery had his faults, but lack of moral courage was not one of them.

The American airborne assault faced a threat from another quarter, this time Washington. Generals Marshall and Arnold suggested a massive airborne attack into the Orléans Gap, the area between the Seine and Loire Rivers southwest of Paris (see map 31.1). Blocking it with ground troops would augment the line of interdiction formed by destroying the Seine and Loire bridges.

Both thought the airborne should be used for a strategic attack rather than for tactical purposes guarding the flanks of the invasion area. The attack would involve the dropping of the 82nd and 101st by parachute, followed twenty-four hours later by a conventional infantry division landed by glider. Transport aircraft could bring in additional troops and equipment once airfields were seized.

It sounded a lot like the costly German airborne operation against Crete, and Eisenhower resisted the idea. He wanted to keep his invasion force concentrated, not spread out where it could be defeated in detail. Ike knew airborne forces underwent an interesting metamorphosis during their employment. Before being dropped, they were the most mobile of troops. They could go anywhere their troop carrier aircraft could fly. Once on the ground, however, their mobility was limited to walking speed.

The use of gliders allowed some vehicles to be delivered while others could be captured. No one at Supreme Headquarters Allied Expeditionary Force (SHAEF) thought this could give the airborne troops the kind of mobility necessary to conduct so deep a raid. Such an operation could strand an airborne force deep in enemy territory during the time critical amphibious landings were under way. Marshall had ended his suggestion with the statement "Please believe that, as usual, I do not want to embarrass you with undue pressure." Marshall's principled deference to an overseas commander gave Ike the choice, and he chose to maintain the current NEPTUNE plan.[9]

CHAPTER THIRTY-THREE

The Paras

The French pioneered the concept of dropping troops from airplanes in World War I, delivering two-man sabotage teams by parachute behind German lines. From this idea, Army Air Service brigadier general Billy Mitchell developed a plan to drop a whole 10,000-man division at once behind the fiercely defended German lines near Metz. Every Allied bomber available would be used, each carrying as many as 10 men. The war ended before the force could be assembled and trained.

In June 1940, Winston Churchill became the father of the British Airborne Forces. In the wake of recent triumphs by the German parachutists in seizing key terrain in Norway and Belgium, Churchill told the head of the military staff of the War Cabinet: "We ought to have a corps of at least 5,000 parachute troops including a proportion of Australians, New Zealanders and Canadians together with some trustworthy people from Norway and France."[1]

By July 1940, British commandos were undertaking parachute training. It was during this time the RAF decided to use obsolescent bombers for troop carrier missions. A belly hatch was provided from which the "stick" (a combat squad of paratroopers) could exit the aircraft. Aircraft available for this work tended to be underpowered and too cramped for an adequate squad of troopers. In particular, the belly hatches were small and slow to exit, resulting in dispersion of the stick.[2] In February 1941, the parachute commandos began active operations. The British used their fledgling airborne capability to destroy an Italian aqueduct at Mount Volturno. By the end of 1941 they had established the 1st Airborne Division.

GLIDERS

Both the Soviets and Germans experimented with parachute and glider infantry between the wars. The Soviets used airborne troops to seize Bessarabia in June 1940. The Germans used paratroopers and glider infantry in their 1940–1941 campaigns in Western Europe and the Mediterranean. The British were initially unaware that the Germans were also using DFS 30 gliders towed by the Junkers 52s to deliver some of their airborne infantry as complete squads.

The DFS 30 was a small glider, able to carry a squad of only eight German infantrymen and no heavy cargo. Its pilots were trained to become part of the infantry squad on landing. The DFS 30 was often fitted with a braking parachute or retrorockets to slow the aircraft on landing.

After observing the successful German parachute and glider assault on Crete in May 1941, the British established the Glider Pilot Regiment. Since the British had captured no German DFS 30s, the Royal Air Force turned to private industry to design its own combat gliders from scratch. This included both the medium Horsa and heavy Hamilcar.

The Horsa could carry up to twenty-nine combat troops, light vehicles, and artillery. Development began in December 1940.[3]

Development of the Hamilcar began in 1941, but it did not enter service until 1943. Its first combat action was on D-Day. The Hamilcar could carry heavy equipment, including a specially designed airborne light tank called the Tetrarch. Only the Halifax four-engine bomber could tow the heavy Hamilcar.[4]

PARATROOPERS

In September 1941 there were enough troops to form the British 1st Parachute Brigade. The following month, General Browning was appointed general officer commanding paratroops and airborne troops. Browning was ordered to form the 1st Airborne Division.[5] The men called themselves "Paras." In North Africa, the German forces facing the Paras gave them another nickname: the Red Devils (*Die roten Teufel*), in honor of their maroon berets and combat audacity. It was in the Mediterranean fighting of 1942–1943 that British and American airborne forces developed a close relationship and standardized Allied airborne tactics and terminology both for the troop carrier aircraft and the troops themselves.

In the fall of 1943, Anglo-American airborne and troop carrier forces concentrated in Britain. They were incorporated in the OVERLORD Plan. A second British airborne division, the 6th, was established. The British had been introduced to the C-47 in North Africa and received a supply of these aircraft to supplement their overworked troop carrier units. The C-47 was capable of towing the medium Horsa gliders.

British ex-bomber troop carrier aircraft included the Albemarle, Stirling, and Halifax aircraft. They were assigned to No. 38 Group, part of the Allied Expeditionary Air Force, by November 1943. The Albemarle was underpowered as a bomber but more capable as a troop carrier and glider tug. The Stirling squadrons were transferred from Bomber Command due to performance problems at higher altitude. Two Halifax squadrons were also transferred from Bomber Command as it standardized on the Lancaster. No. 46 Group of Transport Command flew the C-47, called the Dakota in British service.

By D-Day, the RAF would have available 460 powered aircraft, 1,050 medium Horsa gliders, and 70 heavy Hamilcar gliders. It was this force that would carry the British 6th Airborne Division into Normandy.[6]

CHAPTER THIRTY-FOUR

The Gooney Bird and the WACO

In February 1933, the US Army Air Corps began using modified airliners and other aircraft to provide priority freight service between air depots. By 1939, the 1st Transport Group had been established with about forty planes in four squadrons. The further expansion of this limited force began in June 1940, as the war in Europe increased in intensity.

The troop carrier and paratroops units evolved together. The shortage of transports was so severe it delayed parachutist training at Fort Benning for months after Pearl Harbor. By June 1942, however, the Army Air Force had almost 12,000 medium transport aircraft on order. The I Troop Carrier Command (I TCC) was established at Indianapolis, Indiana, under Brigadier General Harold L. George. In July, the first formal troop carrier group had been created under I TCC.[1] The first American airborne division, the 82nd, was already in advanced training. By the following month, it would split to provide a cadre for the 101st Airborne Division.

The major aircraft type assigned to the troop carrier force was the Douglas C-47, a derivative of the DC-3 airliner, with large cargo doors in the left rear fuselage and other military improvements, including a reinforced floor. The C-47 was the premier troop carrier aircraft of World War II. First delivered just after Christmas 1941, it replaced earlier military versions of the similar DC-2/DC-3 military fleet already in limited service.

New-built and some ex-airliner DC-3 aircraft, with single left-rear passenger door and unreinforced floors, were officially called "C-53s." Often, however, both C-47 and C-53 aircraft were simply referred to as "C-47s."[2] The aircrew nickname was the "Goose," or more commonly, the "Gooney Bird." Radio operator Mike Ingrisano remembers that some of the planes still had the remnants of coffee service equipment in the back:

The C-53 was the airline plane that first entered the TC [troop carrier] service. It had a small rear door usable by people only. And there may have been other differences but that was the most outstanding. My first assignment

Figure 34.1. The C-47 could be used for cargo as well as troop carrier work.
AIR FORCE HISTORICAL RESEARCH AGENCY

was with the 72nd Troop Carrier Squadron in Alliance, Nebraska. I recall a cross-country flight where I noticed that we still had the containers for hot coffee, etc. that used to be used for commercial flight. We flew into LaGuardia, and I was able to visit my folks in Brooklyn. I came back with some of my Dad's homemade red wine and poured it into the coffee dispenser. We had a nice flight back to Nebraska![3]

Both the C-47 and C-53 could carry a full stick of twenty-one paratroopers, although the combat load was actually sixteen to eighteen paratroopers. Some C-47s were fitted with bomb shackles for parapacks, containers of heavy weapons and ammunition that could be dropped with the paratroopers. These were released using a toggle switch in the cockpit. Paracrates and parachute bundles of ammunition, food, and other supplies could also be pushed out the door. The combat crew of a C-47 was four airmen: pilot, copilot, radio operator, and flying crew chief. If the plane was an element leader, it often carried a navigator as a fifth crewman.

WACO

The C-47 was a troop carrier aircraft far superior to its German counterpart, the Ju 52. A separate effort was required to develop an American combat glider to match or better the DFS 30, the aircraft in which the Germans had attacked key targets in Belgium and in Crete in 1940–1941. Like the RAF, the Army Air Force turned to private industry to design a combat glider from scratch.

The Weaver Aircraft Company, or WACO, responded with its Cargo Glider Model 4A (CG-4A), made of canvas-covered tubing with a plywood floor. One glider man recalled that it was like flying inside a box kite. While it was normally referred to as the CG-4A, sometimes the nickname "flying coffin" was used, as one of Weaver's subcontractors was a coffin manufacturer. On occasion, it was also referred to as the WACO (pronounced *wacko*, or *wayco*). The manufacturer preferred the former pronunciation. No one but the British ever called it the "Hadrian," its official RAF nickname. Despite giving it an official designation, the British did not widely use the type.

The C-47 could tow two CG-4As, but this was not popular with the crews. One glider was the standard load. The glider was rated for a maximum speed of 150 mph. No troops were carried inside the C-47 tow aircraft during glider tows. The 300-foot-long tow rope was made of nylon. The scion of the Dupont Chemical Company that produced nylon was a glider enthusiast and had championed this application. Nylon was stronger and more durable than the hemp used by British and German gliders, and American gliders had less of a problem with rope separations than their European counterparts.

An intercom line ran along the rope to provide inter-plane communications. The rope could be released either by the tow aircraft or the glider, but normally it was the glider that released it. The heavy rope snapping back toward the glider could injure or kill the glider pilot; therefore a tow rope release by the tow aircraft was quickly repeated by the glider.

Although the CG-4A had accommodation for a pilot and copilot, a single aviator most often flew it. Sometimes the copilot seat was occupied by one of the passengers to assist the pilot. Visibility to the front was excellent. If the pilot kept the glider above the slipstream of the tow aircraft, the ride was normally fairly smooth. Unlike its German counterpart, the CG-4A could carry an antitank gun, jeep, or almost 4,000 pounds of other cargo.

Jeeps and other such equipment were too heavy to drop by the parachutes of the day. The nose, including the cockpit, folded up over the fuselage so that the heavy items could be easily loaded or unloaded. When carrying a jeep, the pilots feared that too sudden a stop would tear loose the load and crush them. It was yet another good reason for avoiding a crash.

The US Army established glider infantry regiments for its glider fleet of 12,000 aircraft. Each glider could carry up to thirteen troops instead of heavy equipment. American airborne divisions included two regiments of parachute infantry and one regiment of glider infantry. Regimental and divisional artillery also arrived by glider. The glider men were derisively called "glider riders" by the parachutists, at least until the veterans began to see that riding into combat in a glider was at least as dangerous as arriving by parachute.

The army was tardy in recognizing the contribution of its glider pilots, glider infantry, and artillery. Glider pilots received basic infantry skills training and were able to fend for themselves after landing their gliders in combat area. Glider pilots did not receive flight pay and the glider infantry did not receive hazardous duty pay, at least until after D-Day. Glider pilot wings had a "G" emblazoned over the center crest of the standard Army Air Force pilot wings, representing "Glider." The other men in the airborne units and troop carrier groups soon learned that the "G" really stood for "guts."

Supplementing the CG-4A WACO/Hadrian in American service was the larger British Horsa glider. The Horsa was bigger than the CG-4A and could carry twenty-eight troops, two jeeps, or a 75mm howitzer. Like the CG-4A it could accommodate two pilots. The Horsa was not popular with the Americans; it was considered too heavy and awkward. The air-powered brakes seldom worked in combat, and the Horsa needed a fair amount of room to be properly landed. It filled the requirement for a glider larger than the CG-4A and was therefore accepted by the Yanks as unavoidable.

Gooney Birds, WACOs, and Horsas successfully delivered two American airborne divisions to the Cotentin Peninsula on D-Day.

CHAPTER THIRTY-FIVE

Autumn over Germany
(August–December 1943)

The Quadrant Conference began the same day as the Schweinfurt–Regensburg raid and affirmed the necessity of POINTBLANK, as did COSSAC's OVER-LORD Digest. After the Schweinfurt–Regensburg and HYDRA raids, the weather deteriorated over Germany. The Eighth Air Force hit targets in France while it rebuilt decimated bomber units.

Only a few American attacks were accomplished into the Reich, one of which was an area bombing through clouds using the new American H2X bombing radar. Eaker clung to unescorted bombing long after his superiors and subordinates knew that long-range escort fighters were necessary. Eaker was a fighter pilot. When General Arnold appointed him to command American bombers in Europe, he asked Arnold if he was the right man for the job. Arnold replied that he wanted an aggressive commander who would get the job done. That man was Eaker.[1]

Eaker sought economies of scale by planning for bigger bomber formations. He thought three hundred bombers was about right. Perhaps if enough bombers were sent, they would simply be too many for the *Luftwaffe* to down a significant percentage. This put him increasingly at odds with his friend Hap Arnold, who could foresee failure unless something was done about escort fighters quickly. It was time to inflict losses on the *Luftwaffe*, not absorb damage by it.[2]

In October, the skies over Germany began to clear and the Eighth began to pound the aircraft industry again. Targets included an aircraft engine plant at Anklam and the Focke-Wulf fighter factory at Marienburg. The Anklam and Marienburg facilities were destroyed. Although Schweinfurt had been heavily damaged on the first raid, the Germans were scrambling to get the factory complex back into operation. Before they could, the Eighth struck again on October 14, a raid known as "Second Schweinfurt." Another sixty bombers were downed, but nearly 70 percent of Germany's ball-bearing production capability had been lost. Speer again dipped into the ball-bearing stockpile as he continued dispersion of the aircraft production industry.

Figure 35.1. 91st BG B-17 *Virgin's Delight* after bombing Marienburg FW 190
plant. AIR FORCE HISTORICAL RESEARCH AGENCY

Figure 35.2. Marienburg aircraft plant before attack of October 9,
1943. AIR FORCE HISTORICAL RESEARCH AGENCY, KARLSRUHE COLLECTION

Figure 35.3. Marienburg during attack of October 9, 1943. AIR FORCE HISTORICAL RESEARCH AGENCY, KARLSRUHE COLLECTION

Figure 35.4. Marienburg after attack of October 9, 1943. AIR FORCE HISTORICAL RESEARCH AGENCY, KARLSRUHE COLLECTION

The crews who flew the Second Schweinfurt mission called it "Black Thursday." October 1943 became what the British would call "the high tide of American tribulation," with the loss of 175 heavy bombers in only seven bombing missions over Germany, at a rate of 7.3 percent of the force.[3] Many more were damaged beyond repair. After Schweinfurt, the weather over Germany became worse and missions less frequent. This provided some hiatus for the German and American air forces, both deeply wounded by attrition.

From January to October 1943, VIII Bomber Command had lost over 750 heavy bombers, a loss rate of 4.6 percent. The leadership and aircrew of the Eighth Air Force could look back on a long, hard nine months of combat. Almost 300 additional bombers had been downed in the Mediterranean Theater, but their loss rate was lower, at 1.7 percent. The number crunchers had determined that 4 percent was considered an "acceptable" bomber loss per mission.[4] Many Gold Star Mothers would have disagreed.

At that rate of attrition, in twenty missions VIII Bomber Command would lose about half of its original aircraft, so statistically the original crews would have about a 50 percent chance of survival. Eighth Air Force set a quota of twenty-five missions per crew member to complete a combat tour, meaning statistically an airman had a bit less than a 50 percent chance of surviving his tour.[5] During 1943, Eighth Air Force lost a little over a quarter of its available bomber crews a month. Things, as they said, were rough in the ETO.

Thus, by the end of October, the Army Air Force was at the same point that the German air force had been three years earlier over England. The losses could not be sustained.[6] The day air battle had grown to such great fury that it would be statistically safer for an American to be a US Marine assaulting Japanese-held islands than a bomber crewman in Europe. For the Germans, it was safer to be in an SS assault battalion on the Eastern Front than a fighter pilot over Germany.[7]

Between July and December of 1943, the Americans dropped some 4,600 tons of bombs on aircraft factories and ball-bearing plants. German aircraft production had risen from 400 single-engine fighters in January to over 1,000 in July, as the attack against the aircraft industry intensified. With continued bombing, German production fell to less than 700 fighters in December. Without bombing and the subsequent disruption of factory dispersion, some 2,000 fighters might have been produced.[8]

Map 35.1. Eighth Air Force targets, June–December 1943. CRAVEN[9]

POINTBLANK had had a definite effect on German fighter production even if it did not cripple the *Luftwaffe* by December 1943. German leadership also weakened the air defense of Germany. Hitler and Göring's obsession with retaliation meant German production emphasis was on bombers for offense rather than fighters for defense. This was exacerbated by the accelerated vengeance missile weapon production programs initiated after the Hamburg raids.

HUNGER

If 1943 was a time of tribulation for VIII Bomber Command, the autumn of that year began the worst winter of World War II yet for the Germans. There was no chance left to win against the manpower of the East and the material power of the West. Casablanca had introduced the term "unconditional surrender," which for the Germans meant no chance for a just ending to the war. "Total war" was at hand, and for the Reich it meant a fight for survival.[10] On November 4, 1943, Hitler issued his encyclopedic Directive No. 51 to repel the Allied invasion of Western Europe he now felt was inevitable[11] (see appendix 3).

The cold, wet weather threatened the potato crop, adding to the dismay at the surrender of Italy and the Allied juggernaut approaching Germany from the south. The Russians were pushing back the Germans on their front, threatening to overrun the Ukraine, a major food-producing area for the Reich since 1941. Its inevitable loss would be severely felt. By December 1943, German rations of all kinds had been cut, and hunger added to the misery of bombing. Even though both RAF Bomber Command and Eighth Air Force losses had been near catastrophic in the latter half of 1943, this was not visible to the German public, who suffered under sustained round-the-clock bombing.[12]

Ninety percent of the total weight of the RAF bomber offensive had been directed against thirty-eight German urban areas, most of which had populations in excess of 100,000. These communities contained a total of approximately 18,000,000 people, about a quarter of the German population. About 25 percent of the buildings in these communities had been destroyed by October 31.[13]

THE BATTLE OF BERLIN

The Battle of Berlin began with a 450-bomber RAF raid on November 18, 1943. Although other cities were attacked, over 9,000 sorties would be flown against Berlin in the next four months. The Germans fought back hard, downing 650 RAF heavy bombers in the last quarter of 1943. Among the new weapons they used was *Schräge Musik* ("jazz"), automatic cannon mounted vertically behind the pilot of some night fighters. Rather than endure return fire from the bomber's gun turrets, the night fighter could pass beneath its victim and inflict mortal damage.[14] A new airborne radar, the SN-2, was fitted to German night fighters. This equipment was not susceptible to chaff, the aluminum strips that had protected the bombers from German radar since Hamburg the previous summer.

November also saw changes in the German leadership of the night air war. As the British bombing crescendo increased, Hitler fired *XII Fliegerkorps* (Aviation Corps) commander Josef Kammhuber, who had built the night-fighter organization that was keeping pace with Bomber Command technical advances. Kammhuber was sent north to command *Luftflotte 5* in Norway, a backwater by this time.

XII Fliegerkorps was redesignated *I Fliegerkorps* and took control of all radars, fighters, and flak defending Germany, day and night. Ironically, this was the same thing that Kammhuber had been suggesting for years. To replace him, Göring selected *Generalleutnant* Josef Schmid, the same "Beppo" Schmid whose inept intelligence work had contributed to the Battle of Britain fiasco.

II Fliegerkorps was established in *Luftflotte 3* (France and the Low Countries) to coordinate fighter defense of that area.[15] The RAF bombing of German vengeance missile facilities in coastal France in December 1943 temporarily decreased British bombing of Germany. Hitler recognized this fact and regretted that more of these weapons sites were not available to draw away Bomber Command.[16]

Increasingly bad weather shattered the morale of the *Luftwaffe* Wild Boar units even as RAF losses mounted. Wild Boar units were an elite force flying single-engine day fighters at night. Their *30th Fliegerdivision* was quietly disbanded in early 1944 and replaced with the understrength JG300 and JG301 "bad-weather" wings. These units continued to fly both day and night. The instrument-qualified pilots assigned to these wings were in short supply and should have been reserved for night operations only.[17] Even so, another 800 RAF bombers would fall before the end of March 1944.

General Galland observed:

> *In the course of the year 1943 the accent of the Reich's defense shifted more and more towards actions against the daylight raiders. Even though numerically the British raids against Germany were undoubtedly a great trial for the civilian population, the American precision raids were of greater consequence to the war industry. They received priority attention over the British raids on our towns.*[18]

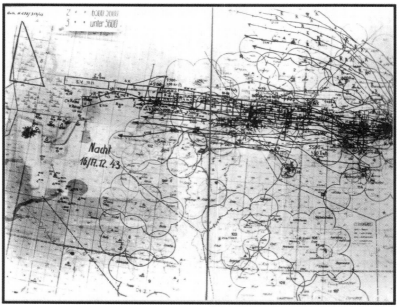

Map 35.2. *Luftwaffe* map of radar-tracked RAF bombers, December 16–17, 1943. AIR FORCE HISTORICAL RESEARCH AGENCY, KARLSRUHE COLLECTION

CHAPTER THIRTY-SIX

Festung Europa (March–December 1943)

Hitler ordered *Generalfeldmarschall* Rommel home before the final Axis defeat in North Africa. Rommel commanded the Axis armies in North Africa from February 1941 until March 1943. After the Sicily invasion and the surrender of Italy, Rommel took charge of the German troops that quickly occupied their former ally. Rommel had previously commanded large numbers of Italy's most capable troops in North Africa. Now he was their country's jailer. His dislike of this duty brought him into conflict with ruthless Nazi SS troops. By January 1944, Hitler had reassigned him to inspect and improve the *Atlantik Wall*.

The German army had the best-trained soldiers in Europe. While they were famous as offensive warriors, they also shined in defense. As the Americans found out to their dismay in the Mediterranean, German minefields, machine guns, and ready reserve troops were in place within *two hours* of German soldiers occupying a new position.

The Germans had had four years to prepare the *Atlantik Wall*.[1] Now Rommel would perfect their earlier efforts. He was given the coastal command from the Netherlands to the Loire River as commander in chief of Army Group B. Essentially, Rommel was now in place to block OVERLORD. The man the Allies had defeated in North Africa would again skillfully oppose them in France.[2]

Years of war had prepared both Rommel and Eisenhower to face one another across the English Channel at the dawn of 1944. Both men had experienced victory and defeat. Now they would face one another in the greatest battle of their careers. Rommel would spend the first five months of 1944 preparing his land army to defend the *Atlantik Wall*. Eisenhower would spend those same challenging days forging a partnership of airmen, soldiers, and sailors to pierce Hitler's Fortress Europe. Rommel's assets were more limited, and he did not enjoy Eisenhower's unparalleled span of control and authority. He did, however, have the ear of Hitler, and would often bypass senior officers to present his opinions directly to the Führer.

As Rommel inspected the defenses, the German army continued to feed irreplaceable manpower into the Eastern Front meat grinder, while simultaneously attempting to stabilize the growing disaster in the Mediterranean. Grimly, the trains had begun to roll in earnest from Occupied Europe to the various

Figure 36.1. General Blaskowitz (left) with Field Marshal Rommel (center, smiling) and Field Marshal von Rundstedt (on right) at a staff conference in Paris. Blaskowitz commanded Army Group G in the south of France; Rommel commanded Army Group B in the north of France; and von Rundstedt's OBW (*Oberkommando Wehrmacht* West—High Command West), controlled both Army Groups. AIR FORCE HISTORICAL RESEARCH AGENCY, KARLSRUHE COLLECTION

death camps in Germany and the German-occupied territories to the east. The war against the Jews and other internal victims of the Reich was in full swing.

The German navy was clearly losing the war at sea. German sailors termed May 1943 as "Black May" because of grievous U-boat losses in the Atlantic. Things had only gotten worse for the submarines for the remainder of the year. Surviving German heavy combatants, the feared surface raiders had been withdrawn from France to Norwegian fjords and Baltic ports. No German warship larger than a destroyer remained on the Channel or Atlantic coast. Only light but potent German forces remained to provide limited protection to coastal naval and merchant shipping.

In France and Belgium, Germany's Western Front, the *Luftwaffe* continued to maintain only two fighter wings, JG2 and JG26 (*Jagdgeschwader* 2 and 26). Only over daytime Germany could the *Luftwaffe* still claim air superiority by inflicting crippling losses on the intruders. The *Luftwaffe* could not understand the intense commitment of the USAAF to daylight bombing. No European, Allied or Axis, thought such attacks viable.

On December 12, 1943, the *Luftwaffe* released the Imminent Danger–West (*Drohende Gefahr West*) Plan. This detailed the aviation and mobile flak forces that would form the defense of Germany to forward bases in France and the Low Countries. A similar plan, Imminent Danger–North (*Drohende Gefahr Nord*) was published for the defense of Scandinavia. The *Luftwaffe* realized that its overburdened air forces would have to move quickly to counter growing Allied strength in the air and on the ground. Defending France, the Low Countries, or Scandinavia would require diluting the defense of the homeland.[3]

CHAPTER THIRTY-SEVEN

Coastal (September 1939–February 1942)

The main target for the Navy during the Eastern campaign still remains Britain.

—ADMIRAL RAEDER'S BARBAROSSA
DIRECTIVE OF MARCH 6, 1941[1]

When considering a cross-Channel invasion, Allied planners had to consider the German navy's ability to move forces along the occupied European coast and to attack approaching Allied vessels. This was a different planning consideration than keeping the *Kriegsmarine* from closing Britain's lifeline across the Atlantic. German naval capability in the Channel and Narrow Seas was never completely suppressed as it was in the mid-Atlantic fight. Yet, the losses sustained by the German defenders were sufficient to allow the passage of the huge Allied invasion fleet in June, 1944.

RAF COASTAL COMMAND

As World War II began, RAF Coastal Command operated armed patrol planes, almost all classified as GR (general reconnaissance) aircraft. For long-range operations, obsolescent flying boats were replaced by the modern four-engine Short Sunderland aircraft beginning in 1938. The Sunderlands were most useful in finding enemy vessels and summoning nearby Royal Navy warships to deal with them.

For operations closer to home, the land-based twin-engine Anson was used. It carried only a few 100-pound bombs and two machine guns. Its combat radius was 60 miles short of the Norwegian coast. Replacement of the Anson by the American-made Lockheed Hudson with a heavier bomb load began in 1939, but only two Anson squadrons had been replaced when the war began.

The Hudson could fly as far as the western Baltic Sea, although the *Luftwaffe* made such a sortie unlikely in daylight. Among Coastal Command's land-

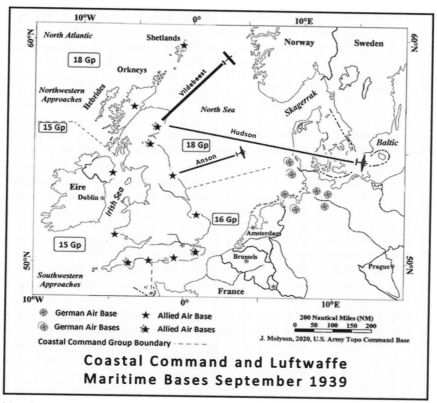

Map 37.1. RAF Coastal Command and Luftwaffe maritime bases in September 1939. MOLYSON

based aircraft, only the Hudson could patrol along portions of Norway's North Sea coastline. Neither the Anson nor the Hudson could take on single-engine German fighters, but they occasionally preyed on unwary enemy patrol aircraft.

At the beginning of the war, Coastal Command had little in the way of intelligence-gathering along the coast other than patrol planes. There were no agents following activity in Continental Europe's ports. Accurately identifying and classifying various vessels, both coastal and transoceanic, was a skill more possessed by Royal Navy ships' officers than RAF aircrew. Available reporting offered little in the way of merchant ship traffic and movement patterns at sea. Methods for determining the speed of various vessels under way from the air had to be developed, learned, and then taught to the aircrew.

The good news, or so it was thought at the time, was that the Norwegians, Danes, Belgians, Dutch, and French on the opposite North Sea and Channel coasts were friendly, and all but the French would likely begin any war involving Germany as neutrals. Therefore, it was doubted there would be much in the way of light German naval forces in need of sinking unless they approached the English coast from their bases in the far eastern North Sea.

THE SCANDINAVIAN CONNECTION

In 1939, Germany was a net importer of many strategic materials. For war production, Germany needed high-grade iron ore mined in Sweden. Germany also needed large quantities of nickel ore for hardened steel used in armor and armor-piercing shells. A major source of nickel was in Canada. Once war began, Hitler turned to nickel supplies mined in neutral Norway and Finnish Lapland. Norway also produced molybdenum used for some types of steel and iron pyrites used to make sulfuric acid and stocks of finished aluminum. Production of Norwegian aluminum was possible due to Norway's abundant hydroelectric power. Germany reciprocated by exporting coal and coke to Scandinavia along the same routes.[2]

Lacking railroad capacity to ship large quantities of minerals between Scandinavia and Germany, the Germans relied on the sea. There were two routes. The route across the Baltic from Luleå, Sweden, to the German Baltic ports was relatively secure but closed by ice in the winter. Ships departing Luleå traveled south along the Swedish coast, transited the Kiel Canal across far northern Germany, then traveled west along the German and Dutch North Sea coast to Rotterdam.

The ice-free coastal route from Narvik to Rotterdam passed to the east of Denmark, and also transited the Kiel Canal to Rotterdam. Once the war started, the British mined this route and threatened German shipping by Royal Navy warships.[3] The Narvik–Rotterdam route was also vulnerable to air attack west of Denmark. From Rotterdam the ore proceeded by barge to the Ruhr area. Emden was an alternative destination, but the route south to the Ruhr was more tenuous. Similarly, other German Baltic ports could receive ore, but again, getting to the Ruhr was challenging. Sadly, it was these facts that led Hitler to invade Denmark and Norway in April 1940.

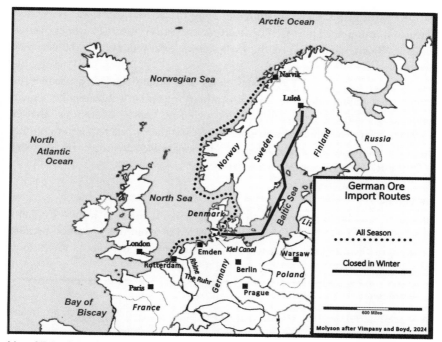

Map 37.2. German iron ore import routes from Scandinavia. MOLYSON[4]

The attack against Norway was extensively supported by German merchant ships, carrying troops and war materials. The prewar restrictions on attacks against merchant ships began to relax, and completely disappeared after Germany occupied France and the Low Countries. By October 1940, the RAF policy regarding enemy merchant ships was "sink on sight."[5]

Since it was impossible to distinguish between a German vessel and that of another country, impressed or contracted into German service, they too became targets. Sweden was a neutral country under the economic thumb of the Germans, at least at this stage of the war. Their ships carried ore to Germany and returned to Sweden with German exports. They therefore were also considered "legitimate" targets.

BLITZKRIEG

Late in May 1940, Hitler struck west to overrun the rest of Continental Europe. Germany seized the available coastal warship, trawler, and transport fleets of France, the Netherlands, Denmark, and Norway, except those vessels that had escaped to England. German shipping along the coastal route was facilitated. Naval and commercial port facilities were also seized. As German armies overran Holland, Belgium, and France, the *Kriegsmarine* followed them to the occupied coasts.

Seizing and occupying coastal ports had unanticipated consequences, namely that maintaining the German military machine would require a great increase in freight movement, including extensive coastal operations. That in turn meant large numbers of transport vessels and the escorts required to protect them. The German air force also had an additional task—to protect this network from the RAF and Royal Navy coastal forces.[6]

SEALION

In July 1940, the Germans began massing a naval force to invade England, Operation *Seelöwe* (SEALION).[7] Hitler wanted to avoid this operation because he thought the English would negotiate an armistice if they could retain their

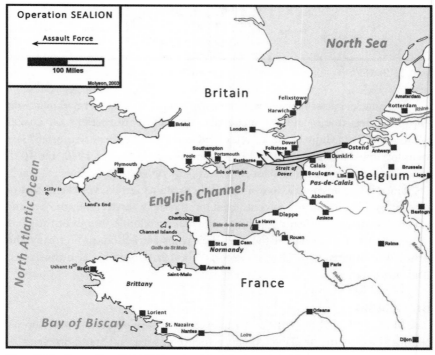

Map 37.3. Operation SEALION, scheduled for late fall, 1940. MOLYSON

empire. This in turn would allow him to turn east against the real enemy, the communist Soviet Union. The German army, underestimating British resolve and defenses, wanted a 200-mile invasion front, essentially much of England's south coast. The *Kriegsmarine*, in negotiation with Hitler and against the German army's unrealistic wishes, reduced the original target area to only 35 miles. The target beachhead was now directly across the Strait of Dover from the Pas-de-Calais.[8]

The *Kriegsmarine*'s motley 2,400-vessel amphibious fleet included various small craft and barges to carry the German army across the Channel. From a contemporary German planning map, the ports of embarkation would be *V Korps* from Ostend, *XIII Korps* from Dunkirk, and *VI Korps* from Calais and Boulogne.[9] The German navy needed the *Luftwaffe* to maintain air superiority over the passage and to defend its fleet preparing in ports from Antwerp to Le Havre.

The Royal Navy and Bomber Command began attacking the assembled German fleet and their ports in September, and by the end of the month had destroyed approximately 10 percent of the invasion vessels in port. Belgian and French port facilities were also damaged or destroyed, which impeded the loading of potential invasion troops. RAF Bomber Command won this phase of the air battle against German coastal shipping.

KRIEGSMARINE COASTAL FORCES

With SEALION postponed and the German invasion fleet dispersed, the *Kriegsmarine* now had three remaining coastal missions in the Channel and North Sea. The first was to support attacks on transatlantic Allied convoys arriving in and departing from Britain. The second mission was closer to home, attacking British coastal convoys in the Channel and adjacent Narrow Seas using mines, destroyers,[10] and *Schnellboote* ("fast boats"). *Schnellboote* were called *S-boots* by the Germans and E-boats[11] by the Allies. The E-boats could lay mines, and they were also heavily armed with torpedoes and heavy automatic weapons.

Almost all E-boat operations were at night, out of sight of defending aircraft and ships. During the day they rested within harbors with extensive antiaircraft protection. A major disadvantage of the E-boat was the lack of an effective embarked radar to find targets. The Germans relied on coastal radars, air and destroyer reconnaissance, and signals intelligence to locate Allied targets. The E-boats were a German threat that would not be neutralized before D-Day, four years later.

The third German coastal naval mission was to defend commerce on the occupied coast from the Spanish border to Norway. This was necessary for the maintenance of the occupation army and air force as well as the civilian economies, now subject to exploitation by Germany. German defensive minefields were laid and maintained by minelayers. British minefields had to be removed using minesweepers. Axis convoys consisting of one or more cargo ships were defended by various kinds of small German warships. All German warships were fitted with extensive batteries of flak, which could be used against attacking aircraft and surface craft. Most coastal warships could both lay and clear mines as required (see appendix 4). The *Kriegsmarine* also operated some coastal artillery and flak batteries.

LUFTWAFFE OVER THE NARROW SEAS

Before and during the Battle of Britain, *Luftwaffe* aircraft attacked British warships and coastal convoys. German aircraft attacked the ships evacuating Allied troops during and immediately after the fall of France. Indirectly, this benefited the German U-boat campaign in the Atlantic, for many of the ships sunk during the evacuations were Royal Navy escort vessels.

By the spring of 1941, most of the *Luftwaffe* was sent east and south to support the army. What remained was *Luftflotte 3*, and it settled into a defensive role during daylight. At night, German aircraft dropped mines outside of English ports, including in the Thames Estuary. They also continued to bomb opportune targets, mainly London and other industrial and port towns.

STRIKE OPERATIONS

By the end of 1940, RAF anti-shipping squadrons had sunk only 6 enemy vessels traveling along the occupied coast and damaged perhaps 14 more, at a cost of 161 aircraft. This was a loss rate of almost 27 aircraft per ship sunk, the equivalent of more than 2 RAF squadrons.[12] Obviously, the unfavorable ratio of ships sunk to aircraft lost had to be reversed. This required a multilevel approach: better intelligence; more and better mission-appropriate aircraft; and better tactics, weapons, and aircrew training.

Sinking port-to-port cargo ships in the Channel and those going to and from Narvik were strategic operations—that is, they struck at the economies of Germany and the occupied countries. Blocking Swedish ore shipments had the same effect as destroying ore-processing facilities in Germany, and the vessels carrying the ore were more vulnerable than well-defended industries in the German homeland.

Planes designed to destroy enemy ships and associated coastal facilities are termed "strike aircraft." The only Coastal Command strike aircraft in 1939 was the obsolete Vickers Vildebeest III, a biplane torpedo bomber of 1924 design. It was charitably rated with a combat radius of perhaps 150 miles at 122 miles per hour, carrying a single torpedo, mounted externally. It had little in the way of self-defense, with one forward-firing machine gun and another rear-facing gun in an open cockpit. A total of only twelve Vildebeest were operational.

By February 1940, the Bristol Blenheim light bomber was operating with Coastal Command.[13] An upgraded fighter version was also provided to counter enemy *Zerstörer* ("heavy fighters") hunting RAF patrol planes. Late in 1940, the two Vildebeest squadrons and one squadron each of Ansons and Blenheim bombers were replace by Bristol Beauforts.[14]

Although its combat debut was delayed by engine problems, the Beaufort torpedo bomber had a combat radius of approximately 640 miles. It was a great improvement over the Vildebeest but required a long, vulnerable gliding approach to deliver its torpedo against a ship. A chronic shortage of torpedoes meant that many if not most Beaufort missions were armed with air-dropped mines or conventional bombs. When armed with bombs, the Beaufort shared a dangerous limitation with the Blenheim. Its bombsight could not hit a ship from medium altitude; therefore, it had to attack from mast height to score a hit. This made it relatively easy to shoot down by the flak guns carried by most coastal vessels.

No. 18 Group, based along the upper east coast of England and Scotland, flew against coastal traffic along the Norwegian coast, mainly vessels bringing ore and finished products south from Narvik and carrying German coke and coal north in trade. By April 1941, Coastal Command No. 16 Group was operating against German vessels in the east Channel and southern North Sea coastlines.

To supplement No. 16 Group, No. 2 Group Bomber Command was ordered to operate its Blenheim bombers against German vessels along the northern French and Dutch coastlines. Two different RAF commands were now in the ship-killing business with Blenheim bombers.

Bomber Command stationed six Blenheims at RAF Manston north of Dover to stop daylight passage of German shipping. The mission was termed CHANNEL STOP. Their effort augmented the large British coastal artillery guns emplaced near Dover. Their assignment at Manston, a fighter base, ensured they would be escorted during their short-range missions.[15]

On April 6, 1941, six Beaufort torpedo bombers of No. 22 Squadron, Coastal Command were sent to attack the battlecruiser *Gneisenau* in Brest Harbor. With extremely bad weather, only one Beaufort, flown by Flight

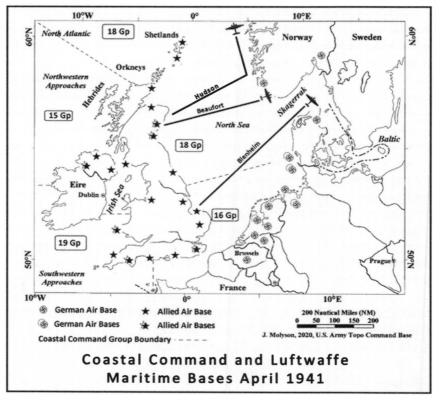

Map 37.4. Coastal Command and *Luftwaffe* maritime bases in April 1941. MOLYSON

Officer Kenneth Clark, found the target. The *Gneisenau* was hit at its dock by the Beaufort's torpedo. Clark and his crew were quickly shot down by some of the 1,000 flak guns defending the port. The Germans were so impressed by the torpedoing of *Gneisenau* that they recovered the four bodies of the downed crew and buried them with full military honors. Clark later received a posthumous Victoria Cross, the highest British award for valor. In April of 2000 Clark's sister presented the award to the entire No. 22 Squadron in perpetuity, stipulating that it honored all four crew members of Clark's Beaufort.

THE BEAU

Later in April, the RAF introduced the Bristol Beaufighter into the Coastal Command strike mission. The Beaufighter, or "Beau," was an evolutionary development of the Beaufort torpedo bomber. This involved much more powerful engines, larger propellers, and longer landing gear. Armed with a cluster of 20mm cannon in the nose and additional machine guns in the wings for attack, and a dorsal turret with machine gun for self-defense, the Beau was arguably the most heavily armed fighter-bomber in the world.

What brought the Beau to Coastal Command was its potential anti-ship capability with forward-firing cannon, machine guns, and bombs. Very fast and maneuverable, it could attack and withdraw quickly. This lessened its exposure to enemy flak—necessary, since the inadequate bombsight forced it to attack from mast height like the Blenheim.

Unescorted single or small units of Coastal Command Beaufighter and Blenheim bombers and Beaufort torpedo aircraft continued to hunt in the Channel and North Sea in irregular patterns to catch the unwary. In the next few months, Coastal Command made 143 attacks, losing 52 aircraft. Bomber Command Blenheims, escorted by Spitfires, made 297 attacks, losing 36 aircraft.

EVOLUTION

The Germans replaced their losses and responded with more antiaircraft guns on their merchant shipping and more escorted small convoys.[16] British attacks were effective enough to drive the Germans to operate mostly at night when possible. This in turn led Coastal Command to improve night tactics, the use of parachute and float flares, and investigate the air-to-surface (ASV) radars currently in use against U-boats to hunt surface ships.

Unfortunately, the overlap between Bomber Command and Coastal Command strike operations was unworkable and lasted only a few months. There was much confusion, lack of coordination, and duplication of effort. By the end of the summer of 1941, it was decided to divide the anti-shipping effort by geographic allocation. Bomber Command retained CHANNEL STOP and the operating area between Cherbourg and Wilhelmshaven.[17] Coastal Command operated outside of this area, that is, on both flanks. This reduced confusion and duplication.

In mid-1941, German and Italian operations in North Africa forced the RAF to shift significant numbers of light and medium bombers from Britain to Egypt and Malta. Aircraft that might have interdicted German coastal operations in the Narrow Seas instead were used against Axis convoys in the Mediterranean. The U-boats and surface raiders were at the height of their effectiveness, a challenge that Coastal Command could not ignore. Many aircraft were also transferred to the antisubmarine mission. This left the Coastal Command anti-shipping force in Britain "back to square one."

BENEFITS

By the fall of 1941, RAF anti-shipping attacks, costly though they were, greatly concerned *Grossadmiral* Erich Raeder, commander in chief of the *Kriegsmarine*. He complained to Hitler that German naval losses to aircraft and mines were intolerable and could only be alleviated by reinforcing the defensive fighters of *Luftflotte 3* on the *Kanalfront*:

> *Losses in October included two steamers and one dredger sunk, and sixteen minesweepers, motor minesweepers and patrol boats damaged, some severely. We cannot afford such losses. . . . The only way to rectify the position at sea is to reinforce the fighter units, an urgently needed step. According to information from the Air Force, this is not possible.*[18]

Increased German defensive measures reduced the efficiency of their coastal operations, resulting in increased transit times between ports and demands for conversion of more vessels to flak ships. Coastal Command attacks on German shipping off the Norwegian coast also might have influenced Hitler to consider the threat of a possible Allied invasion of Norway sometime in 1942. This would immediately cut off the essential ore supplies out of Narvik. Germany was also dependent on the Norwegian fishing industry for their products. A British commando raid and air attacks against German airfields on the Norwegian coast in September must have reinforced Hitler's fear of losing Norway.

CHAPTER THIRTY-EIGHT

The Channel Dash (Winter–Spring 1942)

Three major German combatants—battlecruisers *Gneisenau* and *Scharnhorst* and heavy cruiser *Prinz Eugen* were based at Brest in France. All suffered damage from RAF air attacks which kept them from active operations. Maintenance and repairs to *Scharnhorst* had been delayed by damage to the Brest port facilities, and the ship itself was badly damaged by RAF aircraft during a sea trial run from Brest to La Pallice. Punishing air raids and continuous surveillance prevented them from sneaking out on another Atlantic raiding foray, the very reason they were based at Brest. The British established Operation FULLER to watch over the ships and to intercept them if they left the harbor. Radar-equipped Lockheed Hudsons patrolled the waters off the harbor mouth.

With concerns over the safety of the Norwegian coast, Hitler wanted the ships brought up the Channel to be based in Norway. He ordered planning to begin for Operation CEREBUS, a breakout attempt from Brest, at a conference on January 12, 1942. The ships would leave the harbor in the dark and by daylight would be covered by a rotating escort totaling 250 *Luftwaffe* fighters. General Adolf Galland took personal charge of the air defense. The fighter operation supporting CEREBUS was separately code-named DONNERKIEL ("Thunderbolt"). The *Kriegsmarine* provided a strong squadron of escort vessels to help protect the heavy ships en route.

A patrolling Hudson failed to detect the departure of the big ships on February 11, 1942. A second Hudson, which should have detected the ships moving up the Channel, had returned to base with a malfunctioning radar. Despite courageous but uncoordinated attacks by the RAF and Royal Navy, the ships got through. This action, called the "Channel Dash," was a major embarrassment to the RAF and Royal Navy, whose planes and ships had failed to stop the escape. Both the *Scharnhorst* and *Gneisenau* were damaged by air-delivered mines, but all three big warships made it home to Germany by February 13. Weather, bad luck, and poor coordination, as well as German proficiency and planning, made CEREBUS a *Kriegsmarine* success.

The German celebration was not to last the month. *Scharnhorst* had hit two mines and required extensive repairs at a German shipyard. On February 23, previously undamaged *Prinz Eugen* was torpedoed on the way to Norway by a British submarine and limped back to Germany. Four days later, *Gneisenau*, docked at Kiel, was hit twice in a Bomber Command raid. All three were out of service for months. The German tactical victory of CEREBUS became a strategic defeat.[1] CEREBUS also removed the three heavy warships from the Channel coast, which simplified later planning for the Allied return to France.

That did not, however, save Coastal Command from criticism, to which it responded by pointing out its span of responsibility, relative lack of resources, and attrition rates. Coastal Command's AOC-in-C Air Marshal Philip Joubert demanded more aircraft and sole control of anti-shipping operations in the Narrow Seas and North Sea. Besides CEREBUS, the first three months of 1942 had been costly. Coastal Command sank only 6 ships in that period, losing 55 aircraft, a loss rate of 7.6 aircraft per vessel destroyed. The cost of anti-shipping operations was unsustainable.[2]

Like the weather, the targeting dilemma—fly high and miss, or fly low and die—continued to plague anti-shipping operations. The chance for a Coastal Command aircrew member to survive his first tour of duty of 200 operational hours was less than 18 percent, and surviving a second tour, only 3 percent. This was worse than for Bomber Command aircrews attacking German cities.

Along with the weather improving in the spring of 1942, four squadrons of Hampton torpedo bombers joined Coastal Command. These were surplus aircraft from Bomber Command displaced by more capable aircraft. The Hamptons and their torpedoes supplemented but did not replace the Coastal Command bombers attacking coastal shipping at mast height.

CHAPTER THIRTY-NINE

Strike Wings (July 1942–April 1944)

If you find yourself in a fair fight, your planning is flawed.
—MILITARY AXIOM, VARIOUSLY ATTRIBUTED

Even in improving weather, the cost in aircraft and aircrew in the mast-height attacks remained prohibitive. By July 1942, Coastal Command ordered that no more attacks were to be conducted at low altitude, forcing the aircraft up to medium altitude. After almost three years of combat, there was still no adequate bombsight. The Hamptons were not affected by this order, continuing to deliver their torpedoes flying very low over the water.[1]

It was now that Air Marshal Joubert secured the approval of the Air Ministry to acquire increased numbers of the fast and sturdy Bristol Beaufighters for Coastal Command. He wanted two-thirds of the Beaus to be flak-suppression aircraft, armed with automatic cannon and machine guns, and one-third to carry torpedoes. The torpedo Beaufighters were nicknamed "Torbeaus."[2] Unfortunately, wartime demands for torpedoes and torpedo aircraft delayed delivery of the Torbeaus and the training of their crews.

In addition to acquiring more capable aircraft, it was time to improve the tactics for attacking convoys. A wing in the RAF consisted of three squadrons based at the same airfield. Each wing took its designation from the home airfield. By the summer of 1942, three Beaufighter squadrons were based at RAF North Coates, the North Coates Strike Wing. The strike wing concept had been used in the Mediterranean, where RAF units on Malta had ravaged Axis convoys traveling to Africa, supporting Rommel.

Each Coastal Command strike wing was intended to have two squadrons of flak-suppression Beaufighters and one squadron of Torbeaus. Each squadron had eight aircraft, giving a strike wing twenty-four Beaus. The intention was to attack in full strength to overwhelm the defense rather than in the small flights of aircraft used previously. In addition, an RAF single-engine fighter escort squadron would escort the wing and fend off intercepting German fighters.

The first North Coates Strike Wing attack was in November of 1942, and was not successful, sinking only one vessel and losing three Beaufighters. Two more were lost in landing accidents. Post-strike analysis indicated the fighter escort should be at least two squadrons, and that an advance scout aircraft should locate the target convoy so that the strike wing could properly approach and execute the attack.

In the spring of 1943, more aerial torpedoes were available and the Torbeaus were armed with a reliable weapon. Some of the anti-flak Beaus were armed with 60-pound rockets with high-explosive warheads in addition to their automatic cannon. Others carried bombs. With more training, practice and coordination, and the arrival of good weather, the first successful strike wing attack occurred in April 1943. An escorted convoy of eight ships was attacked and a 5,000 GRT merchant ship sunk. Escorting vessels were damaged, and no aircraft were lost.

The strike wings were tailored to attack convoys with one or more merchant ships, protected by various escorts to sweep mines and provide flak support. The convoys were the unmovable object being hit by the strike wing, the unstoppable force. Bleeding in the attacking planes and target ships began on contact. Attacks were over in just a few vicious minutes. The ships often had fellow sailors to rescue from the water and sometimes a crippled ship to tow to port. Sometimes there was just an oil slick marking a lost vessel's final resting place.

British aircrew were most often lost in the target area, posted as "killed in action" or "missing in action," depending on what was observed from the other wing aircraft. Surviving aircrew in damaged planes who ditched on the way home were most often rescued by the efficient RAF Air Rescue force.

The Hampton torpedo bomber units continued their attacks separate from the strike wings. The Hamptons were much too slow to attack in concert with the faster Beaufighters. The Hamptons were still successful, including on patrols into Norwegian waters. Sometimes British fighters escorted them; sometimes they flew alone or in small flights. Hamptons were also the first Coastal Command strike aircraft to receive ASV radar, improving their ability to find targets at night and in bad weather.

Also in April of 1943, Mosquito fighter-bombers began reequipping some strike squadrons. In November, some strike wing units began flying the Mosquito Mk.XVIII "Tsetse Mosquito." This gunship was equipped with a massive 57mm Molins automatic cannon, which fired a 7-pound projectile with a hardened steel nose. A few hits from this gun could demolish a small surface vessel or sink a U-boat.[3] The 60-pound high-explosive rockets on some Beaufighters and Mosquitoes were replaced with the more accurate 25-pound rocket, with a solid metal warhead. These could easily punch through a U-boat or surface vessel hull, even below the waterline.

In July 1943, some strike aircraft received Gee navigation equipment. The G was for "grid," which it created electronically for the navigator. It allowed for accurate navigation over open water, in bad weather and at night. Used in conjunction with ASV radar, darkness was no longer a cloak for German surface vessels. Radio altimeters, which gave accurate altitude information to pilots, also arrived in Coastal Command. This greatly reduced the challenge of flying over water at night.

TACTICS

To counter German coastal movement by night, the strike units attacked at dawn and dusk and developed night-attack tactics and equipment. Dawn was the most preferable time because approaching from the west, the aircraft caught the silhouettes of the target ships scurrying to port against the sunrise glow. This allowed the most efficient of attacks. The arrival of two squadrons of Beaufighters, firing automatic cannon and machine guns and dropping bombs, caused many flak gunners to abandon their posts by the time the Torbeaus arrived.

Strike wing attacks were conducted in secret to prevent the Germans from exploiting operational procedures. Attacks were always conducted at low level, and included enemy shipping in the Channel and North Sea, and occasionally in the Bay of Biscay. Most attacks were against surface ships rather than submarines. Aircrew casualties continued to be heavy and proportional to those suffered by Bomber Command.[4]

From 1940 until March 1943, Coastal Command strike aircraft had inadequate anti-ship tactics and little fighter escort. The entire RAF based in Britain sank only 107 enemy vessels totaling about 155,076 GRT,[5] at the cost of 648 aircraft, or 4.2 aircraft per enemy ship sunk. In contrast, air-delivered magnetic mines delivered by the RAF sank 369 vessels, losing 329 aircraft, or about 1.1 aircraft per enemy ship sunk. Strike wing attacks beginning in April of 1943 made anti-shipping air attacks more effective.

There were attempts to break up the strike wings for "more important" work. The Beaufighters and Mosquitoes were needed to intercept German heavy fighters trying to shoot down Allied antisubmarine aircraft over the Bay of Biscay. Biscay was another microcosm of hell where the U-boat, not the coastal convoy, was the ultimate prey of Coastal Command.

The strike wings and Hamptons greatly reduced the flow of ore and other products from Narvik to Rotterdam, diverting it to the less efficient port of Essen and impeding its eventual delivery to the Ruhr industrial district. By January, 1944, the Coastal Command strike force was formidable and modern. There were now three designated strike wings and other units using strike wing tactics applicable to their operations.

As D-Day approached in the spring, much of the anti-shipping effort transitioned to protecting the Allied invasion fleet. This meant focusing more against German E- and R-boat operations in the Channel than stopping German convoy movement. (R-boats were motor minesweeper patrol boats, heavily armed with antiaircraft weapons.) About half of Coastal Command was reassigned to the Allied Expeditionary Air Force (AEAF) for the invasion.

Strike wing operations resumed after D-Day on the flanks of the invasion area, further impeding the failing German defense. Coastal shipping continued at a reduced rate. The coastal shipping routes were finally cut between Cherbourg and Le Havre by Operation OVERLORD, but continued on both flanks until Allied armies seized the convoys' ports.

CHAPTER FORTY

Lessons Learned
(August 1941–December 1943)

Between August 1941 and February 1943, the RAF Army Co-operation Command and its single No. 70 group maintained its role as a training and experimentation headquarters, firmly under RAF Fighter Command control. It was the source of much dispute between the War Ministry, in charge of land forces, and the Air Ministry, in charge of the RAF. Air Marshal Barratt, AOC Army Co-operation Command, was often the target of these disputes, but he endured.

THE WDAF

While angry gentlemen in Britain exchanged conflicting staff studies, the British were fighting a shooting war in the Mediterranean against the Germans and Italians. By October 1941, the overall RAF commander in North Africa was Air Marshal Arthur Tedder. Like Eisenhower, Tedder could lead a variety of units and personalities toward a common goal.

As AOC Middle East Command, Tedder revised many policies and eventually helped reverse the series of Allied defeats in the Mediterranean. The RAF and the Royal Army figured out how to get along, and finally, how to correctly apply airpower to the land battle. Tedder emphasized the importance of the center of gravity, the *Schwerpunkt*, on the battlefield. The emphasis on center of gravity had been validated by the *Luftwaffe* during the Battle of France in 1940.

Among Tedder's innovations was the Western Desert Air Force (WDAF).[1] Organized in October 1941, RAF fighters, fighter-bombers, RAF, and Fleet Air Arm land-based light bombers in North Africa were organized under Air Vice Marshal Arthur Coningham. Coningham turned Tedder's ideas into victories.

One of the major developments was the colocation of air and ground command headquarters so that land and air commanders could together draft and execute joint plans. The proximity and prowess of Axis forces made this a marriage of necessity. RAF and (later) the USAAF provided two kinds of support to the Allied armies. *Direct* support was applied in close proximity to friendly

177

armies. *Indirect* support was provided to the army beyond the immediate battle-field, including strikes on enemy ports and cargo ships.

Best practices and lessons learned in the Mediterranean flowed back to Britain, especially after Operation TORCH and the Allied advance into Libya from Egypt. Improved air–ground communication and better reconnaissance over and beyond the battlefield were key ingredients. This allowed commanders, aircrew, and soldiers on the ground to perceive the situation in hours rather than days. Barratt and his principal subordinates championed these reforms in Britain.

During 1942, the RAF and (army) Home Forces accepted the concept of an air observation post (AOP). An experimental unit had deployed to France with the BAFF in 1940 but did not enter combat. Late in 1942, an AOP was established for Operation TORCH in North Africa. The AOP flew light "civilian-type" aircraft which were able to operate from unimproved airstrips in close proximity to the troops they supported. The aircraft of choice were various British-redesigned models of the American Taylorcraft, designated as the Auster.

The Auster was a high-wing monoplane that provided a good view of the surrounding terrain below. The AOP aircraft were able to provide local commanders with battlefield reconnaissance and direct friendly artillery fire. AOP pilots were Royal Army artillerymen trained to pilot the aircraft and provide ground crew support. The AOP itself was also an RAF squadron.[2] The RAF provided aviation and ground crew training and some technical support.

Based on the experience of the WDAF, it was found that direct support to troops in contact with the enemy was best provided by fighter and fighter-bomber aircraft. The biggest problem, one that remains to this day, was distinguishing between friendly and enemy troops in contact in a battle area. This was offset by prearranged recognition signals, low-altitude attack tactics, better air–ground communications, and the activity of the AOPs. Of course, fighters were also necessary to gain and maintain air superiority over the battlefield and the friendly rear area.

For indirect support beyond the battle area, light and medium bombers were the best solution, especially for destroying fixed enemy facilities supporting the enemy army. For more distant targets, heavy bombers were useful against larger facilities such as ports and airfields. Heavy bomber units remained under their own headquarters and were "borrowed" to hit distant targets identified by the WDAF for destruction. The robust light and medium flak defending such important targets could be avoided by bombing from high altitude, and there was no risk of hitting friendly troops.

Among the many new concepts implemented by the Western Desert Air Force in North Africa was the creation of composite air groups of mixed aircraft types. This directly contravened the prewar RAF combat organization by function, that is, Fighter Command, Bomber Command, and Coastal Command. In North Africa, however, the WDAF operated ad hoc composite air groups to effectively support the army. Various composite groups included fighters, fighter-bombers, tactical and photo-reconnaissance aircraft, light and medium bombers, AOPs, and, as necessary, cargo/troop carrier planes.

The headquarters of the composite air group and the army formation it supported were colocated. All the infrastructure of the composite air group was mobile, so that the group could move forward with the army. This included communications. There was much less telephone wire than in the ancient days of 1940, and much more radio capability. This allowed quick identification and attack of targets of opportunity on a rapidly changing battlefield.[3]

When the composite group was adapted in Britain to support the future invasion, it was decided to scale the forces to support a single field army. Exact numbers and types of aircraft would depend on the mission and operational area of the supported army. As the OVERLORD Plan was developed and expanded, the number of Allied field armies increased. Early on it was decided that composite groups formed by the RAF would support British armies; by the RCAF, the Canadian army; and by the USAAF, American armies.

2TAF

After digesting the lessons learned in North Africa and in Exercise SPARTAN, the RAF Army Co-Operation Command (ACC) was redesignated the HQ Tactical Air Force (HQ TAF). This was more than a name change. ACC was a training formation. TAF was an operational combat formation. It was soon realized that the Western Desert Air Force had been the "first" Tactical Air Force, so HQ TAF was redesignated the Second Tactical Air Force (2TAF), absorbing units from Fighter Command, Bomber Command, and other RAF resources.

The reorganization was completed by November 15, 1943, although shifting of some squadrons continued. RAF Fighter Command was split between 2TAF and the Air Defense Great Britain (ADGB) Command.[4] The 2TAF would provide the RAF tactical contingent for OVERLORD. ADGB would provide an umbrella of air security over the burgeoning forces in England being built up for the invasion.

It was Tedder's performance in the Med that later led General Eisenhower to appoint him Deputy Supreme Commander for OVERLORD. Coningham's skillful application of tactical airpower to win battles in turn led Tedder to select him in January 1944 as the AOC Second Tactical Air Force for the invasion of northwestern France.

CHAPTER FORTY-ONE

The PIs and Photo Joes

Once the command of the air is obtained by one of the contended armies, the
war must become a conflict between a seeing host and one that is blind.
—H. G. WELLS[1]

In World War I, the first combat mission for aircraft was reconnaissance. While many other uses were found for planes in combat, reconnaissance remained a major mission. When it became obvious that the average pilot or observer could not remember all the details he had observed, cameras were added to the planes. Aerial reconnaissance photography became an advanced art during the years between the world wars.

The father of American aerial photography was Major Albert W. Stevens. In the 1930s Stevens flew aboard two National Geographic balloon expeditions to altitudes in excess of 70,000 feet. On one of his ascents he took a single photograph that captured half of the state of Indiana. Stevens later joined the Air Technical Intelligence staff at Wright Field, Ohio. His expertise was soon fully utilized in improved aerial photography from military aircraft.[2] From his early efforts would come the many "Photo Joes," American aircrews specially trained to collect critical aerial photography of terrain and enemy forces.

About the same time, in England, MI6 (the Secret Intelligence Service) convinced Australian businessman Sidney Cotton to engage in aerial photography over Germany and Italy during his frequent business and touring trips. What followed was a deluge of photography taken by Cotton in his highly modified personal Lockheed 12 aircraft. Once the war started, the RAF assumed responsibility for this kind of intelligence work.[3]

The RAF established what was to become the Allied Central Interpretation Unit (ACIU) at Medmenham. Medmenham became a mecca for photo interpreters (PIs). This included not only the processing of thousands of photographs, but also the training of hundreds of new PIs to interpret them. RAF Flight

Officer Constance Babington Smith, who first discovered conclusive evidence of the highly secret German V-1 and V-2 missile programs, was a product of this effort.[4] Eventually, the RAF established No. 84 Group for its strategic photo reconnaissance work, and several wings for tactical support to the Commonwealth armies fighting on the Continent after D-Day.[5]

England began World War II using light and medium bombers for photo reconnaissance. Extreme losses soon led the RAF to convert to stripped-down fighter types operating at high speeds and very high altitude to avoid German defenses. These included the trusty Spitfire and later the Mosquito. The American forces arriving in Europe also favored modified fighters, although they and the English still used bombers for missions where little enemy opposition was expected. The Yanks disbanded their obsolete prewar observation squadrons and converted the crews to more survivable aircraft, including the Spitfire PR.XI, the P-38 (as the F-3 and F-5), the P-51 (as the F-6), and the Mosquito Mk.XVI (as the F-8).

As the skill of PIs improved, so did the efforts of camoufleurs[6] on both sides of the Channel. Their job was to develop camouflage to hide critical installations or deceive enemy PIs. PIs looked for straight lines, perfect circles, and bright colors. Such things are called *signatures*, physical characteristics associated with a particular kind of facility that can be observed by a sensor such as a visible light or infrared camera.

Camoufleurs attempted to hide signatures from view. A well-camouflaged target was hard to see and harder to hit.[7] It was a sign of friendly air superiority—for example, when US aircraft began to appear in bright metal natural finishes in 1944. They no longer needed to be hidden by camouflage on their own airfields.

Camouflage included the protection of not only tactical assets but also things of operational and strategic value. The German ability to hide production facilities from RAF and US PIs with elaborate camouflage clearly contributed to Allied difficulties in assessing and focusing the daylight bombing of Germany. It was photoreconnaissance that found many targets for the day and night bombers and allowed evaluation of their efforts with post-strike photography. At night, the blackout of German cities was a simple form of concealment, attempting to blend urban areas into unoccupied farmland. This was a temporary measure at best, for the RAF soon fielded highly skilled airmen adept at the arcane art of night navigation.

These men, called *pathfinders*, would seek out the darkened cities and mark them with incendiary bombs and other devices. Hundreds of RAF heavy bombers would swarm to the scene to drop their deadly cargoes. These pathfinder procedures were not new; they were copied from the Germans who had earlier used them against blacked-out British cities. Like the Germans, the British developed electronic navigation and radar devices to navigate precisely to their targets. By 1943, night was no longer a deterrent for RAF bombers. German cities were in flames.[8]

Not all the aerial photography was aimed at enemy forces and facilities. Much of it supported cartographic activity, as well as familiarization of thousands of new American airmen to their overseas operating areas. The American Air Transport Command used a modified B-24 called a *Peeping Tom* to take movies of the approaches to hundreds of airfields around the world for use by the aircrews. These films were widely distributed and improved the safety and reliability of air cargo movement worldwide.[9]

One of the tougher jobs in the USAAF was training a corps of American PIs to look at, analyze, and accurately report on what was captured in aerial photographs. Awaiting training, some PIs were diverted into non-intelligence work for a time before reporting for PI duty. The work was grueling and mentally demanding. The Americans went through PI school prior to going overseas, and a consolidated training facility was also established at Medmenham for those arriving in Britain.

In 1943, the American PIs that went to North Africa to support Operation TORCH received little or no training at Medmenham, and forgot much of what they had learned in the States. It showed in their work. During an interview of Colonel Elliot Roosevelt of the Photo Reconnaissance Wing of the North African Air Force, the following vignette serves to illustrate the challenge:

Q. What are the shortcomings of the United States photo interpreters, both the Army and the Navy? What do you consider the qualifications for photo interpreters?

A. What do I consider the qualifications? The ability accurately to obtain all the desired information on a photograph for which the mission was run. I'll give you a very good example. I had an American-trained Army photo interpreter in the early days of the Tunisian campaign who had been through interpretation school in the United States. He received a photograph of a certain road in Tunisia. On that road there was what looked like a long train of vehicles, and he said it was an armored column moving toward a certain frontal area. That information was phoned in to Army headquarters, and a division was started that night to meet this armored column which was on the move. Well, about six o'clock that night a British RAF interpreter got hold of that print and said "Hey, there's something wrong here! That is a column of camels—a camel caravan." The word was flashed up to Army headquarters, but by that time the division was on its way and had been moving uselessly against a nonexistent enemy for a period of 7½ hours. That's what I mean by a competent photo interpreter; he must be able to tell exactly what is in the picture, and unless one has had extremely careful schooling, he is apt to say things and express opinions which are not actually true. The photo interpreter who is properly trained never makes a claim unless he is positive.[10]

As time when on, the American photo reconnaissance effort improved, especially with increasing Allied air superiority in all theaters. The same could not be said of the Germans, although they had an early start against Britain. They converted Ju 86P/R, Ju 88D, and Do 17F medium bombers for longer-range strategic reconnaissance. German photographic work over Britain is described in a series of books by British photographer Nigel Clarke.[11] When the war started, German capability over the United Kingdom declined. In July 1943, RAF Wing Commander Asher Lee, an expert on the German air force, visited Washington and revealed the current sad state of the *Luftwaffe's* aerial reconnaissance:

> *In reconnaissance on the Western Front the Germans are covering the sea areas—the Channel, the North Sea, and the Southern Arctic and the Western Approaches (to England)—very efficiently. But in overland reconnaissance of England where they could get up-to-date information from aerial reconnaissance, their work in the past six months has been worse than shocking— it's been negligible, and they have had no reliable coverage at all. They have made various attempts to improve it. . . . But there is no regular long-range overland reconnaissance of England at all. Presumably the German Intelligence has abandoned the idea of getting up-to-date information about England inland from aerial reconnaissance.*[12]

DICING WITH DEATH

As planning for OVERLORD proceeded, American F-5 Lightning aircraft of the 10th Photo Group were used to fly fast and very low along the French and Belgian coasts:

Especially needed by 21st Army Group were low-altitude photographs show-
ing the barriers, mines and other beach defenses in detail. Such an under-
taking had previously been regarded as suicidal because of the bristling flak
defenses which made these French beaches one of the most strongly defended
areas in the world, but at the 10th Photo Group it was felt that the opera-
tion could be carried out by employing to the full the high speed of the P–38
aircraft. The result was a series of "dicing" missions which yielded photographs
invaluable for planning the beach assault. One of the 11 pilots participating
was lost in this dangerous "dicing with death" . . .

To 2nd Lt. (now 1st Lt.) Albert Lanker of the 31st Photo Reconnaissance
Squadron went the honor of being the first Group pilot to fly a minimum-
altitude mission in enemy territory. (Missing in action from a mission on 26
December 1944, to drop photographs to US troops at BASTOGNE, in the
ARDENNES.) The Squadron historian records that Lt. Lanker admitted
being nervous and apprehensive when he took off in his P–38 (F–5), modi-
fied to carry a 12-inch nose camera, at 1711 hours on 6 May. He was 50 feet

Figure 41.1. Workers scatter from "dicing" aircraft. Note beach obstacles being
erected. AIR FORCE HISTORICAL RESEARCH AGENCY, KARLSRUHE COLLECTION

off the ground at DUNGNESS, where he circled and shot across the Channel ten to fifteen feet above the whitecaps.

Near BERCK-SUR-MER [France] he turned around a sand dune to lessen his possibilities as a target. (His pictures later showed the dune to be an enemy gun emplacement!)

Then, gaining speed in a short dive he started his super buzz of the coast. Here, he said, nervousness left him, and he began to enjoy himself immensely. During the four minutes his cameras were operating he encountered five groups of workmen building defenses on the beach.

"I headed straight for every group just to watch them scatter and roll," the lieutenant said. "They were completely surprised—didn't see me until I was almost on top of them."

Near the end of the run Lt. Lanker scaled a cliff, with his left wingtip six feet from its top. A rifleman on top of the cliff fired at him but his shots went wild.

The magnificent pictures which the pilot brought back showed beach defenses in great detail, and workmen ducking to escape the plane which must have seemed aimed straight for their heads.[13]

CHAPTER FORTY-TWO

Big Changes (August–October 1943)

Despite heavy losses to the bombers, VIII Fighter Command's General Hunter refused to put all of his fighters into the escort mission. His Thunderbolts could only escort up to the town of Eupen, Belgium, east of Liège and 15 miles or so from the German border. In any case, the key targets of the German aircraft industry were beyond the reach of the P-47. Hunter still believed in fighter sweeps, somehow hoping the Germans could be provoked into a major air battle that the rugged Thunderbolts would win. He was often wrong but never in doubt.[1]

Meanwhile, the Germans continued to pull fighters in from all battlefronts to reinforce their day air superiority over Germany. *Luftflotte 3* husbanded its aircraft wisely. In 10,000 sorties, VIII Fighter Command had downed only eighty German planes. So it seemed a leadership change was overdue.[2]

By the end of August 1943, General Arnold had had enough. Hunter was promoted out of England into a training command. Replacing him was Major General William Kepner, an outstanding tactician who would use all the technology that Arnold was sending his way.[3] Kepner had worked on the long-range escort program ordered by Arnold in June 1943. Kepner knew that he would be expected to provide better fighter protection to the heavy bombers of the Eighth Air Force.

Arnold also seemed to have mixed feelings about Eaker's performance. Surely he realized that Eaker had received only some 75 percent of the bomber strength envisioned in the POINTBLANK Directive, but Arnold continued to chide Eaker over the fact his raids used only about half of his available strength. The rapid buildup of the Eighth Air Force was partially to blame—huge numbers of aircraft and men were being sent to England—but their arrival there did not make them combat-ready.

There were in-theater modifications that needed to be made to the aircraft. Additional training was necessary for the combat crews and the various maintenance and other specialists that supported them. Each mission into Germany overloaded repair facilities with damaged P-47s, Fortresses, and Liberators. The loss of so many combat crews, support personnel, and aircraft to TORCH the previous year had also taken its toll.[4]

In September 1943, shortly after replacing Hunter, Arnold laid all his cards on the table in a letter to his friend Eaker. The words "or else" were not written, but they were certainly implied.

> *Of grave concern to me is the employment of your fighters. I cannot comprehend what value is derived from the frequently reported so-called offensive fighter sweeps in which the enemy is rarely sighted. Except as a means of consuming gasoline I can see no purpose in this practice. . . . I feel that a vigorous escort can successfully be accomplished if the fighters are less cautious. Higher fighter combat losses than those now reported may result from this policy but will be more than offset by reduced bomber losses. . . . [G]ive this subject your personal attention.*[5]

Of course, emphasis on the fighter sweep originated with the RAF. Hunter adopted the tactic and continued to use it even after the British stopped. The appointment of Kepner to lead VIII Fighter Command was an attempt to rectify that failed policy. Bill Kepner was uninterested in anything except killing German fighters; unproductive fighter sweeps were not his style. He had been a marine and then served on the Western Front as an infantryman in World War I. After the Great War he had become an accomplished balloonist, flying *Explorer I* to over 60,000 feet in 1934. He had attended Tactical School but avoided becoming embroiled in doctrine issues.

After the publication of "Digest of Operation OVERLORD," it was obvious that OVERLORD would be another Dieppe unless something was done about German air superiority. Kepner knew his fighters had to go to where the German fighters were—that's why he had been picked for the job. After working in Washington on the escort fighter issue, Bill Kepner knew that range enhancements were on the way; now he would be in a position to use them wisely.[6]

Kepner immediately began making changes to Hunter's program. Previous orders from Eaker had demanded the P-47s stay close to the bombers. The slow acceleration of the P-47 meant it was unable to effectively respond to enemy fighters closing at high speed.[7] This in turn meant German fighters could "blow through" escort squadrons before the Jugs could effectively react. When Kepner complained to Eaker about close escort and the resulting low scores against German fighters, Eaker told him that his primary mission was to stay with and protect the bombers. The downing of German fighters was secondary.[8]

Kepner's persistence and Arnold's stinging missive began to affect Eaker's policies. In October, Eaker allowed Kepner to open the range of his fighters from the bombers to 250 yards. This would allow for weaving, to permit the Thunderbolts to fly faster while remaining with the bombers. Although the P-47s now had the speed they needed, weaving was wasteful of fuel. Although technical improvements to the Jugs and orders to keep drop tanks until engaged by the enemy should have provided more combat radius, instead, the fuel was consumed while staying in sight of the bombers.

Kepner soon proposed a more liberal escort policy. Some pilots used this change to hunt German fighters away from the immediate area of the bombers. Eaker told Kepner that "leaving the vicinity of the bomber formations to engage in such hostilities should be avoided by individual pilots." So Kepner reluctantly told his fighters to remain close to the bombers. This robbed them of the initiative; they remained just an extension of the bombers' defensive guns.[9] It was impossible to extend the combat radius of the P-47 beyond Eupen, Belgium, near the German border, until this policy too was changed.

Even the Germans noted that the close escort and weaving policies kept the American fighters on the defensive. Göring ordered his interceptors to ignore the escort altogether and go straight for the bombers.[10]

Figure 42.1. P-47 relay escort contrails above a Fortress combat box. While weaving helped to maintain station on bomber formations, it also wasted gas—and lives.
AIR FORCE HISTORICAL RESEARCH AGENCY

BRERETON

In October 1943, the Headquarters of Ninth Air Force under Major General Lewis Brereton were transferred from North Africa to England. Once there, it absorbed some units from Major General Eaker's Eighth Air Force. Ninth Air Force was now a tactical air force, like the previously established 2TAF, dedicated to supporting land operations.

Eighth Air Force gave up all its light and medium bombers and troop carrier aircraft, as well as some fighters, to the Ninth. Ninth's combat commands included the IX Bomber Command (light and medium bombers), the IX Fighter Command (fighters and tactical reconnaissance), and the IX Troop Carrier Command. The transfers would allow Eaker and Brereton to each concentrate on his part of the air war. Eaker was the senior and coordinated the activity of both.

Eighth Air Force became a "pure" strategic air force. Its combat commands included the VIII Bomber Command (heavy bombers) and the VIII Fighter Command (escort fighters and strategic reconnaissance). Ninth began flying diversionary light and medium bomber attacks and provided additional escort fighters for Eighth Air Force missions. These would continue until April 1944. German airfields in France and the Low Countries soon became a favorite target of Brereton's men.

CHAPTER FORTY-THREE

The Fork-Tailed Devil
(October 1943–May 1944)

The P-38 in VIII Fighter Command was reincarnated with the arrival of the 55th Fighter Group from McChord Field, Washington. The 55th was not declared operational until October 15, 1943, the day after Black Thursday. Soon, a second P-38 Lightning group, the 20th, joined the 55th in England. They flew new P-38H models, able to escort bombers over 520 miles using two 75-gallon drop tanks, and out to 575 miles with the Lockheed 150-gallon tanks.

The American P-47 also now received higher-capacity drop tanks to extend its radius out to 425 miles. With more American escort fighters on hand, the RAF Mustang I/II[1] and Typhoon were increasingly tasked to train and operate with the RAF Air-Cooperation Command. These could fight deep into France, far beyond the future invasion area, and well before OVERLORD began.

The return of the Lightning to English skies promised a resolution to the long-range fighter escort issue for American daylight bombing. By the fall of 1943, hundreds of these planes had been successfully employed in the Pacific and Mediterranean.[2] In the Pacific, the P-38 was credited with shooting down more Japanese aircraft than any other fighter.[3] In North Africa, the legend of the fast and maneuverable P-38 grew among German air force pilots. It was soon nicknamed the *Der Gabelschwanz Teufel* ("the fork-tailed devil"). Some sources believe that this nickname was invented by the American propaganda machine, but in any case, the Germans had good cause to respect the Lightning. A German *experten* (ace) wrote:

> *Over Tunisia, my flight encountered four P-38s and we slipped behind them, virtually unnoticed. Although our Gustavs [Bf 109Gs] gave all they could, the distance between us and the Lightnings hardly diminished. At a distance of about 500 meters, I fired all my guns, but my shells exploded behind one of the P-38s. After several more ineffective bursts, the US pilots obviously*

sensed danger. Applying full war-emergency power, they disappeared, leaving us with our mouths wide open. The five-minute chase caused my engine to seize. One of the connecting rods pushed itself right through the cowling.[4]

When the 55th went operational, its P-38s found immediate employment as escorts. The arrival of the Lightning unit could not have been more timely. The Germans were employing increasing numbers of rocket-firing fighters and *Zerstörer* as well as more conventionally equipped fighter aircraft over Germany, beyond the range of the escort P-47. While the 21cm rockets allowed the *Luftwaffe* to attack from outside the range of the defensive .50 caliber guns on the bombers, they also cut into the air-to-air performance of the German planes.

On the November 3 Wilhelmshaven mission, the superior endurance now possessed by the Lightning proved especially valuable during the farthest leg of the journey and made the escort virtually continuous throughout the bomber route. In the Lightnings' encounter with German interceptors, they claimed three enemy aircraft without losing a single P-38.

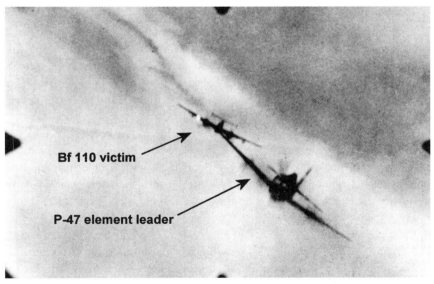

Figure 43.1. Last seconds of a Bf 110 *Zerstörer*. Airspace over Germany was no longer a sanctuary from American escort fighters. NINTH AIR FORCE GUN CAMERA FILM, COURTESY OF JOHN DRUMMOND

Unfortunately, General Eaker's order that escort fighters remain close to the bombers meant that the P-38s could not as effectively destroy German aircraft. Eaker had experienced the extensive bomber losses of the Schweinfurt–Regensburg raid and the subsequent Black Thursday mission. He believed that he finally had an effective way to preserve his bombers over Germany. The Lightnings could probably have destroyed more enemy aircraft, but they remained in close support of the bombers. They warded off attacks and refused to be drawn off in independent combat.[5]

There were four problems associated with the P-38 in England that detracted from its capability as an air-to-air fighter: size and configuration; engine reliability; cockpit heat; and compressibility.

The P-38 was a big aircraft, a third again as big as a Bf 109 or FW 190. Combined with its unusual twin-boom configuration, it was simply easier to see and identify than its opponents. The configuration, with the pilot situated between two engine nacelles, also limited the view below the aircraft. This was ironic in that the P-38 was the first American fighter originally designed with a "bubble" canopy, allowing excellent visibility behind and above the aircraft.

Engine reliability was a factor of special interest for the P-38 force based in England. One author cited poor technical support from the engine manufacturer (Allison), faulty spark plugs from Champion, and the poor quality of high-octane fuel as possible causes for these problems. Due to the design of the nacelles, engine maintenance was also difficult.[6] On average, an engine would fail after seven hours of operation.[7] Perhaps half the P-38s lost in the high-altitude long-range role were lost to engine problems, not enemy action.[8] For whatever reason, the P-38s in the Mediterranean never experienced the engine problems associated with the same aircraft based in England.[9]

Cockpit heating was a special problem for Eighth Air Force P-38 pilots in Northern Europe, who endured high-altitude subzero temperatures for many hours on each mission. Unlike the P-47 and P-51 with simple fuselages, the P-38 cockpit structure was completely separate from the engines. The passive heat from the engines did not warm the cockpit. There was a cockpit heater, but it did not work well. This was more than a comfort issue when the temperature in the cockpit could reach 50 degrees *below* zero.[10] Not only were pilots numbed and frostbitten, but ice would also sometimes form on the inside of cockpits.

Compressibility is a loss of flight control in high-speed dives. The Lightning's high-altitude bomber escort mission also exacerbated this. A long dive in a P-38 under combat power could result in loss of control and subsequently the airplane. The P-47 and P-51 also had problems with this effect, but somehow it became firmly associated with the P-38 fleet. Soon this was common knowledge among both the Lightning pilots and their German counterparts, so that a common *Luftwaffe* escape maneuver while fighting the P-38 was a dive for the deck. The American pilots normally would not follow.

By early 1944, the problem was overcome after extensive flight-testing by Lockheed. The solution was the development of dive flaps, which when opened would slow the aircraft's exceptional dive speed and thus defeat the problem. The fix was delayed when the first P-38 fitted with the new dive brakes was lost in a developmental accident. After testing was complete, it was decided that new-production aircraft would receive the modification and field kits would be manufactured for the existing fleet.

These were assembled at the plant and readied for shipment to Europe where P-38s were to be modified at once, enhancing tremendously their capabilities against German fighters. A total of 425 sets of the flaps and modification kits were loaded aboard a Douglas C-54 four-engine transport for a high-priority flight to England.

Unfortunately the Kondor, the P-38's first European victim, would again play a role in the P-38's combat career. A patrolling RAF Spitfire misidentified the C-54 carrying the entire production run of kits as an FW 200 approaching the United Kingdom. The hapless crew and its priceless cargo went to the bottom of the Atlantic, and the older P-38s in England went without their dive flaps until after D-Day.

All of these problems detracted from the high-altitude long-range escort capability of the P-38. During a four-month period in early 1944, almost 2,000 engine changes were performed on the Lightnings in England. This meant, in effect, that every P-38 in the Eighth Air Force had at least one complete set of engines changed out.

Eventually these problems led to the Lightnings being transferred into the Ninth Air Force in England and the Fifteenth in Italy, where they served with great effectiveness in the ground-attack and low-altitude air superiority role. After all is said and done, Eighth Air Force Lightnings destroyed 1.5 German fighters in combat for every P-38 lost *from all causes*. Possibly, the ratio would have been much more favorable if the high-altitude problems had not occurred.[11]

CHAPTER FORTY-FOUR

Mustang: The Long Reach
(May 1942–May 1944)

*The Mustang could do everything the Spitfire could do in eight minutes, but
it could do it for eight hours.*
—ATTRIBUTED TO GENERAL CHUCK YEAGER

When the VIII Fighter Command Lightnings became operational, a third
major American escort fighter was being delivered to bases in England. It was
the P-51B Mustang, a small, powerful fighter that would soon dominate the
skies of Western Europe. The British had originally contracted North American
Aviation for the aircraft, requesting a design that was optimized for medium- to
low-altitude combat. The airplane was to be powered by an Allison engine, the
same type that equipped the P-40 and P-38. The Allison was a good engine at
medium to low altitudes, and the RAF Mustang I was soon a success.

The British accepted their first Mustang I aircraft at the end of 1941, and
the RAF quickly put it to work. Although many were assigned to tactical reconnaissance squadrons, they were often employed as long-range, low-altitude interceptors and ground-attack aircraft. RAF No. 2 Squadron at Sawbridgeworth was
the first Mustang I operational unit.

On May 10, 1942, the first mission was flown over occupied France when
No. 2 Squadron raided a German airfield just across the Channel. On July 27,
1942, No. 2 Squadron Mustangs did something that no other fighter aircraft
could then do: They took off from Sawbridgeworth and flew straight into Germany to raid targets in the Ruhr area, a distance of more than 250 miles.[1]

It was the first time any Allied fighter aircraft had crossed the German
border. The VIII Fighter Command ignored their capability, perhaps because
their Allison engines would not allow them to operate at high altitude with
the heavy bombers. During the disastrous raid on Dieppe on August 19, 1942,

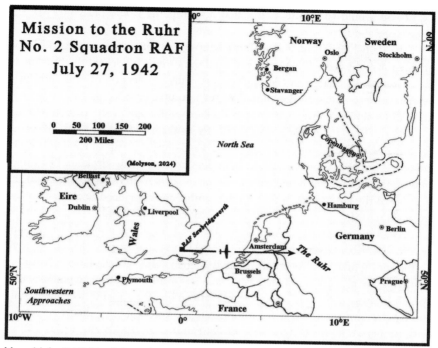

Map 44.1. RAF No. 2 Squadron's Mustang I Mission to the Ruhr, July 27, 1942. It would be almost eighteen months before the combat debut of the USAAF P-51B escort fighter. MOLYSON

the Mustang I drew its first blood. RAF pilot officer Hollis Hills, of Pasadena, California, shot down an FW 190 for the first Mustang "kill." On this same date, the first Mustang was lost.[2]

General Hap Arnold was briefed on the Mustang during his visit to England in the spring of 1942. Arnold and the rest of the USAAF were tired of the continuous British disparaging of US equipment, combined with their enthusiastic opinion of their own. The fact that the little fighter had started as a British project had an unfortunate impact on his opinion, even though both the airframe (North American Aviation) and powerplant (Allison) were being built in America.

The Mustang I eventually entered the USAAF inventory in small numbers as the A-36 Apache. Like the British aircraft, it was intended to be a low-altitude ground-attack plane. Arnold, a champion of the All-American P-38

Lightning, would later sadly admit that his antipathy would delay entry of the long-range P-51.[3]

The British experimented with the Mustang, adding a supercharged Merlin engine for flight tests. The Merlin powered the various models of the Spitfire; in fact, each model change of the Spitfire was really a reflection of more powerful versions of its engines. In the United States, manufacturer North American Aviation did a similar conversion using a Packard-built copy of the British Merlin.

World War I American ace Eddie Rickenbacker flew an RAF Mustang equipped with the Merlin engine in early 1943, during a trip to England. Rickenbacker was convinced the Eighth Air Force needed this airplane. His infectious enthusiasm—combined with favorable reports from other sources, and the support of the air attaché in the London embassy—convinced Secretary of War Stimson to order production of the US version by April 1943.

Assistant Secretary of War for Air Robert Lovett was also a Mustang supporter, and helped overcome internal USAAF bias against the "British" fighter.[4] In the spring of 1943, Lovett also visited England and saw the British Mustang firsthand. He also got the same positive reports from the American embassy that had so impressed Rickenbacker. On his return, he sent a memo to Hap Arnold noting the immediate need for a long-range escort fighter. "This may be met with proper tanks for P-47s," he said, "but ultimately P-38s and P-51s will be needed."[5]

Arnold, the P-38 proponent, thought further development of the Lightning would lead to the range and performance required for long-range escort. Still, Lovett was his boss and he was willing to admit that the Mustang rather than the Lightning might be the answer to the escort problem. Lovett's memo, and Eaker's demands for escort fighters and more bombers to strike deep into Germany, spurred him to action in June 1943. He ordered Major General Giles, his hardworking deputy, to perform an objective review of the aircraft. He sent Giles clear guidance on the matter:

This [Lovett's memo on the P-51] brings to mind very clearly the absolute necessity for building a fighter airplane that can go in and come out with the bombers. Moreover, this fighter has got to go into Germany. Perhaps we can modify some existing type to do the job. . . . About six months remain before the deep penetration of Germany begins. Within the next six months, you have got to get a fighter that can protect our bombers. . . . Get to work on this right away because by January '44, 1 want fighter escort for all our bombers from [the] U.K. into Germany.[6]

The Mustang had long range and sparkling performance. It was as good at high altitude as on the deck. The key to the Mustang's range was the revolutionary wing design developed at North American. The 12-cylinder Packard-Merlin displaced 1,649 cubic inches, ten times the size of a racing-car engine. The Mustang carried 269 gallons of internal fuel, plus two 108-gallon drop tanks, for a total of 485 gallons. The Merlin gave about 4.4 miles per gallon, enough that the Mustang could easily fly and fight over Berlin.

Figure 44.1. P-51 Mustang fighters with 75-gallon drop tanks and D-Day identification stripes. The three closest aircraft are P-51Ds with bubble canopies; the aircraft at bottom is an earlier-model P-51B with conventional canopy. US ARMY AIR FORCES VIA WIKIMEDIA COMMONS[7]

Combined with drop tanks, the aircraft had longer range than a combat-loaded B-17.[8] It was easier to build than either the P-38 or P-47. Triple-ace Bud Anderson said of the P-51, "The Mustang could do everything the Spitfire could do—and better yet, could do it over Berlin, where you never saw Spitfires."[9] It dominated all other fighters, friend and foe, in the theater when it arrived.

The Merlin-powered P-51B/C began arriving in Europe in September 1943, just weeks after the disastrous Schweinfurt–Regensburg raid of August 17. The B and C models were almost identical, but built in separate cities, the B in Los Angeles and the C in Dallas. As they left the depots, they were issued to the new 354th Fighter Group at Boxted in October and November. They were not operational until December. The 354th was a Ninth Air Force unit, but as senior American airman in Britain, Eaker could "borrow" Ninth Air Force aircraft. The Mustangs were added to the fledgling Eighth Air Force long-range escort force.

Like the P-47s, the first new Mustangs were painted dark green and received the white tail and nose QID bands to aid in recognition by bomber gunners. The Jug looked a little like an FW 190 and the Mustang looked a lot like a Bf 109G. Entering combat in the ETO for the first time on December 11, 1943, Mustangs escorted a bomber force to Emden, Germany. Missions followed this to Kiel and Bremen.

With even longer range than their predecessors, the new escorts surprised German twin-engine *Zerstörer*. No longer could these aircraft attack American bombers outside the range of American escort fighters.[10] It was the first stage of failure for specialized German daylight bomber killers. General Kepner said, "They are distinctly the best fighter that we are going to get over here. They are going to be the only satisfactory answer."[11]

The Mustang had arrived.

CHAPTER FORTY-FIVE

Fighter Pilots

There was a map half the size of Rhode Island, and the colonel would pull back the curtain and voila—*the target is Berlin, Hanover, or, in this case, Leipzig. Some would groan when the target looked tough, and some would grin. The guys who grinned were the ones that I wanted with me.*[1]

—P-51 PILOT "BUD" ANDERSON

Of course, all the escort fighters in the world would have been no help to the Eighth Air Force if VIII Fighter Command did not have some of the best fighter pilots in the world. Fighter pilots in the USAAF, RAF, and *Luftwaffe* shared many traits. They were all generally young. Proficiency came from natural talent, learned skills, and flying time—lots of flying time. The showdown over daytime Germany was between American and German fighter pilots.

Line pilots didn't always know what the "Big Picture" was in that place and time. They did develop their own philosophy about combat and they kept it simple. The "team" was not your crew; it was the other pilots in your squadron and your crew chief, who helped keep you alive. An aggressive spirit was an essential part of the fighter pilot mentality. General Chuck Yeager remembered training as a young fighter pilot at Tonopah, Nevada:

Death was our new trade. . . . I had no idea why the German people were stuck with Hitler and the Nazis and could care less. History was not one of my strong subjects. But when the time came, I would hammer those Germans any chance I got. Them or me. Even a "D" history student from Hamlin High knew that it was always better to be the hammer than the nail.[2]

Most fighter pilots were lost during their first ten combat missions. Most of those lost were stragglers, those out of position and vulnerable "tail-end Charlies." Some left their formations to attack German aircraft who were acting as decoys.[3] Most never saw the airplane that shot them down. It was no picnic even for those who made their first ten. On each mission, the end of the day could mean landing in twilight, half-frozen and exhausted from high-altitude flight. Battle damage and weather often complicated returning to base.

From 1939, German pilot training centers had been allocated only a fraction of their fuel requirements.[4] By 1943, German instructor pilots based in Germany were formed into emergency air defense units in addition to their teaching duties. Like fuel shortages, this detracted from the training regimen and the flying hours available to fledgling flyers. German flight training graduates had many less flying hours than their American and British counterparts.

The Americans never experienced these problems. Fuel and serviceable aircraft were abundant. Stateside training bases were far from any fighting front. Chuck Yeager remembered logging 100 hours of flying time his first month of fighter training in 1943. Guys who could not keep up the pace either died or were transferred to less demanding duty.[5]

On average, American pilots arrived in Europe with 450 hours of flying time. New German pilots had only 150 hours. They were normally first sent into

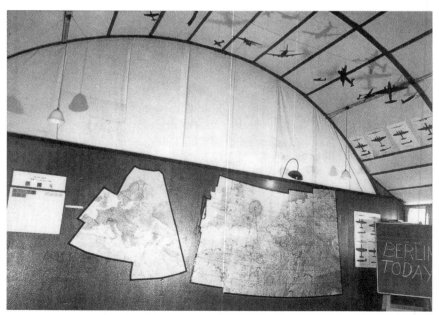

Figure 45.1. Typical fighter ops room: prefabricated Nissen hut, maps, recognition models. AIR FORCE HISTORICAL RESEARCH AGENCY

action on the Eastern Front, which was considered safer than defending the West. Once veterans, these *Alte Hasen* ("old hares") were committed to the Air Battle of Germany. Even with this precaution, more than 5 percent were shot down before their tenth operational flight.[6]

As the weather deteriorated in the late fall of 1943, the differences between increasing numbers of American and the declining numbers of German pilots became clear. With fuel shortages, the superb training program provided to prewar German pilots was no longer maintained. Instrument proficiency was probably the weakest part of American flight training, but it was still far superior to *Luftwaffe* training. German single-engine fighter pilots received little such training.[7] Germany would lose over 60,000 fighter aircraft during the war years, 10,000 of these in non-combat operational accidents often attributed to weather.[8]

Replacing General Hunter in May 1943, Kepner wanted his fighters roaming all over Occupied Europe to clear the way for Eaker's bombers. He therefore worked to get his fighter pilots better instrument training so that they could take off in any weather in which the bombers were capable of flying. With plenty

Figure 45.2. Pilot bails out of his crippled Bf 109 and lives to fight another day.
NINTH AIR FORCE GUN CAMERA FILM, COURTESY OF JOHN DRUMMOND

of fuel, Kepner instituted bad-weather flying training and practice missions to build on the introductory instrument training his pilots had received stateside.

Conversely, the Germans were already feeling the pilot pinch, and little additional training for flying in the weather was conducted. Compounding this problem was the fact that the Americans approached Germany from England or Italy above the weather at high altitude. The intercepting German aircraft had to ascend through the weather, exposing their aircraft to icing and other problems.[9]

Although the German air force had about 70,000 officers and 400 generals in the autumn of 1943, only about 800 were assigned to commander or instructor positions. Shortage of suitable aircraft was not a problem, but losses of experienced commanders and instructors and a dwindling fuel supply strangled German production of proficient new pilots. This would directly contribute to the COSSAC goal of attaining air superiority over the landing area and beyond in France.

CHAPTER FORTY-SIX

Transition (October–December 1943)

The day I saw American fighters over Berlin I knew the jig was up.
—GÖRING TO POSTWAR INTERROGATOR[1]

While Kepner and Eaker attempted to turn around the disastrous loss rates of the Eighth Air Force over Germany, Arnold pressed Air Marshal Portal (RAF chief of air staff) to help with the day offensive. Arnold stated that if the RAF had attacked German airfields on August 17, the Schweinfurt massacre might not have occurred. Arnold proposed postponing delivery of Mustang IIIs to the RAF so that they could be completed as Army Air Force P-51s instead.

While Portal failed to give Arnold all he wanted, he did order increased RAF attacks on German airfields in support of the daylight bombing. He also offered Arnold the use of four squadrons of Mustangs until after D-Day.[2] In response, on October 30, 1943, Arnold ordered all new-production P-51 Mustangs and P-38 Lightnings be sent to the ETO.[3]

Shortly thereafter, Eaker again disappointed Arnold. He agreed with the Ninth Air Force commander, Major General Lewis Brereton, that the incoming P-51Bs would go to the Ninth for tactical support duty. Arnold was incensed; the man who most needed its long-range capability was giving the best escort fighter in the world away for short-range duty. Only after General Kepner intervened did Eaker partially reverse his decision to give up the Mustangs. Eaker sent out a clarification in December identifying the primary tactical role of all fighters in Britain as long-range escort in support of daylight bombing. Unfortunately, it was too late; his days as commanding general of the Eighth Air Force were over.[4]

The tension between friends Arnold and Eaker had come to a head. It was not only the giving up of P-51s to the Ninth Air Force. Arnold knew the Eighth Air Force had never received all the forces it was promised in the POINT-BLANK Directive, yet he expected Eaker to achieve all the things promised by him under that plan. Although Eaker had in fact begun the POINTBLANK campaign at great cost, Arnold believed that Eaker's sympathies were too much with his fliers and the support staff, which kept him from optimizing the forces under his command.

Arnold had earlier replaced General Hunter with Kepner at VIII Fighter Command over Eaker's objections. When Eaker told Arnold he played down the destruction of enemy fighters because it was a secondary job, Arnold knew that he would never make his friend a true escort fighter advocate. There was still too much of the Tactical School mentality, even though Eaker identified himself as a fighter pilot.[5]

On November 1, Arnold split the Twelfth Air Force in North Africa into two parts. A new Fifteenth Air Force was established, with Lieutenant General Jimmy Doolittle as its commander. The Fifteenth, like the Eighth, would be for strategic bombing with heavy bombers and long-range escort fighters. The remainder of the Twelfth AF would be like the Ninth in England, a tactical air force in support of ground operations in Italy.

The Fifteenth Air Force began operations with six heavy bomber groups and four fighter groups flying from Tunisia. Its bomber units were within range of POINTBLANK targets in northern Italy, Austria, and southern Germany. It would grow larger with the addition of other bomber and fighter units, but would always be smaller than the Eighth Air Force based in England.

On November 2, 1943, the Fifteenth Air Force entered the POINT-BLANK effort by raiding the rebuilt Messerschmitt factory at Wiener Neustadt, bombed the previous August. It was estimated that this raid cost the Germans at least one month's production of some 250 planes. A week later, ball-bearing works at Villar Perosa, near Turin, Italy, were struck.[6] POINTBLANK had expanded and the *Luftwaffe* was forced to move more fighters south. German general Adolf Galland believed that the establishment of the Fifteenth Air Force was as important to the success of the American effort as the deployment of long-range escorts in England.[7]

On November 26, 1943, the GAF was up in force as 508 American heavy bombers pounded shipyards and U-boat pens in Bremen. The escorts took a heavy toll of the intercepting Germans, and the heavy bomber losses were in the acceptable range. Hard fighting continued into December, when an eighth P-47 group, the 359th, was established. The range of the P-47 had now been extended out to 420 miles. Three long-range P-38 and P-51B escort groups were now operational. The Germans continued to withdraw fighter strength back into Germany, making it harder for the short-range RAF Spitfires to find air targets over northern France and Holland.

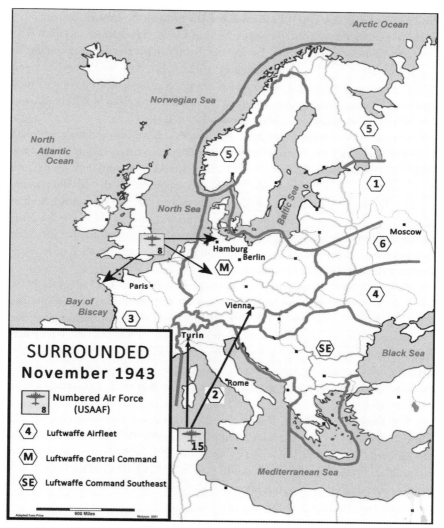

Map 46.1. USAAF numbered air forces with heavy bombers, November 1943.
PRICE[8]

Legend (in map):

**SURROUNDED
November 1943**

- 8 — Numbered Air Force (USAAF)
- 4 — Luftwaffe Airfleet
- M — Luftwaffe Central Command
- SE — Luftwaffe Command Southeast

600 Miles

Adapted from Price   Molyson 2001

SEXTANT-EUREKA (NOVEMBER 23–DECEMBER 6, 1943)

Sextant-Eureka was a split conference held in Cairo, Egypt (Sextant) and Tehran, Iran (Eureka). The United States and Britain used the Sextant session in Cairo to prepare for the Tehran meeting with Stalin. Afterward they returned to Cairo to execute the plans worked out with the Soviets. It was confirmed again at the first Sextant meeting at Cairo that an American would command OVERLORD as supreme Allied commander (SAC).

The assumed candidate for SAC was General Marshall, the man who had built the American citizen army that would face its greatest test at Normandy. Eisenhower knew that his assignment in Italy would be terminated; for balance there must be a British supreme commander appointed in the Mediterranean Theater. Ike had been told he might be returned to Washington as army chief of staff. This was no mean job for an officer who was only a colonel on the army permanent list, although he now enjoyed temporary four-star rank. Ike intended to request assignment as an army group commander under Marshall once Marshall got the OVERLORD command.

At Eureka in Tehran, the proposed date for OVERLORD (May 1, 1944) was revealed to Stalin. Stalin accepted it as a solemn commitment, then pressed for a supreme commander of OVERLORD to be named. Churchill promised to announce one within a few days. Eureka reaffirmed that the Western Allies would respect the Russian viewpoint and requirements as much as possible. OVERLORD would give the Soviets the second ground front against Germany that they had been demanding for two years. [9] The British and Americans then returned to Egypt.

On December 5, 1943, Roosevelt called General Marshall to his villa at Cairo to talk about the supreme Allied commander (SAC) for the invasion of northern France. With Marshall's approval, Roosevelt finally decided that Eisenhower rather than Marshall would command OVERLORD. Marshall was simply too valuable to be spared from Washington, and Ike was the only other man with the credentials to get the job done.

Ike moved to England, bringing his own chief of staff, Lieutenant General Walter Bedell Smith. General Morgan, the former COSSAC, went to work for Smith as deputy chief of staff rather than serving directly under Eisenhower. Ike soon adopted Morgan's basic OVERLORD plan as his own. Less than a month later, Hitler selected *Generalfeldmarschall* Rommel to command the *Atlantik Wall*. [10]

While at the Sextant conference, Arnold pressed for new leadership over the POINTBLANK effort. General Eaker's significant service in the face of fierce enemy action and significant logistical and operational problems was appreciated. Eaker had served over a year in the toughest job in Europe, watching so many of his young aircrew disappear into prisoner-of-war camps, smoking holes, and early graves. Arnold, however, thought it was time for a change.

After Eisenhower was selected as Supreme Allied Commander, General Arnold proposed moving General Spaatz to a new command, United States Strategic Air Forces (USSTAF), which would oversee the activity of both the Eighth and Fifteenth Air Forces. Eaker would move to the Mediterranean as the senior Allied airman in the MTO, while General Doolittle would move from Fifteenth Air Force to command the Eighth. Although Eaker initially resisted the move, it was a promotion and he had earned it. USSTAF was activated at Bushy Park, England, in February.

The USAAF reorganization pleased Eisenhower. Ike would take his three senior airmen from the Mediterranean with him to his new job in England. He had worked with Spaatz and Doolittle in the Mediterranean Theater; he knew and trusted both men. General Eaker would replace RAF Air Vice Marshal Tedder, who was moving to England to become Ike's deputy for OVERLORD.

In December, Kepner, with a new boss on the way, replaced the close escort procedures with a system of relay escort. Instead of joining a particular unit and accompanying it, the fighters would rendezvous with the bomber stream along its route. This allowed encounters with German fighters also headed for the bombers. The first relay escort mission was conducted against a German missile launching site on Christmas Eve, 1943. It was so successful that it replaced close escort altogether within a week, but the fighters were still tied too closely to the bombers once they reached their rendezvous.

On December 30, the biggest daylight raid to date was conducted by Eighth Air Force against Ludwigshafen. P-47s escorted the bombers as far as eastern France, and the three P-38 and new P-51B groups escorted the bombers the rest of the distance into Germany. A total of 658 B-17s and B-24s made the trip, with 28 lost. The loss rate was an almost acceptable 4.2 percent, down from the 26 percent losses suffered by the unescorted Black Thursday raid just two months before.

THE NEW YEAR'S MESSAGE

OVERLORD, the northwestern France invasion, was scheduled for May 1944. ANVIL, a follow-on landing destined for the south of France, was scheduled soon after. It was time to seize permanent day air superiority over France and Germany. With a new POINTBLANK leadership team in place and long-range fighter escorts finally available in England, Arnold delivered his New Year's instructions to the new commanders of the Eighth and the Fifteenth Air Forces unambiguous:

a. Aircraft factories in this country are turning out large quantities of airplanes, engines and accessories.

b. Our training establishments are operating twenty-four hours per day, seven days per week, training crews.

c. We are now furnishing fully all the aircraft and crews to take care of your attrition.

d. It is a conceded fact that OVERLORD and ANVIL will not be possible unless the German Air Force is destroyed.

e. Therefore, my personal message to you—this is a *MUST*—is to, *Destroy the Enemy Air Force wherever you find them, in the air, on the ground and in the factories*[11] (italics added).

CHAPTER FORTY-SEVEN

Casualties (January–June 1944)

At the first meeting of the OVERLORD commanders in January, AOC-in-C Air Vice Marshal Leigh-Mallory optimistically announced that POINT-BLANK had reduced monthly fighter output from 1,500 to 600. What he did not say, or perhaps did not understand, was that remaining German fighter production was more than adequate to offset aircraft losses. Speer's aircraft production dispersal scheme would continue to provide the *Luftwaffe* with all the airplanes it needed, and more.

Invisible to Leigh-Mallory was the real effect of the assault: *Luftwaffe* fighter pilot casualties. On this day in January 1944, there were about 2,300 active fighter pilots in the German air force. By D-Day, half of them would be dead. The Allies dominated the skies over France and were making inroads into the Reich's airspace. Massive British nighttime attacks made the German situation bleak.[1] German fighter pilots had families at home, too. The Germans, however, were not yet defeated.

On the January 11 mission to an aircraft production complex at Oscher-sleben, weather caused most of the escorts to miss rendezvous with the bomber stream. By this time, some 340 *Zerstörer* had been assembled in Germany, their numbers peaking about the same time as the long-range escort fighter strength began to grow in Eighth Air Force. The massed *Zerstörer* and single-engine German fighters attacked the formation of 650 bombers. The very small number of available escort fighters put up a valiant defense, one P-51 pilot winning a Medal of Honor. But it was not enough; rockets broke up formations and individual bombers were shot down by gun attacks. Forty-one bombers were lost and many more damaged beyond repair. The math was simple: Well-escorted raids suffered dramatically less losses than poorly escorted ones.[2]

Spaatz, now the USSTAF commander and senior American airman in Europe, called a meeting on January 24 to coordinate operations between his Eighth and Fifteenth Air Forces and the Ninth Air Force. Spaatz was responsible for integrating Ninth Air Force into POINTBLANK until its forces were needed for the invasion. Spaatz wanted all of his fighters assigned to the most appropriate numbered air force and mission.

The first order of business was to fix the P-51 problem. Spaatz, with Kepner's support, overturned the Eaker–Brereton agreement concerning the P-51 assignments to Ninth Air Force. The Mustangs would now be sent to Eighth Air Force fighter units as they arrived in England. The displaced P-47s from those units, in any case a more capable tactical support fighter than the Mustang, would be transferred to Ninth Air Force. The P-38s would go to the Ninth or the Fifteenth Air Force.[3]

The new commander at Eighth Air Force, Major General Doolittle, inherited the superb organization that Eaker and Kepner had built when it was just reaching its full potential. Escort fighters were now available to take the bombers all the way to any target in Germany. Doolittle would soon order changes in fighter tactics that would make these aircraft even more potent. Eaker had built the team that Doolittle used to win the game.[4]

Doolittle could relate to the men flying the long bomber missions into Germany. On his way from England to Gibraltar just before Operation TORCH, Ju 88C *Zerstörer* had attacked his lone B-17 over the Bay of Biscay. The aircraft had an engine shot out and the pilot was wounded. It was Doolittle's introduction to the *Luftwaffe* day fighter force.[5] Now it was Doolittle's job to cripple it for OVERLORD.

Figure 47.1. "Destroy the Luftwaffe wherever it is found." US ARMY

Doolittle visited Kepner's headquarters to discuss Eaker's restrictive escort rules imposed on VIII Fighter Command. Doolittle knew fighters were offensive weapons and that fighter pilots were trained to be aggressive. They were hunters, not shepherds. They couldn't protect the bombers by remaining too close to them, unable to intercept the equally aggressive German fighter pilots. Doolittle, the man who had led the April 1942 raid on Tokyo, knew a lot about applied aggression.

In Kepner's office, Doolittle noted the Eaker-era sign on the wall. It said:

THE FIRST DUTY OF THE EIGHTH AIR FORCE FIGHTERS IS TO BRING THE BOMBERS BACK ALIVE.

Doolittle ordered Kepner to take down that sign and replace it with a new one:

THE FIRST DUTY OF THE EIGHTH AIR FORCE FIGHTERS IS TO DESTROY GERMAN FIGHTERS.

"You mean you're authorizing me to take the offensive?" Kepner asked.

"I'm directing you to," Doolittle replied.[6]

Kepner was "overjoyed" at Doolittle's new doctrine. Although some fighters would still be assigned escort, most would be free to find the German air force wherever it might be. Doolittle told Kepner, "Flush them out in the air and beat them up on the ground on the way home. Your first priority is to take the offensive."

Doolittle also related that the last sound he heard while leaving Kepner's office was the sign being ripped from the wall. Doolittle was praised by the fighter pilots and condemned by the bomber crews—at least until his new policy began to really hurt the *Luftwaffe*. German general Adolf Galland later said that the day this decision was made, the Germans "lost the air war."[7] It is now recognized by many as Doolittle's most significant command decision while at the Eighth Air Force.

GEFECHTSVERBAND

On January 27, the *Luftwaffe* made its final major changes to daylight air defense prior to D-Day. The headquarters of the Commander *Luftwaffe* Central Region (*Luftwaffe Befehlshaber Mitte*) became a full-fledged Air Fleet headquarters, *Luftflotte Reich* ("Air Fleet Reich").[8] The commander in chief was General Weise, and he worked primarily from the Berlin Air Command Center.

Under *Luftflotte Reich* was *Jagdkorps I* (Fighter Corps I), which controlled all German fighters in Holland and Northwest Germany. The main path for the Eighth Air Force and RAF Bomber Command into northern Germany was the North Sea and the Netherlands. Holland was the graveyard for hundreds of Allied and German aircraft and many airmen classified as MIA (missing in action). Wiese could also call on fighters from adjacent air fleets in emergencies.

Map 47.1. *Luftwaffe* command areas, February–June 1944. The Fifteenth Air Force has moved forward to Foggia, Italy. All targets in Germany and Occupied Europe are in range. MOLYSON AFTER PRICE[9]

Luftflotte 3 (Air Fleet 3) retained control of all German air force units in France and Belgium including *Jagdkorps II* (Fighter Corps II). The two fighter wings of this fighter corps, JG2 and JG26, operated the latest-model FW 190A and Bf 109G fighters. *Jagdkorps II* would be the main fighter opposition to any Allied landing in northern France or Belgium.

Spread in several command centers across France were several regional *Jafü* (*Jagdführers*—"fighter controllers"), experienced fighter pilots who directed the forces of both fighter wings toward points of maximum danger. *Jagdführer* meant "hunting guide" in German. The *Jafü* and the direction system they controlled helped the German fighters find formations containing bombers, avoiding RAF fighter sweeps.[10]

German tactics as well as command arrangements continued to respond to American daylight bombing and the new escort fighters. In Germany, General Galland established large mixed groups of fighters called *Gefechtsverband*. The core of these formations was the *Stürmgruppe* ("assault group"), units of heavily armed FW 190A-8 / R8 *Stürmbock* ("battering ram") aircraft.

Each *Stürmbock* carried two 30mm and two 20mm cannon, as well as two heavy 12.7mm machine guns, about the same caliber as the defensive guns of the American heavy bombers. Extra armor and bulletproof glass protected the pilot and critical areas of the aircraft. All of this added weight to the aircraft, which could no longer hope to match American escort fighters in a dogfight. Protection from Kepner's newly rampaging VIII Fighter Command was necessary.

To provide that protection two *Begleitengruppen* ("escort groups") flying lightly armed and agile Bf 109G-10 fighters escorted the *Stürmgruppe* into the combat area.[11] The idea was for the 109s to attack the escorts while the FW 190s hit the bombers from the stern. In actual attacks, one or two of the 190s would be downed on each pass, but some successful attacks were conducted. *Begleitengruppen* also began escorting the vulnerable *Zerstörer* to the combat area.

The size of the *Gefechtsverband* of 90 to 100 aircraft made assembling it difficult. The weather was almost always a factor. Once the American escorts had fought through the *Begleitengruppen*, then the *Stürmbock* were easy prey. The *Gefechtsverband* became a "Mustang magnet," which often foiled GAF efforts to get an attack started. As German pilot casualties mounted, the tactic was abandoned.

CHAPTER FORTY-EIGHT

Big Week (February 20–25, 1944)

As the Eighth Air Force recovered from the major losses of Black Thursday and began operating longer-range escort fighters, the staff at the Allied Combined Operational Planning Committee (COPC) drafted a document calling for climactic attacks against the German aircraft industry. The name for this new operation was ARGUMENT; its objective was "to conduct a decisive operation against vital targets in the German War Industry, the destruction of which it is estimated can cripple her war potential."[1] To the aircrews who flew it, it was always known as the "Big Week."

At the start of Big Week, Spaatz questioned Doolittle on the soundness of the decision to free the fighters for offensive operations. Perhaps the resentment of the bomber crews had percolated up to USSTAF. Maybe it sounded too much like fighter sweeps. In any case, Doolittle stood his ground. While the Eighth Air Force tripled its fighters and bombers from October 1943 to February 1944, operational *Luftwaffe* strength in the air had hardly increased at all. The flat growth in German fighter pilots, even though more aircraft were available to fly, had terminated German efforts toward a bigger air force. It was time for VIII Fighter Command to seek and destroy.

The primary goal of ARGUMENT was to cripple German fighter production. The plan was finished on November 4, 1943. The tactical air force commanders, IX Air Force's Major General Brereton and AEAF's Air Marshal Leigh-Mallory, informed Lieutenant General Spaatz that they opposed Big Week. They wanted time to train the fighter pilots for close air support for the upcoming invasion. Spaatz declined their request and won the dispute, because Eisenhower knew that Doolittle's men were out killing the *Luftwaffe*. Ike judged that air superiority was more necessary for the invasion than close air support for the troops.[2]

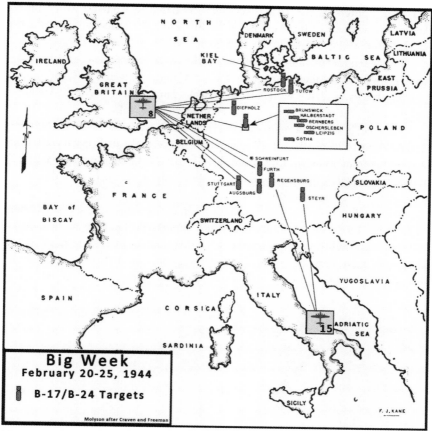

Map 48.1. Big Week targets, February 20–25, 1944. MOLYSON[3]

Operation ARGUMENT planners noted the level of destruction previously wrought on Regensburg, Marienburg, Schweinfurt, Kassel, Hannover, Anklam, and Wiener Neustadt by the Eighth and Fifteenth Air Forces. The new plan envisioned ten B-17 and B-24 combat wings, more than three times as many as had been used to attack Schweinfurt and Regensburg back in August. ARGUMENT would strike new aircraft industry and related facilities dispersed in central and southern Germany. RAF Bomber Command would hit additional targets.

The new targets were at Leipzig, Gotha, Oschersleben, Halberstadt, Bernburg, and Schopau. Leipzig and Oschersleben produced single-engine fighters; Schopau produced synthetic rubber; and the rest produced twin-engine *Zerstörer* and night fighters. Eighth Air Force bombers based in England would hit all. An additional force of bombers from the Fifteenth Air Force would strike the ball-bearing production facility at Stuttgart.

Supplemental medium bomber attacks were envisioned against German airfields in Holland and the Pas-de-Calais, as well as RAF fighter-bomber attacks against enemy airfields within range. The US Ninth Air Force and the 2nd Tactical Air Force would conduct these attacks.

As usual, it was all a matter of weather, and it was mid-February before it seemed right to begin the attack sequence. On the night of February 19, RAF Bomber Command began Operation ARGUMENT by sending a force of 823 bombers to attack Leipzig. An additional 49 bombers were sent on a diversionary minelaying mission to Kiel Bay.

The bomber stream was attacked all the way from the coast of the Netherlands to the target by intermittent flak and almost 700 German night fighters. German night fighters sent to intercept the diversionary force were recalled and also hit the main bomber stream. The town was badly hit, but the attack cost the Brits 83 bombers, 9.5 percent of the force.[4] Bomber gunners and RAF intruders[5]

W.Gr. 21 Rocket Pod

Figure 48.1. A 66-gallon drop tank burns on a rocket-equipped Bf 109. Drop tanks added weight and vulnerability to fighters unless jettisoned before combat.
NINTH AIR FORCE GUN CAMERA FILM, COURTESY OF JOHN DRUMMOND

were able to down only 17 of the German night fighters.[6] RAF Bomber Command losses were heavier than either of the American raids on Schweinfurt. German night defenses were growing ever more effective. Night bombing had become as costly as day bombing to the Allied airmen.

Spaatz sent his daylight bombers the next day knowing that this was the big test for the Army Air Force's daylight precision bombardment strategy. The weather held, and within a week the Eighth and Fifteenth Air Forces had demolished much of the German aircraft industry. Harris's RAF bombers joined the attack again on the night of February 24, with a large raid against Schweinfurt.

The tempo of attack was unrelenting. Escort fighters caught the heavily armed German fighters and *Zerstörer* repeatedly. *Gefechtsverband* tactics were ineffective. The VIII, IX, and XV Fighter Commands, which provided the escort force, claimed over 300 German fighters for the week against 41 escorts lost. Most of the kills were verified with gun camera film. The bomber gunners claimed more. On February 26, the weather reverted to its normal winter pattern and the bombing ended for a time.

What hurt the Germans the most during Big Week was the rapid depletion of experienced pilots, with almost 450 killed. Doolittle's fighters were effectively implementing his offensive doctrine. The Allied bombers damaged or destroyed almost three-quarters of the facilities in which German aircraft were produced. This forced the Germans to salvage and move more of their aircraft industry into less-efficient dispersed sites, some of them underground. It also caused another dip in aircraft production in the months leading up to D-Day. An additional benefit of Big Week was the accelerated withdrawal of more fighters from *Luftflotte 3* in France back into Germany.[7] General Galland of the *Luftwaffe* later said:

> *Only now did the superiority of the American fighters come into its own. They were no longer glued to the slow-moving bomber formation but took the law of action into their own hands. Wherever our fighters appeared, the Americans hurled themselves at them. They went over to low-level attacks on our airfields. Nowhere were we safe from them; we had to skulk on our own bases.*[8]

Big Week attacks directed against the German aircraft industry also impeded the production of the new Me 262 jet fighter. Because of the damage to the factories at Augsburg and Regensburg, a tardily ordered series of 100 planes could not be delivered. Increased difficulties in personnel and material delayed the final course of production for over a month.[9]

On March 16, 1944, Bf 110s of *Zerstörergeschwader* 76 (Destroyer Wing 76) downed 18 B-17s in a mass attack. The escort, however, arrived and shot down 26 of the destroyers, a loss rate of 60 percent for ZG 76. ZG 76 was forced to disband its third group and soon began reequipping with Me 410s.[10] These last Bf 110s flown in the daylight bomber interception role were assigned to other duties.[11]

New tactics failed to rescue the German fighters from further carnage. In March through May 1944, a further 28 *Experten*, whose combined victories over Allied aircraft numbered some 2,100, were lost to POINTBLANK. With the continued decline of training, their experience and skill were gone forever.[12]

Chapter Forty-Nine

Big B and Beyond
(November 1943–March 1944)

A thing of orchestrated hell—a terrible symphony of light and flame.
—Journalist Edward R. Murrow[1]

The Battle of Berlin, beginning on November 18, 1943, would include 16 major RAF raids involving almost 10,000 bomber sorties; 30,000 tons of bombs would be dropped, burning out almost 8 square miles (5,000 acres) of urban area. (In comparison, the atomic bomb attack on Hiroshima burned out approximately 6 square miles.) It extended through Big Week until March 31, 1944, a duration of over four months.

Propaganda chief Goebbels wrote, "Devastation is again appalling in the Government section . . . Alkeet [tank factory] is almost completely destroyed . . . the English aimed so accurately that one might think spies had pointed their way." Actually, it was Mosquito Pathfinder aircraft, not spies, that had helped the RAF bomber streams to find their way to their urban targets in the German capital.[2]

The RAF Official History rated the Battle of Berlin as unsuccessful: "The Battle of Berlin was more than a failure. It was a defeat." Having helped the German day fighters (*Jagdwaffe*) coerce the Americans to suspend their daylight attacks in October 1943, the German night fighters (*Nachjagdwaffe*) now constituted a serious and growing threat to Bomber Command.[3]

The *Nachjagdwaffe* had evolved, as had their night control system. RAF losses were 1,047 aircraft missing during the four-month battle, 1,682 damaged. While the loss numbers were staggering, even worse was the fact that the Germans kept the factories turning out huge amounts of war materiel even as their cities burned. Destruction to Berlin was extensive, what the RAF Official History called "enormous and horrifying damage." The government district of

Berlin, the Wilhelmstrasse, and the Reich Chancellery were in ruins, and extensive areas of Berlin and other selected cities were burned out. Yet, Albert Speer's war economy seemed to thrive.[4]

Most frustrating to the British was that the frayed morale of the German people did not shatter. It was the Blitz repeated with the antagonists reversed in role. The Germans even made jokes about their grim situation. One concerned an imaginary conversation between Propaganda Minister Goebbels and Göring: "Hitler," Goebbels told the *Reichsmarschall*, "has hanged himself." Replied Göring, "There you are—I always said we should win this war in the air!"[5]

DOGFIGHT

When Big Week ended on February 25, it was time for the Americans to join the battered RAF Bomber Command in attacking Hitler's capital. Only by continuing to threaten the capital could Spaatz, Doolittle, and Kepner keep the *Jagdwaffe* fighting and losing rather than reconstituting itself to counter the invasion.

On March 3, 1944, thirty B-17s with fighter escort bombed Berlin by day.[6] The mission was briefed and hundreds of aircraft launched. Weather forced most of them to find alternate targets or turn back, but a B-17 group consisting of two 95th Bomb Group squadrons and one 100th Bomb Group squadron pressed on for the target. Only a few Bf 109s intercepted, one being downed by an alert top turret gunner. Weather over Berlin was so bad that the formation bombed by radar before turning for home. Five B-17s were lost on the return trip, but spirits were high in the Mighty Eighth that night. Big B had been bombed.

Over 700 bombers and 700 escort fighters conducted a more effective attack on March 6. This day saw the worst one-day loss of American heavy bombers in the daylight campaign, with 69 destroyed and another 100 badly damaged. There was no rejoicing in Germany, however. Almost 200 German fighters were claimed shot down by the Eighth Air Force; a loss of even half that number was a disaster for the *Luftwaffe*.

On March 15, a huge dogfight developed over Dümmer Lake in Germany, a landmark on the "Flak Highway" to Berlin. Over 300 German and American fighters clashed at high altitude while 1,200 American heavy bombers continued on unmolested to Berlin; 35 German fighters were downed, as well as 5 escort fighters.[7] A Berlin mission could be bad, very bad, but on this day the American bombers lost only 3 aircraft; 2 were downed by flak, and 1, due to an oxygen system failure. The fifth and last attack in the series was launched on March 22. Further attacks were postponed because of poor bombing weather rather than enemy opposition. Offensive fighter escort had come of age in the Eighth Air Force.[8]

On March 30, weather again had a major impact on Allied heavy bombing, this time during an RAF raid against Nürnberg. Predicted bad weather did not materialize; instead, it was a crystalline night. The bombers' contrails disastrously marked them out in the clear sky over Germany, making them easy targets for the *Nachjagdwaffe* night fighters. In the loose assembly of a night-bomber stream, armed mostly with ineffective 0.303 rifle-caliber machine guns, 95 of 795 bombers were downed—almost 12 percent of the force. The mission became known as the "Nürnberg disaster."

Later in March, the so-called *Jäger* ("Hunter") program to increase production of German fighters was instituted.[9] Although this program performed something of a miracle, actually boosting production at a time when Germany was under increasing bombardment, aircraft production numbers were no longer the determining factor in air superiority over Germany. By this time, the *Luftwaffe* was well into decline due to losses in its fighter pilot corps.

Such losses forced the transfer of pilots from bomber and transport duties, gutting those capabilities without significantly rebuilding the *Jagdwaffe*. Half-prepared youngsters from the truncated flight-training program joined these veterans. Allied pilots soon reported that some German air force fighter pilots were bailing out before a shot was fired in air combat.

Meanwhile, Germany struggled to get its wonder weapons into the fight for day air superiority over the Reich. Me 163 rocket interceptors had a negligible effect on the daylight campaign due to their short range. Hitler's interference and Allied bombing also delayed the effective use of the Me 262 as a fighter until after D-Day.[10]

MISSION ACCOMPLISHED

From Christmas 1943 to April 1, 1944, some 1,200 German fighter pilots died. Rested and refurbished GAF fighter units returning to combat were nominally at 70 to 80 percent of authorized strength. After four days of combat against the American bombers and their escort fighters, the same unit would be at 30 to 40 percent level. If forced to continue fighting, it fell to "tactical zero"—that is, no combat capability due to lack of pilots.

General Galland reported to Göring:

The ratio in which we fight in now is about one to seven. The standard of the Americans is extraordinarily high. The day fighters have lost more than 1,000 aircraft, and among them our best officers. These gaps cannot be filled. During each enemy raid we lose about fifty fighters. Things have gone so far that the danger of a collapse of our arm exists.[11]

Galland pleaded with Göring to form a reserve of rested pilots, diverting some strength into units that would not be committed to air defense. This was close to treason in Hitler's Germany, yet Göring agreed. The carefully husbanded reserve would total 450 men by the end of May, just in time to be consumed by the air activity surrounding D-Day.[12]

TRANSPORTATION AND FUEL

The Mighty Eighth and RAF Bomber Command received new jobs in the so-called Transportation Plan, a priority mission now that D-Day was fast approaching. By April 7, with growing demands to support the Transportation Plan and ever-increasing bomber losses, Bomber Harris had had enough of area-bombing German urban areas. He wrote to the Air Ministry that "the strength of German defences would in time reach a point at which night bombing attacks by existing methods and types of heavy bomber would involve percentage casualty rates which could not in the long run be sustained." The *Luftwaffe* had regained night air superiority over Germany at the same time as they had permanently lost day air superiority over their long-suffering country.[13]

The German oil industry was also on the Combined Bomber Offensive target list. As early as June 1943, American bombers had severely damaged the oil refinery complex at Hüls. Other refineries in occupied countries and Germany were frequent targets of both the RAF and the USAAF. As natural oil refineries were attacked and production reduced, synthetic fuel production at hydrogenation synthetic fuel plants became increasingly important. On May 24, 1944, Göring warned: "What good does it do to strengthen the entire front when the enemy continues to go after the hydrogenation plants? Then flying operations will completely stop and we can disband the Fighter Staff."[14] He was referring to the *Drohende Gefahr West* (Imminent Danger–West) and *Drohende Gefahr Nord* (Imminent Danger–North) plans, which would transfer fighters and flak into an invasion-threatened area.

Now that the *Luftwaffe* was decimated, it was time to strip it of its fuel. On May 27, the Americans turned to the German oil industry as a primary target. Albert Speer decided that the technological war was lost. Over 900 American heavy bombers had attacked several synthetic fuel plants in Germany. The blow was repeated on May 28–29, and in addition, the refinery complex at Ploesti was hit again. The result of these attacks was the immediate loss of half of Germany's fuel production capacity. Added to the hemorrhage of experienced fighter pilots, it was a compound catastrophe for the German air force just before D-Day.[15]

By D-Day most of the Eighth Air Force's P-47s would be transferred to Ninth Air Force in exchange for P-51s. The Jugs sometimes flew escort missions, but increasingly were involved in ground attack, often expending their ammo after failing to find airborne German targets. The Jug was highly effective in the ground-attack mission, and the mission itself was more closely aligned with the Ninth Air Force than the Eighth. Not all the P-47s went to the Ninth Air Force. The 56th and 78th Fighter Groups continued to fly their Thunderbolts with the Eighth Air Force and had a significant role in the continued battle for air superiority over France and Germany.[16]

CHAPTER FIFTY

They Will Be Ours
(November 1943–May 1944)

If you see fighting aircraft over you, they will be ours.
—IKE'S PROMISE TO THE INVASION TROOPS
ON THE EVE OF D-DAY[1]

By November of 1943, major components of the Allied Expeditionary Air Force were assembling. The AEAF was to provide support to the Allied armies that would be landed in France. The British would provide the First Canadian Army and the Second British Army under the 21st Army Group, with air support in the form of "Composite Groups," while the Americans would provide air support to the First US Army and the Third US Army under the 12th Army Group, in the form of "Tactical Air Commands." Each army's tactical air support would be under its operational control and provide direct and indirect support to its ground forces. This would ensure, as Eisenhower said, that aircraft overhead of the ground troops would be Allied.

The AEAF was multinational. The British Second Tactical Air Force would provide fighter, fighter-bomber, light/medium bomber, and Air Observation Post (AOP) support to the British and Canadian Armies. Two RAF Groups would also transport British airborne forces, which operated on the flanks and ahead of the ground armies.

The RAF's No. 38 Group flew ex-bomber aircraft modified to tow gliders and drop parachutists. British airborne forces had been employed successfully in the Mediterranean, and the No. 38 Group (Airborne) RAF was established to support them. The No. 38 Group flew the Albermarle, Stirling, and Halifax aircraft. The No. 46 Group, flying Dakotas (C-47s), was not formally established until January 1944.

Table 50.1. Allied Expeditionary Air Force, November 1943.

Component	Parent Air Force	Field Army Supported	Status	Order of Battle
Second Tactical Air Force	RAF	First Canadian and Second British Armies	Assigned	Photo reconnaissance, tactical reconnaissance, medium and light bomber, fighter and Air Observation Post (AOP) units
No. 38 Group	RAF	Airborne units	Attached	Ex-bomber troop carrier and glider tug units
No. 46 Group	RAF	Airborne units	Planned	C-47 cargo, troop carrier, and glider tug units; not formed until January 1944
Air Defense of Great Britain (formerly Fighter Command)	RAF	—	Attached	Defensive fighters in Britain and over Channel
Ninth Air Force	USAAF	First and Third US Armies	Forming	Photo reconnaissance, tactical reconnaissance, medium and light bomber, fighter, C-47 troop carrier and glider tug units, and Air Observation Post (AOP) units

The American contribution was the Ninth Air Force. The Ninth was a heavy bomber outfit in North Africa, but its top headquarters (and not much else) had been moved to England in October 1943. Unlike the RAF, which "borrowed" No. 38 and 46 Groups for airborne transport, the Ninth Air Force had its own IX Troop Carrier Command. The IX Troop Carrier Command predominantly flew the C-47/C-53 aircraft.

Both strategic bomber forces, Bomber Command and Eighth Air Force, transferred their light and medium bombers to the AEAF. They were ideal for indirect support to the army. Bomber Command and Eighth Air Force were now focused on strategic bombing with heavy bombers. Bomber Command transferred No. 2 Group to 2nd Tactical Air Force (2TAF). Eighth Air Force's light and medium bombers were absorbed into Ninth Air Forces IX Bomber Command. Eighth Air Force also provided Ninth Air Force with much of its troop carrier C-47/C-53 fleet. Finally, Eighth passed most of its Thunderbolts and Lightnings to Ninth Air Force and replaced them with Mustangs as they were delivered to Europe.

The AEAF also partially controlled the Air Defense of Great Britain (ADGB), which was the remnant of the Fighter Command which continued to maintain air superiority over Britain. Some ADGB units extended the Allied air umbrella over the Channel as required to support the invasion and defend London.

By providing composite groups / tactical air commands to ground formations of the same nationality, previous air force–army cooperation procedures developed within each national air force were maintained. As the AEAF squadrons began to train in Britain for their OVERLORD role, they continued to fly other kinds of missions across the Channel. Neither the RAF nor the USAAF could afford to keep so many units in training status for six months. By D-Day, however, both training and continued operational missions had prepared AEAF aircrew to support and protect amphibious and ground operations.

CHAPTER FIFTY-ONE

Sorting Out SHAEF (January–May 1944)

We cannot make war as we ought; we can only make it as we can.
—LORD KITCHENER, BRITISH SECRETARY OF WAR, 1915[1]

When published in July 1943, the "Digest of Operation OVERLORD" provided the basis for all subsequent planning, preparations, and operations related to the invasion.[2] By the end of 1943, the primary objective of gaining air superiority over the invasion area had been achieved. It would be maintained and expanded into Germany by the continuing campaign against the German fighter forces.

In January 1944, General Eisenhower arrived in England and quickly established himself at the Supreme Headquarters, Allied Expeditionary Force (SHAEF). With the invasion army and air force rapidly being assembled, his title transitioned from Supreme Allied Commander to supreme commander, Allied Expeditionary Forces (SCAEF). There would be no "BEF" this time in France; it was a combined effort to free Occupied Europe.

All eyes were now focused on the upcoming invasion, and all eyes were centered on preparing the "Allied Expeditionary Forces." Ike moved SHAEF headquarters to Bushy Park, far outside of London and the machinations of the British government. Soon Ike and his staff had established the collegial atmosphere that always characterized his inner circle. In February, he received orders for SHAEF to invade Western Europe during the late spring of 1944. Now Ike and his staff refined the COSSAC plan to meet the challenges and opportunities presented by the wounded but still-dangerous German military machine across the Channel.

With Eisenhower came his best general officers from the Mediterranean. For his chief of staff, he brought Lieutenant General Walter Bedell Smith, widely known to peers and superiors as "Beetle." COSSAC, Lieutenant General Morgan, became Smith's deputy chief of staff. As deputy supreme commander, Eisenhower brought Air Chief Marshal Tedder, an airman with extensive experience in air support of ground operations in the Mediterranean. Tedder's calm and thoughtful approach was effective both in negotiation and in leadership.

The measure of Eisenhower and Tedder was soon taken by their foes in Germany. German views were colored by their previous experience with both officers in the Mediterranean. In a lecture presented to the *Luftwaffe* Academy, "Invasion Generals, Careers and Assessments," Eisenhower was described as:

an expert on operations of armored formations. He is noted for his great energy and for his hatred of routine office work. He leaves the initiative to his subordinates whom he manages to inspire to supreme efforts through kind understanding and easy discipline. His strongest point is said to be an ability for adjusting personalities to one another and smoothing over opposite viewpoints. Eisenhower enjoys the greatest popularity with Roosevelt and Churchill.[3]

Tedder was described as:

on good terms with Eisenhower, to whom he is superior in both intelligence and energy. The coming operations will be conducted by him to a great extent. He regards the Air Force as "spearhead artillery," rendering the enemy vulnerable to an attack. His tactics in North Africa, Sicily and Italy, based on this theory, provided for air support for the advance of even the smallest Army units . . . Under Tedder's influence the cooperation between the Air Force and Army has become excellent . . . Obviously we are dealing here with one of the most eminent personalities amongst the invasion leaders.[4]

Tedder, the de facto invasion air commander, eventually brought in Air Vice Marshal Sir Arthur Coningham, who had provided critical RAF tactical air support throughout the Mediterranean campaign, to command the 2nd Tactical Air Force. The 2TAF would provide the RAF portion of the Allied Expeditionary Air Force (AEAF), formed to support the invasion.

At the same time as Ike was establishing SHAEF, General Spaatz launched Headquarters US Strategic Air Forces (USSTAF).[5] Spaatz and his USSTAF directly or indirectly controlled all American airpower in England, plus the Fifteenth Air Force in Italy. General Doolittle replaced General Eaker as commander of the Eighth Air Force, and General Brereton moved his Ninth Air Force headquarters up from the Mediterranean. Brereton would provide the American half of the AEAF. Both Doolittle and Brereton reported to Spaatz.

THE BATTLE OF THE GENERALS

By the time American bombers were flying Big Week in February 1944, the AEAF under Air Marshal Leigh-Mallory was well into planning air support for OVERLORD. This included bombing attacks prior to the landings and subsequent support to the troops ashore. Since the AEAF was supposed to be Ike's key air headquarters for OVERLORD, it is curious that none of his Mediterranean coterie was given the job of running it.

Leigh-Mallory was sometimes a difficult character, noted by some historians as taciturn and haughty. His relations with all the other senior airmen were strained, and his demand for total control of airpower for the invasion alienated the strategic bomber commanders. Even Eisenhower had his concerns, noting that Leigh-Mallory "had much fighting experience, particularly in the Battle of Britain, but had not theretofore been in charge of air operations requiring close co-operation with ground troops."[6] His last substantial involvement with army cooperation was in World War I. Leigh-Mallory was also the senior air commander at Dieppe, certainly a sobering thought in picking such a commander for OVERLORD.

Feelings about Leigh-Mallory set the stage for discord among the senior airmen as D-Day approached. From Washington, General Arnold refused to allow the AEAF staff to become a pit into which scarce Army Air Force staff officers would be drawn. He approved few transfers to Leigh-Mallory's headquarters, giving the AEAF a distinctly RAF orientation. Arnold also stated that Brereton's Ninth Air Force would only receive "general operational direction" from Leigh-Mallory.

Arnold appointed Major General William O. Butler to be Leigh-Mallory's American deputy at AEAF but sent little else in the way of real talent to the headquarters. General Butler later complained to General Giles (Arnold's deputy), "I asked for about 5 or 6 officers before I left. . . . So far none of these have arrived and there is no notice on their departure. . . . The Air Force here has furnished a few nondescripts and promises some more of doubtful ability soon."[7]

Harris at RAF Bomber Command wanted no part of Leigh-Mallory; he considered anything other than vigorous pursuit of his night-bombing campaign a useless "diversion." For Spaatz the problem was more of a clash of personalities. Like Harris, Spaatz had no intention of subordinating himself or his men to a commander with no bomber experience. Even worse, the gregarious Spaatz interpreted Leigh-Mallory's demeanor as hostility, to be returned in kind.

Spaatz was a team player and an associate of Eisenhower's since their West Point days. He certainly didn't need Leigh-Mallory to explain the finer points of supporting an amphibious assault, nor would he tolerate the AEAF diverting forces from POINTBLANK. He had volunteered his heavy bomber force in the Mediterranean to support the Salerno landings; he was no stranger to the needs of an invading army. During the Mediterranean fighting, Spaatz had signaled Arnold:

> *When the battle situation requires it, all units, including medium and heavy bombardment, must support the ground operations. Air support of the ground forces, on the other hand, cannot be made effective in the face of air supremacy, superiority, and under certain conditions, even parity on the part of the enemy's air forces. It follows from this that in order for the army to advance, the air battle must first be won.*[8]

Spaatz was aware that the strategic air forces must come under Eisenhower's control at some point. He felt that this point would be March 1, some sixty days prior to the anticipated landings then scheduled for May 1.[9] Spaatz had no problem supporting either Eisenhower or OVERLORD; it was Leigh-Mallory that Spaatz rejected. Spaatz was amazed that Leigh-Mallory "apparently accepts [the] possibility of not establishing air supremacy until [the] landing starts."[10] This was anathema to all that Spaatz and the USAAF had fought for, and reflected Leigh-Mallory's faulty assessment of the Allied air "victory" at Dieppe. A message to the Ninth Air Force from Leigh-Mallory's AEAF in March, at the height of the air battle over Germany, brought the matter to a head:

> *The Supreme Allied Commander has decided that the time has now come for the operations of US IXth Air Force to be directed towards the preparation for Operation "Overlord." Henceforth IXth Air Force will therefore operate exclusively under Allied Expeditionary Air Force and will be released from its commitment to assist US VIIIth Air Force "Pointblank" operations under arrangements made by that Force.*[11]

Leigh-Mallory had issued this order to the Ninth Air Force without coordination with Spaatz, the senior American airman in Europe. This was an unforgivable error in the rarefied atmosphere of general officer politics. Worse still, the note threatened to remove the Ninth Air Force fighter units from their bomber escort role just when they were most needed. Spaatz reacted immediately with a note directly to Leigh-Mallory, "It will be my responsibility to determine how much diversion from POINTBLANK will be allowed for training."[12] No USAAF fighters would be dropping practice bombs while American bombers were being shot down for lack of escort.

Spaatz did allow his subordinate General Doolittle at Eighth Air Force to have his fighters strafe German airfields when returning from escort missions, providing dangerous but productive training for future invasion missions. He called this a "guerrilla war" against the *Luftwaffe*. Ninth Air Force medium bombers continued to pound German airfields, missile sites, rail facilities, and other targets, some of which were relevant to POINTBLANK and some that were not.

Critical Ninth Air Force troop carrier units also continued their training unaware of the controversy between Spaatz and the AEAF. Even Tedder had problems with his fellow RAF colleague, writing later that Leigh-Mallory, "though earnest, zealous and brave, did not inspire confidence as Commander of the Allied Expeditionary Air Forces. . . . I did my best . . . to explain gently . . . that a less brusque manner would pay dividends."[13]

Unfortunately, neither Eisenhower nor Tedder was in a position to demand Leigh-Mallory's removal from his post, so they simply worked around him.

CHAPTER FIFTY-TWO

CROSSBOW (May 1943–May 1944)

On April 15, 1943, the British chiefs of staff and MI6 informed Churchill that the Germans were possibly building vengeance rockets and that London might soon be bombarded. They nominated Churchill's son-in-law, Duncan Sandys, to head a committee to examine this threat. Sandys, a crippled veteran of the Norway campaign and Churchill's son-in-law, tackled the job aggressively.

Figure 52.1. First RAF picture of A-4/V-2 rocket. **A** is V-2 rocket on trailer; **B** are cranes; **C** is the assembly building; **N** is North. AIR FORCE HISTORICAL RESEARCH AGENCY, KARLSRUHE COLLECTION

Sandys established the Bodyline Committee, including representatives from Section 6, British Military Intelligence (MI6) for human intelligence; Central Interpretation Unit (CIU), for photographic intelligence; and selected scientific advisors.[1] To support the committee work Sandys ordered increased photographic reconnaissance of Peenemünde and the areas of France within 130 miles of London. Soon 40 percent of all Allied aerial reconnaissance sorties from England were related to the emerging German missile threat.[2] It was thought that this distance was the maximum range of the hypothetical German rocket weapons.[3]

LARGE SITES

By May, Sandys knew from the photographic evidence that two kinds of missiles were being developed to bombard Britain. Sandys and his Bodyline Committee now needed to know where these weapons would be launched and what kind of vulnerable infrastructure might be associated with their support and use. V-2 "large sites" near the Channel coast were already under construction and easily located, since they were too large to hide effectively.

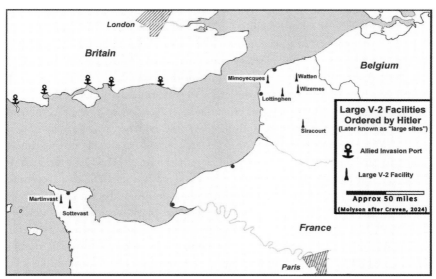

Map 52.1. V-2 large sites ordered by Hitler. MOLYSON AFTER CRAVEN[4]

The Committee assumed—like Hitler, who had ordered them built—that huge bunkers were needed for V-2 launching operations, and that any large sites in France were missile-launching facilities. They had no idea the German army would relegate such costly structures to simple storage duties. Ten days after the August 17, 1943, RAF Peenemünde attack, the Eighth Air Force sent 187 B-17s against the large site at Watten, France. Many of the bombs hit wet concrete in the construction area, freezing forever the violence of the event. This was the first Allied air attack against a V-weapon facility in France. Additional reconnaissance would reveal six more of the large sites, all of which were attacked. These attacks continued through the fall of 1943.

Ski Sites

Having located and begun surveillance of the large sites, the Committee started looking for where the "projectors," or launch ramps, for the smaller V-1 flying bombs might be built. Members of the French Resistance began reporting mysterious new construction activity in the vicinity of, but not directly associated with, the large sites. Frantic construction activity was being accomplished along the Channel coast from Cherbourg to Calais, some 150 miles.

The Germans had drafted large numbers of French laborers to help in the construction of both missile facilities and the *Atlantik Wall*. These men proved to be an intelligence bonanza for the Allies, and one code-named André was perhaps the best source of all. After being hired at one of the construction sites as a clerk, André was able to copy portions of the master plan for the site each morning as his German boss left the office to perform a daily call of nature.[5]

The plans were duly smuggled out to MI6 in London, and, when combined with other tidbits of agent data and photographic evidence, revealed the master pattern of the newly constructed sites.[6] As luck would have it, about this time a prototype air-launched V-1 was released from its Heinkel He 111 carrier aircraft flying out of Peenemünde West. It went awry and crashed into a field in Denmark.

Danish Resistance members provided photographs and some key pieces of wreckage. The Royal Air Force again intensified its photoreconnaissance activity along the Channel coast. In October the first of the so-called ski sites emerged in the photographs. The term "ski site" referred to the hardened V-1 missile storage building, which was curved on one end so that the structure appeared like a ski in profile when seen from above. The curved design prevented a nearby bomb blast from destroying all the V-1s within the shelter.

Each ski site was a cluster of buildings and had one or more launch ramps, the "projectors" sought by the Bodyline Committee. The ramp was the most necessary feature of each site, for the V-1's pulse jet engine could not start until the missile was propelled along the steam-driven catapult to launch speed. Ski sites soon joined the large sites on the so-called NOBALL target list, a tabulation of all German V-weapon facilities in France. Missile storage areas, labor camps, and other key missile-related facilities also became prospective NOBALL targets.[7]

Extensive Allied aerial photoreconnaissance of the French coast corroborated reports from the French underground to reveal the network of sixty-four ski sites being built. This work continued into November, uncovering numerous confirmed and additional suspected launch and support sites. On November 15, 1943, the Bodyline Committee transferred all of its functions to the (British) Air Ministry. So much information was being collected that a simple ad hoc committee could no longer manage it. The activities associated with intelligence collection and attacks against the German V-weapon program were incorporated under the code name Operation CROSSBOW.[8]

There were two clusters of launch sites. The western complex, on the Cotentin Peninsula, was aimed at the major port of Bristol. The eastern complex, on the Pas-de-Calais, was aimed at London.[9] In December 1943, General Eisenhower ordered all sites that appeared more than half complete to be bombed. All fighter-bombers and medium bombers assigned to the AEAF, including both the RAF and USAAF tactical air forces in England, were ordered to begin the attacks.

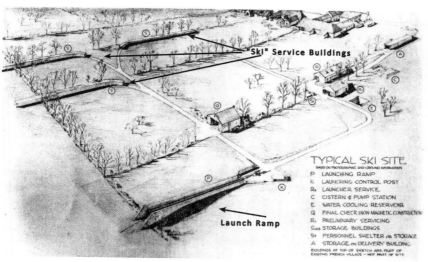

Figure 52.2. Diagram of a typical V-1 ski site at Maisoncelle, France. AIR FORCE HISTORICAL RESEARCH AGENCY, KARLSRUHE COLLECTION

Duncan Sandys knew more about the V-1 than most of the officers in Hitler's personal headquarters, *Oberkommando Wehrmacht* (OKW). The OKW had not been let in on the secret of the V-1 and V-2 weapons until after Hamburg had been destroyed in Operation GOMORRAH and the V-2 research effort at Peenemünde had been severely damaged in Operation HYDRA.

The OKW evaluated their military potential as an alternative to the continuing but inadequate German air force bombing attacks against England. Hitler ordered that the V-weapons were to be used exclusively for attacks on London. He anticipated that such attacks would delay if not prevent an Allied invasion across the Channel. The military men at OKW thought less of the weapons—that "the quantity of high explosive which can be delivered daily is less than that which could be dropped in a major air attack."[10] Thankfully, neither Hitler nor the OKW seriously considered using the missiles against the potential Allied invasion ports along the English Channel.

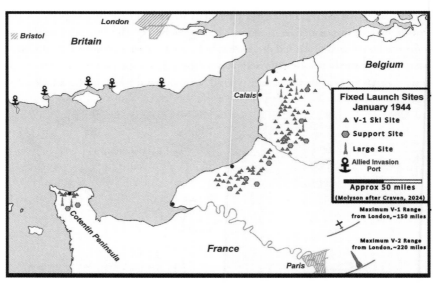

Map 52.2. V-1 and V-2 fixed launch sites as of January 1944.
MOLYSON AFTER CRAVEN[11]

On Christmas Eve, strategic bombers from the Eighth Air Force joined the fight. For the first time Ike interrupted the ongoing strategic bombardment of Germany and the occupied countries to order a direct attack on German forces in France. A total of 722 B-17 and B-24 bombers were sent to bomb the V-weapon sites in the Pas-de-Calais. They were escorted by 541 P-38, P-47, and P-51 aircraft, and no bomber losses were incurred.

Since it was estimated that the V-weapons would begin bombarding London by February 1944, it was necessary to delay the German attack as long as possible. Bombing the launch and launch support infrastructure achieved that goal. Between December 1943 and D-Day (June 6, 1944), over 25,000 sorties were flown to deliver 36,200 tons of bombs on CROSSBOW targets. All but twelve of the originally identified V-1 sites were rendered unusable. Rail and storage infrastructure was also struck. Most importantly, no V-weapons hit London or anywhere else in Britain before D-Day. The cost was 154 aircraft and 771 Allied airmen.

CROSSBOW had the same effect on the V-1 as HYDRA (the attack on Peenemünde) had had on the V-2. It delayed the effective use of a missile weapon until after the OVERLORD landings had been accomplished. The postwar US Strategic Bombing Survey later estimated that if the Germans had not invested so heavily in the V-1 and V-2 programs, some 24,000 additional German fighters could have been produced in 1944–1945. After Hamburg, Hitler might have ordered increased fighter production to defend Germany and its people; instead, the Führer wanted revenge. In exchange for the lost fighter productivity, all V-weapons combined delivered less explosive power on Allied territory than one British 1,000-bomber raid.[12]

General Eisenhower later commented:

It seemed likely that, if the German[13] had succeeded in perfecting and using these new weapons six months earlier than he did, our invasion of Europe would have proved exceedingly difficult, perhaps impossible. I feel sure that if he had succeeded in using these weapons over a six-month period, and particularly if he had made the Portsmouth-Southampton area one of his principal targets, Overlord might have been written off.[14]

CHAPTER FIFTY-THREE

Holding the Fortress (January–May 1944)

Even as the SHAEF headquarters evolved, the brass was also arguing and adjusting boundaries on the other side of the Channel. *Generalfeldmarschall* Rommel, the Desert Fox, was still Hitler's favorite field commander, and arrived in France as commander in chief of Army Group B about the same time that Ike arrived in England. Hitler made him personally responsible for strengthening the *Atlantik Wall* and defeating the expected invasion. Rommel's immediate superior was *Oberbefehlshaber West* (Commander in Chief West), *Generalfeldmarschall* Gerd von Rundstedt. His headquarters was known simply as OKW. Von Rundstedt ran the Western Front (France and the Low Countries) from his headquarters in Paris.

DIFFERENCES

The two field marshals had opposing views on how to defend Fortress Europe. Von Rundstedt had commanded the invasion of France in 1940 when the *Luftwaffe* had reigned supreme over the battlefield. Rommel, conversely, had been run out of Africa largely because of massive Allied air superiority that crippled his support and combat units on the move. Because they were both German field marshals, they were allowed direct access to Hitler.

Rommel wanted the invasion stopped on the beach by massive fortifications and an infantry defense, followed quickly by an armored counterattack to throw the Allies back into the sea.[1] Hitler's Directive No. 51, issued the previous November, clearly described a strong defense of the landing beaches (see appendix 3).

For the Desert Fox, this meant basing the panzer (tank) units very close to likely landing areas where they didn't have to move long distances under the Allied air umbrella. Rommel had no illusions about road marches in daylight. It was Rommel who coined the phrase *Der längste Tag* ("The Longest Day"), considering the day of the initial landing to be the most critical.

238

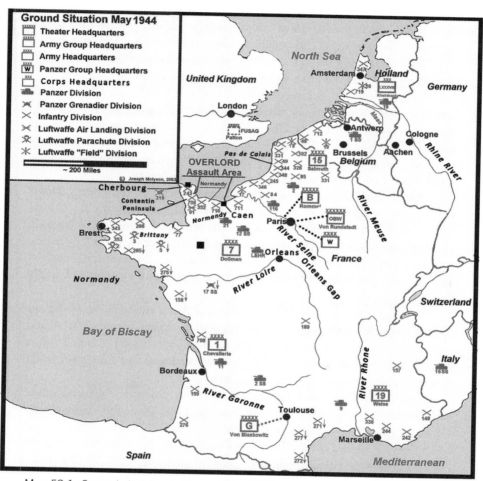

Map 53.1. Ground situation in France, May 1944. The German army and its fortifications in France were heavily reinforced between May 1943 and May 1944. Army Group D became a formal OKW headquarters and two new Army Groups, B and G, were established. MOLYSON AFTER HASTINGS, NATKIEL, AND GRIESS[2]

Von Rundstedt, mindful of his own 1940 blitzkrieg victory in France that had resulted in the Dunkirk evacuation, discounted the power of Allied aircraft and insisted the panzers be held farther back. Although he never served in North Africa, he had observed the failed RAF "lean forward" offensive and the disastrous Dieppe landings. The Allied troops would be allowed to establish a fragile foothold, landing much of their valuable equipment on the beach but trapped in place by the strong coastal defenses. Then the massed panzers in reserve would push them back into the sea, a replay of the Dunkirk debacle.

General Geyr von Schweppenburg, commander of Panzer Group West, agreed with and supported von Rundstedt's plans.[3] Although the "massed panzers" were assigned to Panzer Group West, the tanks were not to move until released by Hitler himself. Panzer Group West was under von Rundstedt administratively, but directly under Hitler operationally. They were strictly trained as an attack force; they had no assigned geographic area to defend.

Despite Directive No. 51 and the forward beach defense strategy, Hitler favored von Rundstedt's ideas of concentrating panzers centrally for a mass attack, but still insisted they remain under his personal control. Von Rundstedt, Rommel, and von Schweppenburg all assumed that Hitler would rapidly release the tanks under his control when the invasion started. This practically ensured that German armor would not be used at the appropriate moment and fatally delayed their use on D-Day.

Hitler assured von Rundstedt and Rommel that a strong *Luftwaffe* fighter reserve would be rushed into France when the invasion started. This should restore German air superiority over the landing area. Strong armored forces covered by strong air forces would be concentrated, and von Rundstedt could unleash blitzkrieg on the trapped Allied armies.

Von Rundstedt divided France and the Low Countries into two areas, each defended by an army group. South of the Loire River was Army Group G, under *Generaloberst* Johannes Blaskowitz. This was considered the area of lesser threat. Assigned to Army Group G were the *1st* and *19th Armees*. The *1st Armee* defended the Bay of Biscay coast south of the Loire, while the *19th Armee* defended the French Mediterranean coast. Inland from the line of infantry divisions defending the coastlines were four powerful Panzer Group West armored divisions—three panzer divisions, and one panzer grenadier (mechanized infantry) division.

North of the Loire River, from Brittany in the west to Holland in the east, was Army Group B under Rommel. Just across the Channel from the Pas-de-Calais loomed the menacing but totally fictitious FUSAG, the First US

Army Group. This diversionary force was "commanded" by the much-respected General George Patton. Eisenhower hoped to hold the interest of Hitler and Rommel as long as possible with this decoy force.

The German *7th Armee* was deployed west of Caen, defending Normandy, the Cotentin Peninsula, and Brittany. Unknown to the Germans, it was the *7th Armee* that would face the actual invasion. Centered on the Pas-de-Calais was the *15th Armee*, defending the coast from Caen all the way to the estuary of the Rhine River in Holland.[4] Further northeast in Holland was the independent *LXXXVIII Korps*, all infantry, well dug in on difficult ground.

OBSTACLE

In the first six months of 1944, the Allies amassed over 1 million ground troops, 16 million tons of supplies, 3,500 artillery pieces, 4,200 tanks, and 137,000 other vehicles in England.[5] This vast ground army would have to cross the English Channel before it could begin fighting. The Channel was a major obstacle that kept the Nazis out of England in 1940 and the Allies out of France until 1944.

Even three months after D-Day, Eisenhower could not hope to land enough troops to fight all the divisions available to von Rundstedt in France and the Low Countries. The Allied invasion army in England was smaller than the German army, and it had to be moved piecemeal across the Channel, making it subject to German countermeasures, weather, and tides.

Eisenhower did not know that Hitler had hobbled the German defense by retaining direct control of German armor. Ike did know, however, that the Germans had the advantage of interior lines of communication. Each part of the German perimeter could be reinforced as required to counter an Allied invasion. The Germans could move forces within their area, unless impeded by Allied aircraft, more easily than the Allies could move around it.[6]

The Allies realized that the *7th Armee* and its part of the perimeter would have to be separated from the rest of the German forces so that the odds could be tipped in favor of the smaller Allied ground forces. Movement in and out of the *7th Armee* sector must be prevented, and German units within it pinned down by Allied aircraft. German mobility was the most critical target of Allied airpower.

The effort to deplete and sequester the *7th Armee* started with the information campaign of which FUSAG was a part. To reinforce the perception that they would land in the Pas-de-Calais, the Allies developed a "two-for-one" rule. For every target struck by aircraft in Normandy, two similar targets must be struck in the Pas-de-Calais.[7] This operation, code-named FORTITUDE, was an incredibly successful deception. Hitler built the toughest section of the *Atlantik Wall* and deployed the biggest of the four German field armies in France to protect the Pas-de-Calais. The Germans were lured away from Normandy and the *7th Armee* sector to fight the FUSAG landings that would never occur.

The crippling of the German fighter force accomplished by the Eighth Air Force from January to April 1944 meant the initial landings and follow-on support could proceed with minimal *Luftwaffe* interference. Von Rundstedt would not get his blitzkrieg. The *7th Armee* would fight alone under the crushing weight of Allied air superiority.

Still, more was needed to ensure an Allied victory.

CHAPTER FIFTY-FOUR

Trains (February–May 1944)

Railways are the arteries of modern armies. Vitality decreases when they are blocked and terminates when they are permanently severed.
—(British) Imperial Strategy, 1906[1]

Selected as the target for OVERLORD, the *7th Armee* occupied a zone bounded on the east by the Seine and on the south by the Loire. This part of France must be isolated by interdiction from potential supplies and reinforcements. Eisenhower's main concern was for the panzer and panzer grenadier formations located in northern France and Holland but outside the *7th Armee* sector. If they were moved into the battle zone early enough, they could easily push the invaders back into the sea. If these units could be kept out of the *7th Armee* area for an extended period, the defending Germans could be overwhelmed.

It was known from the Italian campaign raging to the south that interdiction by blocking railroads impeded rapid movement of the German army, which was heavily dependent on trains to move their armored divisions. Tanks were not designed for long road marches, and the numerous infantry divisions of the 15th, 1st, and 19th *Armees* also threatened the invasion force if they could be quickly moved to the targeted *7th Armee* area. Trains were necessary for the long-distance movement of these units, too. The German infantry units moved mainly on foot or by horsepower; only a fraction of its units even had trucks.

Years of battle attrition and the bombing of vital tank, motor transport, and tire factories had, in the words of Charles Winchester, "demodernized" the German army.[2] So the trains needed to be stopped, either at the river crossings or somewhere else on the route.

If this could be accomplished, it would be easier to move Allied troops across the Channel and into the battle area than German troops from eastern or southern France. The buildup of Allied power in the *7th Armee* sector could then overwhelm the defenders. The bottom line was a numbers game: The Allies had to move their forces across the Channel faster than the Germans could move theirs across France.

THE TRANSPORTATION PLAN

The German dependence on railroads had caught the eye of operational planners at AEAF, and by January they were completing plans for a concerted air effort against the French railway system. Initial bombing efforts and collateral French casualties had angered even some pro-Allied Frenchmen. This in turn resulted in a letter on January 10, 1944, from COSSAC (Lieutenant General Morgan) to AEAF AOC Leigh-Mallory on the potential costs and benefits of such a campaign.[3]

By January 25, a letter by the AEAF intelligence chief noted that Leigh-Mallory was "particularly anxious to deal with the railroads before D-Day so that his aircraft could concentrate on German road traffic once the invasion began." Leigh-Mallory felt that the anti-railroad interdiction campaign was worthwhile, leaving the questions of French casualties to the chiefs of staff. It was also noted that General Spaatz was "very anxious to find targets for the US strategic bomber force in support of OVERLORD, particularly for periods when the weather over Germany made POINTBLANK impossible."[4] The great railway bombing saga began in earnest.

General Eisenhower was aware of the German transportation vulnerabilities, both because of strategic intelligence forwarded to him from Washington and from tactical intelligence gathered by various Allied forces operating out of England. In early February, the air staff in Washington sent General Spaatz a completed study called "Creation of the Air Situation Necessary for OVERLORD and Air Operations in Support of OVERLORD." Appended to this study was a plan called TOPFLIGHT, calling for the destruction of bridges and other rail facilities in eastern France.

Headquarters Army Air Force in Washington estimated that the railroads carried 75 percent of German long-haul military freight, while the inland waterways (rivers and canals) carried another 20 percent. Only 5 percent was carried by motor vehicles. Bombing could damage or destroy fixed railroad facilities while locomotives, rolling stock (railroad cars), motor vehicles, and barges could be destroyed by bombing and strafing.[5]

The US Army Air Forces confidential magazine *Impact*, required reading for American aircrew and their generals, analyzed the weaknesses of the European railroad system:

It is a fundamental industry, being essential to all components of the civilian and war economies. It cannot be moved or dispersed. It is so large that it cannot be well defended. It is almost impossible to camouflage effectively. It cannot go underground. Targets are so numerous that there is almost always some part of the system which is not cloud-obscured despite general overcast weather. They are also so varied that they can be attacked by all kinds of aircraft. Heavy attacks within a certain area can be compensated for in part by shifting to road or water transport, but lost capacity cannot be balanced by expansion somewhere else as is the case in manufacturing. Finally, the effects of air attack are cumulative because the capital investment is exceptionally high and damage cannot be replaced at a rate comparable to the potential rate of new damage. As a result, policing costs [costs associated with reattacking the system as it is repaired] are low and enemy recuperation is slow.[6]

ZUCKERMAN

Ike directed Tedder to find a way to interdict the railways serving the *7th Armee*. Tedder turned to British physician and scientist Solly Zuckerman to develop a detailed interdiction plan. Zuckerman had come to work for the RAF in 1940, evaluating the effects of bomb blasts on personnel protected by various kinds of shelters. He used monkeys as test subjects, and his results were of great interest in a country undergoing the rigors of the Blitz. Zuckerman was considered the father of operational research—the application of scientific methods to study economic and military systems.

Later, Zuckerman was brought down to the Mediterranean as a scientific advisor for Tedder. Zuckerman documented his war service in a book, *From Apes to Warlords*. Working with primates required him to wear leather gauntlets for protection; unfortunately, he never learned to wear kid gloves in his career when working with general officers. He had little patience for the military mind-set.

Zuckerman's ideas became the core of the finalized AEAF "Transportation Plan" published on February 12, 1944. Bombing had already begun, but this marked the official beginning of the Plan. The Plan called for air interdiction attacks on seventy-eight key railroad marshaling yards and related facilities in France and Belgium.[7]

Marshaling yards are facilities in which a main railway line is split into numerous parallel tracks. This allows for railcars to be maintained, traded between trains or rerouted to other rail lines. Zuckerman noted that marshaling yards seemed to be the ideal target, as the clustered tracks were easy to damage using high-explosive bombs. Destruction of the repair and maintenance facilities and spare locomotives in the yards would be a secondary benefit.

Zuckerman had recommended a similar campaign in the Sicily–southern Italy attacks, and the resulting bombing had been judged a success. Unfortunately, Tedder assigned Leigh-Mallory and Zuckerman to champion the Plan before the other senior air commanders, not an inspired choice. Both men had an uncanny ability to irritate rather than convince their audience.

Both Harris and Spaatz resisted participation in the Transportation Plan; they felt it diverted their forces from POINTBLANK and the night campaign against German cities. Tedder quickly became aware that neither Harris nor Spaatz was willing to work or even accept coordination from Leigh-Mallory.[8] They had serious concerns about diverting their effort to such targets, especially since the marshaling yards of interest were well within range of Coningham's 2TAF and Brereton's Ninth Air Force medium bombers. Why divert the heavy bombers from their continued attack on the German homeland?

Figure 54.1. B-26 Marauder bombing marshaling yard. AIR FORCE HISTORICAL RESEARCH AGENCY

The 2TAF operated the Mosquito VI, the American-built Boston III (A-20), and Mitchell (B-25) bombers. The standard Ninth Air Force medium bomber in England was the B-26 Marauder. The Ninth also had significant numbers of A-20 light bombers, the same type of aircraft that had opened the American bombing campaign back in July 1942. The RAF and USAAF had been bombing targets in France with light and medium bombers for years and their crews were highly skilled and courageous.

Allied light and medium bombers often flew diversionary missions to decoy German fighters away from daylight strategic bombing. They were also bombing suspected German vengeance weapons sites in France. Existing interdiction targets attacked were the German supply system, including airfields and air depots; stocks of equipment; and logistical facilities. Now the Mosquitoes, Mitchells, Bostons, A-20s, and B-26s were directed against marshaling yards.

Unfortunately, marshaling yards in France often had civilian dwellings for the workers clustered around them in adjacent villages and towns. This was no problem when the targets were in Axis countries. Now the Allied air forces would be bombing in France and Belgium. Harris brought his concerns to his immediate boss, RAF Chief of Air Staff Portal. Bomber Command was not trained or equipped for daylight precision attack of marshaling yards, or anything else.

Harris estimated that he would kill 80,000 to 100,000 French civilians, and many more thousands would be maimed. Harris commanded a bomber force that emphasized massed attack against area targets. Harris had no problem killing German civilians, but the French populace was another matter. Bomber Command was a mace, not a rapier, so he was sincere if overly pessimistic in his opinion. Ike and Tedder refuted the estimates and countered that only a successful OVERLORD could free the French from the Nazi yoke.

Choke Points and Oil

A second proposal for crippling the *Luftwaffe* and the German army in France came from operational planners within the RAF and USAAF. They proposed and championed interdiction of targets other than marshaling yards, including key bridges, tunnels, and other "choke points." Such places were harder to repair than marshaling yards, and most were located outside of heavily populated areas. Attacks against German airfields in France, a long-standing Allied effort, would also intensify.

General Spaatz felt Zuckerman's Transportation Plan would not paralyze the German rail network as claimed. He proposed a third alternative: to continue and intensify the attacks on the German synthetic fuel industry. Germany had no domestic natural oil resources, depending on imports and the conversion of abundant coal reserves into gasoline. Now with the advance of the Russians from the east and the Allies from the south, Germany's oil imports were threatened.[9]

Even though attacks on synthetic fuel plants might not slow the German army before the invasion, such attacks in the long term would stop enemy movement altogether. It would keep German fighters on the ground and turn the panzers into static pillboxes. Fuel was too critical a commodity for the Germans not to defend.[10]

In the event, there were sufficient resources to proceed with all three options: hit the marshaling yards; hit the choke points; and hit the synthetic fuel industry. All three could be considered *air interdiction*, preventing the flow of vital materials to the enemy fighting forces, including the *7th Armee*.

CHAPTER FIFTY-FIVE

Compromises (April–May 1944)

Leigh-Mallory and Zuckerman faded to the background as Eisenhower and Tedder continued to sell the Transportation Plan to Spaatz and Harris. Churchill intervened. He was no fan of killing French civilians, especially so close to their liberation. The prime minister told Ike, "Postwar France must be our friend. It is not alone a question of humanitarianism. It is also a question of high state policy."[1] Churchill was particularly sensitive to the use of Harris's bombers at night; he feared they would cause most of the deaths.

Tedder would not wait for blanket authority to hit all the targets; he put RAF Bomber Command to work right away on the targets already approved by the chiefs of staff. When ordered to suspend night bombing and begin daylight-only precision bombing of French targets, Harris skillfully rebuilt Bomber Command to meet the new requirements. This eliminated Churchill's fear of night area bombing of French towns adjacent to interdiction targets.

Harris's heavy bombers began attacking daylight transportation targets on March 6, 1944. The *Luftwaffe* generally did not appear except for intense flak defending some targets. It was not enough. The first target was a marshaling yard at Trappes, France. In the next few weeks Bomber Command bombed fourteen more French transportation targets, including marshaling yards at Aulnoye, Le Mans, Amiens, Longeau, Courtrai, and Laon.[2]

During the attack on the Vaires marshaling yard, the British bombers ravaged not only the target but also the *Waffen SS Division Frundsberg* whose troop trains happened to be on the sidings of the yard. Adjacent to the troops were cars full of mines, which amplified the German casualties. After the raid, relief troops collected nearly 1,200 identity disks from the dead.[3]

Although bombing accuracy was satisfactory, civilian casualties were also substantial. Two attacks against Le Mans and Lille alone killed over 500 civilians. The German press hypocritically protested "the Anglo-American terrorist bombings." An RAF target was the rail center at Rouen. Rouen, it will be remembered, was the town in which the English had burned Jeanne d'Arc. A

Figure 55.1. Shattered rolling stock in marshaling yard. NATIONAL ARCHIVES AND RECORDS ADMINISTRATION

French newspaper opined, "So, as in the past, France is atrociously ravaged by a ferocious adversary, always the same one after ten centuries."[4]

The Resistance movement in France and Belgium added to the weight of the Allied air attack. As Allied aircraft pounded various targets, French and Belgian operatives cut railroad tracks, sabotaged locomotives, and attacked supply trains.[5] The attacks against the German rail system were round-the-clock, just like the strategic bombing of Germany.

For Eisenhower, it was never a matter of POINTBLANK and RAF night bombing of Germany versus the Transportation Plan, but rather his control of sufficient airpower to make the invasion a success. Ike insisted the Strategic Air Forces, the American Eighth Air Force (Spaatz and Doolittle), and RAF Bomber Command (Harris) be under his command when needed. Eisenhower's Mediterranean experience reinforced this conviction.[6]

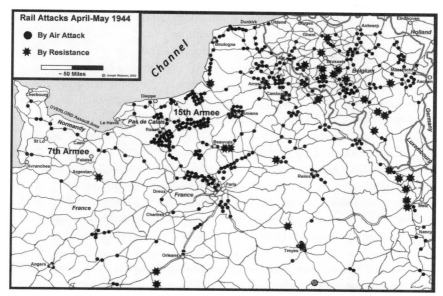

Map 55.1. Rail attacks by Allied aircraft and the French Resistance on marshaling yards, bridges, and other transportation targets, April–May 1944. MOLYSON

On March 25, about six weeks after the formal Transportation Plan was published by the AEAF, a meeting was held between Eisenhower and the senior air commanders in London to finally settle the matter. Ike had one objective: to ensure that the air forces would support OVERLORD during the critical period before, during, and after the landings. Tedder continued to champion the Transportation Plan with Eisenhower's support. Ike was willing to accept even "a small reduction" in railway traffic into the *7th Armee* sector.

Spaatz spoke up for his "Oil Plan," the campaign against the German synthetic fuel industry, but did not make his case to the others. Spaatz could not promise to completely shut off the fuel before the invasion. That was a showstopper. He delayed raising the issue again.

Harris had little left to champion; night bombing was getting as expensive as day bombing. Lucrative night targets were getting scarce. There was no nighttime equivalent to the P-51. German radar-directed night fighters and flak were making life increasingly difficult for Bomber Command. Harris was also surprised how effective his bombers were against the marshaling yards at Trappes and the other targets. In the end Harris and Spaatz agreed to bomb transportation targets; they had little choice.

Air Chief Marshals Portal and Tedder crafted a compromise that made the subordination of the heavy bombers to Eisenhower more palatable. Eisenhower would get heavy bomber support in executing the Transportation Plan. Tedder and not Leigh-Mallory would be the link between Ike and bomber commanders Spaatz and Harris. "The Supreme Commander has designated the Deputy Supreme Commander [Tedder] as responsible for supervision of all [air] operations concerned with 'POINTBLANK' and 'OVERLORD.'"[7]

Leigh-Mallory accepted a reduced role.[8] Tedder, Spaatz, and Harris would all perform functions Leigh-Mallory had thought belonged to him. In the final analysis, his AEAF consisted only of the RAF 2nd Tactical Air Force (2TAF) and the US Ninth Air Force. Tedder would direct all OVERLORD air operations. Leigh-Mallory, Spaatz, and Harris would operate as equals under Tedder's control.[9] Spaatz was also authorized to continue POINTBLANK and oil attacks when there were no suitable OVERLORD targets for his heavy daylight bombers and escorts.

General Montgomery, the overall ground commander for OVERLORD, was confident that the Transportation Plan and the OVER-LORD landings would succeed despite the heavy odds against him and his troops. On April 7, 1944, Montgomery made a presentation to the king, the prime minister, Eisenhower, and other assembled civilian and military leaders at his headquarters in St. Paul's School, London.

Montgomery stated that only seven and two-thirds divisions could be landed in France in the initial attack. It would take three months to transport all thirty-five Allied divisions in Britain to France. The Allies had their own choke points, landing all troops and their equipment over five open beaches and through two limited-capacity artificial harbors.

There would be fifty-five German divisions in the West on D-Day. The lengthy buildup was risky, but the Allies were relying on air supremacy to immobilize German divisions and keep the *Luftwaffe* at bay. The Transportation Plan was critical to OVERLORD's success.[10]

Three days later, Ike issued his formal directive to Leigh-Mallory, Spaatz, and Harris. It called for all Allied air forces to: assist the landings; maintain the combined bomber offensive; maintain air superiority over France; and attack rail communications in France and Belgium.[11] Eisenhower, the great compromiser, had focused his disparate air commanders on the main goal of the European War—the liberation of France.

The American and British strategic air forces continued their campaign against Germany at a reduced tempo. No one wanted to throw away the accomplishments of POINTBLANK; if the air attacks into Germany were called off now, the German fighter forces might be able to rebound before D-Day. Tedder also ordered Spaatz to make CROSSBOW—attacks against German vengeance weapons sites along the French coast—and not POINTBLANK his highest priority. Now both CROSSBOW and the Transportation Plan were to divert heavy bombers away from POINTBLANK.

CHAPTER FIFTY-SIX

Mort pour la France (April–May 1944)

The French government recognized those French civilians and Allied soldiers who were killed during the Liberation with the honorific MORT POUR LA FRANCE, meaning, literally, "died for France." The phrase also appeared on American graves in Normandy after the invasion, along with flowers.

Even with Eisenhower and Tedder firmly in control of Allied airpower preparing for D-Day, the dispute about marshaling yards as transportation targets was not over. The British War Cabinet met on April 27 on the issue of French casualties and what they called the "Marshaling Yards Plan." On Saturday, April 29, 1944, Churchill tried once more to convince Eisenhower about the potentially disastrous French casualties that could result by completing the marshaling yard attacks.

The British War Cabinet wanted a revision of the plan to exclude targets with potential French casualties in excess of 100 to 150 souls. They also wanted reconsideration of other kinds of interdiction or destruction of German military materiel. Significantly, the War Cabinet demanded that Churchill send a message directly to the American president after appropriate review by Eisenhower.

Two days later the British War Cabinet issued an adverse report on the Transportation Plan results. D-Day was only five weeks away and the marshaling yard targets were not yet yielding the desired results. As the Transportation Plan missions were flown, the JIC (Joint Intelligence Subcommittee, British War Cabinet) collected information from various sources to evaluate its effectiveness in support of OVERLORD. The May 1 weekly update echoed earlier JIC reports:

Effect on Transportation.—Heavy damage to main lines and marshalling yards in France and the Low Countries is being repaired reasonably quickly, at least to the extent required for military purposes. Locomotive, rolling-stock

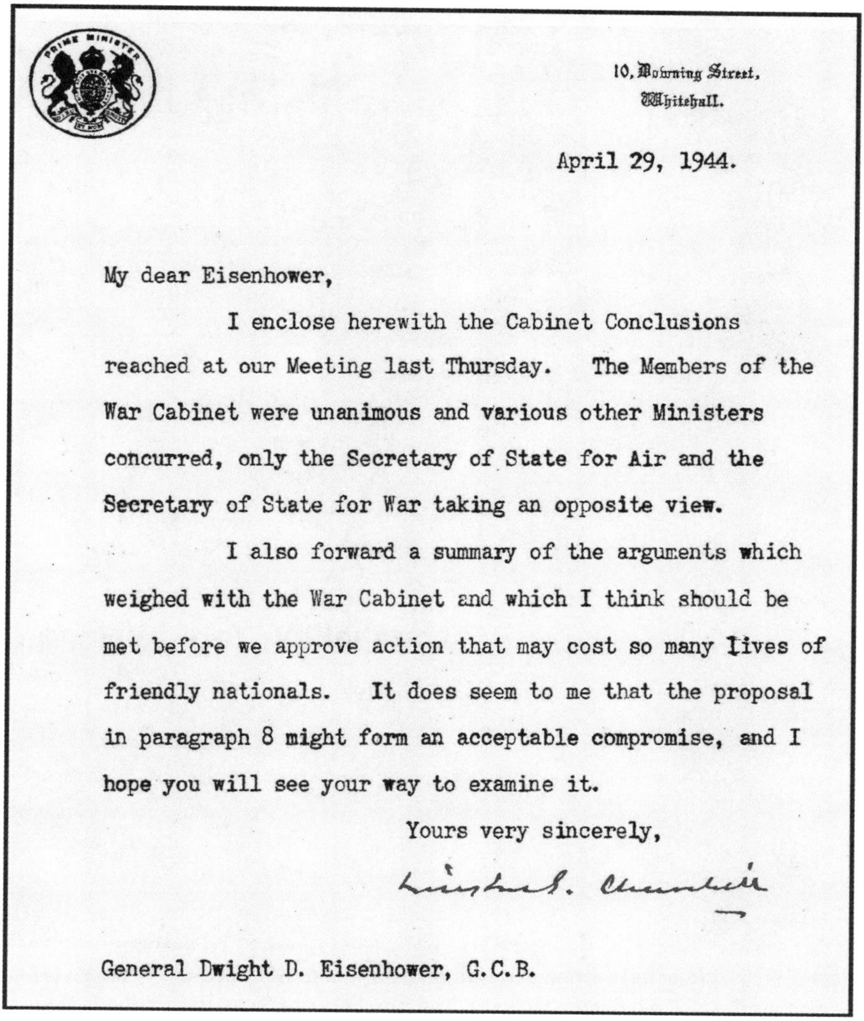

10, Downing Street,
Whitehall.

April 29, 1944.

My dear Eisenhower,

      I enclose herewith the Cabinet Conclusions reached at our Meeting last Thursday. The Members of the War Cabinet were unanimous and various other Ministers concurred, only the Secretary of State for Air and the Secretary of State for War taking an opposite view.

      I also forward a summary of the arguments which weighed with the War Cabinet and which I think should be met before we approve action that may cost so many lives of friendly nationals. It does seem to me that the proposal in paragraph 8 might form an acceptable compromise, and I hope you will see your way to examine it.

                Yours very sincerely,

                Winston S. Churchill

General Dwight D. Eisenhower, G.C.B.

Figure 56.1. Churchill's memo to Eisenhower on possible French casualties caused by the Transportation Plan. NATIONAL ARCHIVES AND RECORDS ADMINISTRATION, RECORD GROUP 331, BOX 66

Marshalling Yard Village

Figure 56.2. What Tedder and Zuckerman said was most effective: A-20s accurately hit the Busigny marshaling yard. The bombers are flying toward the bottom of the picture. The explosions are grouped in three parallel tracks, each representing a squadron dropping their bombs on cue by their lead bombardier. The two tracks on the right demolish the marshaling yard; the track on the left misses. AIR FORCE HISTORICAL RESEARCH AGENCY, KARLSRUHE COLLECTION

Marshalling Yard   Village

Figure 56.3. What Churchill and the RAF and USAAF targeting staffs feared most: A model village for railway workers at Busigny is hit by mistake in a subsequent attack. Note the smoke from the previous attack's bomb impacts. Possible causes are bad setting on the leader's bombsight or misidentification of the village as part of the marshaling yard. The bomb impacts are grouped close together (precision) but are not accurate on the intended target. AIR FORCE HISTORICAL RESEARCH AGENCY, KARLSRUHE COLLECTION

*and repair facilities, particularly heavy cranes, have been considerably dam-
aged and cannot be repaired for many months. Nevertheless, enemy military
traffic is not at present being appreciably hindered and the weight of disloca-
tion is falling primarily on French civilian traffic.*[1]

On May 3, a high-level meeting was held at SHAEF. Chaired by Tedder
and attended by Leigh-Mallory and Zuckerman, it was called to consider
alternatives to the marshaling yard targets being hit in the Transportation Plan.
Tedder, having read the reports coming out of the JIC, knew more needed to
be done. The answer—"Bridges!"—was being loudly shouted from the sidelines
by frustrated RAF and USAAF targeting personnel, and even Zuckerman had
considered the bridge solution.

It was recommended that only the Seine bridges to the east of the *7th Armee*
be attacked before the invasion, but not the Loire bridges to the south until after
D-Day. Attacking both the Seine and Loire bridges would tip the Germans off
that the landing would occur in Normandy rather than where they expected it,
in the Pas-de-Calais. It was also recommended that the Meuse bridges to the
east of the *15th Armee* in the Pas-de-Calais be bombed again to make it appear
that the invasion would occur in the Pas-de-Calais area. Of course, bombing the
Meuse bridges also cut off some rail communications with Germany.

At the meeting, it was asked if adding bridges as targets canceled the Transportation Plan marshaling yard campaign. Chairman Tedder emphasized that
the supreme Allied commander (Eisenhower) insisted it continue.[2]

Watching French casualties mount as D-Day approached, Churchill heeded
the War Cabinet and referred the matter directly to President Roosevelt. In a
message sent on May 7, Churchill noted that the military was doing everything
possible to minimize casualties. Leaflets and other means were used to warn
people away from likely targets, but Frenchmen were still dying. He concluded
his message to Roosevelt as follows:

*The War Cabinet shares my apprehensions of the bad effect which will be pro-
duced up the French population by these slaughters . . . Accordingly they ask
me to invite you to consider the matter from the highest political standpoint
and to give us your opinion as a matter between governments. It must be
remembered on the one hand that this slaughter is among a friendly people
who have committed no crimes against us, and not among the German foe
with all their record of cruelty and ruthlessness.*[3]

Churchill went on about ardent support of OVERLORD, but he also stated that his War Cabinet wanted to cancel the Transportation Plan and end excessive French casualties. Roosevelt refused to intervene from across the Atlantic. Roosevelt went on to say that although he regretted the death of so many civilians, he would not second-guess the judgment of the invasion's military leaders from across the Atlantic.[4]

The bombing continued and the invasion approached. Each casualty was a necessary death for France.

CHAPTER FIFTY-SEVEN

The Bridge at Vernon (May 1944)

Although the May 3 SHAEF meeting to discuss alternatives to marshaling yards designated the Eighth Air Force to hit the rail bridges, the airmen within the AEAF (2TAF and Ninth Air Force) were also eager to try their luck against bridge targets. It was thought the use of medium bombers and even fighter-bombers would be "technically practicable."

American officers with recent experience in Italy stated that bridges were not extraordinarily tough targets; in fact, they were relatively easy to damage. Air Marshal Sir John Slessor, the senior RAF officer in Italy, stated unequivocally that bridges had emerged as worthwhile targets. Of the twenty-five cuts made by Allied aircraft in the Italian railway network, sixteen had been made by demolishing a bridge.[1]

Slessor also marveled at how accurately medium bombers in Italy had hit and destroyed bridge targets using level-bombing techniques. Light and medium bombers were to be used to attack some bridges in France and Belgium, where it was hoped they could repeat the accomplishments of their Mediterranean counterparts. Dive-bombing by P-47 Thunderbolts was also an effective way to bring down a bridge.

In dive-bombing, the pilot of the attacking aircraft descends at a steep incline, drops his bomb at the appropriate altitude, and then pulls up sharply. This is opposed to level bombing, when a bomb-aimer or bombardier normally releases the ordnance using a precision bombsight while the pilot holds the aircraft on a steady course,

In 1941, American airmen had observed the effectiveness of the German Ju 87 Stuka dive-bomber against the Allies in Western Europe. The Stuka was a highly capable ground support aircraft but was very vulnerable to enemy fighters, as demonstrated in the Battle of Britain. Later, they were employed successfully in Russia and in the Mediterranean until the advent of better Allied fighters in those theaters.

Figure 57.1. Why the Allied air forces preferred bridges: Accurate and precise bombing of Mantes-Gassicourt bridge by USAAF medium bombers in May 1944; west is top of photo. Note the twelfth-century Notre Dame de Mantes Church on the west bank of the Seine, which was undamaged. General Patton's first foothold across the Seine was established here on August 19, 1944, but his assault troops had to cross the river west (top) to east (bottom) in assault boats and over a narrow dam until a replacement treadway bridge build by US Army combat engineers was built. AIR FORCE HISTORICAL RESEARCH AGENCY, KARLSRUHE COLLECTION

The USAAF acquired a few Douglas SBD Dauntless dive-bombers from a navy contract and designated the aircraft the A-24. In navy service, the Dauntless dive-bomber was the deadliest ship-killer in the Pacific War. In early 1942 the army used the A-24 operationally only in the South Pacific, and the planes were soon relegated to secondary roles. The A-24 was replaced by the A-20 and B-25 level bombers. No A-24s were sent to Europe by the USAAF.

In September 1943, an enterprising officer, Major Glenn Duncan of the 353rd Fighter Group, suggested that the new P-47D Thunderbolt would be an excellent dive-bomber. He was soon chartered to develop the tactics necessary to use the Thunderbolt in this way. Without dive flaps or a bombsight, and using drop-tank shackles to hold the bombs, Duncan soon accomplished his objective. Additional help with tactics development came from Italy, where the Jug was already being successfully employed as a dive-bomber. By November P-47s carrying 500-pound bombs had attacked a German airfield near Saint-Omer, France. It was the first of many such attacks before and after D-Day.[2]

Major Duncan's pioneering dive-bombing work would soon be applied to the bridge problem. Brigadier General Frederic H. Smith Jr., second-highest-ranking US officer at Headquarters AEAF, developed a plan to use P-47s to bomb the Seine bridges. It is believed that Smith's plan caught the attention of Churchill, ensuring quick approval by Leigh-Mallory.[3]

On May 7 the Ninth Air Force's 363rd Fighter Group conducted trial attacks with P-47s each armed with two 1,000-pound bombs. At Vernon, France, twelve P-47s descended from overcast skies at noon to hit a steel railway bridge.

The first plane dropped its bombs into the northern bridge abutment at point-blank range, then jinked away through heavy rapid-fire flak. By the time

Figure 57.2. The ruined railroad bridge at Vernon, France. AIR FORCE HISTORICAL RESEARCH AGENCY, KARLSRUHE COLLECTION

the sixth plane attacked, the north end of the steel rail bridge had dropped into the Seine. Two more planes managed to drop the entire span into the Seine, partially blocking the river. The rest of the aircraft flattened a nearby ammunition facility. Two Thunderbolts were lost, but the use of fighter-bombers to attack bridges was affirmed.[4]

The rest of the 363rd Fighter Group struck other bridges at nearby Mantes, but their tough concrete construction defied Allied bombs until the fuse settings were adjusted for delayed detonation. On May 8, additional bridges were attacked near the Belgian frontier. These bridges carried traffic from Germany itself, and their destruction partially isolated both the *7th* and *15th Armees.*

Medium and light bombers and fighter-bombers of the Ninth Air Force and 2TAF soon joined in the interdiction attacks against bridges. By May 27, of the roughly 1,000 sorties that had been flown against bridges, fighter-bombers, including P-47s, P-51s, Typhoons, and Spitfires, had flown more than half.[5] Fourteen bridges were destroyed or rendered unusable. The bridge attacks would continue through D-Day.

Chapter Fifty-Eight
CHATTANOOGA (May 1944)

If you were flying down the length of the train and it exploded in front of you, you had it right then. Nothing to do but pat you in the face with a shovel.
—Lieutenant Colonel William R. Dunn, P-47 pilot[1]

On May 21, two weeks before D-Day, Allied fighter-bombers began Operation CHATTANOOGA, a massive hunt across France and Belgium, cutting deeply into German transportation capability. In military terms it was "armed reconnaissance," a nice way of telling the pilots to go out and kill something important. The "important" targets in this case were locomotives, railcars, and barges.

Figure 58.1. Strafing barges: Waterways carried 20 percent of German war materiel. NINTH AIR FORCE GUN CAMERA FILM, COURTESY OF JOHN DRUMMOND

Eisenhower stockpiled 1,000 new locomotives and 20,000 railcars in England to replace French equipment his raging airmen destroyed in this campaign.[2] CHATTANOOGA was designed to make even functioning railroad lines unusable to the Germans. Some of the French locomotives lost their steam spectacularly as .50 caliber bullets punched holes in their boilers. Such damage was seldom fatal to the locomotive; the holes were easily patched and the engine returned to service.[3] Without the marshaling yard repair facilities, however, such repairs were more problematical.

Figure 58.2. P-47 pilot hits an ammunition train car as seen from his wingman's gun camera. NINTH AIR FORCE GUN CAMERA FILM, COURTESY OF JOHN DRUMMOND / NATIONAL ARCHIVES AND RECORDS ADMINISTRATION REF. 342-FH-3A18011-54056AC

Although the French were warned to avoid rail travel, unfortunately some were killed in strafing attacks. Canal barges were also strafed in order to prevent Germans from using this method of transportation. Former Eagle Squadron pilot Bill Dunn had his own opinions about strafing trains:

Well, it could be a lot of fun—depends on how you did it. Yes, it's pretty wild to see all that steam go flying up in the air after you've hit the boiler good. Of course it's a lot more fun if the train was carrying ammunition, but also a little more dangerous as well. That makes it more of a 4th of July fireworks show than just the locomotive. But shooting up a locomotive was interesting if you did it right.

There are lots of tricks to the trade, you know, in attacking a locomotive or train. The Germans used to put flak cars in front and back of the train, and a great number of people made the fatal mistake of attacking the train head-on or astern and flying down the length of the train, shooting up each carriage or car in turn. Dead ducks they were, as they gave the ground gunners a no-deflection shot at them—just head-on shooting or right up the guy's rear end as he passed overhead.

But if you attacked the train from about 30 degrees or so from the beam, giving the gunners some deflection, you could normally get in and out without any problem. Another thing, too, was if the train was carrying ammunition and blew up in front of you; you could go through the flying debris reasonably safely if you were flying through at a 30- or 40-degree angle. But if you were flying down the length of the train and it exploded in front of you, you had it right then. Nothing to do but pat you in the face with a shovel.[4]

CHAPTER FIFTY-NINE

Reactions (May 1944)

Even with the rail bridges added to the Transportation Plan, bombing of the marshaling yards with French civilian casualties continued. Finally, on May 25, General Charles de Gaulle's French Committee for National Liberation (FNCL) had had enough. They delivered a strong note to the American embassy in Algiers that was forwarded by cable to London. Despite their objections, the Transportation Plan would continue until after D-Day.

On May 27, a summary of the results of the Transportation Plan was issued. It was the first report to show truly positive results.[1] The plan was working now that bridges had been added as targets. Since the attacks started on February 9, seventy-two marshaling yards and related facilities had been attacked, of which forty-two were either destroyed or operating on a very restricted basis. Thirty-eight attacks had also been made on fourteen bridges, cutting at least ten rail lines.

Repair efforts had finally fallen behind the attacks, and attempts were made only in those locations where small efforts yielded good dividends. Much of the German east–west traffic had been stopped or diverted far south of Paris, the intended effect. French civil traffic had ceased in the area. Over 6,000 French and Belgian civilians would die in the Transportation Plan attacks by June 1, as well as over 3,200 Germans. Despite the FNCL cautions, the Resistance movements accepted the civilian casualties as the cost of liberation—*C'est la guerre*. The civilians living close to rail facilities were less generous, although the report noted that those not directly affected by the raids soon forgot them.

By the end of May, less than a week before D-Day, Bomber Command had struck 95 percent of its assigned targets, dropping some 35,000 of the 48,000 tons of bombs used so far. The AEAF (Ninth Air Force and 2TAF) also had attacked some 95 percent of its targets, delivering over 8,000 tons. The Eighth Air Force had hit 90 percent of its transportation targets by the end of May, using over 4,000 tons of bombs, while continuing to hit POINTBLANK and other strategic targets. The transportation crunch blocked not only German troop movements but also the cement and coal necessary to continue construction of V-weapons sites and the *Atlantik Wall*. This slowed work on these vital programs to a crawl.

Shortage of materials, particularly cement and land mines, due both to production and to transportation difficulties, affected all fortification work. The shortage of cement, critical even at the outset of the winter construction program, was greatly intensified by the Allies' all-out rail bombing and barge-strafing offensive. For example, late in May the German LXXXIV Corps in Holland received 47 carloads of cement in a three-day period, against a minimum *daily* need of 240 carloads.

Two days after this report was made, the flow of cement to the *7th Armee* area stopped altogether as trains had to be diverted to carrying more urgently needed freight. The cement works in Cherbourg were forced to shut down for lack of coal. Plans were then made to bring up cement by canal to Rouen and ship by sea to the *7th Armee* area, but this was a last-minute solution and could never be tried out.[2] In any case, Coastal Command strike wings would have interdicted this resupply effort.

On June 3, the German air force operations staff reported that German railway officials were doubtful if any more effort should be expended to repair the rail system because of the extent of the damage. The *Luftwaffe* was just as dependent as the army on rail transportation. When de Gaulle met with the prime minister the following day, he was more interested in maintaining the ability to communicate with his FNCL headquarters in Algiers than with Churchill's apology for French casualties. Politics and de Gaulle's intended role as the savior of the French were preeminent. A military man, he understood that defeating the Germans was a costly undertaking. Losing to them was worse. This was fortunate, since many French towns were targeted on the "First Line of Interdiction" to have their streets blocked by rubble from bombing.[3]

The 2TAF, Eighth and Ninth Air Forces, and RAF Bomber Command flew more than 100,000 interdiction sorties in support of OVERLORD before the landing began. By D-Day all the Seine bridges had been dropped or rendered unusable. This effectively cut off rapid movement between the *7th Armee* and 15th *Armee*. The Germans did not deduce that the invasion was aimed at Normandy, possibly because they assumed the bombing was meant to prevent reinforcement of the 15th *Armee* from the west.

The isolation of the *7th Armee* would be completed by the bombing of key roads and railroads and direct attack against German units in the Orléans Gap between Paris and Orléans. After D-Day the bridges along the Loire River were also struck. Hundreds of locomotives and thousands of railcars were also destroyed. Along with this rolling stock, fixed railroad facilities including roundhouses, water towers, and maintenance sheds were leveled.[4]

Figure 59.1. Flak was a continuous threat to Allied aircraft even after *Luftwaffe* fighters were depleted in France. AIR FORCE HISTORICAL RESEARCH AGENCY, KARLSRUHE COLLECTION

The Transportation Plan and the bridge attacks crippled the rail network, forcing increased utilization of scarce German motor transport. It took about 180 trucks to replace one train. Allied airpower would in fact make it easier for the Allies to move a division across the Channel than for the Germans to move a division across the Seine into Normandy. Once there, the Allied division had superb twenty-four-hour mobility while its German counterpart could only move on the roads at night.[5]

After his capture, an RAF officer interrogated the director of railway operations for OKW, Colonel Hans Höffner. The RAF officer asked, "Which events did you dread most during the bombing offensive before the invasion? What did you fear most as regards its effects after the invasion?" Höffner replied, "We dreaded attacks on bridges most, and they actually proved extremely serious, and secondly, attacks on workshops and coaling plants—that is, attacks on communications centers, owing to their effect on repair and coal installations."

The RAF officer, perhaps a marshaling yard proponent, attempted to clarify the effectiveness of bridge bombing: "As regards bridges, what I meant by my last question was not so much which causes did you dread most, but which effects did you fear most of all before the invasion?"

Höffner said firmly, "We dreaded attacks on bridges the most."[6]

CHAPTER SIXTY

Airfields and Radars (January–May 1944)

Even as the controversy raged over French marshaling yards, American daylight attacks against German airfields in France, Belgium, and Holland that began in July 1942 continued. Bad-weather days in Germany allowed targets in the clear in France to be attacked. On February 5, 1944, for example, seven *Luftwaffe* airfields were hit by 441 B-17s and 106 B-24s, escorted by 542 P-47s from the Eighth Air Force.

The weather that day was excellent; total enemy opposition was fifteen fighters, with four destroyed and five probably destroyed. Some flak was encountered at the coast and moderate-intensity flak was seen over the targets. One B-24 was lost to enemy aircraft, and another went down for unknown causes. Two B-17s too damaged to land were abandoned by parachute over England. Seventy-two B-17s and twenty B-24s were reported damaged. Bombing results were good. Hangars, repair shops, barracks, and aircraft and storage facilities at the various bases were destroyed or damaged.[1]

ASSAULT ON THE AIRFIELDS

The P-47 matured in the dive-bomber role. On March 17, 1944, fifteen bomb-equipped P-47s escorted by thirteen other "clean" Thunderbolts hit the major German fighter base at Soesterberg, Holland. Photographed on March 25, 1944, the following assessment was made:

> *The damage to the A/F [airfield] is mainly in the area that encloses Hangars, Repair Shops, Offices and Stores. All 3 hangars are severely damaged, 5 medium buildings either destroyed or severely damaged, 1 small building gutted and another severely damaged.[2]*

By May 3, some forty-one airfields had been identified for destruction. The criteria for an airfield to become a target were fairly simple: location within 130 miles of the OVERLORD assault area, and having functional aircraft maintenance facilities.[3] By destroying these key airfields the *Luftwaffe* would have as far to fly to the invasion area as the Allies based in England. There were too many additional German dispersal landing strips without facilities to cover adequately, especially since many of them were unidentified.

The excitement of airfield attacks could become a deadly fixation, as noted by Captain John Godfrey: "Each time I'd tell myself this was the last [pass], but eagerness overcame caution . . . until on the fifth pass the firing at me was so heavy I could literally smell the hot lead around me."[4]

Target airfields ranged from Brest eastward to the Pas-de-Calais and into Holland.[5] The main *Luftwaffe* aircraft repair facilities in France were severely degraded by bombing. A few remaining aircraft factory and related aviation support facilities were also attacked before D-Day.

Airfield bombing in France and Belgium contributed to POINTBLANK by destroying German aircraft and reducing the German air force capability to fly in more fighters from Germany once the invasion began. In addition, the approach of German bombers from distant bases allowed more time for Allied fighters to intercept and destroy them. The paucity of remaining German fighters under *Luftflotte 3* in France changed the threat picture for Allied aircraft. As in the old Circus/Rhubarb days of 1941–1942, flak became the main danger to

Figure 60.1. Strafing inhibited German use of their airfields. Note the ubiquitous Thunderbolt. The target aircraft is a French-built LeO 45 taken into German service. AIR FORCE HISTORICAL RESEARCH AGENCY, KARLSRUHE COLLECTION

Allied aircraft. For the medium bombers, attack altitude was changed to 10,000 feet. This was above the light flak (which was effective up to 7,500 feet) and below the heavy flak (ineffective below 13,000 feet).[6]

So depleted was the *Luftwaffe* that for two weeks before D-Day it carried out no reconnaissance over southern and southwestern England, depriving the German High Command of important knowledge which would have indicated the probable direction of the Allied assault.[7] After all, most of the invading Allied army and its invasion fleet were there.

The German air force planned to fly in about 500 fighters from Germany once the landings occurred. Göring had ordered the preparation of appropriate airfield facilities to receive the reinforcements. Aggressive bombing of the airfields ruined these preparations, such as they were.[8] It was a kind of interdiction against air forces similar to the transportation interdiction being inflicted on the ground forces. An aggressive commander running *Luftflotte 3* might have fared better in competing with priority programs like the V-weapons sites and the *Atlantik Wall*.

Generalfeldmarschall Hugo Sperrle—having led the German air force in France since the Battle of Britain days, and now in command of *Luftflotte 3*—was unable to keep pace with Allied damage to his airfields. Therefore, the ability to receive air reinforcements from Germany was limited. *Luftflotte 3* was a victim of interdiction just as real as that against the *7th Armee*. Total Allied air superiority on and after D-Day and the poorly trained *Luftwaffe* pilot force doomed the reinforcement effort to failure.

Figure 60.2. Würzburg-Reise coastal early warning radar. AIR FORCE HISTORICAL RESEARCH AGENCY, KARLSRUHE COLLECTION, GREEN PHOTO 058

KILLING THE RADARS

The final interdiction effort was against German information and the ability to collect it. On May 10, most of the German coastal radars were taken out. Of special note were rocket-firing Typhoon fighters that destroyed many of these facilities. A few were left standing so that they could play their role in the deception effort. During the last two weeks of May, Allied strategic and tactical air forces carried out attacks on enemy batteries and radar sites along the English Channel coast. By the first week of June, the strikes had destroyed about 80 percent of German coastal radar capability.[9]

Total cost for the interdiction campaign against the *7th Armee* and *Luftflotte 3* was some 2,000 Allied aircraft and some 12,000 crewmen. Thousands more were lost attacking POINTBLANK targets. More Allied airmen died in the European Theater of Operations while preparing for OVERLORD during the first five months of 1944 than would die on land, sea, and air on D-Day.[10]

Normandy, however, was now ripe for invasion.

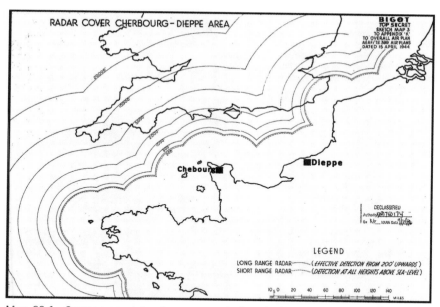

Map 60.1. German coastal radar coverage before the Typhoon anti-radar campaign. NATIONAL ARCHIVES AND RECORDS ADMINISTRATION

CHAPTER SIXTY-ONE

To Cross the Narrow Seas (May 1944)

General Morgan's COSSAC Plan envisioned D-Day to occur in May of 1944. This would be the beginning of the so-called "campaigning season," with generally good weather, passable dirt roads, and long daylight hours. It was the same reasoning Hitler's generals used to begin *Fall Gelb* (Case Yellow) back in 1940. After studying the plan, possible German strategy, and the strength of the German army, Eisenhower and Montgomery expanded the invasion from three to five amphibious divisions.

Figure 61.1. Higgins landing craft plant in New Orleans. The author's grandfather, a World War I veteran, worked at this plant. NAVAL HISTORY AND HERITAGE COMMAND PHOTO

The number of landing craft became a critical planning criterion. Operations in Italy had consumed large quantities of the vessels, and some US production was also diverted to the Pacific Campaign. Each amphibious assault reduced the number of landing craft available. It would take time to build enough additional craft to meet the five-division requirement.

The invasion of Southern France, Operation ANVIL, was postponed until August of 1944 as a supporting attack after the main landing in the north. This made more landing craft available for the OVERLORD effort. In the end, it was decided to reschedule D-Day for early June. Meanwhile, the Allied airmen continued to pound the Germans throughout Occupied Europe.

The Allied air forces had completed the missions determined by a president, prime ministers, generals, weather, and fate. They had defeated the U-boats in the Atlantic. They had driven the German commerce raiders far from the convoy routes. This allowed the buildup in Britain, without which no invasion would have been possible.[1]

Fortress Britain itself was defended from invasion across the Narrow Seas. The RAF maintained air superiority over the homeland and adjacent waters. In 1940, the BEF at Dunkirk was saved from the *Luftwaffe*, allowing it to evacuate, reconstitute, and reequip. The German SEALION invasion fleet was decimated and dispersed. The British army had time to rebuild and introduce new equipment and tactics battle-tested in the Mediterranean. By May, 1944, the Allied air forces had also delayed the onslaught of V-1 and V-2 missiles until the attacks could be endured after D-Day.

Coastal Command, attacking with aircraft and mines and in concert with Royal Navy mining and light forces, depleted *Kriegsmarine* threats that could have threatened the approaching Allied invasion fleet. The RAF went on to attack the German coastal convoy system and the ports from which they sailed. The threat posed by German coastal warships led to the development of RAF Coastal Command strike wings, especially created to defeat small German warships and coastal convoys in the Channel, the Bay of Biscay, and the North Sea. Essential traffic between Norway and Rotterdam was diverted east into Essen and the Baltic ports, poor substitutes for the Rotterdam–Rhine–Ruhr route.

Strategic attack of German installations and military and naval forces began in 1939 and greatly expanded by the end of 1941 (see appendix 2). Such attacks required aircraft able to carry and deliver adequate bomb loads to targets in occupied territory and to the German homeland. It was quickly determined that air superiority was necessary to get the bombers to their targets in daytime.

Some theories and techniques had to be reinvented. The RAF was unable to deplete the German fighter force in the "lean forward" attacks of 1941–1942. The Germans simply would not come up and fight unless the circumstances were heavily weighted in their favor. The Americans were more successful in bringing up defending fighters because of daylight bombing. The doctrine developed at the Tactical School was flawed because it failed to address the inevitable improvement in fighter aircraft.

Enemy fighters could inflict crippling losses on the self-defending heavy bombers, contrary to Tactical School theory. The big bombers were too effective for the defenders to ignore, especially when they began to erode the German aircraft industry. Attacking them and the longer-ranged escort fighters caused a downward spiral of the German fighter pilot force, both in quantity and quality. The result was the eclipse of German airpower over France months before the invasion.

The RAF and USAAF, in conjunction with their national armies, built fleets of transport aircraft that could carry cargo and troops quickly from where they were based to where they were needed. Huge numbers of aircraft, supplemented by newly developed gliders, were required to train the airborne troops as well as to deliver them to their target. Thousands of aircraft and tons of critical equipment were carried and supported around the world thanks to an efficient logistical network. By 1944, the Allies were able to land complete airborne divisions in enemy territory and sustain them by air.

Inability to provide air support to the BEF and failure to interdict the 1940 blitzkrieg made the RAF reluctant to engage in further army cooperation. Fortunately, the Mediterranean experience showed that neither an army nor its air force can survive for long without a joint effort against the enemy. By 1943, COSSAC had clearly identified the necessity of crippling the German logistics network in France. Allied airpower was necessary to keep German war materiel from getting from point A to point B. It was also necessary to defend the skies above the invading army and the navy that delivered it to France.

All of these efforts came to fruition in May, 1944. It was easier and safer to move an Allied division across the Channel than to move a German division from Paris to Caen. It was only the boats that delayed the liberation. When D-Day happened, after more than four years of total war, the Allies were going back into France with a smaller army than the German defenders. They were going back to win. No more Gallipolis; no more Dunkirks.

By D-Day, Eisenhower's airmen had won the great struggle for control of the air over Normandy and the Narrow Seas that had begun in the summer of

1940. His son John, a shiny new army lieutenant who had just graduated from West Point, joined Ike for a tour of the crowded beaches of Normandy on June 24. He was treated to a jeep tour of the recent battleground. The roads were clogged with dust and trucks and troops:

> *Fresh out of West Point, with all its courses in conventional procedures, I was offended at this jamming up of traffic. It wasn't according to the book. Leaning over Dad's shoulder, I remarked, "You'd never get away with this if you didn't have air supremacy."*
>
> *I received an impatient snort:*
> *"If I didn't have air supremacy, I wouldn't be here."* [2]

Appendix 1: World War II Combat Aircraft Characteristics

Combat aircraft evolved quickly during World War II, with several generations of planes overlapping. Attrition dictated that aircraft manufacture proceeded at an accelerated rate, and competition ensured that only the best designs endured. Both engines and airframes evolved to meet existing and emerging requirements. There were several types of combat aircraft in World War II, some of which persist today in more modern form.

FIGHTERS

Fighters were designed to fight other aircraft, including enemy fighters. Generally, these aircraft were armed with machine guns or automatic cannon, sometimes both. Escort fighters were provided additional fuel capacity, with increased volume of internal fuel cells or externally mounted drop tanks. Interceptors were fighters specially designed to climb to high altitude to destroy enemy bombers and reconnaissance aircraft. Fighters that had enhanced ordnance to attack ground targets were fighter-bombers. Ground attack weapons included batteries of machine guns, bombs, and, later, rockets.

BOMBERS

Bombers were aircraft that were designed to drop ordnance on ground targets. Such weapons included bombs and unguided rockets and missiles. Level bombers dropped their ordnance from a relatively constant altitude. Their effectiveness was dictated by the stability of the aircraft and accuracy of their aiming device, or bombsight. Dive-bombers dropped their bombs by pointing their aircraft toward their targets and releasing the ordnance at as low an altitude as possible. Dive-bombers had bombsights optimized for this kind of attack.

During World War II, bombers were also arbitrarily categorized by their size and weight-carrying ability. Heavy bombers, also called strategic bombers, were designed to penetrate into the enemy heartland to attack essential industries, energy production, and lines of communication. As World War II progressed, new heavy bomber models had four engines. They most often attacked from medium to high altitude. They had relatively large crews (up to eleven men) and were equipped with defensive machine guns which could defend the aircraft from all directions. Among the crew was normally a navigator to find the target and a bombardier to aim and release the weapons, which were almost always some type of bomb.

Medium bombers were intermediate between light and heavy bombers. They had the range to penetrate beyond the immediate land battlefield but not into the enemy heartland. Their targets included troop concentrations, supply and fuel dumps, essential local industries and food production, and lines of communication. Their crews often contained a navigator or bombardier, sometimes both.

Light bombers tended to have the smallest crews and carry the least bomb load. Often the pilot aimed and released the bombs or rockets. Light bombers had one or two engines. Most dive-bombers were light bombers. They normally attacked from low to medium altitude and were often well armed with ground-attack guns as well as bombs or rockets. They were not intended to attack much beyond the current ground battle area and were often equipped with only one or a few defensive machine guns.

TRANSPORTS

Transport aircraft were designed to carry groups of non-crew personnel and cargo. Strategic transports could deliver personnel and cargo to distant locations and normally had four engines and a crew of five or more people, including the pilots, a navigator, a flight engineer, and a radio operator. Tactical transports had smaller crews, cargo capacity, and range. Some were designed as troop carriers and dropped paratroopers. Some troop carriers were equipped to tow troop and cargo gliders.

Appendix 2: Levels of Engagement

In military and naval combat operations, there are three basic levels of engagement.

First, the *tactical* level of engagement involves a single or closely related group of objectives in a limited area. For example, combat on or above a battlefield would be tactical in nature. Procedures for winning tactical combat are called *tactics*. Large-scale tactical combat is called *battle*.

Second, the *operational* level of engagement involves a single or closely related group of objectives in a broad area, called a theater of operations. It often involves a series of battles called a *campaign*. For example, the series of battles between Allied forces and German submarines in World War II was an antisubmarine campaign. Thus the "Battle of the Atlantic" is more properly

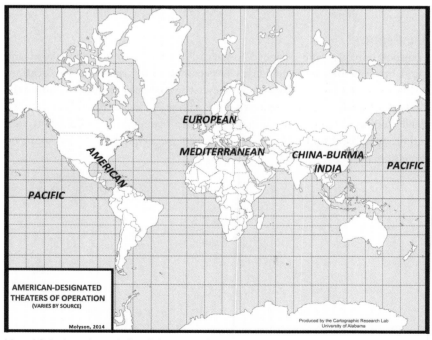

Map A2.1. American-defined theaters of operation in World War II. MOLYSON

referred to as the "Atlantic Campaign." Procedures for winning campaigns are often established in *plans*.

Third, the *strategic* level of engagement involves multiple objectives in a broad area, sometimes as large as a continent, or the entire planet. It always includes the homeland of one or more of the combatants. It is conducted in a series of battles or campaigns. For example, the series of air campaigns against the British and German heartlands were strategic in nature, as opposed to the tactical air campaigns conducted against the Allied and German military forces. A procedure for winning at the strategic level is called a *strategy*.

Appendix 3: Führer Directive No. 51[1]

(Translated excerpt, italics added)

Führer Headquarters
3 November 1943

Top Secret

The Führer
OKW/WFSt/Op. No. 662656/43 gm., Chefs

27 Copies
Copy No.____

Directive No. 51

For the last two and one-half years the bitter and costly struggle against Bolshevism has made the utmost demands upon the bulk of our military resources and energies. This commitment was in keeping with the seriousness of the danger, and the over-all situation. The situation has since changed. *The threat from the East remains, but an even greater danger looms in the West: the Anglo-American landing!* In the East, the vastness of the space will, as a last resort, permit a loss of territory even on a major scale, without suffering a mortal blow to Germany's chance for survival.

Not so in the West! If the enemy here succeeds in penetrating our defenses on a wide front, consequences of staggering proportions will follow within a short time. All signs point to an offensive against the Western Front of Europe no later than spring, and perhaps earlier.

For that reason, I can no longer justify the further weakening of the West in favor of other theaters of war. I have therefore decided to strengthen the defenses in the West, particularly at places from which we shall launch our long-range war against England. For those are the very points at which the enemy must and will attack; there—unless all indications are misleading—will be fought the decisive invasion battle.

Holding attacks and diversions on other fronts are to be expected. Not even the possibility of a large-scale offensive against Denmark may be excluded. It would pose greater nautical problems and could be less effectively supported from the air but would nevertheless produce the greatest political and strategic impact if it were to succeed.

During the opening phase of the battle, the entire striking power of the enemy will of necessity be directed against our forces manning the coast. Only an all-out effort in the construction of fortifications, an unsurpassed effort that will enlist all available manpower and physical resources of Germany and the occupied areas, will be able to strengthen our defenses along the coasts within the short time that still appears to be left to us. . . .

Should the enemy nevertheless force a landing by concentrating his armed might, he must be hit by the full fury of our counterattack. For this mission ample and speedy reinforcements of men and materiel, as well as intensive training, must transform available larger units into first-rate, fully mobile general reserves suitable for offensive operations. The counterattack of these units will prevent the enlargement of the beachhead and throw the enemy back into the sea. . . .

The anticipated strong attacks by air and sea must be relentlessly countered by Air Force and Navy with all their available resources. I therefore order the following:

a) Army:
> . . . *Sufficient mobility for all panzer and panzer grenadier divisions in the West,* and equipment of each of those units by December 1943, with 93 Mark IV tanks or assault guns, as well as large numbers of antitank weapons. . . .

b) Luftwaffe:
> The offensive and defensive effectiveness of Luftwaffe units in the West and in Denmark will be increased to meet the changed situation. *To that end, preparations will be made for the release of units suited for commitment in the anti-invasion effort—that is, all flying units and mobile Flak artillery that can be spared from the air defenses of the home front,* and from schools and training units in the Zone of the Interior. All those units are to be earmarked for the West and possibly Denmark.
>
> The Luftwaffe ground organization in southern Norway, Denmark, northwestern Germany, and the West will be expanded and supplied in a way that will—by the most far-reaching decentralization of [our] own forces—deny targets to the enemy bombers and split the enemy's offensive effort in case of large-scale operations. *Particularly important in that connection will be our fighter forces. Possibilities for their commitment must be increased by the establishment of numerous advanced landing fields. Special emphasis is to be placed on good camouflage.* I expect also that the

Luftwaffe will unstintingly furnish all available forces, by stripping them from less threatened areas.

c) Navy:

The Navy will prepare the strongest possible forces suitable for attacking the enemy landing fleets. Coastal defense installations in the process of construction will be completed with the utmost speed. The emplacing of additional coastal batteries and the possibility of laying further flanking minefields should be investigated. . . .

I expect that all agencies will make a supreme effort toward utilizing every moment of the remaining time in preparing for the decisive battle in the West. All authorities will guard against wasting time and energy in useless jurisdictional squabbles and will direct all their efforts toward strengthening our defensive and offensive power.

Signed:
Adolf Hitler

Appendix 4: German Coastal Warships

Table A4.1. Types of German coastal warships.[1]

Type	Allied Equivalent	Mission
Zerstörer	Destroyer	Defense against aircraft and warships; armed with medium- and light-caliber guns and torpedoes
Torpedo boat	Corvette, sloop, or destroyer escort	Small escort-type vessel for defense against aircraft and warships; armed with medium- and light-caliber guns and torpedoes
S-boat	Motor torpedo boat or American PT boat	Called "E-boat" by Allies, meaning "enemy boat"; armed with two torpedoes and medium- and light-caliber antiaircraft guns
Minenleger	Minelayer	Places naval minefields; a variety of German and captured ships, including naval and former civilian vessels, were used
Minensuchboot (M-boot)	Minesweeper	Clears enemy and maintains friendly minefields; secondary antiaircraft vessel
Räumboot (R-boot)	Motor minesweeper	Clears enemy and maintains friendly minefields; secondary antiaircraft vessel; general inshore patrol and flak ship
Vorpostenboot (VP-boot)	Patrol boat or armed trawler	Used for coastal surveillance; a variety of slower converted civilian vessels were used in this role as sentry vessels
Sperrbrecher	Large minesweeper	Originally used to escort blockade breakers through friendly defensive minefields and to remove enemy mines laid in cleared lanes; a variety of slower vessels were used in this role; later became the most heavily armed German flak ship
Unterseebootjäger	Submarine chaser	Primary mission was patrol but had some antisubmarine capability
Tross-schiffe	Military transport	Used to carry military supplies and fuel
Steamer	Steamer	Merchant ship of various sizes
Coastal tanker	Coastal tanker	Primary mission is to move fuel and lubricants between ports
Coastal freighter	Coastal freighter	Primary mission is to move raw material or finish products between ports

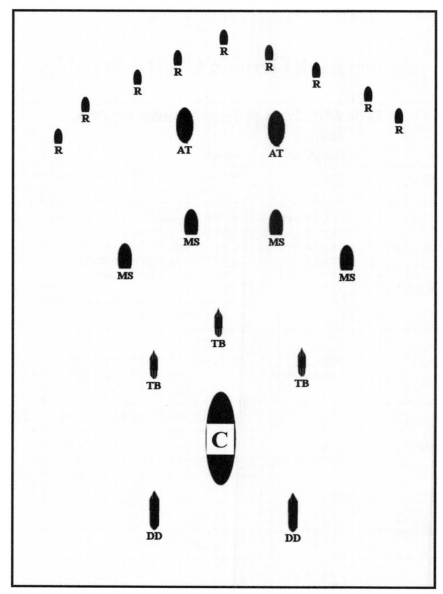

Figure A4.1. Typical German coastal convoy: C = coastal transport; AT = armed trawler; DD = destroyer; TB = torpedo boat; MS = minesweeper; R-boat = motor minesweeper. All the vessels are heavily armed with antiaircraft weapons.[2] MOLYSON AFTER RÜGE

Acknowledgments

I want to thank my family—most of all, my wife Margaret, daughters Elizabeth and Katherine, sons-in-law Justin and David, and granddaughters Mia and Anna—for their continued support of my late-in-life career move. I would also like to thank my friend Dr. James Arnold, who helped ferret out ambiguities and terms unfamiliar to most people.

I also want to thank all the airmen I served with during my thirty-two years in the US Air Force. They inspired me to do my best because they always did theirs. I did my intelligence training at an Air Force school, but I got my education through having an airman's get-it-done attitude, working with pilots, intel guys, ops guys, maintainers, and other airmen who put the mission and the team first.

God bless you all!

Notes

PREFACE
1. Drummond, John "Ace." Oral history interview by Colonel Joseph Molyson, USAFR (Ret.), January 22, 2003.

INTRODUCTION
1. Many authors used the word *Wehrmacht* rather than the more correct *Heer*.

CHAPTER 1: THE CHANNEL AND THE NARROW SEAS
1. Map based on Wesley Frank Craven and James Lea Cate, eds. *The Army Air Forces in World War II, Vol. II, Europe: Torch to Pointblank, August 1942 to December 1943* (Washington, DC: Office of Air Force History, US Air Force, 1983), 215; and Peter C. Smith, *Naval Warfare in the English Channel 1939–1945* (Barnsley, South Yorkshire, UK: Pen & Sword Books, Ltd., 2007), x.
2. Smith, *Naval Warfare in the English Channel 1939–1945*, x.

CHAPTER 3: THE AIRPOWER FACTOR
1. See Joseph Molyson, *Six Air Forces Over the Atlantic* (Mechanicsburg, PA: Stackpole Books, 2024).
2. "Co-Operation" is the British term for army–air force coordination of selected operations. The American term is "Cooperation."

CHAPTER 4: ARSENAL (MARCH 1935–AUGUST 1941)
1. General of the Air Force H. H. Arnold, *Global Mission* (New York: Harper Brothers, 1949), 177–78.
2. Eric Larrabee, *Commander in Chief* (Annapolis: Naval Institute Press, 1987) Kindle Edition, 214.
3. Adapted from Wesley Frank Craven and James Lea Cate, eds. *The Army Air Forces in World War II, Vol. VII, Services Around the World* (Washington, DC: Office of Air Force History, US Air Force, 1983), 228.
4. Alexander J. Field, *The Economic Consequences of the US Mobilization for the Second World War* (New Haven: Yale University Press, 2022), 5.
5. National World War II Museum, New Orleans, Louisiana.
6. Field, *The Economic Consequences of the US Mobilization for the Second World War*, 7.
7. Ibid.
8. Not all of these products originated in the United States (Source: National World War II Museum, New Orleans, Louisiana).

9. Arnold, *Global Mission*, 291.

10. David F. Trask, "Political-Military Relations," in *The D-Day Encyclopedia*, eds. David G. Chandler and James Lawton Collins (New York: Simon & Schuster, 1994), 429.

11. Maj. Gen. Heywood S. Hansell Jr., "USSAF Plans and Strategic Targets," in *Impact* 4 (May–August 1944), ed. James Parton (Harrisburg, PA: National Historical Society, 1980), v–vi.

CHAPTER 5: THEORY INTO PRACTICE (1914–1939)

1. John Terraine, *The Right of the Line: The Royal Air Force in the European War, 1939–1945* (London, UK: Hodder and Stoughton, Ltd., 1985), 10–11.

2. Author's italics, quoted from "The Bomber Will Always Get Through," *Air and Space Forces Magazine*, July 1, 2008, accessed January 22, 2024, https://www.airandspaceforces.com/article/0708keeperfile/.

3. Terraine, *The Right of the Line*, 23.

4. Stephen L. McFarland and Wesley Phillips Newton, *To Command the Sky* (Washington, DC: Smithsonian Institution Press, 1991), 3–4.

CHAPTER 6: DARKNESS (SEPTEMBER 1939–FEBRUARY 1942)

1. Winston S. Churchill, *The Second World War, Vol. II: Their Finest Hour* (Boston, MA: Mariner Books, 1985), 405.

2. Ibid., 567.

3. Ronald H. Bailey and the Editors of Time-Life Books, *The Air War in Europe* (Chicago, IL: Time-Life Books, 1981), 54.

4. John Weal, *Osprey Aircraft of the Aces, Vol. 29: Bf 109F/G/K Aces of the Western Front*, ed. Tony Holmes (Oxford, UK: Osprey Books, 1999), 34–36.

5. Mike Spick, *Luftwaffe Fighter Aces* (Mechanicsburg, PA: Stackpole Books, 1996), 132–34.

6. Air Marshal Sir Charles Portal, quoted in Earl R. Beck, *Under the Bombs* (Lexington: University of Kentucky Press, 1986), 2–3.

CHAPTER 7: BOMBER CREWS

1. Terraine, *The Right of the Line*, 462.

2. Martin Middlebrook, *The Schweinfurt–Regensburg Mission* (New York: Charles Scribner's Sons, 1983), 260.

3. Ibid., 259–60.

CHAPTER 8: LÜBECK (FEBRUARY–DECEMBER 1942)

1. Quoted in "Air Power," Air & Space Forces Association, accessed February 24, 2024, https://secure.afa.org/quotes/Quotes_81208.pdf.

2. Eric Niderost, "Terror by Night," *Military Heritage,* February 2001, 48–55, 87.

3. Dr. Walter Kudrycz, "A Practical Prophet? Arthur Harris, the Legacy of Lord Trenchard, and the Question of 'Panacea' targeting," *Royal Air Force Airpower Review* V, no. 1 (Spring 2002): 30–33.

4. Nicolaus von Below, *At Hitler's Side*, trans. Geoffrey Brooks (London, UK: Greenhill Books, 2001), 145.

5. Quoted in Martin Middlebrook and Chris Everitt, *The Bomber Command War Diaries 1939–1945* (Leicester, UK: Midland Publishing, 1996), 261.

6. Adapted from Alfred Price, *The Luftwaffe Data Book* (Mechanicsburg, PA: Stackpole Books, 1997), 57–60; Middlebrook and Everitt, *The Bomber Command War Diaries 1939–1945*, 250–62.

7. Col. Homer Case, transcript of interview by the Assistant Chief of Air Staff for Intelligence, Undated 1942, in File 142.05-3, Albert F. Simpson Historical Research Center, Air University, Maxwell AFB, AL.

8. The "mines" were air-dropped 1,500-pound anti-ship mines that were more powerful than contemporary British high-explosive bombs. They were fused to explode on contact with the ground and could level a city block. The Germans were also dropping their own 1,100- and 2,200-pound mines on British cities at this time.

9. These were anti-ship mines adapted to the urban bombing mission.

10. Beck, *Under the Bombs*, 1–2.

CHAPTER 9: COOPERATION (JUNE 1940–AUGUST 1941)

1. Quoted in Terraine, *The Right of the Line*, 380.

2. "Directive to AOC-in-C Army Co-Operation Command," in Matthew Powell, *The Development of British Tactical Air Power, 1940–1943* (London, UK: Palgrave Macmillan, 2016), 233–34.

CHAPTER 10: ALLIES (DECEMBER 1941–MARCH 1942)

1. John S. D. Eisenhower, *Allies: Pearl Harbor to D-Day* (New York: Da Capo Press, 2000), 14.

2. Ibid., xxi.

3. The theater of operations is a designated geographic area with military objectives limited to that region. It normally includes an active combat zone supported by a communications zone.

4. Maj. Gen. Heywood S. Hansell Jr., "USSAF Plans and Strategic Targets," in *Impact* 4 (May –August 1944), ix.

5. Formally designated *État Français* ("French State").

6. Alan F. Wilt, "Prelude," in *The D-Day Encyclopedia*, eds. David G. Chandler and James Lawton Collins (New York: Simon & Schuster, 1994), 432.

7. Ira C. Eaker, "The Evolution of Air Command." In *Impact* 1 (April–August 1943), ed. James Parton. Harrisburg, PA: National Historical Society, 1980, xiii.

8. Quoted in Michael R. Howard, *The Mediterranean Strategy in the Second World War* (London, UK: Greenhill Books, 1993), 21–22.

CHAPTER 11: BOLERO (JULY 1941–APRIL 1942)

1. John T. Corell, "The Third Musketeer," *Air and Space Forces Magazine*, December 2014, page 61, accessed March 25, 2024, https://www.airandspaceforces.com/PDF/MagazineArchive/Magazine%20Documents/2014/December%202014/1214musketeer.pdf.

2. Col. Beirne Lay Jr., "The Background," in *Impact* 5 (September–December 1944), ed. James Parton (Harrisburg, PA: National Historical Society, 1980), viii.

3. Corell, "The Third Musketeer," 60.

4. Actually, the Arnold Line already existed as the North Atlantic Ferry Route. Deliveries of American-built Lockheed Hudson maritime bombers using this route had commenced in February 1939.

5. In fighters, these were hung from modified bomb racks with the necessary plumbing to transfer fuel from the tank to internal fuel cells of the aircraft. Initial designs were not intended for combat.

6. Wesley Frank Craven and James Lea Cate, eds. *The Army Air Forces in World War II, Vol. I: Plans and Early Operations, January 1939 to August 1942* (Washington, DC: Office of Air Force History, US Air Force, 1983), 643.

7. "Operation Bolero I and II," P-38 Home Page, n.d., n.p., August 14, 2000, available at http://members.xoom.com/_XMCM/tguettle/bolero1.html.

8. Chuck Yeager and Leo Janos, *Yeager* (New York: Bantam Books, 1985), 246.

9. Martin Caidin, *Fork-Tailed Devil: The P-38* (New York: ibooks, inc., 2001), 87.

10. Eisenhower, *Allies: Pearl Harbor to D-Day*, 64.

11. Eaker, "The Evolution of Air Command," xiii.

Chapter 12: *Kanalfront* (January 1941–August 1942)

1. Each German fighter squadron consisted of nine to twelve aircraft.

2. Adapted from Price, *The Luftwaffe Data Book*, 31–32, 42–43.

3. David Stubbs, "A Blind Spot? The Royal Air Force and Long-Range Fighters, 1936–1944," *Journal of Military History* 78, no. 2, 677–79.

4. In RAF parlance, a wing consists of three squadrons with the same aircraft normally based on the same or nearby airfields.

5. Terraine, *The Right of the Line*, 284–85.

6. Weal, *Osprey Aircraft of the Aces, Vol. 29: Bf 109F/G/K Aces of the Western Front*, 34.

7. Ibid., 11–12.

8. Capt. Eric Brown, "Flying FW 190 Kurt Tank's Butcher Bird," *Aviation History* (October 2000), 46–57.

9. John Starkey, *The RAF's Cross-Channel Offensive* (Philadelphia: Pen & Sword Press, 2022), 150–51.

10. John Weal, *Osprey Aircraft of the Aces, Vol. 9: Focke-Wulf FW 190 Aces of the Western Front* ed. Tony Holmes (Oxford, UK: Osprey Books, 1998), 6–12.

11. Jerry Scutts, *Spitfire in Action* (Carrollton, TX: Squadron/Signal Publications, Inc., 1980), 26.

Chapter 13: Death of a Kondor (August 1942)

1. USAAF photo from *This Day in Aviation*, accessed May 9, 2024, www.thisday inaviation.com/14-august-1942/lockheed-p-38f-lightnings-at-iceland-lt-shahans-41 -7540-is-at-the-left/.

2. Overprint of CIA Base Map 504778 10-81, Perry-Castañeda Library, University of Texas at Austin, accessed May 9, 2024, https://maps.lib.utexas.edu/maps/europe/iceland_pol81.jpg.

3. Warren M. Bodie, *Lockheed P-38 Lightning* (Hiawassee, GA: Widewing Publications, 1991), 103; Caidin, *Fork-Tailed Devil*, 49; and Maurer Maurer, ed., *World War II Combat Squadrons of the United States Air Force* (Woodbury, NY: Smithmark Publishers, Inc., 1992), 160–61.

4. Bodie, *Lockheed P-38 Lightning*, 103.

CHAPTER 14: THE NEW GUYS (MAY–AUGUST 1942)

1. Former 8th Air Force ball turret gunner John Day. Col. Joseph T. Molyson, USAF, 16 April 2002, at the 390th Bomb Group Museum.

2. Kenn C. Rust, *The 12th Air Force in World War II* (Temple City, CA: Historical Aviation Album, 1975), 11–12.

3. Sam McGowan, "Low-Level Run at Ploesti," *WWII History*, May 2003, 66–69.

4. Balloon barrages were clusters of unmanned balloons tethered to the ground with cables, intended to wreck low-flying aircraft encountering them. Both sides employed these passive defenses.

5. Caidin, *Fork-Tailed Devil*, 108.

6. McFarland and Newton, *To Command the Sky*, 171.

7. Ibid., 84–85, 91.

8. Lt. Gen. Ira C. Eaker, transcript of US Air Force oral history interview by Arthur Marmor, January 1966, in File K239.0512-626, Albert F. Simpson Historical Research Center, Air University, Maxwell AFB, AL, 9.

9. Roger A. Freeman, *The Mighty Eighth* (London, UK: Cassell & Co., 2000), 9–10.

10. "VIII Bomber Command I," American Air Museum in Britain, accessed May 22, 2024, https://www.americanairmuseum.com/archive/mission/viii-bomber-command-1.

11. Third *Staffel* (Squadron)/*Jagdgeschwader* (Fighter Wing) 2.

12. Freeman, *The Mighty Eighth*, 11–12.

CHAPTER 15: JUBILEE (JUNE–AUGUST 1942)

1. Quoted in Terraine, *The Right of the Line*, 559.

2. Eisenhower, *Allies: Pearl Harbor to D-Day*, 92–95.

3. Henry L. deZeng IV, *Luftwaffe Airfields 1935–45 France*, page 4, accessed May 23, 2024, http://www.ww2.dk/Airfields%20-%20France.pdf.

4. Donald L. Caldwell, *JG 26: Top Guns of the Luftwaffe* (New York: Ivy Books, 1991), 118–19.

5. "The Dieppe Raid," *British Forces in World War II*, n.d., n.p. November 13, 2001, available at http://british-forces.com/world_war2/Campaigns/dieppe.html.

6. A "sortie" is one flight by one aircraft.

7. Starkey, *The RAF's Cross-Channel Offensive*, 176–77.

8. "BR 1736(26) Royal Navy Staff History: Raid on Dieppe," Warships1 Web Site, n.d., n.p., online, March 26 2002, available at http://www.warships1.com/W-hist/.

CHAPTER 16: DECISIONS, DIVERSIONS, AND MISSTEPS (JULY–OCTOBER 1942)

1. General der Flieger Adolf Galland, *The First and the Last* (Cutchogue, NY: Buccaneer Books, 1997), 132.

2. McFarland and Newton, *To Command the Sky*, 171.
3. Wesley Frank Craven and James Lea Cate, eds. *The Army Air Forces in World War II, Vol. IV: The Pacific: Guadalcanal to Saipan August 1942 to July 1944* (1949; new imprint, Washington, DC: Office of Air Force History, United States Air Force, 1983), 49.
4. Caidin, *Fork-Tailed Devil*, 97.
5. Quoted in Bodie, *Lockheed P-38 Lightning*, 207.
6. Ibid.
7. Spick, *Luftwaffe Fighter Aces*, 100.
8. Caidin, *Fork-Tailed Devil*, 109.
9. Grover C. Hall Jr., *1,000 Destroyed: The Life and Times of the 4th Fighter Group* (Fallbrook, CA: Aero Publishers, Inc., 1978), 21–22; Roger A. Freeman with Alan Crouchman and Vic Maslen, *Mighty Eighth War Diary* (New York: Jane's, 1981), 17.
10. Hall Jr., *1,000 Destroyed*, 21–22; Freeman et al., *Mighty Eighth War Diary*, 17–19.
11. Ibid., 16.
12. Ibid., 19.

CHAPTER 17: TORCH (NOVEMBER–DECEMBER 1942)
1. Base Map produced by the Cartographic Research Lab, University of Alabama.
2. Eisenhower, *Allies: Pearl Harbor to D-Day*, 144.
3. "Air-landed" troops are those carried by troop transport aircraft, and are not necessarily paratroopers.

CHAPTER 18: AUTUMN OVER FRANCE (NOVEMBER–DECEMBER 1942)
1. John J. Sullivan, *Overlord's Eagles* (Jefferson, NC: McFarland & Company, Inc., Publishers, 1997), 30.
2. Col. Raymond F. Toliver and Trevor J. Constable, *Horrido! Fighter Aces of the Luftwaffe* (New York: Bantam Books, 1977), 264.
3. Lt. Gen. Archie Old Jr. transcript of US Air Force oral history interview by Hugh N. Ahmann, 26 October–2 November 1982, in File K239.0512-1357, Albert F. Simpson Historical Research Center, Air University, Maxwell AFB, AL, 183.
4. McFarland and Newton, *To Command the Sky*, 92–93.
5. Galland, *The First and the Last*, 140–41.
6. Spick, *Luftwaffe Fighter Aces*, 145–47.
7. Ibid., 158.
8. McFarland and Newton, *To Command the Sky*, 96.
9. Col. L. C. Craigle, Col. M. S. Roth, and Col. J. F. Philips, transcript of interview by the Assistant Chief of Air Staff for Intelligence, 12 January 1943, in File 142.052-Craigle, Albert F. Simpson Historical Research Center, Air University, Maxwell AFB, AL, 6.

CHAPTER 19: THE END OF THE BEGINNING (JANUARY 1943)
1. Albert Speer, *Inside the Third Reich*, trans. Richard and Clara Winston (New York: Macmillan, 1970), 263–64, 290–91, 303.
2. Air Marshal Portal quoted in Beck, *Under the Bombs*, 39–46.

3. A gross registered ton (GRT) is a measure of ship cargo, volume rather than weight. One GRT is equal to one hundred cubic feet of cargo storage capacity.

4. Marshal of the RAF Sir John Slessor, "Cooperation between Land, Seas and Air," in *Impact* 1 (April–August 1943), ed. James Parton (Harrisburg, PA: National Historical Society, 1980), xvii–xviii.

5. Joint Intelligence Subcommittee (JIC) of the Joint Planning Staff of the (UK) War Cabinet, "German Reactions to the US-British Operation," Unnumbered JIC Report, 17 February 1944, in JCS Geographic File 1942–1945, Records Group 218, National Records and Archives Administration Archive II, College Park, MD, page 12.

6. James Parton, in foreword to "The Evolution of Air Command," in *Impact* 1 (April–August 1943), ed. James Parton (Harrisburg, PA: National Historical Society, 1980), x.

7. Eisenhower, *Allies: Pearl Harbor to D-Day*, 248.

CHAPTER 20: THE MED (JANUARY–DECEMBER 1943)

1. Eisenhower, *Allies: Pearl Harbor to D-Day*, 323.

2. Ibid., 360–61.

CHAPTER 21: RADAR

1. "Radar" stands for "*RA*dio *D*etection *A*nd *R*anging."

2. Middlebrook and Everitt, *The Bomber Command War Diaries 1939–1945*, 26–27; "Freya Radar," Radartutorial.eu, accessed May 26, 2024, https://www.radartutorial.eu/19 kartei/11.ancient/karte001.en.html.

CHAPTER 22: FLAK

1. Quoted in Edward B. Westermann, *Flak German Anti-Aircraft Defenses 1914–1945* (Lawrence: University Press of Kansas, 2001), 4.

2. Westermann, *Flak German Anti-Aircraft Defenses 1914–1945*, 9–10.

3. "German Antiaircraft Ceilings," *Tactical and Technical Trends*, No. 25, May 20, 1943, accessed March 8, 2024, https://www.lonesentry.com/articles/ttt07/german-an tiaircraft-ceilings.html. Approximate ranges based on a study of multiple sources with multiple variables. Flak guns could also fire at ground targets. Flak guns could not fire straight up. Generally, aircraft above 10,000 feet were engaged only by heavy flak guns.

4. Terraine, *The Right of the Line*, 90.

5. Westermann, *Flak German Anti-Aircraft Defenses 1914–1945*, 139.

6. McFarland and Newton, *To Command the Sky*, 54.

7. Westermann, *Flak German Anti-Aircraft Defenses 1914–1945*, 2–3.

8. Ibid., 259.

9. Kenneth P. Werrell, *Archie, Flak, AAA, and SAM: A Short Operational History of Ground-Based Air Defense* (Honolulu, HI: University Press of the Pacific, 2002), 34–43.

10. Ibid., 42.

CHAPTER 23: INTO THE REICH (JANUARY–APRIL 1943)

1. Middlebrook and Everitt, *The Bomber Command War Diaries 1939–1945*, 348.

2. Ibid., 348–49.

3. Freeman et al., *Mighty Eighth War Diary*, 35.

4. Edwin P. Hoyt, *Angels of Death: Göring Luftwaffe* (New York: Tom Doherty Associates Books, 1994), 227–28.

5. Spick, *Luftwaffe Fighter Aces*, 147.

6. Galland, *The First and the Last*, 148–49.

7. Freeman et al., *Mighty Eighth War Diary*, 32–73. Map based on Craven and Cate, eds., *The Army Air Forces in World War II, Vol. II, Europe: Torch to Pointblank*, 215.

8. Ibid., 150.

9. Ibid., 150–51.

10. Heinz Knoke, *I Flew for the Führer*. trans. R. H. Barry (Novato, CA: Presidio Press, 1991), 93–97.

11. Hoyt, *Angels of Death*, 254.

12. Galland, *The First and the Last*, 187.

CHAPTER 24: THE TYRANNY OF RANGE (JANUARY–JULY 1943)

1. Stubbs, "A Blind Spot?," 673–77.

2. Wesley Frank Craven and James Lea Cate, eds. *The Army Air Forces in World War II, Vol. VI: Men and Planes.* (Washington, DC: Office of Air Force History, United States Air Force, 1955, new imprint, 1983), 196–97.

3. Scutts, *Spitfire in Action*, 11.

4. Jerry Scutts, *Osprey Aircraft of the Aces, Vol. 24: P-47 Thunderbolt Aces of the Eighth Air Force*, ed. Tony Holmes (Oxford, UK: Osprey Books, 1998), 7.

5. Scutts, *Osprey Aircraft of the Aces, Vol. 24: P-47 Thunderbolt Aces of the Eighth Air Force*, 7.6.

6. Bodie, *Lockheed P-38 Lightning*, 207.

7. Scutts, *Osprey Aircraft of the Aces, Vol. 24: P-47 Thunderbolt Aces of the Eighth Air Force*, 7.

8. Sullivan, *Overlord's Eagles*, 29.

9. Ibid., 199–201.

10. Colin D. Heaton, "Wolfpack Ace Robert S. Johnson," *Military History*, August 1996, 26–32.

11. Mr. Robert S. Johnson, transcript of US Air Force oral history interview by Lt. Col. John N. Dick, 9 February 1977, in File K239.0512-1074, Albert F. Simpson Historical Research Center, Air University, Maxwell AFB, AL, 48–56.

12. Robert S. Johnson, *Thunderbolt!* (Spartanburg, SC: The Honoribus Press, February 1999), 171–92.

CHAPTER 25: LITTLE FRIENDS (JANUARY–AUGUST 1943)

1. Military term for dropping items no longer required from an aircraft.

2. Paul Stoddard, "Escort Spitfire: A Missed Opportunity for Longer Reach?," Royal Aeronautical Society, accessed January 24, 2024, https://www.aerosociety.com/news/escort-spitfire-a-missed-opportunity-for-longer-reach/; Freeman et al., *Mighty Eighth War Diary*, 54, 66, 79.

3. Hoyt, *Angels of Death*, 254, 228.

4. The IG Farben nitrate works was used to manufacture explosives.

5. Freeman et al., *Mighty Eighth War Diary*, 78–84; "Operation Blitz Week," *Codenames Operations of World War II*, accessed May 28, 2024, https://codenames.info/operation/blitz-week/.

6. Freeman et al., *Mighty Eighth War Diary*, 78–84; "Operation Blitz Week," *Codenames Operations of World War II*; map based on Craven and Cate, eds., *The Army Air Forces in World War II, Vol. II, Europe: Torch to Pointblank*, 667.

7. Scutts, *Osprey Aircraft of the Aces, Vol. 24: P-47 Thunderbolt Aces of the Eighth Air Force*, 35.

8. Kit C. Carter and Robert Mueller, compilers, *US Army Air Forces in World War II Combat Chronology 1941–1945* (Washington, DC: Center for Air Force History, 1991), 166.

9. Knocke, *I Flew for the Führer*, 207.

10. Middlebrook, *The Schweinfurt–Regensburg Mission*, 28.

11. Martin W. Bowman, *The USAAF Handbook 1939–1945* (Mechanicsburg, PA: Stackpole Books, 1996), 255.

12. McFarland and Newton, *To Command the Sky*, 92–93, 107–09.

13. Air Commodore A. H. C. Sharp and Wing Commander J. Roland Robinson, transcript of a briefing to General Arnold by the Assistant Chief of Air Staff for Intelligence, 10 August 1943, in File 142.05-7, Albert F. Simpson Historical Research Center, Air University, Maxwell AFB, AL, 8.

14. Sir Charles Webster and Noble Frankland, *The Strategic Air Offensive against Germany, Vol. II: Endeavour* (London, UK: HMSO, 1961), 78.

15. McFarland and Newton, *To Command the Sky*, 106–07.

16. Edwin P. Hoyt, *Angels of Death: Göring Luftwaffe* (New York: Tom Doherty Associates Books, 1994), 252.

17. McFarland and Newton, *To Command the Sky*, 106–07.

CHAPTER 26: GOMORRAH (JULY 25–AUGUST 3, 1943)

1. Galland, *The First and the Last*, 155.

2. W. A. Jacobs, "British Strategic Air Offensive," in *Case Studies in Strategic Bombardment*, ed. R. Cargill Hall (Washington, DC: Center for Air Force History, US Air Force, 1998), 125–26.

3. Jacobs, "British Strategic Air Offensive," 127.

4. Middlebrook and Everitt, *The Bomber Command War Diaries 1939–1945*, 411–12.

5. Walter J. Boyne, *Clash of Wings World War II in the Air* (New York: Touchstone, 1997), 318.

6. Middlebrook and Everitt, *The Bomber Command War Diaries 1939–1945*, 413–14.

7. Edward Jablonski, *Airwar, Vol. II* (Garden City, NY: Doubleday & Company, Inc., 1979), 40–41.

8. Ibid., 160.

9. Boyne, *Clash of Wings World War II in the Air*, 296.

CHAPTER 27: SURROUNDED (JULY 1–AUGUST 13, 1943)

1. Luftwaffe Command Central in German is *Luftwaffenbefehlshaber Mitte*. Luftwaffe Command Southeast is *Luftwaffenkommando Süd Ost*. German areas after Price, *The Luftwaffe Data Book*, 93–95.

2. McGowan, "Low-Level Run at Ploesti," 66–67.

3. McGowan, "Low-Level Run at Ploesti," 66–73, 88; Galland, *The First and the Last*, 189; Bowman, *The USAAF Handbook 1939–1945*, 254–55.

4. Stephen E. Ambrose, *The Supreme Commander* (Jackson: The University of Mississippi Press, 1999), 246–47.

5. Galland, *The First and the Last*, 190.

Chapter 28: The Schweinfurt–Regensburg Raid (August 17, 1943)

1. Knocke, *I Flew for the Führer*, 98.

2. Hall, *1,000 Destroyed: The Life and Times of the 4th Fighter Group*, 30.

3. Gen. Curtis E. LeMay, "The Command Realities," *Impact* 5 (September–December 1944, ed. James Parton (Harrisburg, PA: National Historical Society, 1980), xiii.

4. Wesley Frank Craven and James Lea Cate, eds. *The Army Air Forces in World War II, Vol. III: Europe: Argument to V-E Day, January 1944 to May 1945* (1951; new imprint, Washington, DC: Office of Air Force History, United States Air Force, 1983), 681–87; Middlebrook, *The Schweinfurt–Regensburg Mission*, 9–14; Marshall L. Michel, *Schweinfurt–Regensburg: 1943* Osprey Air Campaign Series (Oxford, UK: Osprey Publishing Ltd., 2020), 64–65. Base Map from Thomas E. Greiss, ed., *West Point Atlas for the Second World War: Europe and the Mediterranean* (Wayne, NJ: Avery Publishing, 1984), Plate 2.

5. Alfred Price, "Against Regensburg and Schweinfurt," *Air & Space Forces* (September 1, 1993), accessed January 20, 2024, https://www.airandspaceforces.com/article/0993regensburg/.

6. Middlebrook, *The Schweinfurt–Regensburg Mission*, 320.

7. Quoted in Johannes Steinhoff, Peter Pechel, and Dennis Showalter, *Voices from the Third Reich* (New York: Da Capo Press, 1994), 197–98.

8. Donald L. Miller, *Masters of the Air* (New York: Simon & Schuster, 2006), 199.

9. John Sweetman, *Schweinfurt* (New York: Ballantine Books, Inc., 1971), 119.

10. Allen Andrews, *The Air Marshals: The Air War in Western Europe* (New York: William Morrow and Company, Inc., 1970), 227–28.

11. Middlebrook, *The Schweinfurt–Regensburg Mission*, 324.

12. Ibid., 86.

13. McFarland and Newton, *To Command the Sky*, 129.

Chapter 29: HYDRA (August 17–18, 1943)

1. "Outer space," by international agreement, is any altitude beyond 50 miles.

2. Michael J. Neufeld, *The Rocket and the Reich* (Cambridge, MA: Harvard University Press, 1996), 193.

3. Kenneth B. Werrell, *The Evolution of the Cruise Missile* (Maxwell AFB, AL: Air University Press, September 1985), 43.

4. James McGovern, *Crossbow and Overcast* (New York: William Morrow and Company, Inc., 1964), 29–30.

5. Middlebrook and Everitt, *The Bomber Command War Diaries 1939–1945*, 422–24.

6. McGovern, *Crossbow and Overcast*, 1964), 33.

7. Andrews, *The Air Marshals*, 237.

8. Neufeld, *The Rocket and the Reich*, 264.

9. Hoyt, *Angels of Death*, 248.

10. Williamson Murray, *Strategy for Defeat: The Luftwaffe 1933–1945* (Osceola, WI: Motorbooks International Publishers & Wholesalers, 1998), 156.

11. Galland, *The First and the Last*, 161–64.

CHAPTER 30: COSSAC AND OVERLORD (JANUARY–JULY 1943)

1. Forrest C. Pogue, *United States Army in World War II, European Theater: The Supreme Command* (Washington, DC: Center of Military History United States Army, 1989), 24, accessed June 15, 2024, https://www.ibiblio.org/hyperwar/USA/USA-E-Supreme/.

2. "In Desperate Battle: Normandy 1944," Valour and Horror, Second World War, Canadian History, World War II Page, n.d., n.p., July 7, 2000, available at http://www.valourandhorror.com/BC/Backg/big_week%20.htm.

3. Terraine, *The Right of the Line*, 564.

4. Ibid., 544–46.

5. Chief of Staff to the Supreme Allied Commander, "Attainment of the Necessary Air Situation," Appendix K to COSSAC (43) 28 undated 1943, in File 505.14-3, Albert F. Simpson Historical Research Center, Air University, Maxwell AFB, AL.

6. Reprinted in Gordon A. Harrison, *United States Army in World War II, European Theater: Cross-Channel Attack* (Washington, DC: Center of Military History United States Army, 1989), 450-456.

CHAPTER 31: THE PLAN (JULY–NOVEMBER 1943)

1. Pogue, *United States Army in World War II, European Theater: The Supreme Command*, 103.

2. Harrison, *United States Army in World War II, European Theater: Cross-Channel Attack*, 76–77.

3. Joint Planning Staff of the (UK) War Cabinet, "Operation OVERLORD," J.P. Report (43) 260, 3 August 1943, in SHAEF SGS Minutes Decimal File, May 1943–August 1945, Records Group 331, National Records and Archives Administration Archive II, College Park, MD, 1.

4. Harrison, *United States Army in World War II, European Theater: Cross-Channel Attack*, 72.

5. Ibid.

6. Pogue, *United States Army in World War II, European Theater: The Supreme Command*, 106; Chief of Staff to the Supreme Allied Commander, "Requirements for a Tactical Air Force," COSSAC Study No. 2, undated 1943, in File 505.13-3, Albert F. Simpson Historical Research Center, Air University, Maxwell AFB, AL.

7. Pogue, *United States Army in World War II, European Theater: The Supreme Command*, 107–15.

CHAPTER 32: TROOP CARRIER

1. Col. R. B. Bagby, G-2 SHAEF, memorandum to General Nevins, subject: Troop Carrier: Airborne Operations, March 7, 1944, in Box 11 of the James M. Gavin Papers, US Army Heritage and Education Center, Carlisle Barracks, PA.

2. Gregor Ferguson and Kevin Lyles, *The Paras 1940–1984*, Osprey Elite Series, Vol. 21, ed. Martin Windrow (London, UK: Osprey Books, 1984), 3–4.

3. Chief of Staff to the Supreme Allied Commander, "Requirements for a Tactical Air Force," COSSAC Study No. 2.

4. Harrison, *United States Army in World War II, European Theater: Cross-Channel Attack,* 75.

5. James M. Gavin, transcript of US Army oral history interview by Lt. Col. Donald G. Andrews, USA, and Lt. Col. Charles H. Ferguson, USA, 1975, in File Box 1 of the James M. Gavin Papers, US Army Heritage and Education Center, Carlisle Barracks, PA.

6. Pogue, *United States Army in World War II, European Theater: The Supreme Command,* 119–20.

7. Richard G. Davis, "IX Troop Carrier Command," in *The D-Day Encyclopedia,* eds. David G. Chandler and James Lawton Collins (New York: Simon & Schuster, 1994), 400.

8. Omar Bradley, *A Soldier's Story* (New York: Henry Holt and Company, 1951), 234.

9. Pogue, *United States Army in World War II, European Theater: The Supreme Command,* 120.

CHAPTER 33: THE PARAS

1. Quoted in "The Beginnings," British First Airborne Division Living History Association, n.d., n.p., online, July 19, 2002, available at http://www.britishairborne.org/.

2. Ferguson and Lyles, *The Paras 1940–1984,* 3.

3. Stephen E. Ambrose, *Pegasus Bridge* (New York: Simon & Schuster, Inc., 1985), 52.

4. Alexander Morrison, *Silent Invader* (London, UK: Airlife Publishing, Ltd., 2002), 43.

5. Ferguson and Lyles, *The Paras 1940–1984,* 8–9.

6. Richard Townshend Bickers, *Air War Normandy* (London, UK: Leo Cooper, 1994), xiv.

CHAPTER 34: THE GOONEY BIRD AND THE WACO

1. C. V. Glines, "Troop Carriers of WWII," *Air Force Magazine,* February 1999, n.p., online, March 12, 2000, available at http://www.afa.org/magazine/0299troop.html.

2. Irving Brinton Holley Jr., *United States Army in World War II, Special Studies, Buying Aircraft: Materiel Procurement for the Army Air Forces* (Washington, DC: Center of Military History United States Army, 1989), 577.

3. Michael N. Ingrisano Jr., 316th Troop Carrier Group Association, interviewed by author, January 5, 2003.

CHAPTER 35: AUTUMN OVER GERMANY (AUGUST–DECEMBER 1943)

1. Corell, "The Third Musketeer," 60.
2. McFarland and Newton, *To Command the Sky*, 113.
3. Terraine, *The Right of the Line*, 550.
4. Charles W. McArthur, *History of Mathematics, Vol. 4: Operational Analysis in the US Army Eighth Air Force in World War II* (Providence, RI: American Mathematical Society, 1990), 73–83.
5. Murray, *Strategy for Defeat: The Luftwaffe 1933–1945*, 342.
6. Terraine, *The Right of the Line*, 550.
7. Williamson Murray and Allan R. Millett, *A War to Be Won: Fighting the Second World War* (Cambridge, MA: The Belknap Press, 2000), 316–17.
8. Walt W. Rostow, *Pre-Invasion Bombing Strategy* (Austin, TX: University of Texas Press, 1981), 26.
9. Craven and Cate, eds. *The Army Air Forces in World War II, Vol. III, Europe: Argument to V-E Day*, 667.
10. Galland, *The First and the Last*, 190–91.
11. von Below, *At Hitler's Side*, trans. Geoffrey Brooks (London, UK: Greenhill Books, 2001), 184.
12. Air Marshal Sir Charles Portal quoted in Beck, *Under the Bombs*, 83, 93, 99–100.
13. Strategic Intelligence Branch, G-2 European Theater of Operations (US Army), "An Evaluation of Military Effects of RAF Bombing of Germany," 1 March–31 December 1943, in 519.553-3, Albert F. Simpson Historical Research Center, Air University, Maxwell AFB, AL, 2–3.
14. Spick, *Luftwaffe Fighter Aces*, 149.
15. McFarland and Newton, *To Command the Sky*, 47–50, 54–60.
16. von Below, *At Hitler's Side*, 187.
17. Galland, *The First and the Last*, 177–78.
18. Ibid., 178.

CHAPTER 36: FESTUNG EUROPA (MARCH–DECEMBER 1943)

1. Ambrose, *The Supreme Commander*, 152.
2. Eisenhower, *Allies: Pearl Harbor to D-Day*, 331.
3. Westermann, *Flak German Anti-Aircraft Defenses 1914–1945*, 258–59.

CHAPTER 37: COASTAL (SEPTEMBER 1939–FEBRUARY 1942)

1. Quoted in Denis Richards and Hilary St. George Saunders, *Royal Air Force 1939–1945, Vol. I: The Fight at Odds* (London, UK: HMSO, 1993), 343. The Barbarossa Directive was in reference to the invasion of the Soviet Union.
2. Roy Conyers Nesbit, *The Strike Wings* (Barnsley, South Yorkshire, UK: Pen & Sword Books, Ltd., 2012), 18.
3. John Vimpany and David Boyd, *To Force the Enemy off the Sea* (Warwick, UK: Helion & Company, 2022), 13.

4. Ibid., 13–15.

5. Richards and Saunders, *Royal Air Force 1939–1945, Vol. I: The Fight at Odds*, 352.

6. Robert Jackson, ed., *Kriegsmarine* (Osceola, WI: MBI Publishing, 2001), 153.

7. "Zusammendruck Dover-Lille Op. Karte Chef," 8 Things You Need to Know About the Battle of Britain, Imperial War Museum, accessed April 13, 2024, https://www.iwm.org.uk/history/8-things-you-need-to-know-about-the-battle-of-britain.

8. In French, the Strait of Dover is called the Pas de Calais. Note that in referring to the strait, no hyphens are used, unlike the French region of the Pas-de-Calais.

9. "Zusammendruck Dover-Lille Op. Karte Chef," 1:250,000, Der Kanal Blatt Nr. 1 overprint, Niel Kagan and Stephen G. Hyslop, *Atlas of World War II* (Washington, DC: National Geographic, 2018), 48–49.

10. The Germans operated both destroyers and torpedo boats in this role. German destroyers were equivalent to British destroyers, while torpedo boats were equivalent to British corvettes.

11. "E" for "enemy."

12. These numbers do not include aircraft lost or ships sunk during the abortive Operation SEALION.

13. Roy Conyers Nesbit, "Blenheims and Beauforts," *Royal Air Force Historical Society Journal*, no. 33 (United Kingdom: Royal Air Force Historical Society, 2005), 39.

14. Ibid., 41.

15. Richards and Saunders, *Royal Air Force 1939–1945, Vol. I: The Fight at Odds*, 354.

16. Ibid.

17. Jackson, ed., *Kriegsmarine*, 157.

18. Richards and Saunders, *Royal Air Force 1939–1945, Vol. I: The Fight at Odds*, 357.

CHAPTER 38: THE CHANNEL DASH (WINTER–SPRING 1942)

1. Richards and Saunders, *Royal Air Force 1939–1945, Vol. I: The Fight at Odds*, 357–75.

2. Denis Richards and Hilary St. George Saunders, *Royal Air Force 1939–1945, Vol. II: The Fight Avails* (London, UK: HMSO, 1993), 94–95.

CHAPTER 39: STRIKE WINGS (JULY 1942–APRIL 1944)

1. Richards and Saunders, *Royal Air Force 1939–1945, Vol. II: The Fight Avails*, 95.

2. Richards and Saunders, *Royal Air Force 1939–1945, Vol. II: The Fight Avails*, 96.

3. Andrew D. Bird, *A Separate Little War* (London, UK: Grub Street, 2003), 9–11.

4. Nesbit, *The Strike Wings*, 13.

5. A GRT, or gross register ton, is the equivalent of a 100 cubic feet of cargo space. It is a common measure of vessel cargo capacity.

CHAPTER 40: LESSONS LEARNED (AUGUST 1941–DECEMBER 1943

1. "Western Desert" refers to the Sahara Desert, located to the west of Cairo and the critical Suez Canal.

2. Powell, *The Development of British Tactical Air Power, 1940–1943*, 190–91.

3. Ibid., 207–08.

4. Terraine, *The Right of the Line*, 602.

CHAPTER 41: THE PIS AND PHOTO JOES

1. Quoted in "Air Power," Air & Space Forces Association.

2. "A Brief History of Air Force Scientific and Technical Intelligence," US Air Force History Support Office Web Page, n.d., n.p., online, July 28, 2000, available at http://www.airforcehistory.hq.af.mil/online/santihist.htm.

3. Sebastian Cox, "photographic reconnaissance," in *The Oxford Companion to WWII*, eds. I. C. B. Dear and M. R. D. Foot (New York: Oxford University Press, 1995), 887.

4. Chris Staerck, *Allied Photo Reconnaissance of World War II* (San Diego, CA: Thunder Bay Press, 1998), 11.

5. Cox, "photographic reconnaissance," in *The Oxford Companion to WWII*, 887.

6. "Camoufleurs" are specialists in developing and using camouflage.

7. Roy M. Stanley II, *To Fool a Glass Eye* (Washington, DC: Smithsonian Institution Press, 1998), 10.

8. Ibid., 11–20.

9. Joe Rychetnik, " 'Hi' Broiles Logged a Million Miles in Peeping Tom while Filming Airfields around the World," *Aviation History* (November 2000), 74.

10. Col. Elliot Roosevelt, transcript of interview by A-2, ACAS Intelligence, 30 July 1943, in File 152.052 Roosevelt, Albert F. Simpson Historical Research Center, Air University, Maxwell AFB, AL.

11. By Nigel Clarke: *Adolf Hitler's Holiday Snaps: Luftwaffe Target Reconnaissance: Avon, Cornwall, Devon, Dorset, Hampshire, Isle of Wight, Somerset, 1939–1942*; *Adolf Hitler's British Holiday Snaps: Luftwaffe Aerial Reconnaissance of England, Scotland and Wales*; and *Adolf Hitler's Home Counties Holiday Snaps: Berkshire, Essex, Kent, London, Surrey, Sussex, 1939–1942*.

12. Wing Commander Asher Lee, transcript of interview by the Assistant Chief of Air Staff for Intelligence, 29 July 1943, in File 152.052 Lee, Albert F. Simpson Historical Research Center, Air University, Maxwell AFB, AL.

13. "Reconnaissance in a Tactical Air Command," XIX TAC Report, 13 February 1945, n.p., online, May 15, 2001, available at http://militaryhistory.archives.webjump.com/.

CHAPTER 42: BIG CHANGES (AUGUST–OCTOBER 1943)

1. Military aphorism sometimes attributed to Lt. Col. Gene Ziemba, USAF (Ret).

2. Sullivan, *Overlord's Eagles*, 33.

3. Quoted in McFarland and Newton, *To Command the Sky*, 114–15.

4. James Parton, *Air Force Spoken Here* (Maxwell AFB, AL: Air University Press, March 2000), 330–35.

5. Quoted in McFarland and Newton, *To Command the Sky*, 113.

6. McFarland and Newton, *To Command the Sky*, 117.

7. Sullivan, *Overlord's Eagles*, 35.

8. Ibid., 36.

9. McFarland and Newton, *To Command the Sky*, 140.

10. Galland, *The First and the Last*, 187.

Chapter 43: The Fork-Tailed Devil (October 1943–May 1944)

1. These were the original RAF Mustangs used for low-level operations.
2. Bodie, *Lockheed P-38 Lightning*, 191.
3. Caidin, *Fork-Tailed Devil*, 9.
4. German ace Hans Pichler quoted in Caidin, *Fork-Tailed Devil*, 116.
5. Craven and Cate, eds., *The Army Air Forces in World War II, Vol. III, Europe: Argument to V-E Day*, 10.
6. Bodie, *Lockheed P-38 Lightning*, 191, 207–08.
7. Caidin, *Fork-Tailed Devil*, 403.
8. Ibid., 201.
9. Bodie, *Lockheed P-38 Lightning*, 188–91.
10. Caidin, *Fork-Tailed Devil*, 403.
11. Lockheed test pilot Tony DeVier quoted in Caidin, *Fork-Tailed Devil*, 181.

Chapter 44: Mustang: The Long Reach (May 1942–May 1944)

1. John Rickard, *North American Mustang Mk I*, 7 June 2007, accessed February 7, 2024,
   http://www.historyofwar.org/articles/weapons_MustangI.html.
2. Larry Davis, *P-51 Mustang in Action* (Carrollton, TX: Squadron/Signal Publications, Inc., 1981), 7.
3. Sullivan, *Overlord's Eagles*, xiii.
4. Ibid., 39–40.
5. Quoted in Sullivan, *Overlord's Eagles*, 46.
6. Ibid., 46–47.
7. USAAF, photographed for a series of US 8th Air Force publicity pictures for widespread distribution (photo was taken from a B-17G bomber of the 91st Bomb Group), public domain, via Wikimedia Commons.
8. Clarence E. "Bud" Anderson with Joseph P. Hamelin, *To Fly and to Fight* (New York: St. Martin's Press, 1990), 7, 104.
9. Ibid., 75.
10. Davis, *P-51 Mustang in Action*, 24.
11. General Kepner quoted in Jerry Scutts, *Osprey Aircraft of the Aces, Vol. 1: Mustang Aces of the Eighth Air Force*, ed. Tony Holmes (Oxford, UK: Osprey Books, 1995), 12.

Chapter 45: Fighter Pilots

1. Anderson and Hamelin, *To Fly and to Fight*, 90.
2. Yeager and Janos, *Yeager*, 16.
3. P-38 pilot Ray Crawford quoted in Bodie, *The Lockheed P-38 Lightning*, 165.
4. Field Marshal Erhard Milch, GAF (Ret.), "The Allied Combined Bomber Offensive: Two German Views (Part 1)," *The Combined Bomber Offensive: Classical and Revolutionary, Combined and Divided, Planned and Fortuitous*, ed. Noble Frankland

(Washington, DC: Office of Air Force History, 1968); Air War College Nonresident Studies Site, "AWCGate," n.d., n.p., July 5, 2001, available at http://www.au.af.mil/au/awc/awcgatecbo-afa/cbo05.htm.

5. Yeager and Janos, *Yeager*, 11–12.

6. Galland, *The First and the Last*, 167–70.

7. McFarland and Newton, *To Command the Sky*, 79.

8. John Ellis, *World War II: A Statistical Survey* (Facts on File: Higgins-McArthur / Longino & Porter, Inc., 1972), 258.

9. McFarland and Newton, *To Command the Sky*, 126.

CHAPTER 46: TRANSITION (OCTOBER–DECEMBER 1943)

1. Jablonski, *Airwar, Vol. IV: Wings of Fire*, 57.

2. McFarland and Newton, *To Command the Sky*, 139–40.

3. Andrews, *The Air Marshals*, 245.

4. McFarland and Newton, *To Command the Sky*, 146.

5. Ibid., 145–47.

6. Kenn C. Rust, *Fifteenth Air Force Story in World War II* (Temple City, CA: Historical Aviation Album, ca. 1976), 7.

7. Galland, *The First and the Last*, 190.

8. Luftwaffe Command Central in German is *Luftwaffenbefehlshaber Mitte*. Luftwaffe Command Southeast is *Luftwaffenkommando Süd Ost*. German areas after Price, *The Luftwaffe Data Book*, 93–95.

9. Eisenhower, *Allies: Pearl Harbor to D-Day*, 418.

10. The term "Supreme Allied Commander (SAC)" was superseded by Supreme Commander, Allied Expeditionary Force.

11. Quoted in Craven and Cate, eds., *The Army Air Forces in World War II, Vol. III, Europe: Argument to V-E Day*, 8.

CHAPTER 47: CASUALTIES (JANUARY–JUNE 1944)

1. Eisenhower, *Allies: Pearl Harbor to D-Day*, 438–39.

2. Bodie, *The Lockheed P-38 Lightning*, 192.

3. McFarland and Newton, *To Command the Sky*, 157.

4. LTG James H. Doolittle and Col Beirne Lay Jr., "Daylight Precision Bombing," in *Impact* 6 (January–April 1945), ed. James Parton (Harrisburg, PA: National Historical Society, 1980), xiii.

5. Colin Heaton, "Jimmy Doolittle and the Emergence of American Air Power," *World War II*, May 2003, 49.

6. Gen. James H. Doolittle with Carroll V. Glines, *I Could Never Be So Lucky Again* (New York: Bantam Books, 1992), 352.

7. Quoted in Doolittle and Lay, "Daylight Precision Bombing," xv.

8. McFarland and Newton, *To Command the Sky*, 119.

9. Price, *The Luftwaffe Data Book*, 93–95.

10. McFarland and Newton, *To Command the Sky*, 118–19.

11. Spick, *Luftwaffe Fighter Aces*, 150.

Chapter 48: Big Week (February 20–25, 1944)

1. Combined Operational Planning Committee, "PLAN—ARGUMENT," November 29, 1943, COPC/S.2071, in File 508.401, Albert F. Simpson Historical Research Center, Air University, Maxwell AFB, AL.

2. McFarland and Newton, *To Command the Sky*, 171.

3. After Craven and Cate, eds., *The Army Air Forces in World War II, Vol. III, Europe: Argument to V-E Day*, 34. William B. Breuer, *Secret Weapons of World War II* (New York: John Wiley & Sons, Inc., 2000), 180.

4. Middlebrook and Everitt, *The Bomber Command War Diaries 1939–1945*, 473.

5. RAF night intruders were normally radar-equipped Mosquito fighters.

6. Christopher Shores, *Duel for the Sky* (London, UK: Grub Street, 1999), 163–65.

7. Doolittle and Glines, *I Could Never Be So Lucky Again*, 367.

8. Galland, *The First and the Last*, 206.

9. Ibid., 192.

10. By the fall of 1944, the Me 410 *Zerstörer* were also driven from Germany's daylight skies.

11. Jerry L. Campbell, *Messerschmitt Me 110 in Action* (Carrollton, TX: Squadron / Signal Publications, Inc., 1977), 48.

12. McFarland and Newton, *To Command the Sky*, 171.

Chapter 49: Big B and Beyond (November 1943–March 1944)

1. Statement in a radio broadcast after his flight in an RAF Lancaster bomber attacking Berlin, quoted in "Air Power," Air & Space Forces Association.

2. Group Captain Dudley Saward, "Attacks by Night," *Impact* 6 (January–April 1945), ed. James Parton (Harrisburg, PA: National Historical Society, 1980), x.

3. Ibid.

4. Terraine, *The Right of the Line*, 557.

5. Ibid.

6. Galland, *The First and the Last*, 192.

7. Eric Hammel, *Air War Europa Chronology* (Pacifica, CA: Pacifica Press, 1994), 262–63.

8. Johnson, *Thunderbolt!*, 266–70.

9. Portal quoted in Beck, *Under the Bombs*, 121; and Speer, *Inside the Third Reich*, 332–33.

10. Hugh Morgan and John Weal, *Osprey Aircraft of the Aces, Vol. 17: German Jet Aces of World War 2*, ed. Tony Holmes (Oxford, UK: Osprey Books, 1998), 17–18.

11. Galland, *The First and the Last*, 195.

12. Ibid., 200–01.

13. Andrews, *The Air Marshals*, 251.

14. Quoted in Westermann, *Flak German Anti-Aircraft Defenses 1914–1945* (Lawrence: University Press of Kansas, 2001), 265.

15. Speer, *Inside the Third Reich*, 332–33, 346–49.

16. Scutts, *Osprey Aircraft of the Aces, Vol. 24: P-47 Thunderbolt Aces of the Eighth Air Force*, 64–65.

CHAPTER 50: THEY WILL BE OURS (NOVEMBER 1943–MAY 1944)
1. Quoted in McFarland and Newton, *To Command the Sky*, 239.

CHAPTER 51: SORTING OUT SHAEF (JANUARY–MAY 1944)
1. Quoted in Terraine, *The Right of the Line*, 683.
2. Joint Planning Staff of the (UK) War Cabinet, "Operation OVERLORD," reproduced in Gordon A. Harrison, *United States Army in World War II, European Theater: Cross-Channel Attack*, 450–56.
3. Quoted in Thomas E. Griess, ed., *West Point Atlas for the Second World War: Europe and the Mediterranean* (New York: Square One Publishers, 2002), 264.
4. Ibid.
5. Richard G. Davis, "Pointblank versus Overlord: Strategic Bombing and the Normandy Invasion," *Air Power History* 41, no. 2 (Summer 1994), 4.
6. Dwight D. Eisenhower, *Crusade in Europe* (Baltimore, MD: Johns Hopkins University Press, 1997), 221.
7. Sullivan, *Overlord's Eagles*, 52.
8. Ibid., 12.
9. Davis, "Pointblank versus Overlord," 5.
10. Sullivan, *Overlord's Eagles*, 53.
11. Ibid., 55.
12. Ibid., 55.
13. Ibid., 53.

CHAPTER 52: CROSSBOW (MAY 1943–MAY 1944)
1. Adam L. Gruen, *Preemptive Defense: Allied Air Power Versus Hitler's V-Weapons, 1943–1945*, US Army Air Forces in World War II (Washington, DC: Air Force History and Museums Program, 1998), 8–10.
2. Quoted in Craven and Cate, eds., *The Army Air Forces in World War II, Vol. III, Europe: Argument to V-E Day*, 89.
3. Ibid.
4. Map based on Craven and Cate, eds., *The Army Air Forces in World War II, Vol. II, Europe: Torch to Pointblank*, 94.
5. Breuer, *Secret Weapons of World War II*, 180.
6. George Kent, "The Man Who Saved London," in *Secrets & Spies* (Pleasantville, NY: Reader's Digest Association, 1964), 277–82.
7. Breuer, *Secret Weapons of World War II*, 180–82.
8. Gruen, *Preemptive Defense: Allied Air Power Versus Hitler's V-Weapons, 1943–1945*, 16–17.
9. Craven and Cate, eds., *The Army Air Forces in World War II, Vol. III, Europe: Argument to V-E Day*, 95.

10. General Walter Warlimont, *Inside Hitler's Headquarters 1939–45*, trans. R. H. Barry (Novato, CA: Presidio Press, 1964), 403.

11. Map based on Craven and Cate, eds., *The Army Air Forces in World War II, Vol. II, Europe: Torch to Pointblank*, 94.

12. Neufeld, *The Rocket and the Reich*, 273–74.

13. Eisenhower and other Allied leaders of the time used the "the German" to refer to the German enemy in general.

14. Eisenhower, *Crusade in Europe*, 260.

CHAPTER 53: HOLDING THE FORTRESS (JANUARY–MAY 1944)

1. Field Marshal Erwin Rommel, *The Rommel Papers*, trans. and ed. Sir B. H. Liddell Hart (New York: Da Capo Press, 1953), 455.

2. Harrison, *United States Army in World War II, European Theater: Cross-Channel Attack*, Map V; Max Hastings, *Das Reich* (New York: Jove Books, 1983), xii–xiii; Richard Natkiel, *Atlas of World War II* (1985; new imprint, Greenwich, CT: Brompton Books Corporation, 1999), 170; *German Order of Battle. The Directory Prepared by Allied Intelligence of Regiments, Formations, and Units of the German Armed Forces* (1944; new imprint; Mechanicsburg, PA: Stackpole Books, 1994), B35; and Griess, ed., *West Point Atlas for the Second World War: Europe and the Mediterranean*, 270.

3. Ibid., 455–66.

4. Harrison, *United States Army in World War II, European Theater: Cross-Channel Attack*, Map V.

5. William M. Hammond, "The US Army Campaigns of World War II: Normandy," United States Army Center for Military History, n.d., n.p., July 28, 2000, available at http://www.army.mil/cmh-pg/brochures/normandy/nor-pam.htm.

6. Alfred Goldberg, "Air Campaign OVERLORD: To D-Day," in *D-Day: The Normandy Invasion in Retrospect*, ed. Eisenhower Foundation (Lawrence: University of Kansas Press, 1971), 63.

7. Lt. Col. Maris McCrabb, "Drohende Gefahr West: The Pre-Normandy Air Campaign," *Airpower Journal* (Summer 1994), n.p., April 11, 2000, available at http://www.airpower.maxwell.af.mil/airchronicles/apj/apj94/mccrabb2.html.

CHAPTER 54: TRAINS (FEBRUARY–MAY 1944)

1. Quoted in Rostow, *Pre-Invasion Bombing Strategy*, 18.

2. Charles Winchester, "Advancing Backwards: The Demodernization of the German Army in World War II," *Osprey Military Journal* (January–February 2000), 18.

3. Lt. Gen. Morgan COSSAC, to CINC AEAF, subject: "Overlord" Bombing Policy, January 10 1944, in SHAEF SGS Minutes Decimal File, May 1943–August 1945, Records Group 331, National Records and Archives Administration Archive II, College Park, MD.

4. Major General P. G. Whiteford, ACS G-2 (Intelligence Division) AEAF, to Maj. Gen. H. R. Bull, Maj. Gen. C. A. West, and Brig. K. McLean. Subject: Letter. "Overlord" Bombing Policy (untitled), January 25, 1944. In SHAEF SGS Minutes Decimal File,

May 1943–August 1945, Records Group 331. National Records and Archives Administration Archive II, College Park, MD..

5. Brigadier General L. S. Kuter, Assistant Chief of Air Staff, Plan, memorandum to Lt. Gen. Carl Spaatz, Commander USSTAF, subject: Air Operations in Western Europe, February 4, 1944, in File 167.04-27, Albert F. Simpson Historical Research Center, Air University, Maxwell AFB, AL.

6. "Transportation," in *Impact* 7 (May–July 1945), ed. James Parton (Harrisburg, PA: National Historical Society, 1980), 37.

7. ACM Trafford Leigh-Mallory, Air Commander in Chief AEAF, to Gen. Dwight D. Eisenhower Supreme Allied Commander SHAEF, subject: Attacks on Rail Targets in Enemy-Occupied Territories, March 10, 1944, in SHAEF SGS Minutes Decimal File, May 1943–August 1945, Records Group 331, National Records and Archives Administration Archive II, College Park, MD.

8. Andrews, *The Air Marshals*, 260–62.

9. Shawn P. Keller, Major USAF, "Turning Point: A History of German Petroleum in World War II and Its Lessons for the Role of Oil in Modern Air Warfare" (research paper, ACSC, Air University, Maxwell AFB, AL, undated).

10. MG Haywood S. Hansell Jr., *The Air Plan that Defeated Hitler* (Atlanta, GA: Higgins-McArthur / Longino & Porter, Inc., 1972), 235.

CHAPTER 55: COMPROMISES (APRIL–MAY 1944)

1. Eisenhower, *Crusade in Europe*, 232.

2. Dr. Silvano Wueschner, *The "Transportation Plan": Preparing for the Normandy Invasion* (Maxwell AFB, AL: Air University History Office, 2019).

3. Murray, *Strategy for Defeat: The Luftwaffe 1933–1945*, 194.

4. Sullivan, *Overlord's Eagles*, 99.

5. Hammond, "The US Army Campaigns of World War II: Normandy."

6. Eisenhower, *Crusade in Europe*, 222.

7. AVM J. M. Robb, Secretary General Staff SHAEF, "Direction of Operations of Allied Air Forces Against Transportation Targets," April 15, 1944, in SHAEF SGS Minutes Decimal File, May 1943–August 1945, Records Group 331, National Records and Archives Administration Archive II, College Park, MD.

8. Eisenhower, *Allies: Pearl Harbor to D-Day*, 444–47.

9. Sullivan, *Overlord's Eagles*, 14–16.

10. Eisenhower, *Allies: Pearl Harbor to D-Day,* 455.

11. Rostow, *Pre-Invasion Bombing Strategy*, 6.

CHAPTER 56: *MORT POUR LA FRANCE* (APRIL–MAY 1944)

1. Joint Intelligence Subcommittee of the Joint Planning Staff of the (UK) War Cabinet, "Effects of the Allied Bombing Offensive on the German War Effort with Particular Reference to "Overlord," JIC Report (44) 177, 1 May 1944, in SHAEF SGS Minutes Decimal File, May 1943–August 1945, Records Group 331, National Records and Archives Administration Archive II, College Park, MD.

2. Minutes of meeting of the Office of the Deputy Supreme Commander SHAEF on the topic of Alternate Plans for the Employment of Strategic Bomber Forces Meeting, May 3, 1944, in SHAEF SGS Minutes Decimal File, May 1943–August 1945, Records Group 331, National Records and Archives Administration Archive II, College Park, MD.

3. Edward L. Loewenheim, Harold D. Langley, and Manfred Jones, eds., *Roosevelt and Churchill: Their Secret Wartime Correspondence* (New York: Saturday Review Press / E. P. Dutton & Co., Inc., 1975), 494–95.

4. No Date/Time Group Message, President Roosevelt, to Prime Minister Churchill, May 11, 1944, in SHAEF SGS Minutes Decimal File, May 1943–August 1945, Records Group 331, National Records and Archives Administration Archive II, College Park, MD.

Chapter 57: The Bridge at Vernon (May 1944)
1. Sullivan, *Overlord's Eagles*, 76.
2. Ibid., 86–88.
3. Rostow, *Pre-Invasion Bombing Strategy*, 63–64.
4. Ibid., 117–18.
5. 1Lt Lyne M. Shackelford, Assistant Secretary SHAEF General Staff, memorandum to Lt Gen W. Bedel Smith, Chief of Staff SHAEF, subject: Summary of results of attacks on rail transportation targets, May 27, 1944, in SHAEF SGS Minutes, Decimal File, May 1943–August 1945, Records Group 331, National Records and Archives Administration Archive II, College Park, MD.

Chapter 58: CHATTANOOGA (May 1944)
1. Lt. Col. William R. Dunn, transcript of US Air Force oral history interview by Maj. Gilmartin and Captains Porter and High, 2 November 1973, in File K239.0512-922, Albert F. Simpson Historical Research Center, Air University, Maxwell AFB, AL, 47.
2. Albert Marrin, *Overlord D-Day and the Invasion of Europe* (New York: Atheneum, 1982), 36.
3. Frederick A. Johnsen, "Working on the Railroad," *Airpower* 32, no. 3 (May 2002): 49.
4. Lt. Col. William R. Dunn, transcript of US Air Force oral history interview by Gilmartin et al., 47.

Chapter 59: Reactions (May 1944)
1. Shackelford, Summary of results of attacks on rail transportation targets, May 27, 1944.
2. Jason Pipes and Aryo L. Vercamer, "The West on the Eve of D-Day," World War II Axis Military History Day-by-Day, n.d., n.p., online, April 27, 2000, available at http://www.uwm.edu/~jpipes/eve44.html.
3. Eisenhower, *Allies: Pearl Harbor to D-Day*, 467–68.

4. James F. Dunnigan and Albert A. Nofi, *Dirty Little Secrets of World War II* (New York: William Morrow and Company, Inc., 1994), 250.

5. Eisenhower, *Allies: Pearl Harbor to D-Day*, 460.

6. Sullivan, *Overlord's Eagles*, 165.

CHAPTER 60: AIRFIELDS AND RADARS (JANUARY–MAY 1944)

1. Combined Operational Planning Committee, "France: Airdromes & Airdrome Installations," *Airfield Attack Reports*, February 5, 1944, File 520.3651, Albert F. Simpson Historical Research Center, Air University, Maxwell AFB, AL.

2. Combined Operational Planning Committee, "Sosterberg [*sic*] Airdrome & Chartres A/D," *Airfield Attack Reports*, March 17, 1944, File 520.3651, Albert F. Simpson Historical Research Center, Air University, Maxwell AFB, AL; Combined Operational Planning Committee, "Immediate Interpretation Report No. K.1942: Soesterberg A/F," March 26 1944, File 520.3651, Albert F. Simpson Historical Research Center, Air University, Maxwell AFB, AL.

3. Minutes of meeting of the Office of the Deputy Supreme Commander SHAEF on the topic of Alternate Plans for the Employment of Strategic Bomber Forces Meeting, May 3, 1944, in SHAEF SGS Minutes, Decimal File, May 1943–August 1945, Records Group 331, National Records and Archives Administration Archive II, College Park, MD.

4. Sullivan, *Overlord's Eagles*, 106.

5. *Wings at War Series, Vol. 2: Sunday Punch in Normandy* [1992] (Washington, DC: Center for Air Force History, US Air Force, undated, new imprint), 7.

6. Sullivan, *Overlord's Eagles*, 107.

7. Goldberg, "Air Campaign OVERLORD: To D-Day," 62.

8. James H. Kitchens III, PhD, "The *Luftwaffe* and D-Day," Lecture to the Ninth AF Conference "D-Day Remembered," University of New Orleans, New Orleans, LA, April 30, 1994.

9. "1944," RAF History Page, n.d., n.p., November 13, 2001, available http://www raf.mod.uk/history/line1944.html.

10. Terraine, *The Right of the Line*, 627.

CHAPTER 61: TO CROSS THE NARROW SEAS (MAY 1944)

1. See Molyson, *Six Air Forces Over the Atlantic*.

2. John Eisenhower quoted in Richard P. Hallion, *The US Army Air Forces in World War II, D-Day 1944: Air Power Over the Normandy Beaches and Beyond* (Washington, DC: Air Force History and Museums Program, 1995), 44.

APPENDIX 3: FÜHRER DIRECTIVE NO. 51

1. Harrison, *United States Army in World War II, European Theater: Cross-Channel Attack*, 455, 464–67.

Appendix 4: German Coastal Warships

1. *Jane's Fighting Ships of World War II* [1946] (New York: Crescent Books, 1994 reprint), 141–54; Jak P. Mallmann Showell, *The German Navy in World War Two* (Annapolis, MD: Naval Institute Press, 1979), 94–99; Gordon Williamson, *Kriegsmarine Coastal Forces*, New Vanguard 151 (New York: Osprey, 2009), 6–22.

2. Friedrich Rüge, *Sea Warfare 1939–1945*, trans. Commander M. G. Saunders, RN (London, UK: Cassell & Company Ltd., 1957), 199–202.

Selected Bibliography

Administrative Preparations, The. RAF Narrative, Vol. II. London, UK: Air Historical Branch, Air Ministry. Released July 11, 1984. PDF. Accessed September 27, 2023. https:// www.raf.mod.uk/our-organisation/units/air-historical-branch/second -world-war-campaign-narratives/liberation-of-north-west-europe-vol-ii-the administrative preparations/.

Airgood, Roger. 440th Troop Carrier Group History Project oral history, courtesy of Randolph Hils, October 24, 1992.

"Air Power." Air & Space Forces Association. Accessed February 24, 2024. https://secure .afa.org/quotes/Quotes_81208.pdf.

Air War College Nonresident Studies Site. "AWCGate," n.d., n.p. July 5, 2001. Available at http://www.au.af.mil/au/awc/awcgatecbo-afa/cbo05.htm.

Allied Expeditionary Air Force (AEAF). *Principal Airfields within 100 & 130 Miles of Caen.* Annex K to Operation Neptune Overall Air Plan Sketch Map 2. AEAF/TS399/Air Plans AEAF, 15 April 1944. In WWII Combat Operations REPORTS 1942–1946 Records Group 18. National Records and Archives Administration Archive II, College Park, MD.

Ambrose, Stephen E. *Pegasus Bridge.* New York: Simon & Schuster, Inc., 1985.

———. *The Supreme Commander.* Jackson: University of Mississippi Press, 1999.

Anderson, Clarence E. "Bud," with Joseph P. Hamelin. *To Fly and to Fight.* New York: St. Martin's Press, 1990.

Andrews, Allen. *The Air Marshals: The Air War in Western Europe.* New York: William Morrow and Company, Inc., 1970.

Arnold, H. H. General of the Air Force. *Global Mission.* New York: Harper Brothers, 1949.

Assistant Chief of Air Staff for Intelligence, US Army Air Force. Interview of Col. Elliot Roosevelt by Lt. Col. Palmer Dixon, 30 July 1943. File 152.052 Roosevelt. Albert F. Simpson Historical Research Center, Air University, Maxwell AFB, AL.

Assistant Chief of Air Staff for Intelligence. Interview of Col. P. W. Tibbets, 20 February 1943. File 142.052 Tibbets. Albert F. Simpson Historical Research Center, Air University, Maxwell AFB, AL.

Bailey, Ronald H., and the Editors of Time-Life Books. *The Air War in Europe.* Chicago, IL: Time-Life Books, 1981.

Baxter, I. M. "Defending the Fatherland." *Military Illustrated,* no. 145 (June 2000): 16–23.

Beck, Earl R. *Under the Bombs.* Lexington: University of Kentucky Press, 1986.

"The Beginnings." British First Airborne Division Living History Association, n.d., n.p. July 19, 2002. Available at http://www.britishairborne.org/.

Bekker, Cajus. *The Luftwaffe War Diaries.* Translated by Frank Ziegler. New York: Da Capo Press, 1994.

Bickers, Richard Townshend. *Air War Normandy*. London, UK: Leo Cooper, 1994.

Bird, Andrew D. *A Separate Little War*. London, UK: Grub Street, 2003.

Bodie, Warren M. *The Lockheed P-38 Lightning*. Hiawassee, GA: Widewing Publications, 1991.

Bowman, Martin W. *The USAAF Handbook 1939–1945*. Mechanicsburg, PA: Stackpole Books, 1996.

———. *Confounding the Reich*. Barnsley, South Yorkshire, UK: Pen and Sword Aviation, 2004.

———. *Mosquito Fighter / Fighter Bomber Units of World War 2*. Combat Aircraft 9. New York: Osprey Publishing, 2008.

Bradley, Omar. *A Soldier's Story*. New York: Henry Holt and Company, 1951.

"A Brief History of Air Force Scientific and Technical Intelligence." US Air Force History Support Office Web Page, n.d., n.p. July 28, 2000. Available at http://www.airforcehistory.hq.af.mil/online/santihist.htm.

BR 1736 (26) Royal Navy Staff History—Raid on Dieppe. Battle Summary No. 33, Historical Section, Admiralty. Accessed August 20, 2023. https://www.navy.gov.au/sites/default/files/documents/Battle_Summary_33.pdf.

Breuer, William B. *Secret Weapons of World War II*. New York: John Wiley & Sons, Inc., 2000.

Brown, Capt. Eric. "Flying FW 190 Kurt Tank's Butcher Bird." *Aviation History* (October 2000).

Buckton, Henry. *Friendly Invasion Memories of Operation Bolero*. Chichester, UK: Phillimore & Company, 2006.

Caidin, Martin. *Fork-Tailed Devil: The P-38*. New York: ibooks, inc., 2001.

Caldwell, Donald L. *JG 26: Top Guns of the Luftwaffe*. New York: Ivy Books, 1991.

Caldwell, Donald L., and Richard Muller. *The Luftwaffe Over Germany: Defense of the Reich*. Barnsley, South Yorkshire, UK: Frontline Books, 2014.

Campbell, Jerry L. *Messerschmitt Me 110 in Action*. Carrollton, TX: Squadron / Signal Publications, Inc., 1977.

Carter, Kit C., and Robert Mueller, compilers. *US Army Air Forces in World War II: Combat Chronology 1941–1945*. Washington, DC: Center for Air Force History, US Air Force, 1991.

Case, Col. Homer. Transcript of interview by the Assistant Chief of Air Staff for Intelligence, Undated 1942, in File 142.05-3, Albert F. Simpson Historical Research Center, Air University, Maxwell AFB, AL.

Chandler, David G., and James Lawton Collins, eds. *The D-Day Encyclopedia*. New York: Simon & Schuster, 1994.

Chester, Major Michael C. To Lt. Gen. James M. Gavin. Letter, March 30. 1959. Box 11 of the James M. Gavin Papers, US Army Heritage and Education Center, Carlisle Barracks. PA.

Chicken, Stephen. *Overlord Coastline*. New York: Hippocrene Books, Inc., 1993.

Chief of Staff to the Supreme Allied Commander (COSSAC). *Attainment of the Necessary Air Situation*. Appendix K to COSSAC (43) 28 Plan, 1943. In File 505.14-3. Albert F. Simpson Historical Research Center, Air University, Maxwell AFB, AL.

———. *Operation OVERLORD Beaches and Ports France and the Low Countries Beaches and Theoretical Beach Capacities and Major Port Capacities*. COSSAC (43) 28 Map

MA. Undated 1943. In Box 11 of the James M. Gavin Papers. US Army Heritage and Education Center, Carlisle Barracks, PA.

———. *Requirements for a Tactical Air Force*. COSSAC Study No. 2, undated 1943. In File 505.13-3. Albert F. Simpson Historical Research Center, Air University, Maxwell AFB, AL.

———. *Support of Military Operations by Resistance Groups in France*. Appendix P to COSSAC (43) 28 Chief of Staff to the Supreme Allied Commander, undated 1943. In File 505.14-3. Albert F. Simpson Historical Research Center, Air University, Maxwell AFB, AL.

Chiefs of Staff (COS) Committee of the Joint Planning Staff of the (UK) War Cabinet. *Bombing Policy in Connection with Overlord*. COS Report (44) 125 t, 17 April 1944. In SHAEF SGS Minutes Decimal File, May 1943–August 1945, Records Group 331. National Records and Archives Administration Archive II, College Park, MD.

Chrastil, Rachel. *Bismarck's War: The Franco-Prussian War and the Making of Modern Europe*. New York: Basic Books, 2023.

Churchill, Winston S. *The Second World War, Vol. II: Their Finest Hour*. Boston, MA: Mariner Books, 1985.

———. *The Second World War, Vol. III: The Grand Alliance*. Boston, MA: Mariner Books, 1985.

Clarke, Nigel J. *Adolf Hitler's Holiday Snaps: Luftwaffe Target Reconnaissance: Avon, Cornwall, Devon, Dorset, Hampshire, Isle of Wight, Somerset, 1939–1942*. Lyme Regis, Dorset, UK: Nigel J. Clark Publications, 1995.

———. *Adolf Hitler's Home Counties Holiday Snaps: Berkshire, Essex, Kent, London, Surrey, Sussex, 1939–1942*. Lyme Regis, Dorset, UK: Nigel J. Clark Publications, 1996.

———. *Adolf Hitler's British Holiday Snaps: Luftwaffe Aerial Reconnaissance of England, Scotland and Wales*. Stroud, UK: Fonthill Media, 2012.

Colley, David P. *The Road to Victory: The Untold Story of WWII's Red Ball Express*. Washington, DC: Brassey's, 2000.

Combined Chiefs of Staff. *Air Operations Against the German and French Navies*. CCS 256, 18 June 1943. In JCS Geographic File 1942–1945, Records Group 218. National Records and Archives Administration Archive II, College Park, MD.

———. *Air Operations Against the German and French Navies*. CCS 256/1, 18 June 1943. In JCS Geographic File 1942–1945, Records Group 218. National Records and Archives Administration Archive II, College Park, MD.

———. *Air Operations Against the German and French Navies*. CCS 256/2, 28 June 1943. In JCS Geographic File 1942–1945, Records Group 218. National Records and Archives Administration Archive II, College Park, MD.

Combined Operational Planning Committee. "PLAN–ARGUMENT," November 29, 1943. COPC/S.2071. Group Captain E. J. Corbally. File 508.401. Albert F. Simpson Historical Research Center, Air University, Maxwell AFB, AL.

———. "France: Airdromes & Airdrome Installations." *Airfield Attack Reports*, February 5, 1944. In File 520.3651. Albert F. Simpson Historical Research Center, Air University, Maxwell AFB, AL.

———. "Sosterberg [*sic*] Airdrome & Chartres A/D." *Airfield Attack Reports*, March 17, 1944. In File 520.3651. Albert F. Simpson Historical Research Center, Air University, Maxwell AFB, AL.

————. *"Soesterberg A/F." Immediate Interpretation Report No. K.1942*, March 26, 1944. In File 520.3651. Albert F. Simpson Historical Research Center, Air University, Maxwell AFB, AL.

Cooper, Alan. *Air Battle of the Ruhr*. Shrewsbury, UK: Airlife, 1992, 1983.

Corell, John T. "The Third Musketeer." *Air and Space Forces Magazine* (December 2014). Accessed March 25, 2024. https://www.airandspaceforces.com/PDF/Magazine Archive/Magazine%20Documents/2014/December%202014/1214musketeer.pdf.

Cox, Sebastian. "Photographic Reconnaissance." In *The Oxford Companion to WWII*, eds. I. C. B. Dear and M. R. D. Foot (New York: Oxford University Press, 1995).

Craigle, Col. L. C., Col. M. S. Roth, and Col. J. F. Philips. Transcript of interview by the Assistant Chief of Air Staff for Intelligence, 12 January 1943, in File 142.052-Craigle, Albert F. Simpson Historical Research Center, Air University, Maxwell AFB, AL.

Craven, Wesley Frank, and James Lea Cate, eds. *The Army Air Forces in World War II, Vol. I: Plans and Early Operations, January 1939 to August 1942*. Washington, DC: Office of Air Force History, US Air Force, 1983.

————. *The Army Air Forces in World War II, Vol. II: Europe: Torch to Pointblank, August 1942 to December 1943*. Washington, DC: Office of Air Force History, US Air Force, 1983.

————. *The Army Air Forces in World War II, Vol. III: Europe: Argument to V-E Day, January 1944 to May 1945*. Washington, DC: Office of Air Force History, US Air Force, 1983.

————. *The Army Air Forces in World War II, Vol. IV: The Pacific: Guadalcanal to Saipan August 1942 to July 1944* (1949; new imprint, Washington, DC: Office of Air Force History, United States Air Force, 1983).

————. *The Army Air Forces in World War II, Vol. VI: Men and Planes*. Washington, DC: Office of Air Force History, US Air Force, 1983.

————. *The Army Air Forces in World War II, Vol. VII: Services Around the World*. Washington, DC: Office of Air Force History, US Air Force, 1983.

Davis, Kenneth S. *Dwight D. Eisenhower: Soldier of Democracy*. New York: Konecky & Konecky, 1945.

Davis, Larry. *P-51 Mustang in Action*. Aircraft No. 45. Carrollton, TX: Squadron/Signal Publications, Inc., 1981.

Davis, Richard G. *Carl Spaatz and the Air War in Europe*. Washington, DC: Center for Air Force History, US Air Force, 1983.

————. "Pointblank versus Overlord: Strategic Bombing and the Normandy Invasion." *Air Power History* 41, no. 2 (Summer 1994): 4–13.

Dear, I. C. B., and M. R. D. Foot, eds. *The Oxford Companion to WWII*. New York: Oxford University Press, 1995.

de Planhol, Xavier, and Paul Claval. *An Historical Geography of France*. Translated by Janet Lloyd. Cambridge, UK: Cambridge University Press, 1994.

Deichmann, General der Flieger Paul. *German Air Operations in Support of the Army*. Maxwell AFB, AL: Air University Press, June 1962.

Deighton, Len. *Blood, Tears and Folly*. Edison, NJ: Castle Books, 1999.

Delve, Ken. *The Source Book of the RAF*. Shrewsbury, UK: Airlife Publishing, LTD., 1994.

deZeng IV, Henry L. *Luftwaffe Airfields 1935–45: Belgium and Luxembourg*. August 2014 ed. Accessed August 27, 2023. www.ww2.dk/Airfields%20-%20Austria%20 [1937%20Borders].pdf.

———. *Luftwaffe Airfields 1935–45: Denmark*. August 2014 ed. Accessed August 27, 2023. www.ww2.dk/Airfields%20-%20Denmark.pdf.

———. *Luftwaffe Airfields 1935–45: France*. June 2014 ed. Accessed August 27, 2023. www.ww2.dk/Airfields%20-%20France.pdf

———. *Luftwaffe Airfields 1935–45: General Information*. June 2014 ed. Accessed August 27, 2023. www.ww2.dk/Airfields%20-%20General%20Introduction.pdf.

———. *Luftwaffe Airfields 1935–45: Germany*. June 2014 ed. Accessed August 27, 2023. www.ww2.dk/Airfields%20-%20Germany%20[1937%20Borders].pdf.

———. *Luftwaffe Airfields 1935–45: Netherlands*. August 2014 ed. Accessed August 27, 2023. www.ww2.dk/Airfields%20-%20Netherlands.pdf.

———. *Luftwaffe Airfields 1935–45 Romania*. December 2014 ed. Accessed August 27, 2023. www.ww2.dk/Airfields%20-%20Romania.pdf.

"The Dieppe Raid." *British Forces in World War II*, n.d., n.p. November 13, 2001. Available at http://british-forces.com/world_war2/Campaigns/dieppe.html.

Dildy, Douglas C. *Big Week Operation Argument 1944*. Osprey Air Campaign Series, Vol. 27. Oxford, UK: Osprey Publishing Ltd., 2022.

———. *Dunkirk 1940: Operation Dynamo*. Osprey Campaign Series, Vol. 219. Oxford, UK: Osprey Publishing Ltd., 2010.

———. *Fall Gelb 1940 (1)*. Osprey Campaign Series, Vol. 264. Oxford, UK: Osprey Publishing Ltd., 2014.

———. *Fall Gelb 1940 (2)*. Osprey Campaign Series, Vol. 265. Oxford, UK: Osprey Publishing Ltd., 2015.

Doolittle, Lt. Gen. James H. Oral history by US Air Force Historical Division, 23 June 1965. File K239.0512-623. Albert F. Simpson Historical Research Center, Air University, Maxwell AFB, AL.

———. US Air Force oral history by Brig Gen. George W. Goddard, 20 July 1967. File K239.0512-998. Albert F. Simpson Historical Research Center, Air University, Maxwell AFB, AL.

———. Oral history by Prof. Ronald Schaffer, California State University, 24 August 1979. File K239.0512-1206. Albert F. Simpson Historical Research Center, Air University, Maxwell AFB, AL.

Doolittle, Lt. Gen. James H., with Carroll V. Glines. *I Could Never Be So Lucky Again*. New York: Bantam Books, 1992.

Doolittle, Lt. Gen. James H., and Col. Beirne Lay Jr. "Daylight Precision Bombing." *Impact* 6 (January–April 1945). Harrisburg, PA: National Historical Society, 1980.

Dornberger, Walter. *V-2*. Translated by James Cleugh and Geoffrey Halliday. New York: Viking Press, 1954.

Dougherty, Martin J. *Military Atlas of Air Warfare*. New York: Chartwell Books, 2014.

Drummond, John "Ace." Oral history interview by Col. Joseph Molyson, USAFR, January 22, 2003.

Dunn, Lt. Col. William R. Oral history by Major Gilmartin et al., 2 November 1973. US Air Force Historical Division, File K239.0512-922. Albert F. Simpson Historical Research Center, Air University, Maxwell AFB, AL.

Dunnigan, James F., and Albert A. Nofi. *Dirty Little Secrets of World War II*. New York: William Morrow and Company, Inc., 1994.

Eaker, Lt. Gen. Ira C. US Air Force oral history by. Dr. Goldberg and Dr. Hildreth, 22 May 1962. File K239.0512-627. Albert F. Simpson Historical Research Center, Air University, Maxwell AFB, AL.

———. US Air Force oral history by Arthur Marmor, January 1966. File K239.0512-626. Albert F. Simpson Historical Research Center, Air University, Maxwell AFB, AL.

———. "The Evolution of Air Command." *Impact* 1 (April–August 1943). Harrisburg, PA: National Historical Society, 1980.

Economic Warfare Division, American Embassy, London. *Study of the Effects of the Air Attacks on Hamburg*, 3 January 1944. In 519.553-3. Albert F. Simpson Historical Research Center, Air University, Maxwell AFB, AL.

Eisenhower, Dwight D. *Crusade in Europe* [1948]. Baltimore, MD: Johns Hopkins University Press, 1997.

———. US Air Force oral history by Brig. Gen. George W. Goddard, undated. File K239.0512-999. Albert F. Simpson Historical Research Center, Air University, Maxwell AFB, AL.

Ellis, John. *World War II: A Statistical Survey*. Facts on File: Higgins-McArthur / Longino & Porter, Inc., 1972.

Engelmann, Joachim. *V1: The Flying Bomb*. Atglen, PA: Schiffer Publishing Ltd., 1992.

Faber, Harold, ed. *Luftwaffe: A History*. New York: Quadrangle / New York Times Book Company, 1977.

Ferguson, Gregor, and Kevin Lyles. *The Paras 1940–1944*. Osprey Elite Series, Vol. 21. Edited by Martin Windrow. London, UK: Osprey Books, 1984.

Field, Alexander J. *The Economic Consequences of the US Mobilization for the Second World War*. New Haven: Yale University Press, 2022.

Fisher, Ernest F. "German Signal." *The D-Day Encyclopedia*. Edited by David G. Chandler and James Lawton Collins. New York: Simon & Schuster, 1994.

Fleming, Peter. *Operation Sea Lion*. New York: Simon & Schuster, 1957.

Foot, M. R. D. "Reconnaissance." *The Historical Encyclopedia of World War II*. Edited by Marcel Baudot, et al., trans. Jesse Dilson. New York: Facts on File, 1997.

Ford, Ken. *St. Nazaire 1942*. Osprey Campaign Series, Vol. 92. Oxford, UK: Osprey Publishing Ltd., 2001.

———. *Dieppe 1942. Prelude to D-Day*. Osprey Campaign Series, Vol. 127. Oxford, UK: Osprey Publishing Ltd., 2003.

Forsyth, Robert. *FW 190 Sturmböcke vs. B-17 Flying Fortress Europe 1944–45*. Oxford, UK: Osprey Publishing Ltd., 2009.

———. *Me 210/410 Zerstörer Units*. Combat Aircraft 131. New York: Osprey Publishing, 2019.

———. *Stalingrad Airlift 1942-43*. Osprey Air Campaign Series. New York: Osprey Publishing, 2023.

Freeman, Roger A. *Raiding the Reich*. London, UK: Arms and Armour Press, 1997.

———. *The Mighty Eighth*. London, UK: Cassell & Company, 2000.

———. *The Mighty Eighth War Manual*. London, UK: Cassell & Company, 2000.

Freeman, Roger A., with Alan Crouchman and Vic Maslen. *Mighty Eighth War Diary*. New York: Jane's, 1981.

Galland, Adolf, General der Flieger. *The First and the Last*. Cutchogue, NY: Buccaneer Books, 1997.

Gavin, Lt. Gen. James M. US Army Military History Institute oral history by Lt. Col. Donald G. Andrews, USA. and Lt. Col. Charles H. Ferguson, USA, undated 1975. Box 1 of the James M. Gavin Papers. US Army Heritage and Education Center, Carlisle Barracks, PA.

"German Antiaircraft Ceilings." *Tactical and Technical Trends*, no. 25 (May 20, 1943). Accessed March 8, 2024. https://www.lonesentry.com/articles/ttt07/german-anti aircraft-ceilings.html.

German Order of Battle: The Directory Prepared by Allied Intelligence of Regiments, Formations, and Units of the German Armed Forces, 1944. Mechanicsburg, PA: Stackpole Books, 1994.

Glines, C. V. "Troop Carriers of WWII." *Air Force Magazine* (February 1999), n.p. March 12, 2000. Available at http://www.afa.org/magazine/0299troop.html.

Goldberg, Alfred. "Air Campaign OVERLORD: To D-Day." *D-Day: The Normandy Invasion in Retrospect*. Edited by the Eisenhower Foundation. Lawrence: University of Kansas Press, 1971.

Goulter, Christina J. M. *The Forgotten Offensive: The Royal Air Force Coastal Command's Anti-Shipping Campaign, 1940–1945*. London, UK: Frank Cass, 1995.

Griess, Thomas E., ed. *West Point Atlas for the Second World War Europe and the Mediterranean* [1984], 2nd ed. New York: Square One Publishers, 2002.

Gruen, Adam L. *Preemptive Defense: Allied Air Power versus Hitler's V-Weapons, 1943–1945*. The US Army Air Forces in World War II. Washington, DC: Air Force History and Museums Program, 1998.

G-2, US Army Air Force. Interview of 1 Lt. W. J. Cantwell, 15 March 1944. Major William H. Rhodes. File 142.05-8. Albert F. Simpson Historical Research Center, Air University, Maxwell AFB, AL.

Hale, Julian. *The Blitz: 1940–41*. Osprey Air Campaign Series. Oxford, UK: Osprey Publishing Ltd., 2023.

Hall, Grover C., Jr. *1,000 Destroyed: The Life and Times of the 4th Fighter Group*. Fallbrook, CA: Aero Publishers, Inc., 1978.

Hallion, Richard P. *The US Army Air Forces in World War II, D-Day 1944: Air Power Over the Normandy Beaches and Beyond*. Washington, DC: Air Force History and Museums Program, 1995.

Hammel, Eric. *Air War Europa Chronology*. Pacifica, CA: Pacifica Press, 1994.

Hammond, William M. "The US Army Campaigns of World War II: Normandy." United States Army Center for Military History, n.d., n.p. July 28, 2000. Available at http://www.army.mil/cmh-pg/brochures/normandy/nor-pam.htm.

Hansell, Maj. Gen. Heywood S., Jr. Oral history by the Department by the US Air Force Academy (USAFA). 19 April 1967. File K239.0512-629. Albert F. Simpson Historical Research Center, Air University, Maxwell AFB, AL.

———. *The Air Plan that Defeated Hitler*. Atlanta, GA: Higgins-McArthur / Longino & Porter, Inc., 1972.

————. "USSAF Plans and Strategic Targets." *Impact* 4 (May–August 1944). Harrisburg, PA: National Historical Society, 1980.

Harris, Sir Arthur, Marshal of the RAF. *Bomber Offensive*. Mechanicsburg, PA: Stackpole Books, 1990.

Harrison, Gordon A. *United States Army in World War II, European Theater: Cross-Channel Attack*. Washington, DC: Center of Military History United States Army, 1989.

Hastings, Max. *Das Reich*. New York: Jove Books, 1983.

Heaton, Colin. "Jimmy Doolittle and the Emergence of American Air Power." *World War II* (May 2003).

Held, Werner, and Holger Nauroth. *The Defense of the Reich*. New York: Arco Publishing, Inc., 1982.

Henry, Paul F. "VIII Fighter Command." *The D-Day Encyclopedia*. Edited by David G. Chandler and James Lawton Collins. New York: Simon & Schuster, 1994.

Higham, Robin. "Technology and D-Day." In *D-Day: The Normandy Invasion in Retrospect*. Eisenhower Foundation. Lawrence: University of Kansas Press, 1971.

Hill, Steven D. "Invasion! Fortress Europe." *Naval Aviation News* 76, no. 4 (May–June 1994): 31–35.

Hincliffe, Peter. *The Other Battle: Luftwaffe Night Aces versus Bomber Command*. Edison, NJ: Castle Books, 2001.

Hinsley, F. H. "Deception." *The D-Day Encyclopedia*. Edited by David G. Chandler and James Lawton Collins. New York: Simon & Schuster, 1994.

————. "Intelligence." *The D-Day Encyclopedia*. Edited by David G. Chandler and James Lawton Collins. New York: Simon and Schuster, 1994.

Hogg, I. V. *German Secret Weapons of World War II*. New York: Arco Publishing, Inc., 1970.

Holley, Irving Brinton, Jr. *United States Army in World War II, Special Studies, Buying Aircraft: Materiel Procurement for the Army Air Forces*. Washington, DC: Center of Military History, United States Army, 1989.

Howard, Michael. *The Mediterranean Strategy in the Second World War*. London, UK: Greenhill Books, 1993.

Hoyt, Edwin P. *Angels of Death: Göring Luftwaffe*. New York: Tom Doherty Associates Books, 1994.

"In Desperate Battle: Normandy 1944." Valour and Horror, Second World War, Canadian History, World War II Page, n.d., n.p. July 7, 2000. Available at http://www .valourandhorror.com/BC/Backg/big_week%20.htm.

Informational Intelligence Summary No. 44-32, *German Aircraft and Armament*. Washington, DC: Office of the Assistant Chief of Air Staff, Intelligence, 1944.

Ingrisano, Michael N., Jr. *Valor without Arms*. Bennington, VT: Merriam Press, 2001.

————. 316th Troop Carrier Group Association. Interviewed by author, January 5, 2003.

Jablonski, Edward. *Airwar, Vol. II* (Garden City, NY: Doubleday & Company, Inc., 1979).

Jackson, Robert, ed. *Kriegsmarine*. Osceola, WI: MBI Publishing, 2001.

Jacobs, W. A. "British Strategic Air Offensive." In *Case Studies in Strategic Bombardment*, edited by R. Cargill Hall. Washington, DC: Center for Air Force History, US Air Force, 1998.

Jefford, C. G., Wing Commander. *RAF Squadrons*. Shrewsbury, UK: Airlife Publishing Ltd, 2001.

Johnsen, Frederick A. "Working on the Railroad." *Airpower* 32, no. 3 (May 2002): 48–49.

Johnson, Robert S. US Air Force oral history by Lt. Col. John N. Dick, 9 February 1977. File K239.0512-1074. Albert F. Simpson Historical Research Center, Air University, Maxwell AFB, AL.

———. *Thunderbolt!* Spartanburg, SC: Honoribus Press, 1999.

Joint Intelligence Subcommittee (JIC) of the Joint Planning Staff of the (UK) War Cabinet. "Operations 'Overlord' and 'Anvil,'" 1 February 1944. JIC Memorandum for Information Number 3. In JCS Geographic File 1942–1945, Records Group 218. National Records and Archives Administration Archive II, College Park, MD.

———. "German Reactions to the US-British Operation," 17 February 1944. Unnumbered JIC Report. In JCS Geographic File 1942–1945, Records Group 218. National Records and Archives Administration Archive II, College Park, MD.

———. "Effects of the Allied Bombing Offensive on the German War Effort with Particular Reference to 'Overlord,'" 1 May 1944. JIC Report (44) 177. In SHAEF SGS Minutes Decimal File, May 1943–August 1945, Records Group 331. National Records and Archives Administration Archive II, College Park, MD.

Joint Planning Staff of the (UK) War Cabinet. "Operation OVERLORD," 3 August 1943. In SHAEF SGS Minutes Decimal File, May 1943–August 1945, Records Group 331. National Records and Archives Administration Archive II, College Park, MD.

Kagan, Niel, and Stephen G. Hyslop. *Atlas of World War II.* Washington, DC: National Geographic, 2018.

Keegan, John. *The Second World War.* New York: Penguin Books, 1990.

Keller, Shawn P., Major, USAF. "Turning Point: A History of German Petroleum in World War II and Its Lessons for the Role of Oil in Modern Air Warfare." Research paper, ACSC, Air University, Maxwell AFB, AL, undated.

Kent, George. "The Man Who Saved London." In *Secrets & Spies.* Edited by Reader's Digest Association. Pleasantville, NY: Reader's Digest Association, 1964.

Kepher, Stephen C. *COSSAC: Lt. Gen. Sir Frederick Morgan and the Genesis of Operation Overlord.* Annapolis, MD: Naval Institute Press, 2020.

Kitchens, James H., III, PhD. "The Luftwaffe and D-Day." Lecture. Ninth AF Conference, "D-Day Remembered," University of New Orleans, LA, April 30, 1994.

Kloeppel, Maj. Kirk M. "The Military Utility of German Rocketry during World War II." Air University Research Report, March 1997, n.p., online. Accessed May 30, 2002. http: //research.maxwell.af.mil/papers/student/ay1997/acsc/97-0609O.pdf.

Kluss, Lt. Col. W. L. Interview by the Assistant Chief of Air Staff for Intelligence, 27 May 1942. File 142.05-3. Albert F. Simpson Historical Research Center, Air University, Maxwell AFB, AL.

Knocke, Heinz. *I Flew for the Führer.* Translated by R. H. Barry. Novato, CA: Presidio Press, 1991.

Kohn, Richard H., and Joseph P. Harahan, ed. "World War II." *Air Superiority: World War II and Korea.* Washington, DC: Office of Air Force History, US Air Force, 1983.

———. *Air Interdiction World War II, Korea, and Vietnam.* Washington, DC: Office of Air Force History, US Air Force, 1986.

Kudrycz, Dr. Walter. "A Practical Prophet? Arthur Harris, the Legacy of Lord Trenchard, and the Question of 'Panacea' Targeting." *Royal Air Force Airpower Review* V, no. 1 (Spring 2002): 30–42.

Kuter, Brig. Gen. L. S. Assistant Chief of Air Staff, Plans Memorandum. To Lt. Gen. Carl Spaatz. Subject: Air Operations in Western Europe, February 4, 1944. File 168.04-27. Albert F. Simpson Historical Research Center, Air University, Maxwell AFB, AL.

Lay, Col. Beirne, Jr. "The Background." *Impact* 5 (September–December 1944). Harrisburg, PA: National Historical Society, 1980.

Lee, Wing Commander Asher. Interview by the Assistant Chief of Air Staff for Intelligence, 29 July 1943. File 152.052 Lee. Albert F. Simpson Historical Research Center, Air University, Maxwell AFB, AL.

Leigh-Mallory, ACM Trafford, Air Commander in Chief AEAF. To Gen. Dwight D. Eisenhower. Subject: Attacks on Rail Targets in Enemy-Occupied Territories, March 10, 1944. SHAEF SGS Minutes Decimal File, May 1943–August 1945, Records Group 331. National Records and Archives Administration Archive II, College Park, MD.

LeMay, Gen. Curtis E. "The Command Realities." *Impact* 5 (September–December 1944), ed. James Parton (Harrisburg, PA: National Historical Society, 1980).

Loewenheim, Edward L., Harold D. Langley, and Manfred Jones, eds. *Roosevelt and Churchill: Their Secret Wartime Correspondence.* New York: Saturday Review Press / E. P. Dutton & Co., Inc., 1975.

Mahurin, Bud. *Hitler's Fall Guys.* Atglen, PA: Schiffer Publishing Ltd., 1999.

Man, John. *D-Day Atlas: The Definitive Account of the Allied Invasion of Normandy.* New York: Facts on File, 1994.

Marrin, Albert. *Overlord D-Day and the Invasion of Europe.* New York: Atheneum, 1982.

Marshall, Tim. *Prisoners of Geography.* London, UK: Elliot and Thompson, 2015.

———. *The Power of Geography.* New York: Scribner, 2021.

Mason, Frank. *Luftwaffe Aircraft.* New York: Crescent Books, 1986.

Maurer, Maurer, ed. *Air Force Combat Units of World War II.* Washington, DC: Office of Air Force History, US Air Force, 1983.

———. *World War II Combat Squadrons of the US Air Force.* Woodbury, NY: Smithmark Publishers, Inc., 1992.

McArthur, Charles W. *History of Mathematics, Vol. 4: Operational Analysis in the US Army Eighth Air Force in World War II.* Providence, RI: American Mathematical Society, 1990.

McCrabb, Lt. Col. Maris. "Drohende Gefahr West: The Pre-Normandy Air Campaign." *Airpower Journal* (Summer 1994). Accessed August 21, 2023. https://www.airuniversity.af.edu/Portals/10/ASPJ/journals/Volume-08_Issue-1-Se/1994_Vol8_No2.pdf.

McFarland, Stephen L., and Wesley Phillips Newton. *To Command the Sky.* Washington, DC: Smithsonian Institution Press, 1991.

———. "The American Strategic Air Offensive Against Germany in World War II." In *Case Studies in Strategic Bombardment,* edited by R. Cargill Hall. Washington, DC: Center for Air Force History, US Air Force, 1998.

McGovern, James. *Crossbow and Overcast*. New York: William Morrow and Company, Inc., 1964.

McGowan, Sam. "Low-Level Run at Ploesti." *WWII History* (May 2003).

McNab, Chris. *Order of Battle: German Luftwaffe in WWII*. London, UK: Amber Books, 2009.

Message 241315B, May 1944. USSTAF (Spaatz). To ETOUSA for relay AGWAR, May 24, 1944. SHAEF SGS Minutes Decimal File, May 1943–August 1945, Records Group 331. National Records and Archives Administration Archive II, College Park, MD.

Message, May 5, 1944, 4 p.m. American Embassy, Algiers. To American Embassy, London, May 5, 1944. SHAEF SGS Minutes Decimal File, May 1943–August 1945, Records Group 331. National Records and Archives Administration Archive II, College Park, MD.

Message, No Date/Time Group. President Roosevelt. To Prime Minister Churchill, May 11, 1944. SHAEF SGS Minutes Decimal File, May 1943–August 1945, Records Group 331. National Records and Archives Administration Archive II, College Park, MD.

———. General Eisenhower. To General Arnold, September 3, 1944. File 519.553-2, "An Evaluation of the Effects of the Bomber Offensive on 'Overlord' and 'Dragoon.'" Albert F. Simpson Historical Research Center, Air University, Maxwell AFB, AL.

Messenger, Charles. *The D-Day Atlas: Anatomy of the Normandy Campaign*. New York: Thames & Hudson, 2004.

Michel, Marshall L. *Schweinfurt–Regensburg: 1943*. Osprey Air Campaign Series. Oxford, UK: Osprey Publishing Ltd., 2020.

Middlebrook, Martin. *The Schweinfurt–Regensburg Mission*. New York: Charles Scribner's Sons, 1983.

Middlebrook, Martin, and Chris Everitt. *The Bomber Command War Diaries 1939–1945*. Leicester, UK: Midland Publishing, 1996.

Milch, Field Marshal Erhard, GAF (Ret.). "The Allied Combined Bomber Offensive: Two German Views (Part 1)." *The Combined Bomber Offensive: Classical and Revolutionary, Combined and Divided, Planned and Fortuitous*, ed. Noble Frankland. Washington, DC: Office of Air Force History, 1968.

Miller, Donald L. *Masters of the Air*. New York: Simon & Schuster, 2006.

Ministry of Home Security, Research and Experiments Department. *The Economic Effects of Attacks in Force on German Targets*. In 519.553-3. Albert F. Simpson Historical Research Center, Air University, Maxwell AFB, AL.

Minutes of meeting. Debriefing Conference, Operation Neptune, 82nd Airborne Division, August 13, 1944. Box 11 of the James M. Gavin Papers. US Army Heritage and Education Center, Carlisle Barracks, PA.

———. Alternate Plans for the Employment of Strategic Bomber Forces, Office of the Deputy Supreme Commander SHAEF, May 3 1944. SHAEF SGS Minutes Decimal File, May 1943–August 1945, Records Group 331. National Records and Archives Administration Archive II, College Park, MD.

Molyson, Joseph T., Jr., *Six Air Forces over the Atlantic*. Mechanicsburg, PA: Stackpole Books, 2024.

Morgan, Lt. Gen. Frederick. COSSAC. To CINC AEAF. Subject: "Overlord" Bombing Policy, January 10, 1944. SHAEF SGS Minutes Decimal File, May 1943–August 1945, Records Group 331. National Records and Archives Administration Archive II, College Park, MD.

Morgan, Hugh, and John Weal. *Osprey Aircraft of the Aces, Vol. 17: German Jet Aces of World War 2*, ed. Tony Holmes. Oxford, UK: Osprey Books, 1998.

Morrison, Alexander. *Silent Invader*. London, UK: Airlife Publishing, Ltd., 2002.

Murray, Williamson. *Strategy for Defeat: The Luftwaffe 1933–1945*. Osceola, WI: Motorbooks International Publishers & Wholesalers, 1998.

Murray, Williamson, and Allan R. Millett. *A War to Be Won: Fighting the Second World War*. Cambridge, MA: Belknap Press, 2000.

Nagorski, Andrew. *1941: The Year Germany Lost the War*. New York: Simon & Schuster, 2019.

Natkiel, Richard. *Atlas of World War II*. Greenwich, CT: Brompton Books, 1999.

Nesbit, Roy Conyers. "Blenheims and Beauforts." *Royal Air Force Historical Society Journal*, no. 33. United Kingdom: Royal Air Force Historical Society, 2005.

———. *The Strike Wings*. Barnsley, South Yorkshire, UK: Pen & Sword Books, Ltd., 2012.

Neufeld, Michael J. *The Rocket and the Reich*. Cambridge, MA: Harvard University Press, 1996.

Niderost, Eric. "Terror by Night." *Military Heritage* (February 2001).

"1944." RAF History Page, n.d., n.p. November 13, 2001. Available at http://www.raf.mod.uk/history/line1944.html.

Old, Lt. Gen. Archie, Jr. US Air Force oral history by Hugh N. Ahmann, 26 October–2 November 1982. File K239.0512-1357. Albert F. Simpson Historical Research Center, Air University, Maxwell AFB, AL.

"Operation Blitz Week." *Codenames Operations of World War II*. Accessed May 28, 2024. https://codenames.info/operation/blitz-week/.

"Operation Bolero I and II." P-38 Home Page, n.d., n.p. (August 14, 2000). Available at http://members.xoom.com/_XMCM/tguettle/bolero1.html.

Overprint of CIA Base Map 504778 10-81. Perry-Castañeda Library, University of Texas at Austin. Accessed May 9, 2024. https://maps.lib.utexas.edu/maps/europe/iceland_pol81.jpg.

Parton, James. "The Evolution of Air Command." *Impact* 1 (April–August 1943). Harrisburg, PA: National Historical Society, 1980.

———. *Air Force Spoken Here: General Ira Eaker and the Command of the Air*. Bethesda, MD: Adler & Adler, 1986.

Pavelec, Sterling Michael. *Airpower Over Gallipoli 1915–1916*. Annapolis, MD: Naval Institute Press, 2020.

Paxton, James. "Pointblank." *The D-Day Encyclopedia*. Edited by David G. Chandler and James Lawton Collins. New York: Simon & Schuster, 1994.

Piekalkiewicz, Janusz. *The Air War: 1939–1945*. Translated by Jan van Huerck. Harrisburg, PA: Historical Times, Inc., 1985.

Pimlott, Dr. John. *Luftwaffe*. Osceola, WI: Motorbooks, 1998.

Pipes, Jason, and Aryo L. Vercamer. "The West on the Eve of D-Day." World War II Axis Military History Day-by-Day, n.d., n.p. April 27, 2000. Available at http://www .uwm.edu/~jpipes/eve44.html.

Planning and Preparation of the AEAF for the Landings in Normandy. RAF Narrative, Vol. I. London, UK: Air Historical Branch, Air Ministry, released July 11, 1984. PDF. Accessed September 27, 2023. https:// www.raf.mod.uk/our-organisation/units/ air-historical-branch/second-world-war-campaign-narratives/liberation-of-north -west-europe-vol-i/.

Pogue, Forrest C. *United States Army in World War II, European Theater: The Supreme Command.* Washington, DC: Center of Military History, United States Army, 1989.

Powell, Matthew. *The Development of British Tactical Air Power, 1940–1943.* London, UK: Palgrave Macmillan, 2016.

Price, Alfred. *Luftwaffe Handbook 1939–1945.* New York: Charles Scribner's Sons, 1977.

———. *The Last Year of the Luftwaffe.* Osceola, WI: Motorbooks International Publishers & Wholesalers, 1991.

———. "Against Regensburg and Schweinfurt." *Air & Space Forces,* September 1, 1993. Accessed January 20, 2024. https://www.airandspaceforces.com/article/0993 regensburg/.

———. "Electronic Warfare." *The D-Day Encyclopedia.* Edited by David G. Chandler and James Lawton Collins. New York: Simon & Schuster, 1994.

———. "Third Air Force." *The D-Day Encyclopedia.* Edited by David G. Chandler and James Lawton Collins. New York: Simon & Schuster, 1994.

———. *The Luftwaffe Data Book.* Mechanicsburg, PA: Stackpole Books, 1997.

———. "Electronic Navigation Systems." *The Oxford Companion to World War II.* Edited by I. C. B. Dear and M. R. D. Foot. New York: Oxford University Press, 2001.

———. "Electronic Warfare." *The Oxford Companion to World War II.* Edited by I. C. B. Dear and M. R. D. Foot. New York: Oxford University Press, 2001.

Probert, Henry. "84th Composite Group." *The D-Day Encyclopedia.* Edited by David G. Chandler and James Lawton Collins. New York: Simon & Schuster, 1994.

"Psychological Bombing by the AAF." *Impact* 6 (January–April 1945). Harrisburg, PA: National Historical Society, 1980.

Pyle, Ernie. *Brave Men.* New York: Henry Holt and Company, 1944.

"Reconnaissance in a Tactical Air Command." XIX TAC Report, 13 February 1945, n.p. May 15, 2001. Available at http://militaryhistory.archives.webjump.com/.

Recognition Pictorial Manual FM 30-30. Washington, DC: War Department, undated.

Richards, Denis, and Hilary St. George Saunders. *Royal Air Force 1939–1945, Vol. I: The Fight at Odds.* London, UK: HMSO, 1993.

———. *Royal Air Force 1939–1945, Vol. II: The Fight Avails.* London, UK: HMSO, 1993.

———. *Royal Air Force 1939–1945, Vol. III: The Fight Is Won.* London, UK: HMSO, 1993.

Rickard, John. *North American Mustang Mk I.* June 7, 2007. Accessed February 7, 2024. http://www.historyofwar.org/articles/weapons_MustangI.html.

Rise and Fall of the German Air Force 1933–1945, The. Air Ministry Pamphlet No. 248. A.C.A.S.[I], 1948 (HMSO Reprint, 2001).

Roba, Jean-Louis. *The Luftwaffe in Africa 1941–1943.* Havertown, PA: Casemate Publishers, 2019.

Robb, AVM J. M. *Direction of Operations of Allied Air Forces Against Transportation Targets.* Secretary General Staff SHAEF, April 15, 1944. SHAEF SGS Minutes Decimal File, May 1943–August 1945, Records Group 331. National Records and Archives Administration Archive II, College Park, MD.

Rommel, Field Marshal Erwin. *The Rommel Papers.* Translated and edited by Sir B. H. Liddell Hart. New York: Da Capo Press, 1953.

Rostow, Walt W. *Pre-Invasion Bombing Strategy: General Eisenhower's Decision of March 25, 1944.* Austin: University of Texas Press, 1981.

Rüge, Friedrich. *Sea Warfare 1939–1945.* Translated by Commander M. G. Saunders, RN. London, UK: Cassell & Company Ltd., 1957.

Rust, Kenn C. *The 9th Air Force in World War II.* Fallbrook, CA: Aero Publishers, Inc., 1970.

———. *The 12th Air Force in World War II.* Temple City, CA: Historical Aviation Album, 1975.

———. *Fifteenth Air Force Story in World War II.* Temple City, CA: Historical Aviation Album, ca. 1976.

———. *Eighth Air Force Story in World War II.* Temple City, CA: Historical Aviation Album, 1978.

Rychetnik, Joe. " 'Hi' Broiles Logged a Million Miles in Peeping Tom while Filming Airfields around the World." *Aviation History* (November 2000).

Saward, Group Captain Dudley. "Attacks by Night." *Impact* 6 (January–April 1945). Harrisburg, PA: National Historical Society, 1980.

Scott, Peter. *The Battle of the Narrow Seas.* Annapolis, MD: Naval Institute Press, 1945.

Schuster, Cdr. Carl O. "Weather War." *Command* 13 (November–December 1991): 70–73.

Scutts, Jerry. *Spitfire in Action.* Aircraft No. 39. Carrollton, TX: Squadron/Signal Publications, Inc., 1980.

———. *Osprey Aircraft of the Aces, Vol. 1: Mustang Aces of the Eighth Air Force.* Edited by Tony Holmes. Oxford, UK: Osprey Books, 1995.

———. *Osprey Aircraft of the Aces, Vol. 24: P-47 Thunderbolt Aces of the Eighth Air Force.* Edited by Tony Holmes. Oxford, UK: Osprey Books, 1998.

Second World War Airborne Forces, The. Air Ministry Publication No. 3231. Air Ministry (A.H.B.), 1951 (Naval & Military Press Reprint, undated).

Seydewitz, Max. *Civil Life in Wartime Germany.* New York: Viking Press, 1945.

Shackelford, 1Lt Lyne M. Assistant Secretary SHAEF, General Staff. To Lt. Gen. W. Bedell Smith, Chief of Staff SHAEF. Subject: Summary of results of attacks on rail transportation targets, May 27, 1944. SHAEF SGS Minutes Decimal File, May 1943–August 1945, Records Group 331. National Records and Archives Administration Archive II, College Park, MD.

Sharp, Air Commodore A. H. C., and Wing Commander J. Roland Robinson. Transcript of a briefing to General Arnold by the Assistant Chief of Air Staff for Intelligence, 10 August 1943. File 142.05-7. Albert F. Simpson Historical Research Center, Air University, Maxwell AFB, AL.

Sheppard, Alan. *France 1940.* Osprey Campaign Series, Vol. 3. Oxford, UK: Osprey Publishing Ltd., 1990.

Shores, Christopher. *Duel for the Sky*. London, UK: Grub Street, 1999.

Shores, Christopher, and Chris Thomas. *2nd Tactical Air Force, Vol. 1. Spartan to Normandy June 1943 to June 1944*. Hersham, Surrey, UK: Classic, 2004.

Showell, Jak P. Mallmann. *The German Navy in World War Two*. Annapolis, MD: Naval Institute Press, 1979.

Simons, Graham M. *Consolidated B-24 Liberator*. Barnsley, South Yorkshire, UK: Pen & Sword Aviation, 2012.

Slessor, Sir John, Marshal of the RAF. "Cooperation between Land, Seas and Air." *Impact* 1 (April–August 1943). Harrisburg, PA: National Historical Society, 1980.

Smith, Col. Truman. Transcript of US Army Air Forces briefing, 22 December 1943. File 142.05-10. Albert F. Simpson Historical Research Center, Air University, Maxwell AFB, AL.

Smith, Lt. Gen. W. Bedell, Chief of Staff SHAEF. To CG USSTAF, AOCINC Bomber Command and Air Commander-In-Chief AEAF. Subject: Letter. Air Support of "Overlord" during the Preparatory Period, April 20, 1944. SHAEF SGS Minutes Decimal File, May 1943–August 1945, Records Group 331. National Records and Archives Administration Archive II, College Park, MD.

Smith, Peter C. *Naval Warfare in the English Channel 1939–1945*. Barnsley, South Yorkshire, UK: Pen & Sword Books, Ltd., 2007.

———. *The Battle of the Narrow Seas*. Annapolis, MD: Naval Institute Press, 2009.

Speer, Albert. *Inside the Third Reich*. Translated by Richard and Clara Winston. New York: Macmillan, 1970.

Spick, Mike. *Luftwaffe Fighter Aces*. Mechanicsburg, PA: Stackpole Books, 1996.

Staerck, Chris. *Allied Photo Reconnaissance of World War II*. San Diego, CA: Thunder Bay Press, 1998.

Stanley, Roy M., II. *To Fool a Glass Eye*. Washington, DC: Smithsonian Institution Press, 1998.

Starkey, John. *The RAF's Cross-Channel Offensive*. Philadelphia: Pen & Sword Press, 2022.

Steinhoff, Johannes, Peter Pechel, and Dennis Showalter. *Voices from the Third Reich*. New York: Da Capo Press, 1994.

Stoddard, Paul. "Escort Spitfire: A Missed Opportunity for Longer Reach?" Royal Aeronautical Society. Accessed January 24, 2024. https://www.aerosociety.com/news/escort-spitfire-a-missed-opportunity-for-longer-reach/.

Strahan, Jerry E. *Andrew Jackson Higgins and the Boats that Won World War II*. Baton Rouge: Louisiana State University Press, 1998.

Strategic Intelligence Branch, G-2, US Army, European Theater of Operations. *An Evaluation of Military Effects of R.A.F. Bombing of Germany*, 1 March–31 December 1943. In 519.553-3. Albert F. Simpson Historical Research Center, Air University, Maxwell AFB, AL.

———. *An Evaluation of Military Effects of R.A.F. Bombing of Germany*, 1944. In 519.553-3. Albert F. Simpson Historical Research Center, Air University, Maxwell AFB, AL.

Stubbs, David. "A Blind Spot? The Royal Air Force and Long-Range Fighters, 1936–1944." *Journal of Military History* 78, no. 2 (April 1, 2014). Accessed January 29, 2024. www.smh-hq.org/jmh/jmhvols/782.html.

Suchenwirth, Prof. Richard. *Command Leadership in the German Air Force*. Maxwell AFB, AL: Air University Press, July 1969.

Sweetman, John. *Schweinfurt*. New York: Ballantine Books, Inc., 1971.

Swift, Michael, and Michael Sharpe. *Historical Maps of World War II Europe*. London, UK: PRC Publishing Ltd., 2000.

Sykes, H. C. "Bill." *RAF Strategic Bombing: From Art to Science and Back*. Coningsby, UK: Battle of Britain Memorial Flight, 1989. Accessed February 18, 2003 http://www .stable.demon.co.uk/general/bomb.htm. (Website no longer active.)

Target: German Fighter Industry." *Impact* 3 (January–April 1944). Harrisburg, PA: National Historical Society, 1980.

Taylor, Phillip M. "Allied Propaganda." *The D-Day Encyclopedia*. Edited by David G. Chandler and James Lawton Collins. New York: Simon & Schuster, 1994.

Tent, James Foster. *E-Boat Alert: Defending the Normandy Invasion Fleet*. Annapolis, MD: Naval Institute Press, 1996

Terraine, John. *The Right of the Line: The Royal Air Force in the European War, 1939–1945*. London, UK: Hodder and Stoughton, Ltd., 1985.

This Day in Aviation. Accessed May 9, 2024. www.thisdayinaviation.com/14-august-1942/ lockheed-p-38f-lightnings-at-iceland-lt-shahans-41-7540-is-at-the-left/.

Thomsen, Paul A., and Joshua Spivak. "Through an Interrogator's Eyes." *Military History* (April 2002): 59–64, 74.

Tilley, Col. Reade F. US Air Force oral history by Mr. Frederick D. Claypool, 4TFW/ HO, 15 August 1985. File K239.0512-1757. Albert F. Simpson Historical Research Center, Air University, Maxwell AFB, AL.

TM-E 30-451. *Handbook on German Military Forces, 15 March 1945* (Washington, DC: War Department, 1945), Figure 15. Accessed May 20, 2021. HyperWar: Handbook on German Military Forces (chapter 10) (ibiblio.org).

Toliver, Col. Raymond F., and Trevor J. Constable. *Horrido! Fighter Aces of the Luftwaffe*. New York: Bantam Books, 1977.

"Transportation." *Impact* 7 (May –July 1945). Harrisburg, PA: National Historical Society, 1980.

Trask, David F. "Political–Military Relations." *The D-Day Encyclopedia*. Edited by David G. Chandler and James Lawton Collins. New York: Simon & Schuster, 1994.

Tuchman, Barbara W. *The Guns of August*. New York: Macmillan, 1962.

United States Strategic Bombing Surveys: European War, September 30, 1945; new imprint, Maxwell AFB, AL: Air University Press, 1987.

Unwin, Peter. *The Narrow Sea*. London, UK: Headline Book Publishing, 2003.

US Army Air Force. Compilation of interviews by various Air Intelligence Contact Units at AAF Redistribution Centers, 13 April 1945. File 142.05-11. Albert F. Simpson Historical Research Center, Air University, Maxwell AFB, AL.

US Joint Chiefs of Staff. *Specific Actions for the Defeat of Germany and Her Satellites, 1944*. JCS 580, 18 November 1943. In JCS Geographic File 1942–1945, Records Group 218. National Records and Archives Administration Archive II, College Park, MD.

Vimpany, John, and David Boyd. *To Force the Enemy off the Sea*. Warwick, UK: Helion & Company, 2022.

von Below, Nicolaus. *At Hitler's Side*. Translated by Geoffrey Brooks. London, UK: Greenhill Books, 2001.

von Luck, Col. Hans. Conversation with Major Joseph T. Molyson, USAFR, May 7, 1985.

Waddell, Lt. Col. Hugh B. Interview by the Assistant Chief of Air Staff for Intelligence, 25 November 1942. File 142.05-3. Albert F. Simpson Historical Research Center, Air University, Maxwell AFB, AL.

Wakefield, Ken. *Operation Bolero: The Americans in Bristol and the West Country 1942–45.* Manchester, UK: Crecy Books, 1994.

Warlimont, Gen. Walter. *Inside Hitler's Headquarters 1939–45.* Translated by R. H. Barry. Novato, CA: Presidio Press, 1964.

Weal, John. *Osprey Aircraft of the Aces, Vol. 9: Focke-Wulf FW 190 Aces of the Western Front*, ed. Tony Holmes. Oxford, UK: Osprey Books, 1998.

———. *Osprey Aircraft of the Aces, Vol. 25: Messerschmitt Bf 110 Zerstörer Aces of the World War 2.* Oxford, UK: Osprey Books, 1999.

———. *Osprey Aircraft of the Aces, Vol. 29: Bf 109F/G/K Aces of the Western Front*, ed. Tony Holmes. Oxford, UK: Osprey Books, 1999.

Webster, Sir Charles, and Noble Frankland. *The Strategic Air Offensive against Germany, Vol. I: Preparation.* London, UK: HMSO, 1961.

———. *The Strategic Air Offensive against Germany, Vol. II: Endeavour.* London, UK: HMSO, 1961.

———. *The Strategic Air Offensive against Germany, Vol. III: Victory.* London, UK: HMSO, 1961.

———. *The Strategic Air Offensive against Germany, Vol. IV: Annexes and Appendices.* London, UK: HMSO, 1961.

Werrell, Kenneth B. *The Evolution of the Cruise Missile.* Maxwell AFB, AL: Air University Press, September 1985.

———. *Archie, Flak, AAA, and SAM: A Short Operational History of Ground-Based Air Defense.* Honolulu, HI: University Press of the Pacific, 2002.

Westermann, Edward B. *Flak German Anti-Aircraft Defenses 1914–1945.* Lawrence: University Press of Kansas, 2001.

Whiteford, Maj. Gen. P. G., Assistant Chief of Staff G-2 (AEAF). To Maj. Gen. H. R. Bull, Maj. Gen. C. A. West, and Brig. K. McLean. Subject: Letter. "Overlord" Bombing Policy (untitled), January 25, 1944. In SHAEF SGS Minutes Decimal File, May 1943–August 1945, Records Group 331. National Records and Archives Administration Archive II, College Park, MD.

Williamson, Gordon. *Kriegsmarine Coastal Forces.* New Vanguard 151. New York: Osprey, 2009.

———. *E-Boat vs. MTB: The English Channel 1941–1945.* Duel 34. New York: Osprey, 2011.

Willmott, H. P., Charles Messenger, and Robin Cross. *World War II.* New York: DK Publishing, 2004.

Wings at War Series, Vol. 2: Sunday Punch in Normandy [1992]. Washington, DC: Center for Air Force History, US Air Force, undated, new imprint.

Wood, Tony, and Bill Gunston. *Hitler's Luftwaffe.* London, UK: Salamander Books, 1997.

Wood, W. J. A. (ed.). Defence of the Reich (*Reichsverteidigung*), 3 June 1944. Translation of Enemy Documents. RAF Air Historical Branch (A.H.B.) 6. Copied May 1963.

Worrall, Richard. *Battle of Berlin 1943–44*. Osprey Air Campaign Series. Oxford, UK: Osprey Publishing Ltd., 2019.

———. *The Italian Blitz 1940–43*. Osprey Air Campaign Series. Oxford, UK: Osprey Publishing Ltd., 2020.

———. *The Ruhr 1943*. Osprey Air Campaign Series. Oxford, UK: Osprey Publishing Ltd., 2021.

———. *Hamburg 1940–45*. Osprey Air Campaign Series. Oxford, UK: Osprey Publishing Ltd., 2024.

Wragg, David. *RAF Handbook 1939–1945*. Sutton Publishing, 2007.

Wueschner, Dr. Silvano. *The "Transportation Plan": Preparing for the Normandy Invasion*. Maxwell AFB, AL: Air University History Office, 2019.

Wynn, Humphrey, and Susan Young. *Prelude to Overlord*. Novato, CA: Presidio Press, 1983.

Yeager, Chuck, and Leo Janos. *Yeager*. New York: Bantam Books, 1985.

Zaloga, Steven J. *Operation POINTBLANK 1944*. Osprey Air Series, Vol. 236. Oxford, UK: Osprey Publishing Ltd., 2011.

———. *Brittany 1944*. Osprey Campaign Series, Vol. 320. Oxford, UK: Osprey Publishing Ltd., 2018.

———. *Operation Crossbow 1944*. Osprey Air Campaign Series. Oxford, UK: Osprey Publishing Ltd., 2018.

———. *German Guided Missiles of World War II*. New York: Osprey Publishing, 2019.

———. *Ploesti 1943*. Osprey Air Campaign Series. Oxford, UK: Osprey Publishing Ltd., 2019.

"Zusammendruck Dover-Lille Op. Karte Chef." 8 Things You Need to Know about the Battle of Britain, Imperial War Museum. Accessed April 13, 2024. https://www.iwm.org.uk/history/8-things-you-need-to-know-about-the-battle-of-britain.

Index

air-to-air victory, of USAAF, 59–62
air-to-surface vessel (ASV), 115, 169
air traffic control, 64
Air War Plans Division Plan 1
  (AWPD-1), 44
Allied aircraft: air superiority gained
  for, 275–77; bombers in, 187,
  201–2; flak threat to, 93–97,
  269; Hamburg's round-the-
  clock bombing by, 115–16;
  radar taken out by, 273; railroad
  systems attacked by, *251*; types
  of, 278–79
Allied air forces, 9–10, 71–72, 172,
  261
Allied Central Interpretation Unit
  (ACIU), 180–81
Allied Expeditionary Air Force
  (AEAF), 139, 144–45, 224–26,
  225, 245–47
Allied forces: CCS of, 40; fighters
  in, 211, 217, 273; Hitler with
  French port landing of, 72;
  Normandy invasion with
  available, 135–36; OVERLORD
  Operation field armies as, 179;
  7th Armee and power buildup
  of, 243–44; supplies amassed
  by, 241; SYMBOL meeting,
  86; Vichy French air bases
  threatening, *42*
Allied invasion, 2, 8–10, 72, 132, 252
American, British, and Canadian
  (ABC) governments, 16
American Lend-Lease aid, 14, 16
ammunition train, explosion, *265*
amphibious divisions landing, 137
amphibious raid, 68–72

Anderson, Bud, 197, 199
Anglo-American terrorist bombings,
  249
Anglo-French alliance, 33
antiaircraft defenses, 93–94, *94*
anti-shipping squadrons, 166–68, 170,
  172
anti-ship tactics, 6, 36, 175–76, 290n8
ANVIL Operation, 207–8, 275
AOC. *See* Air Officer Commander
AOP. *See* air observation post
AOR. *See* area of responsibility
Arcadia Conference (December 22,
  1941–January 14, 1942), 39–40
area of responsibility (AOR), 49, *50*,
  54
Argentia Conference (August 9–12,
  1941), 16–17
ARGUMENT Operation, 214–18
armed reconnaissance, 264
Armée de l'Air, from France, 18–19
Armstrong, Frank, 66
Army Co-Operation Command
  (ACC), 37–38, 179
Arnold, Henry ("Hap"), 14, 40, 44,
  187; Eaker and tension with,
  203–4; operational instructions
  from, 207–8; P-47 range
  extended by, 113
Arnold Line, 46, *46*, 292n4
"Arsenal of Democracy," 13
assault group (*Stürmgruppe*), 213
ASV. *See* air-to-surface vessel
Atlantic Squadron, 11
Atlantik Wall, 134, 157, 206, 242, 267
atomic bomb project, 68
"Attainment of the Necessary Air
  Situation" (Morgan), 133

About the Author

Colonel Joseph T. Molyson Jr. is a retired thirty-two-year career intelligence officer and veteran of the United States Air Force. His last assignment was Assistant Deputy Commander for Operations (Intelligence), Headquarters Air Force Reserve Command. He was a squadron and wing chief of intelligence during Operation Desert Storm and Air Force Reserve Command senior crisis action team director during operations responding to the September 11, 2001, attacks. He lives outside of Atlanta, Georgia. His previous book, *Six Air Forces Over the Atlantic*, was published in 2024.